THE GATES
OF GAZA

THE GATES OF GAZA

ISRAEL'S ROAD TO SUEZ AND BACK,
1955-1957

Mordechai Bar-On

ST. MARTIN'S PRESS
NEW YORK

© MORDECHAI BAR-ON 1994

TRANSLATED BY RUTH ROSSING

ORIGINALLY PUBLISHED IN HEBREW BY AM OVED LTD, TEL AVIV 1992

THE MAP OF THE SINAI CAMPAIGN ON THE JACKET AND ON PAGE XII
IS REPRODUCED COURTESY OF THE ORION PUBLISHING GROUP.

FIRST PUBLISHED IN THE UNITED STATES OF AMERICA 1994

PRINTED IN THE UNITED STATES OF AMERICA

ISBN 0-312-10586-X

LIBRARY OF CONGRESS CATALOGING-IN-PUBLICATION DATA

BAR-ON, MORDECHAI, 1928-
    [SHA'ARE 'AZAH. ENGLISH]
    THE GATES OF GAZA : ISRAEL'S ROAD TO SUEZ AND BACK, 1955-1957 /
MORDECHAI BAR-ON.
    P. CM.
    INCLUDES BIBLIOGRAPHICAL REFERENCES AND INDEX.
    ISBN 0-312-10586-X.
    1. ISRAEL—MILITARY POLICY. 2. NATIONAL SECURITY—ISRAEL.
3. SINAI CAMPAIGN, 1956. 4. ISRAEL—FOREIGN RELATIONS. I. TITLE.
UA853.I8B29513 1994
956.9405'2—DC20   93-42414
                                                           CIP

INTERIOR DESIGN BY DIGITAL TYPE & DESIGN

For
Erela

C·O·N·T·E·N·T·S

P·R·E·F·A·C·E
AND
A·C·K·N·O·W·L·E·D·G·E·M·E·N·T·S

For most of the stormy period that this book covers, it was my fortune to serve as head of the Israeli Defense Force's Chief of Staff's Bureau and as General Moshe Dayan's private secretary. I was witness to and actively involved in most of the events described. I also had the rare privilege of recording the history of that tempestuous time on three occasions: In the course of the events themselves, it was my duty to ensure daily notations in the chief of staff's Bureau Diary; about a year after the Sinai Campaign, at the request of Moshe Dayan, I compiled and adapted the diary notations into a book called *Challenge and Quarrel;* and 30 years later, when most of the archive materials on that period were declassified, I once again investigated the events for my doctoral dissertation at the Hebrew University of Jerusalem.

The chief of staff's Bureau Diary, which Moshe Dayan also used when he wrote parts of his book *Diary of the Sinai Campaign* and his autobiography *Milestones,* comprises seven volumes of daily records detailing the discussions and events that took place in the bureau. These notations were made on the spot or, at the very latest, in the evening of the same day. The diary is accompanied by seven volumes comprising most of the important documents that then passed through the bureau's secretariat. These volumes are now in the IDF archives and are not yet accessible to researchers.

Challenge and Quarrel is a semiofficial summary of the major events that led up to the Sinai Campaign and that determined its progress. When writing it I relied mainly on the diary notations and its appendixes, as well as on material made available to me for that purpose by Shimon Peres, then director general of the Defense Ministry; by the late Colonel Nehemia Argov who, until his tragic death, served as Ben-Gurion's military secretary; and by Haim Yisraeli, then and now private secretary of the defense minister. For many years the book was classified "Top Secret." Only recently has it been published by the Ben-Gurion Research Center at the University of the Negev. Although it was written without the benefit of time perspective and without access to contemporary documents from other sources and countries that could shed light on events from other vantage points, I believe that it is an important primary resource for researchers of the period, as it provides a very detailed contemporary view of events as perceived in the chief of staff's Bureau.

The present book, written some 35 years later, is the result of an attempt to reconsider the events of that period using recently declassified sources and with the benefit of the perspective of time. I relied here on the Israeli defense establishment sources as well as on many diaries and memoirs of the participants published since the events took place, British Foreign Office and U.S. Department of State documentation, and Israeli Foreign Ministry records now open to public scrutiny in the State of Israel Archives. Not all the important papers have been declassified—Soviet and Egyptian records are not accessible, and even French documentation is only partially available. But I believe that the abundance of material that is accessible allows today's researcher reliably to follow the course of events and even to understand causal and circumstantial relationships, as well as the implications and meanings of those events in the general historical context within which they occurred.

I doubt if I have been able—or have even really wanted—to sever my own personal ties with that period; but I can assure readers that I have tried honestly to take advantage of the passage of time in order to, at the very least, report the events without embellishment. I do not believe that it is the historian's task to judge the figures at the center of action that he describes and elucidates, although most of us only rarely manage to overcome our human tendency to do so. In my opinion the historian's first duty is to relate the events as they took place and to provide sufficient explanations, in terms of the circumstances in which the central figures acted, of their motivations, and of the logic dictating their decisions. All this I have tried to do, and I hope that I have been successful. I leave it to readers to make their own judgments and draw their own lessons, if any such can be gained from history at all. The eighteenth-century Italian philosopher Giambattista Vico said that we would never be able to understand fully the material world that God had created. Not so human society and its history; these man can understand, since they are his own handiwork to which he has intimate access. I leave readers to judge whether my own intimate acquaintance with the events that I have studied has helped or handicapped me in understanding the truth.

Many books have been written on the Suez crisis, but for readers of English, this volume may provide a new vantage point. My entire research has focused on the Israeli perspective. I do not presume to tell the entire truth, but I hope to present and analyze truthfully the perspective of an important participant.

Many people helped me complete this book and I would like to thank those most responsible. First and foremost I am sincerely grateful to my teachers and mentors, Professor Yehoshafat Harkaby and Professor Emanuel Sivan, from whose inestimable guidance I benefited. Mr. Haim Yisraeli, the veteran private secretary to all Israeli ministers of defense, was unstintingly generous with his encouragement and assistance, prodding me when I grew slack. Thanks also to the Leonard Davis Institute for International Relations at the Hebrew University of Jerusalem for generous financial and administrative help. The employees of the State of Israel Archives, working under the most trying of conditions, provided me with that same gracious and constant assistance that so many researchers have enjoyed. I am indebted to my colleagues and the directors of the Ben-Gurion Research Center at Sde Boker; they form a community of scholars to whom the single researcher looks for intellectual invigoration and sustenance so vital to academic activity.

Special thanks to my Hebrew editor, Attalia Silber, whose talent and insistence turned the often convoluted doctoral dissertation I had written in very cumbersome Hebrew into a readable, fluent, and lucid book. Working with her was not only a great pleasure but also helped me to understand better what I myself had written. Ruth Rossing, who translated the book into English, was also a great pleasure to work with.

Last but not least, I dedicate this book to my wife Erela. She too helped me weed out what was unnecessary, misleading, and incorrect in my book. Her patience during the extended period of the book's composition, which took me away from my family for many long days, and her profound participation in the experiences and events described in the book have made her an integral part of it.

Mordechai Bar-On
JERUSALEM
SPRING 1992

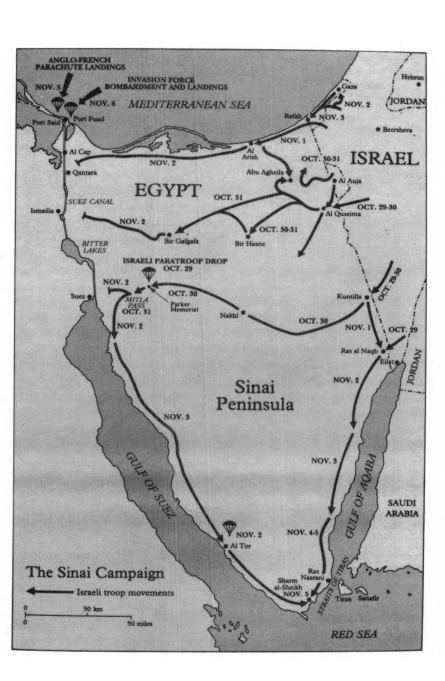

ANGLO-FRENCH
PARACHUTE LANDINGS
NOV. 5

INVASION FORCE
BOMBARDMENT AND LANDINGS
NOV. 6

MEDITERRANEAN SEA

Port Said   Port Fuad

Al Cap

NOV. 2

Qantara

Gaza
NOV. 2

JORDAN
Hebron

Beersheva

Rafah
NOV. 3

Al
Arish
NOV. 1

OCT. 30-31

ISRAEL

EGYPT

Ismailia

SUEZ CANAL

NOV. 2

OCT. 31

Abu Agheila

Al Auja

OCT. 29-30

Bir Gafgafa

OCT. 30-31

Bir Hasne

Al Quseima

BITTER
LAKES

ISRAELI PARATROOP DROP
OCT. 29

NOV. 2

Suez

MITLA
PASS
OCT. 31

OCT. 30
Parker
Memorial

NOV. 2

Nakhl

OCT. 30

Kuntilla

OCT. 29-30

NOV. 1

OCT. 29

Ras al Naqb

Eilat

JORDAN

NOV. 2

Sinai
Peninsula

NOV. 3

GULF OF SUEZ

NOV. 3

GULF OF AQABA

SAUDI
ARABIA

The Sinai Campaign

Israeli troop movements

0   50 km
0   50 miles

NOV. 2

Al Tor

NOV. 4-5

Ras
Nasrani

Sharm
al-Sheikh
NOV. 5

STRAITS OF TIRAN

Tiran   Sanafir

RED SEA

I
...

THE EGYPTIAN-CZECH ARMS DEAL:
THE FORMATION OF A NATIONAL EMERGENCY

"Last week, Egypt signed a commercial agreement with Czechoslovakia for a supply of weapons to her. This agreement stipulates that Egypt shall pay for these weapons with products such as cotton and rice." With this announcement, made at the opening of a photography exhibit in Cairo on Tuesday, September 27, 1955, Egypt's prime minister, Gamal Abdul Nasser, confirmed rumors that had been rife in the West for several days. "We have accomplished one of the revolution's aims," Nasser went on, "namely, the creation of a strong national army." He concluded with a brief explanation of the new "commercial transaction," which would quickly become known throughout the world as the Egyptian-Czech arms deal.[1]

Members of the American intelligence community had unsuccessfully tried to prevent the announcement; at the very least, they were determined to limit its potential damage. According to Mohamed Hassanein Heikal's memoirs, word of the arms deal with Czechoslovakia had begun to spread by mid-September. The American government decided to send an emissary to Cairo to urgently warn the Egyptian leader of the serious implications of his decision. For that task it chose Kermit Roosevelt, a senior Central Intelligence Agency (CIA) officer responsible for Middle East affairs who had known Nasser from the early days of the Egyptian revolution. Nasser, preferring to avoid such pressure and seeking to present his American guest with a fait accompli, decided to announce the transaction as quickly as possible. His only scheduled public appearance was the less-than-spectacular opening of an Egyptian army photography exhibit attended by only some 70 people.[2] The announcement took the Israelis by surprise.[3] The full blow, however, was only felt several days later, when the scope of the transaction began to emerge. At the time David Ben-Gurion—still serving only as defense minister under Moshe Sharett, who replaced Ben-Gurion as prime minister when the "Old Man" (as Ben-Gurion was often referred to) retired to a kibbutz in the Negev for a year in December 1953—was engrossed in the complicated task of forming the new government coalition that he was to lead in the wake of the July elections to the Third Knesset.

The first Israeli discussions on the deal were held in Tel Aviv on the day after the announcement, in the office of Moshe Dayan, chief of staff of the Israeli Defense Forces (IDF). Those assembled had not yet begun to feel the deep anxiety that was to accompany Israeli security discussions within a few weeks. It was obvious that, at this initial meeting, the full scope and repercussions of the arms transaction had not yet sunk in, and Moshe Dayan's chief fears were that arms shipments to Israel would cease, since the West would now try to appease the Egyptians in any way possible.[4] The fact that the chief of staff had not cancelled his plans for an extended holiday in Europe was another indication that the implications had not been fully perceived those first days.

The Egyptian announcement came while the Israeli government was in recess for the High Holy Days. Moshe Sharett, still formally in office, was a frustrated and embittered "lame duck" prime minister. His diary notations those first few days only cursorily referred to the news from Egypt. On September 28, the day after the announcement, Sharett met with the American ambassador to Israel, Edward Lawson, to discuss American arms supplies to Egypt, an issue apparently on the agenda between Egypt and the United States. Sharett's detailed diary notations indicate that he did not even mention the startling news from Cairo. On September 30 his Foreign Ministry advisors counseled Sharett to convene an extraordinary cabinet session, "in order to demonstrate Israel's concern at the risk of a new arms race." Sharett took the advice and even noted in his diary that he wished he had thought of it himself.[5]

For several years Israel had been accustomed to occasional reports of arms deals between an Arab state and a Western one. Thus far, however, none of these transactions exceeded "reasonable" dimensions; and none of them had fundamentally altered the balance of power. When an Arab state bought 20-some tanks or 12 jets, Israel's response was immediate and vociferous, but it was never seriously concerned.

At the beginning of the 1950s, Middle East arms supplies were regulated through an apparatus set up under the Tripartite Declaration issued by the three great Western powers in May 1950.[6] The rules of the game were over-turned when the Soviet Union joined the Middle East arms race: Not being a signatory to that 1950 declaration, it was unlikely that the Soviet Union would feel bound by the restraints that had heretofore characterized Western arms supplies. Prime Minister Sharett aptly described the difference: "A new and powerful force, the Soviet arming of Egypt, has intruded into this incomplete and unstable equilibrium and overturned the balance. And this [change] is not merely the difference between varying degrees of gray; this is the difference between black and white. . . ."[7]

Sharett convened the government for an extraordinary session on October 3, 1955, one of the intermediate days of the Succot holiday. Most of the speakers at the session addressed the need for immediate counterbalancing of arms supplies from the United States as well as a security guarantee. An official statement was issued at the conclusion of the session:

> The Government expresses its serious concern in light of the imminent reinforce-ment of Egypt's armed power which is liable to further exacerbate the disparity and encourage Egypt to aggression towards Israel. It has been agreed that if the reports of significant armament supplies to Egypt are borne out, the Government shall be empowered to take any steps necessary to increase Israel's defensive power by pur-chasing further armaments.

The restrained and cautious wording attests well to the uncertainties that still existed in Jerusalem.

But this was only an interim statement, made before the government had adequate opportunity seriously to consider the challenge Nasser had posed. Soon enough, proposals and demands were heard for preemptive military action to improve Israel's geostrategic position before the effects of the arms deal could make themselves felt.

Such proposals first came from two unexpected quarters. Isser Harel, head of the Mossad—the central Israeli intelligence agency—and chairman of the Intelligence Inter-Services Committee, who had in the past opposed Ben-Gurion's proposals to occupy the Gaza Strip, now proposed such action to Moshe Sharett. Harel contended that the Mossad, which was in constant contact with the CIA, had received signals that an Israeli strike against Egypt would not be inimical to U.S. interests. Indeed, a telegram had arrived two days earlier from Washington summarizing discussions between Kermit

Roosevelt and a Mossad agent; Roosevelt had expressed surprise at Israel's silence and noted that no one would oppose Israel if it struck Egypt once the arms had arrived.[8] Harel believed that Washington was interested in overthrowing Nasser's regime and thus proposed immediate implementation of the plan to occupy the Gaza Strip, before any process of appeasement could begin in the West and the chance be lost. Two weeks later Harel sent the prime minister and the defense minister a detailed and well-argued plan for a military initiative against Egypt. According to the Mossad head:

> The express and secret aims of the Egyptian military junta are hegemony in the Arab world, an increased sphere of influence and military adventurism . . . the military junta will take every opportunity to attempt to implement its threats to destroy Israel. . . . The [delivery of] arms is no more than a well-prepared plan to achieve total and immediate advantage over Israel. . . . The goal is to surprise Israel by gaining unchallenged superiority over it.

Harel's conclusions are far-reaching:

> Israel therefore cannot wait until the initiative passes to Egypt. Egypt's present regime . . . must fall and the Egyptian army must be broken before it has time to use the arms. . . . The immediate aim must be directed at breaking the backbone of the Egyptian army. . . . When this corps is destroyed, the military junta's regime will fall apart.

Harel concludes with a recommendation for immediate action.[9]

The second proposal came from an even more surprising quarter. In mid-October Colonel Katriel Shalmon, Israeli military attaché in Washington, arrived with a message for Moshe Sharett and Ben-Gurion written by himself and two others—Abba Eban, Israel's ambassador to Washington and at the United Nations, and Reuven Shiloah, Israeli minister and special envoy in Washington responsible for CIA contacts. The signals Harel had received from CIA personnel may also have influenced Eban and the others, who concurred with his evaluation that the Egyptian-Czech deal had created a special situation between Israel and the Western powers who shared a common interest in bringing Nasser down:

> This agreement [i.e., the Czech deal] implicitly jeopardizes Western influence in the region and also threatens the very existence of the State of Israel. The necessary conclusion from this development is the need for a timely halt to Soviet penetration and the introduction of radical reform in the Arab world, including toppling the Nasser regime. It is reasonable to assume that there are Western powers who will cooperate with Israel in planning and implementing this daring mission. [From Israel's point of view this] latest development [must be considered] a highly serious threat to Israel's security. We must assume that the Soviet arms [supply] will be massive, effective and uninterrupted, accompanied by technical advisors to instruct the Egyptians in its

use. We are faced with the bleak prospect of our enemy's reinforcement with the support of the second greatest power on earth. We are consequently confronted by a degree of danger which we have never known.

Eban, Shiloah, and Shalmon recommended "that Israel opt for a plan of action to overthrow Nasser's regime, be it on our own or jointly with the Western powers." The right time for action, they believed, was the spring of 1956; until then, Israel had to acquire "a counterbalancing arms supply, a security guarantee and a secret pact for close cooperation [with the United States] in order to alter the situation in the Middle East. . . . If necessary, the military aim must be . . . to strike a decisive blow at the Egyptian army, which is the keystone of the entire regime."[10]

Moshe Sharett was alarmed by the far-reaching proposal and wrote in his diary, "I did not expect Eban to also be moved to desperation." Sharett weighed the alternatives but quickly rejected the recommendation.

> If the bonfire is rekindled in the Middle East—and this time by our own hands—who among us can predict the outcome? . . . After all, we cannot wipe Egypt off the face of the earth; she will always be our neighbor. Will she not be even more disposed to hate and vengeance against Israel? What is our vision in this land—war to the end of time and life by the sword?[11]

Defense Minister Ben-Gurion's reaction is succinctly presented in a telegram from Colonel Nehemia Argov, his military secretary, to Moshe Dayan in Paris: "The 'Old Man' had reached the same conclusions as Katriel Shalmon and the others even before talking to Katriel." Unfortunately, this remark does not clarify whether Ben-Gurion viewed Nasser's elimination as a feasible plan of action or whether he merely concurred that it was advisable.

In the meantime, the Americans and the British considered the move and concluded that the damage could not be undone, but could at least be restricted to prevent Nasser's total identification with the Soviet camp. In his first official reaction, American Secretary of State John Foster Dulles even expressed a note of empathy for Nasser's move: It was understandable, he maintained, for a country sincerely perceiving itself to be at risk to seek defensive weapons from any possible quarter.[12]

At the end of October, Britain's Sir Ivone Kirkpatrick, permanent under secretary of state, sent a memo to Foreign Secretary Harold Macmillan, summing up his position on the Middle East: "Israel must to be made to understand that the West could not afford to estrange the Moslems. Otherwise the Arab States will fall entirely away, come under Russian domination, and it will then be impossible for the West effectively to protect Israel."[13]

Typically, Moshe Sharett wavered. In his diary he records, "For some time I have not been admitting even to myself just how deeply . . . confounded I am at not finding my way through the dense tangle created by the blatant Soviet intrusion into the Middle East. . . . I am at a loss, and the feeling that I am not holding the wheel firmly and am not taking definitive action . . . hurts my pride and troubles me sorely."[14] At any rate, it was clear that a decision for any far-reaching initiatives would have to wait until Ben-Gurion recovered from a sudden illness (see below) and a new government was formed.

In the meantime, public anxiety gathered momentum. The exact extent of the arms sale had not yet become common knowledge those first few days of October; but it was already clear that the amounts and types of weapons could not be matched by the IDF. Azriel Carlebach, one of the senior journalists of the time, published a vigorous editorial in *Ma'ariv,* Israel's leading evening daily, warning of Egyptian aggression, since Nasser himself admitted that the arms were intended to attack "only Israel."[15] The editors of other papers concurred, publishing articles calling for a preemptive strike. Right-wing commentator Dr. Y. Margolin wrote: "With no illusions we must declare that the State of Israel is heading for a serious military confrontation with our Arab neighbors." Professor Benjamin Akzin, a prominent right-wing intellectual, rejected the term "preemptive strike" and argued that it was a defensive war that was being considered, as it was Israel's right to attack in order to defend its very existence: "The circumstances, i.e., the actions of foreign states, are imposing war on Israel."[16]

Unsurprisingly, the radical right *Herut* newspaper immediately raised a hue and cry: "The danger to Israel is no longer for the future," it editorialized on September 29. "If time had been working to our disadvantage until now and any day's delay in action automatically increased the cost of such action—then from this point on, the pace will quicken." The obvious conclusion was that it was Israel's duty "to implement today what will become impossible tomorrow. . . . Let us not sit idly by in the face of this most dangerous threat to Israel's very existence." Three days later the *Herut* editorial declared that "Israel must put an end to the atmosphere of 'anxiety' and argumentation; she must take action immediately, and on all fronts—both in order to prevent the *delivery* of the weaponry to Egypt and to prevent its *receipt* by the Egyptians." The broad hint was made explicit on October 5: "If an Arab attack is inevitable, Israel views a preventive war as necessary . . . because she will not be able to fight a defensive war on her own territory."[17]

Even the General Zionists, ordinarily the voice of moderation, were swept up in the general atmosphere. Centrist Liberal Party head Peretz Bernstein wrote in the *Haboker* paper: "A war which we initiate carries with it all the serious risks of any war. . . . I would hesitate to recommend so dangerous a course were it not for the fact . . . that an Arab war against us . . . is aimed at wiping the State of Israel off the map by destroying its population."[18] Even *Davar,* the moderate and faithful organ of the Labor movement, took up the alarm. Its October 2 editorial declared that "The arms were purchased solely for planned aggression against Israel. . . . The Egyptian ruler and the other Arab rulers believe it their right to foreclose Israel's possibility of self-defense, just as they deny the very existence of our state."[19]

But more than the editorials, it was the newspaper headlines that expressed (and fanned) the increasing anxiety and confusion that began to take hold of the Israeli public: "Fears of an Israeli preventive war!" "Next year—an attempt to breach the Eilat blockade." "Nasser declares Czech arms aimed at Israel." "A time of danger, a time of opportunity." "Anything can happen now along Israel's borders."

In mid-October a U.S. congressional delegation headed by C. J. Zablocki visited Israel. The delegates' impression of the Israeli *zeitgeist* was reflected in their report to Congress: "The mood was one of uncertainty if not depression, and a growing sense of isolation."[20] The Western capitals began to fear an Israeli act of desperation, fears exacerbated by Abba Eban's cutting remarks in an interview broadcast on national American television, in which he affirmed Israel's desire to settle its disagreement with the Arabs amicably, but without sitting by "like a rabbit" waiting to be devoured.

On October 10 the Knesset met in an extraordinary session.[21] Member of the Knesset (MK) Ya'acov Meridor of Herut and MK Peretz Bernstein of the General Zionists raised urgent proposals for the agenda. The Egyptian-Czech arms deal, Meridor stated, was liable to "put into question the future of our nation here, our very existence and well-being." He viewed the government's failure to convene the Knesset on its own initiative as a sign of "weakness" and "fatal confusion." Bernstein also saw the Czech deal as "a revolution . . . utterly transforming the situation throughout the world." A "second round" of warfare between Israel and its Arab neighbors, heretofore not entirely seriously considered, suddenly grew more palpable and threatening. "It is hard to imagine that [Nasser] would make this move if he didn't intend to use the arms. . . . We must consider the serious intention now issuing from Egypt . . . to attempt to destroy Israel."

The full Knesset discussion was held a few days later in a tense atmosphere and stretched on for many hours. Moshe Sharett, then both prime minister and foreign minister, opened with an impassioned description of "serious events threatening the future [of Israel]" and "the bleak prospect of decisive military superiority" that Egypt was acquiring through the Czech deal, which endangered Israel to an extent "unknown since the War of Independence." Sharett quoted at length from the threats and vilifications pouring out of Egyptian radio and newspapers and condemned the hypocritical policies of the Soviet Union, which repeatedly declared its peaceful intentions and desire to reduce international tensions, while at the same time sending vast amounts of arms to Egypt. He also attacked the Western powers' policy of appeasement toward Nasser and refuted the argument that the balance of power between Israel and the Arabs lay in Israel's favor. "The quality [of our manpower]," Sharett said, ". . . can never fully make up for tremendous numerical advantage . . . in view of the imminent . . . crucial reinforcement . . . of Egypt's armed strength which has taken us by surprise, our demand is for weapons! Lots of good, cheap weapons!" Fervently he concluded: "From here in this house, in this our capital, we call to the citizens of Israel, to the Jewish people throughout the Diaspora, and to the entire world for weapons for Israel!"

Menachem Begin spoke on behalf of the opposition, sharply criticizing the government's failures. He did not believe in the call to arms, he said, because no country would supply Israel with the weapons it needed: "Let us not mince words. We declare openly and simply: we must act to prevent a war of destruction. . . . In these troubled times there is no adventurism more reckless . . . more dangerous to our very existence and more threatening to our children's future than inaction."

One after another the parliamentarians, in various styles and tones, reiterated the same point: The Czech deal threatened Israel's existence and presented a most palpable danger. Egypt seriously planned to destroy Israel and thus a state of emergency had to be declared, all resources had to be mustered, and arms had to be requested from the West immediately. Many speakers even hinted that, if all else failed, Israel might be forced to initiate war. If the United States did not provide Israel with armaments and security guarantees, said MK Yitzhak Raphael of the National Religious Front, "she cannot demand that we sit with our hands folded and wait for the [death] sentence to be carried out." MK Yitzhak Ben-Aharon of the left-wing Ahdut Avodah—Poalei Zion Party said, "Let [the nation] defend itself with arms . . . so that the noose is not tied around our neck while we sit quietly and await our fate."

Only the dovish Mapam Party warned against hasty initiatives. "The dangers of adventurism must not distort our view of just how serious our position is," cautioned MK Israel Barzilai. He advocated

> watchfulness and military readiness . . . a strengthened security system, improved methods of active defense, an attempt at mobilizing the great powers toward a cooperative effort to defuse the [tensions in the] region, ceaseless striving for peace, neutrality—with these we can break through the isolation, with these we can win friends, forge defensive strength, reinforce our independence and security.

The bulk of Sharett's response was directed at what needed to be done on the domestic front:

> We must now pull together to mobilize all our capabilities, which may be limited but are not insignificant . . . to take a stand and defend the ramparts. . . . True, it has been said that the sluice gates, opened wide to the flow of Soviet arms to Egypt, portend an upheaval in our political and security situation. Countering this revolution there must be another revolution within our country, a revolution of concepts and of efforts.

An overwhelming majority of the Knesset declared its "concern in view of the large armaments shipments to Egypt. . . . These shipments . . . will be directed by [Israel's] enemies to a war of destruction against her. . . . The Knesset charges the government with mobilizing the people and the State against the dangers." The import of the Knesset discussion was declarative rather than operative, but it genuinely reflected the anxiety that had gripped the entire nation. The nation, however, found more direct means of expressing its mood.

Growing anxiety led the population at large to interpret this call from the Knesset podium simply, directly, and literally: The Israeli people had to mobilize themselves and place at the government's disposal enough financial resources to acquire weapons once the markets were open to Israel. More than anything else, the spontaneous generation of the "Voluntary Defense Fund" expressed the atmosphere and mood of the country during the autumn of 1955. On the day of the Knesset debate, a young boy came to the Ministry of Defense offices in Tel Aviv asking to see the minister. When the excited youngster was directed to one of the clerks, he gave him a handful of small coins that he had been saving for his bar mitzvah, to buy defensive weapons for Israel. The next day an old woman appeared offering her own contribution—a gold bangle. By noontime three more donors showed up, the director general of the Ministry was informed and subsequently reported to the prime minister. It was by now clear that the phenomenon was no mere coincidence and that provisions would have to be made to deal with the additional contributions that could be expected.[22] And indeed the next few days saw an increasing flow of donations, ranging from 100 Israeli lira (IL), which a Nes Ziona shoemaker had borrowed from the bank, to IL 20,000 from the works committee of a major construction company.

The prime minister's office and the Defense Ministry decided to take advantage of and encourage the spontaneous outpouring. On Israeli radio Moshe Sharett issued an appeal for contributions to the Voluntary Defense Fund: "The decisive military advantage which will soon be held by a nation intent on laying Israel to waste, endangers the State and each and every one of us. Let every citizen prove that he senses the danger and is ready to take his stand. It is time to work for the defense of Israel."[23] While he was making his plea, his staff reported that the flow of contributions had already passed the million lira mark. The newspapers joined in, publishing "price lists" of various weapons so that the public could not just contribute money but actually "buy" arms.

By the last week in October, people were coming to the Defense Ministry in droves and the director general had to make special arrangements to handle the flow of money. Special bank accounts were opened and up-to-date figures of donations were published every evening by the Defense Ministry. In ten days, IL 5 million had been collected. On October 23 the government decided to encourage the generosity without direct involvement and announced that "inasmuch as the Government does not wish to mar the spirit of volunteerism, a commission of public figures with no Government representatives will be set up."[24] Three former chiefs of staff headed the commission: Generals Ya'acov Dori, Yigael Yadin, and Mordechai Makleff. Special bureaus were opened throughout the country. Bulletins were issued and public institutions, works committees, trade unions, factories, and industrial plants were systematically canvassed for funds. On November 3 an enormous parade was held in Tel Aviv, as children and teenagers held banners with slogans such as "Arms for the IDF—Our Answer to Those Conspiring Against Us." The slogan "Arms for Israel," stylized into the figure of a tank, was printed by the thousands and pasted all over the public bulletin boards. Eventually a total of IL 20 million was collected for the Voluntary Defense Fund—no mean feat in those days, albeit not enough for all the arms procurement needs created in 1956, and the government eventually had to impose a special "defense tax."

This enthusiasm not only expressed the Israeli public's willingness to mobilize itself, but also gave vent to the foreboding and anxiety provoked by the Egyptian arms deal. The Voluntary Defense Fund was a consequence of the mood, but it also reinforced it; its activities crystallized the collective sense of national emergency.[25]

The feeling of crisis in Israel during the autumn months of 1955 was also the result of growing tensions on the Armistice Demarcation lines, especially along the Egyptian border. In response to an Israeli raid on an Egyptian military camp north of Gaza in February 1955, the Egyptians organized irregular guerrilla units—"Fedayun"—and began to provoke incidents along the border. Tensions continued intermittently throughout the spring and summer of 1955, and General E.L.M. Burns, chief of staff of the U.N. Truce Supervision Organization (UNTSO), and U.N. Secretary General Dag Hammarskjold were frustrated in their efforts to achieve an agreed settlement.[26] On August 22, 1955, an IDF patrol overran two Egyptian outposts. In retaliation, the Egyptians sent Fedayun units deep into Israeli territory; for four days, from August 26 through August 30, they terrorized the south of Israel, reaching as far as the citrus groves of Rehovot and Rishon Le-Zion, only ten miles south of Tel Aviv. Eleven Israelis were killed and nine wounded, and several installations damaged. The Israeli army responded with a large attack on the Khan Yunis police fortress during the night between August 31 and September 1, killing 72 Egyptians and wounding 58. The IDF suffered one casualty and 11 injuries. The police fortress was totally destroyed.[27]

On September 8 a rather balanced U.N. Security Council resolution called for both sides to exercise restraint and to cooperate with the U.N. observers in order to defuse the situation along the cease-fire lines.[28] Fedayun incursions were halted for several months and incidents along the Gaza Strip did decrease, but tensions remained high. In September and October the focus moved south to the demilitarized zone of Nitzana along the old road from Beersheba to Ismailiyah. The disputes there arose from differing interpretations of the relevant articles of the 1949 Armistice Agreements. The argument had remained unresolved for years and was further inflamed at the end of 1953 when Israel established the settlement of Ketziot within the demilitarized zone. The Egyptians claimed that Israel was engaged in military actions disguised as agricultural or police actions. Israel countered that the Egyptians were violating the agreement by exceeding permitted troop concentrations in the area, and at several points were even going beyond the international border itself. In response to Egyptian dismantling of border

signposts set up jointly by the Israelis and U.N. observers, two IDF compa-
nies entered the demilitarized zone on the morning of September 21, 1955,
overran the old Turkish buildings housing the U.N. troops, and chased the
Egyptian guards away. On October 2 the Israeli army recalled its units from
the zone but tensions still ran high; the Egyptians opposed the fact that
General Burns had granted permission to Israel to retain several "police-
men" in the zone.

The Egyptian-Czech arms deal exacerbated these old frictions. Besides
the ever-present danger of all-out war looming on the horizon, it now
seemed that the recurrent feuds along its borders would also make it more
difficult for Israel to defend its interests. All these smoldering points of
minor friction were at any minute liable to ignite and explode the entire
powder keg.

At this stage it was clearly in Egypt's interest to play for time. Egypt's
fear of a serious Western response to the arms transaction dictated moderation and restraint, as did the need to wait until the new Soviet weapons had
arrived and had been assimilated into Egyptian military arsenals. The massive Western intervention in Guatemala and Iran a few years earlier and the
elimination of the pro-Soviet governments there were still fresh in the minds
of Egypt's leadership. Dr. Mahmoud Fawzi, Egypt's foreign minister, tried
to placate the Western powers and in a television broadcast considered the
possibility of an Israeli preventive strike: "If the Israelis truly understood
our policies and intentions, they would never reach such a conclusion."[29]

Several days after the sale was announced, Nasser informed the British
ambassador to Egypt that he did not intend to disrupt the economic and
social programs that he had prepared for Egypt for the sake of an adventure
against Israel. Trying to soothe the ambassador, he added that increased
Russian intervention in Egypt was not expected.[30] Egypt's official propaganda organs were also restrained during those first weeks after the transaction was made public. On October 4 Nasser told Tom Littel of the Arab
News Service that the deal was intended to fill "certain gaps in the arms supply of the Egyptian army. It was not intended to rearm entirely the Egyptian
army. It did not mean a change in Egyptian policy."[31]

But the dramatic transaction had its own dynamics. Having dared to challenge the West and involve his country with the Communist bloc, Nasser's
prestige soared. His new image as a powerful leader in the Arab world called

for personal self-assertion and national defiance.[32] Shortly before the announcement of the arms sale, he had instructed heavy naval guns to be placed in Ras Nassrani, opposite the narrows leading into the Gulf of Eilat, and had intensified the blockade of the Straits of Tiran, which had been in effect formally since the beginning of the 1950s but had not been particularly problematic since shipping to and from Eilat was light.[33] Now the Egyptians also prohibited Israeli planes from overflying the area, forcing El Al to halt flights to and from South Africa along this route. And in juxtaposition to the moderate and conciliatory tones of official Egyptian diplomacy and its press pronouncements to the West, Egyptian Arabic-language radio broadcasts and newspaper editorials aimed at the local Egyptian population and the entire Arab world became increasingly insolent and aggressive.

The autumn of 1955 brought with it a heavy sense of dread and fear for the Israeli public. Not all Israelis agreed with Ben-Gurion and Dayan in their day-to-day security policy; but all Israelis did share the sense that the existence of the State of Israel had been jeopardized.

The historian must be very cautious in generalizing about moods and feelings of large groups of people, since the moods and feelings attributed to the "public" in fact often reflect a ruling elite. In this case, however, it is difficult not to be impressed by the widespread expressions of anxiety exhibited by large sectors of the entire Israeli population and by its impact on decision making. Recognizing and acknowledging this popular atmosphere of crisis and emergency, therefore, is a vital precondition to understanding the actions taken by Israel's political leadership.

2

STATUS ASSESSMENT

The IDF, the Foreign Ministry, and the Defense Ministry, together responsible for the entire range of Israel's foreign and defense policies, needed more than spontaneous reactions, public declarations, and information picked up from the media. These establishments were also affected by the growing anxiety, but professionalism dictated that they examine the problem more closely and then take action to avert the worst. After several days of confusion, Foreign and Defense Ministry officials energetically began to seek ways to discover the details of the deal, assess the situation, and consider suitable responses.

The events of 1956 in the Middle East cannot be understood without looking at the assessments made by the Israeli defense establishment and the way in which the Israeli defense leadership viewed Egyptian intentions; this is even more important than Egypt's intentions themselves, because Israel initiated most of the actual events that involved it with Egypt that year. Gamal Abdul Nasser's intentions toward Israel influenced the course of events in the region primarily not by what was said, but by how it was perceived by the Israelis, because though Egyptian intentions seldom materialized into actions, the conclusions drawn from them did indeed.[1]

* * *

The first problem at IDF General Staff headquarters in assessing the new situation was that of intelligence gathering. As quickly as possible, reliable information had to be obtained on the scope of the transaction, the dates of delivery, the kinds of arms included, and the ability of the Egyptian army to integrate the new weapons into its ranks. One month after the sale had been made public, the deputy chief of the IDF Intelligence Branch, Colonel Yuval

Ne'eman, relayed the first details. Extremely cautious, and relying on confirmed sources only, he indicated moderate quantities of armaments: ". . . we have information on the purchase of T-34 tanks and Stalin-3 tanks, 50 MiG-15 warplanes as well as a dozen or so jet bombers of an unidentified model." He was not yet able to identify more details, but Chief of Staff General Dayan, impressed by newspaper reports throughout the world of large quantities of weapons, insisted that it had to be assumed that the deal was much larger both quantitatively and qualitatively.[2]

IDF intelligence was faced with a very thorny problem. All earlier Mideast arms transactions had been concluded with Western democracies, with whom Israel had various kinds of relations; thus for the most part it was not difficult, sooner or later, to discover their nature, extent, and delivery dates. A deal with the Soviet Union was a different story, as it was completely opaque to Israeli intelligence.[3] Only when the arms had reached Egypt and had been delivered to military bases would it be possible to gather bits of information and put them together one by one to get a full picture. In the meantime, the very mystery created a profound sense of dismay. Moreover, Western political constraints clearly did not apply in the Soviet Union, and thus there was no way of knowing just how far things would go. Were there any limits to the USSR's desire to penetrate the Mideast and increase its influence there?

At a general staff meeting called by Moshe Dayan immediately after his return from the European holiday he had cut short, he said that

> Egypt would not be making a deal like this with Czechoslovakia for small pickings. It does not matter if we have information today about 100 tanks or 200 tanks. We must assume that Egypt will be getting any amount it wants from the East. For Soviet Russia, six or eight submarines make no difference; it's only by our standards that it sounds fantastic. We must leave behind us the perceptions we had gotten used to in the Middle East until now.[4]

The IDF learned the full scope and details of the deal only three months later, but the jigsaw puzzle of intelligence information had begun to take shape earlier and the basic facts were already very clear at the beginning of November, when IDF aerial photographs of Egyptian airfields revealed the first MiG deployments. The Egyptian-Czech transaction announced by Nasser in September included the following main items: 170 T-34 medium tanks, 60 Stalin-3 heavy tanks, 200 BTR armored personnel carriers, 100 S.U.-100 armored mobile anti-tank guns, 80 122-mm Howitzers, 60 152-mm or 122-mm (long-range) field artillery pieces, 200 57-mm anti-tank guns, 100 30-mm light anti-aircraft guns, 34 85-mm heavy anti-aircraft guns, 90 to 100 MiG-15 jet fighters, 48 Iliushin-28 jet bombers, 20 Iliushin-14 transport planes, 4 radar installations, 2 Skori destroyers, 4 minesweepers, 12 torpedo boats, and 6 submarines. The deal also called for considerable amounts of ammunition, spare parts, general equipment, vehicles, and large quantities of small arms.[5]

Reading this list in 1992, when each side in the Middle East conflict has access to thousands of tanks and many hundreds of modern fighter planes, it is hard to comprehend the shock that gripped the Israeli army in the autumn of 1955. But it should be recalled that, until then, Mideast arms deals had not exceeded 30 to 40 tanks and one or two dozen fighter planes at a time. The armaments at the disposal of the Arab states up to then, although quantitatively superior to Israel's, did not raise urgent concern in Israel. Until the autumn of 1955 Israel had some 50 British Meteor and French Ouragan fighter planes to Egypt's 80-odd first-generation jets (mainly Vampires). Egypt had only some 170 outdated World War II tanks, against Israel's 100 similar tanks and another 30 more sophisticated AMX-13 tanks that were on the way from the French production line.

At the beginning of the 1950s the balance of arms in the Middle East was coordinated within the framework of the May 1950 Tripartite Declaration signed by the United States, Great Britain, and France—the main Mideast arms suppliers. These countries formed the Near East Arms Control Commission (NEACC), which met periodically to supervise all arms sales to Mideast states. According to American Secretary of State John Foster Dulles, Western policy on arms supplies to the Middle East was guided by the desire to keep from upsetting the balance of power and avoid an arms race in the region.[6]

Because Israel never had a numerical armaments edge over the aggregate arsenal of its neighboring Arab states, it always sought to acquire more weapons and to upgrade its existing supply through the introduction of more modern arms. At the beginning of the 1950s, however, this was not a pressing need. Israel began to feel increased urgency only in 1953, when Great Britain and the United States became more intensively involved in the Middle East within the framework of Western defense plans, which necessitated increased arms sales to some Arab states.[7] Even then, however, Israel viewed this not as an immediate concern but rather as an ongoing challenge requiring constant vigilance.

The Egyptian-Czech arms deal changed the prevailing situation overnight. When Egypt received everything promised by the Russians it would be capable of deploying over 500 up-to-date tanks in the field and over 200 first-line jet fighters in the air. In other words, Egypt's arsenal alone would be three times larger than what Israel had or could expect to acquire in the near future.

The Israeli general headquarters (GHQ) estimated that the major shift in the arms balance would be one of quality. The MiG-15 was a second-generation jet whose performance was considerably superior to that of Israel's Meteors and Ouragans. Its maximum speed was 520 knots per hour; the Ouragan could do only 440. Comparable disparities existed in maximum altitude, maneuverability, and payload. The IDF's M-3 Sherman tanks had guns accurate up to a range of 800 to 1,000 meters; the Soviet tanks supplied to Egypt had an accuracy range exceeding 2,000 meters. At a range of 1,000 meters, the penetration power of guns on the M-3 Sherman tank was less than 100 mm of steel. The Soviet-supplied tanks had guns with a penetration power over 200 mm. The 30 AMX-13 tanks about to be delivered to Israel could not significantly change this new situation.

The presence of MiG-15s and Iliushin-28s, together with T-34 and Stalin-3 tanks on future battlefields, altered the balance of arms drastically and raised great concern among the higher echelons of the IDF. It put paid to the hitherto prevailing assumption that the numerical imbalance of weapons could be overcome by the quality of IDF manpower: even the most courageous of pilots could not outfly faster planes, and even the most daring of gunners could not hit tanks outside their range. At every level, the enemy's technology could not be offset by bravery, quick thinking, or audacity alone. The Egyptian-Czech arms deal suddenly made it questionable whether the Israeli army could still rely on its vaunted superiority in manpower.

The scope of the arms deal was so dramatic that it called for far-reaching interpretation. Many observers and even intelligence officers felt that the amount of weapons flowing into Egypt suggested that they were not intended for the Egyptian army alone. They looked for secret Soviet plots that could explain the enigma. Noted British analyst Sefton Delmar, for example, published a "scoop" concerning a secret document purporting to prove the existence of a Soviet conspiracy to attack France in North Africa by shipping arms to the emerging Arab states in the region. Delmar contended that the Soviets were exploiting the Israeli-Egyptian conflict to camouflage their own plans to strike at France and thereby weaken the North Atlantic Treaty Organization (NATO), thus paving their way to Europe.[8]

Israel's Military Intelligence Branch also made some far-ranging assumptions. At the end of January 1956 the head of Military Intelligence had written, "If these numbers prove to be true, what we have here is a supply beyond Egypt's ability to assimilate it easily. Egypt may be planning to become a supplier for other Arab countries, such as Syria and Saudi Arabia."[9] From today's perspective it is obvious that these were unfounded guesses only; but they reveal the depth of the shock and astonishment that gripped Israel's security leadership as the scope and nature of the sale became clear.

Until the arms deal was made public, the Israeli Command had estimated that Israeli forces were capable of repulsing all unified Arab armies and therefore could deter the Arabs from attacking Israel. The new assessment, however, was that the arms deal had deprived the Israeli army of its deterrent power; at the very least, it was severely shaken.[10] Israel's defense and security decision makers tended to believe that Nasser would exploit the shift in the balance of arms and would attack Israel as soon as his army had absorbed the new weapons and completed its preparations, perhaps as early as in the summer of 1956.

When the Israeli army did reach the Sinai peninsula during the Sinai Campaign, it became apparent that 12 months had not been enough time for the Egyptian army to entirely assimilate those arms; but a year earlier, and throughout most of 1956, the coming war was spoken of as if it were a dead certainty. Early in December 1955 Ben-Gurion told the chief of staff: "I presume that they will attack at the beginning of the summer. We must not assume that they won't attack. It is only logical that they will attack when they feel that they can win."[11] And on January 15, 1956, he spoke frankly with the U.S. ambassador to Israel, telling him that Nasser would probably think he should attack Israel by June or July. It could not be assumed that Nasser would wait too long after making the necessary preparations and assimilating the new weapons, because if he did, Israel would also acquire arms and then his chances of winning would decrease.[12]

The chief of staff concurred, albeit more cautiously. In an address to senior commanders in mid-January 1956 he said,

> Will there be a war in 1956? And if so, will it be initiated by the enemy? It is difficult to answer these questions not just because none of us can rely on hard information about an Egyptian decision, even if any such Egyptian decision exists. . . . I don't think that when the Egyptians made the deal with the Czechs they said to themselves, "We'll buy these weapons and those weapons, and when they're delivered and assimilated into our army, then we'll attack." . . . *But I do believe that, in the absence of any Israeli-American transaction, the Czech deal has facilitated a situation in which [the Egyptians] may start a war.*[13] [Emphasis added.]

This forecast—that the Egyptians were liable to initiate a war sometime in the summer of 1956, when they had achieved decisive arms superiority—lay at the heart of all Israeli considerations and decisions that year.

In their desire to mollify the West, Nasser and his aides tried to downgrade the significance of the sale; the Israeli military establishment, however, could not be placated. In the autumn of 1955 IDF intelligence accumulated a great deal of material from Arab media, which included inordinate numbers of threats, boasts, and declarations about a forthcoming "second round." Such threats were not new in the Arab media, but now the references increased and the possibility became more palpable, intensified by newly acquired Arab self-assurance in the wake of the Czech deal and by a sense of confidence in their ability to win the next confrontation. Israel viewed the Arabic-language media as a good indicator of the moods prevailing in the Egyptian street. Although radio broadcasts and newspaper editorials obviously did not reflect operative plans and specific decisions, they had considerable influence on Israeli military assessments, especially since within a few months, once the Egyptian army had assimilated the new weapons, it would indeed clearly be capable of turning these moods into operative plans.

The IDF assessments were also influenced by the increasing assertiveness of the Egyptian military leadership in the wake of the Czech deal. On October 20, 1955, the Egyptian chief of staff declared, "Egypt can overwhelm the IDF with its current force, even if there are some weak points in the areas of air and sea. Egyptian superiority will be total when the Czech weapons arrive and training is completed." [14]

IDF evaluations considered more than radio broadcasts; they were also based on the changes in Nasser's pan-Arab policy. Israeli intelligence had already monitored these changes during the first months of 1954, long before it was made public in Nasser's declaration of his pan-Arab orientation on the second anniversary of the Egyptian revolution. From then on, the Israeli issue seemed to have become a chief Egyptian priority, and Egypt's aggressive policy toward Israel was intensified: The restrictions imposed on Israeli shipping through the Suez Canal since 1948 were made even more stringent; Egypt increased its participation in the Arab economic boycott against Israel; the Fedayun were sent into Israeli territory to strike at civilian targets; and finally, the air and sea blockade in the Straits of Tiran was stepped up. Thus by the fall of 1955, only a very few Israelis were prepared to challenge the assumption that the destruction of Israel was one of the central goals of the new Egyptian regime.

It has been argued that the change in Nasser's regional policies, particularly his initiative to the Soviet bloc for arms, came about after, and in response to, the Gaza raid at the end of February 1955, in which Israeli paratroops attacked an Egyptian army camp north of Gaza City.[15] This has often been cited as an instance of "self-fulfilling fear," the aggressive Israeli security policies of 1954 and early 1955 playing a decisive role in forming Nasser's belligerent policies toward Israel. In later years Nasser himself referred at length to the Gaza raid as an instrumental factor in his decision to approach the Russians for arms. "The smoke of the attack on Gaza on February 28, 1955," he said in the opening address to the People's Council in June 1957, "revealed a dangerous truth: that Israel is not only the stolen territories behind the armistice lines, but also the spearhead of imperialism. . . . This truth was a turning point in our thinking and in the course of events in the entire region."[16]

Unfortunately, this overlooks the facts, because Egypt's intensified aggression against Israel began long before the Gaza raid. This is substantiated by Baruch Kimmerling's study of the prominence of the Israeli-Arab conflict between 1949 and 1967 as reflected in Israeli newspaper headlines. His findings indicate that the most noticeable increase in the level of violence along the borders took place in 1953 and 1954, not in 1955.[17]

The turning point occurred in 1954 when Nasser crystallized his new general policy based on a pan-Arab orientation. Indeed, already in 1953, in the wake of the disturbed security situation, Ben-Gurion devoted three months to an examination of the Israeli army's preparedness for a "second round" and submitted his conclusions to the government on October 19, 1953, shortly before he left the prime minister's office.[18] And in the winter of 1954, when Prime Minister Moshe Sharett visited him at Kibbutz Sde Boker, Ben-Gurion expressed his concern at the increasing indications of Arab intentions to renew hostilities against Israel.[19]

Ben-Gurion's originally positive opinion of the new Egyptian regime had taken an about-face. In 1952 he had welcomed the Egyptian revolution; addressing the Knesset on August 18, 1952, he said:

There may also be positive trends toward healing and progress in this tempestuous development. Where there are, we welcome them. . . . The State of Israel wants to see a free, independent, progressive Egypt, and to the extent that the present Egyptian rulers try to uproot domestic corruption and set their country on the path to cultural and social progress—we can only wish for the success of their venture with all sincerity.[20]

But three years later he said:

Domestic reforms—lowering the rate of illness, educating the people, developing the land, raising the status of the fallah [Egyptian peasant], in whose name the revolution was allegedly carried out—seem to have been postponed to the far-distant future in favor of external political ambitions. . . . The rulers of Egypt seem to have concluded that it is easier to win victories on the foreign policy front than to reform the unfortunate and shameful domestic situation, and in order to gain Arab hegemony the tyrants of Egypt have apparently decided that the easiest and cheapest way is by attacking Israel.[21]

In 1955 Ben-Gurion read Nasser's essay "The Philosophy of the Revolution," published at the end of 1954[22]; at the end of 1955 and the beginning of 1956 he repeatedly referred to it and cited from it. On January 2, 1956, he opened a foreign policy debate at the Knesset and said, "The Egyptian tyrant has published a brochure called 'The Philosophy of the Revolution' . . . the pamphleteer reveals to us the three ambitions guiding his action: (a) to stand at the head of the Arab people; (b) to be leader of the Islamic people; (c) to be speaker for the African continent."[23]

The essay also taught Ben-Gurion that Nasser's desire to destroy Israel was deep-rooted and that it was central to his national vision. Nasser's entire national Arab consciousness had been nurtured in the student demonstrations against the Balfour Declaration in which he had participated. During the 1948 Israeli War of Independence his awareness grew:

We understood that Rafah was not the final border of our country and that our . . . security required us to defend the borders of our brethren [the Palestinians], with whom fate had destined us to live in this region. . . . I returned home after the siege [of Faluja] and the battles in Palestine and the entire area seemed a single unity, which I could never again divide in my mind into separate parts.[24]

Ben-Gurion overestimated the importance of the essay. Nasser's work was intended for the general public and should not be viewed as an operative political plan. But the fact that Ben-Gurion attached a great deal of significance to it and considered it clear evidence of the true nature of the regime in Cairo and a faithful diagram of its plans is important in itself, especially since intelligence reports based on secret discussions held at the time in Egypt confirmed this view.

✻ ✻ ✻

The conviction that the Arab states were serious in their intentions to launch another war against Israel was not new. As early as July 1949, the Foreign Ministry had opened a special file, "The Renewal of War,"[25] after Arab leaders and the Arab media began expressing hopes of a "second round." Three months after the signature of the Armistice Agreement with Jordan, for example, General Sir John Bagot Glubb Pasha, commander of the Arab Legion, told the *mukhtars* (local notables) of the Ramallah district "to keep their weapons in readiness for the next round."[26] On June 28, 1949, Radio Baghdad announced, "We shall never stop planning for the day of vengeance, for the second round in which the Jews will be driven from our land."[27] On July 4, 1949, the Egyptian daily *Akhbar al-Yawm* editorialized: "The Palestinian war has not ended! The Egyptian blood which has watered the land of Palestine is a marker, and we must march in the direction to which it points so that we may gain the victory which our holy saints desired."[28]

The Israeli Foreign Ministry's Research Department and the GHQ's Intelligence Branch regularly distributed material such as this to a wide circle in the officer corps and to senior government officials; and although they did not adduce any immediate operative interpretation, it is only logical to assume that, over time, this came to influence their view of Arab intentions. Even Elias Sasson, a senior Foreign Ministry official and Middle East expert, who always advocated moderation and dialogue with the Arabs, had concluded at the beginning of 1950 that the Arab world was heading for a second confrontation: "All information reaching us from the Arab lands foretells doom," he wrote.[29]

But this was not just an assumption held by high officials of the Israeli foreign and defense establishments; this was a deep-seated and widespread popular belief in the gravity of the Arabs' intentions to renew hostilities and destroy Israel as soon as they considered themselves capable of so doing. In October 1955 most Israelis were sure that Nasser and his colleagues would let no chance go by to try a strike against Israel, once and for all to remove the stain of defeat and avenge the shame of the 1948 Arab rout.

This deep conviction in the Arab desire to destroy Israel was accompanied by a no less profound sense of self-righteousness. In the 1950s most Israelis were too involved in the issue to be able to view it objectively and see that the Arabs, too, had their own anxieties and fears of Israeli aggrandizement. For most Israelis, the conflict shaped since the War of

Independence limited their perspective. Their images had crystallized during the hostilities of 1948; if this was how one began reckoning history, then the conflict in the mid-1950s could only be seen as one between a defensive Israel, protecting its very existence, and the belligerent Arabs, intent on Israel's destruction. This view provided Israel's security establishment with two important assets: a wide public consensus on security issues and total civilian willingness to fight in the wars.

Thus for quite some time before the Czech transaction, the Israeli military establishment and the Israeli public had assessed Arab intentions in general, and Egyptian intentions in particular, as aggressive; until the transaction, however, the general feeling had been that such intentions could not be realized or effected. The new arms sale provoked fears of Nasser's having acquired the ability to realize these intentions, and therefore the assessment that eventually emerged was that he was liable to embark on a "second round" sometime in the summer of 1956.

In retrospect, this evaluation seems groundless, not only because the Egyptian army had not assimilated the new weapons, but also because it is now clear that the arms deal was prompted less by anti-Israeli plans than by inter-Arab rivalries: Nasser bitterly opposed the Baghdad Pact and Western defense plans for the Middle East and nurtured hopes for the unification of the Arab world. But it is in the light of the assessment of Nasser's ambitions and new capabilities held by most Israelis at the time that we must consider Ben-Gurion's statement immediately after the Sinai Campaign that "a serious and direct danger hung over our heads."[30] More than describing an objective danger that existed at the time, his words expressed the way in which he, his government, and his colleagues in the security establishment perceived the situation after the Czech sale. The fear that the Arabs intended to destroy Israel was so profound that Israel's leaders could not but view the arms deal, which afforded Nasser the capability of realizing these intentions, as a grave danger that had to be averted.

Even Foreign Ministry officials, including the usually more moderate Moshe Sharett, concurred. They too were distressed and perceived the new situation as a crisis and threat. There was no disagreement on the significance of the arms deal for Israel; the issues under occasional dispute were the present degree of risk, how immediate it was, and what countersteps should be taken.

3
...

CRISIS DIPLOMACY

Israeli Foreign Ministry officials were now confronted with the urgent need to pressure the Western powers into taking immediate and firm action against the Egyptian-Czech deal, while also furnishing Israel with arms to redress the imbalance and providing it with security guarantees. Moshe Sharett decided to take advantage of the upcoming Geneva conference of the four Great Power foreign ministers to impress upon them Israel's growing anxieties and to urge them to help Israel in its moment of duress. Ben-Gurion was not enthusiastic about Sharett's proposed trip: "It's only worth going for one thing—to talk to the French about arms."[1] But he did not object, and Sharett, who was still prime minister, left for Europe on Sunday, October 23, 1955.

During Sharett's nine days in Paris and Geneva, he held scores of meetings with journalists, Western diplomats, and world leaders. He met twice with American Secretary of State John Foster Dulles and twice with Great Britain's Foreign Secretary Harold Macmillan. He met with French Prime Minister Edgar Faure and Foreign Minister Antoine Pinay. He even spoke with Soviet Foreign Minister Vyacheslav Molotov.[2] But other than some arms transactions with the French, the trip produced neither a substantial arms supply nor any other immediate political achievements. Furthermore, most of the Western diplomats viewed Sharett's appearance in Geneva, in the midst of discussions on major global problems, as an unwelcome nuisance. Sharett himself was at first skeptical about the value of his trip.[3] But ultimately it took a dramatic and unexpected turn and had major repercussions throughout the world.

Sharett's meetings with the British foreign secretary were very disappointing. Macmillan was careful not to deviate from the fundamental line formulated in the Alpha Plan (see chapter 9): that Israel would not be offered any substantial arms supplies or security guarantees until it demonstrated flexibility and showed a readiness to make territorial concessions in the framework of an overall agreement with the Arabs. "Macmillan's response was vague, hollow and negative," Sharett wrote in his diary. "[H]e rejected any security treaty, objected to arms provisions to reach parity with Egypt, and advocated a peace settlement requiring concessions."[4] In his diary Evelyn Shuckburgh, Great Britain's deputy undersecretary for African and Near East Affairs, who took minutes at the meeting, recorded that Sharett played his strongest card and hinted that Israel might be forced to initiate a preventive war,[5] but even this thinly veiled threat could not shake the British position.

There was no significant movement at the second meeting with Macmillan, which took place in Geneva on October 31, the last day of Sharett's European stay. "Macmillan made an emotional and sincere attempt to win me around," Sharett wrote; and when they parted Macmillan said to Eliahu Elath, Israel's ambassador to Great Britain, who was present at the meetings, "If only you knew how hard it is for me to talk to you this way!"[6] But the practical outcome was nil. Shuckburgh's minutes record Macmillan's unequivocal response: Great Britain opposed guarantees to Israel beyond what was stipulated in the Tripartite Declaration of 1950 and refused to be a party to an accelerated Near East arms race. Referring to the possibility of a preventive war, he warned Israel explicitly: "In the long run such methods always turned against those who used them." He again proposed a general settlement and urged Sharett to consider concessions, which the two sides would ultimately be forced to make if they seriously desired to reach any agreement.[7] "In terms of the actual result and the climate of relations," Sharett summed up, "it was a total disappointment."[8]

The discussions with Dulles were different in style but not in essence. "We found Dulles genial in tone but unyielding in content," wrote Abba Eban in his memoirs. "His refusal of arms was no longer stated as a theological principle. It was a pragmatic and conditional refusal."[9] The arms balance, Dulles told the Israelis, had not yet shifted to Israel's disadvantage. And at any rate, the United States did not want to get involved with the issue of Near East arms, which had up to then been the responsibility of the European allies. Sharett wrote that

Dulles was more flexible and incisive than Macmillan. . . . he was very concerned about the change that had taken place, tried to reassure us by reiterating the U.S. administration's positive attitude toward Israel and the American public's strong support . . . [but] fundamentally, his position did not differ from Macmillan's—what was required was a general agreement with the Arabs, which would necessitate concessions. A security guarantee was not practical at the moment, America was totally opposed to supplying arms in order to rectify the imbalance caused by the Czech deal. He only added that if we submitted a modest request for arms he would consider it with an open mind.[10]

Sharett came away "utterly disappointed." Eban also admitted that the discussion was "undeniably negative." Beyond a lukewarm promise to consider a "modest request" for arms "there was not a single bright spot."

The second meeting took place on October 30, producing nothing new, though Sharett was slightly encouraged. If nothing else, he felt that he himself had forcefully, clearly, and energetically presented his case before the secretary of state. Dulles repeated the formulas agreed on beforehand with Macmillan: A security treaty was out of the question at the moment, although he did not totally reject the possibility at a later stage. As far as weapons were concerned, he was prepared to review a list of defensive weapons submitted by Israel. More than anything, he reiterated the need for a general agreement between Israel and the Arab states that would also obligate Israel to make concessions.[11]

Dulles was more moderate in tone for three reasons. First, at this stage the Americans still believed Nasser could be kept from going over to the Russians entirely and thus the United States refrained from officially joining the Baghdad Pact, which was intended to establish a Western line of defense against the USSR and to which Egypt was vehemently opposed. But should it become necessary, Dulles wanted to reserve the option of counterbalancing such a move by granting Israel security guarantees, and perhaps even weapons. Second, U.S. elections were scheduled for the following year, and the secretary of state could not ignore the impact of the "Jewish vote" and the opinions of respected congressmen who pressed for aid to Israel. Finally, Dulles wanted to keep up Israeli hopes lest it be driven to desperate measures. Indeed, Dulles's ambassador to Tel Aviv believed that "Israeli talk on preventive war is no idle talk. It may well open war, if it will not get weapons. Its isolation, the blockades in the Suez and the Straits of Aqaba and the recurrent attacks in its territories—push it to acts of desperation."[12]

The American diplomats accompanying Dulles also did their best to keep Israel's hopes for assistance alive. In the meetings with their Israeli colleagues they spoke of Israel's ultimately receiving "some arms," but were careful to warn against hasty moves.[13] Francis Russell, one of the senior

American officials present, even hinted that the United States would take steps against any party initiating aggression: "We cannot undertake to intervene in every border incident, but we can ensure intervention if one side captures territory with the intention of retaining it."[14]

In fact, America's assistant secretary of defense had just sent the Joint Chiefs of Staff a directive from the National Security Council (NSC) to plan the measures the United States would have to take if major armed conflict broke out between Israel and its Arab neighbors: "The United States must be prepared to take action against a state which the U.N. or the U.S. itself decides is responsible for aggression and which refuses to retreat behind the Armistice lines." Among other measures advocated were imposing a trade embargo, cutting off financial and economic aid, and freezing financial assets. The NSC also suggested that military action be considered, such as a naval blockade effected jointly with England and perhaps also with France and Turkey. The directive specifically referred to possible provocations, among which ". . . the possibility that Israel might initiate or threaten to initiate a 'preventive war' is the most immediate danger."[15]

At the time, Sharett knew nothing of this directive; but he well understood the implications of Russell's veiled threat and of the repeated American references to the 1950 Tripartite Declaration: "Let us assume that a new, revised and amended edition of the 'Tripartite' [Declaration] were issued," he wrote in his diary. "[U]nder current circumstances, could it not be directed mainly against us, that is, intended to stop us from a preventive offensive?"[16]

After much delay Sharett also managed to meet with the Soviet foreign minister. The meeting was doomed to failure from the outset and soon deteriorated into bitter and sterile recriminations. "The disagreement," Sharett wrote, "or rather the quarrel, was always on the verge of erupting. We maintained a verbal cordiality, but were clearly at each other's throats."[17]

Israel derived no practical benefit from this rare meeting. But it was not only the Israeli foreign minister who labored under the impact of Molotov's aggressive and intractable mood. The Geneva conference ultimately failed because, in the estimation of the Western representatives, the Russians had hoped to make political gains from increased global tensions. In his memoirs U.S. President Eisenhower wrote, "It seems to me that the Soviets decided to take steps which they knew would increase tensions and intensify the Cold War."[18]

Sharett was deeply frustrated during his entire European stay:

> I was crushed by despair. With the exception of the surprising results of my meeting with Faure, my diplomatic mission had proved fruitless and I seemed doomed to return empty-handed. Worse yet, I had only myself to blame for the failure. Had I not made the trip, the disaster would not have been so obvious. Now it will be clear to one and all that . . . the democratic West has turned its back on us. . . . Israel's position has been weakened instead of strengthened; its cause has been abandoned instead of embraced.[19]

As far as the political facts are concerned, Sharett was right: His trip to Paris and Geneva made it crystal clear that the West had no intention of redressing the upset arms balance. But he was wrong about public opinion; and indeed, as his journey drew to an end, his spirits rose. "I do not regret the trip," he wrote Ben-Gurion. "[O]ur explanations and warnings had to be voiced, with the result that our interests have merited a great deal of publicity all over the world."

The psychological impact of Sharett's trip was unexpected. Rumors abounded that Israel, pushed to desperation in the tense atmosphere that had characterized the Middle East since the Czech deal, might initiate hostilities. Moshe Sharett also did not hesitate to harp on this theme and replied to journalists' questions that "He who asks this question attests that he too has considered preventive war as a logical option out of the existing situation."[20] Moreover, the Geneva Foreign Ministers' talks were disappointing and had proved to be of little value in any of the areas discussed. Against this background, Sharett managed to steal the show. "According to New York reports," he wrote in his diary, "our appearance in Geneva took center stage in the press, on television and on radio. The only serious competition came not from the official Geneva conference but from Princess Margaret, as the whole world waited to hear whether she would decide to get married or break it off." Philip Benn, reporter for the Israeli daily *Ma'ariv* and member of Sharett's entourage, wrote:

> Moshe Sharett may not be coming back from his trip with weapons from America . . . or with Molotov's promise to call off the Czech arms deliveries to Egypt, but it is already abundantly clear that his mission has accomplished one important goal: it has secured world opinion against unilaterally arming the Arabs and brought this problem to the forefront of world politics.[21]

The Israeli foreign minister was besieged by reporters and photographers who had come in droves to Paris and Geneva for the summit meeting and who hoped to elicit from him some of the drama missing from the rest of the conference. The reporters hung on his every word. When Sharett left the meeting with Dulles at the Hotel du Rhone in Geneva, he was stunned:

> I have never seen anything like it in my entire life—I had no idea anything like this could even happen. Hundreds, literally hundreds, of reporters and scores of photographers crowded around us. . . . "Do you understand what's happening?" asked Dan Avni, the Israeli delegation's press attaché. "There hasn't been tension like this surrounding any one of the 'Big Four.' All interest and anticipation is focused on you."[22]

On his return, at the airport in Lod, Sharett summed up his trip:

> . . . The situation in the Middle East was not on the official conference agenda, but the appearance of the Israeli delegation in Paris and Geneva drew a great deal of attention . . . to the drastic change in the Middle East balance of power. The center of gravity has therefore shifted—Israel's security and Middle East regional stability took a central place on the actual world agenda and became a sort of focus point for the Geneva meetings.[23]

In the weekly Foreign Ministry report the trip was described as "one of the climaxes of the State of Israel's political and propaganda efforts since its founding." [24]

In terms of real political results, however, there wasn't much to report. Other than his own eloquence, Moshe Sharett had only one weapon to wield in his diplomatic encounters: the threat of a preventive strike. And although Sharett was adamantly opposed to the idea, he did not hesitate to use the threat to stir up the rumors that had already begun to circulate throughout political and media circles. He referred to it, for example, upon his arrival at the Geneva airport, making world headlines: "PM Sharett said today that he 'hoped to God his country would not be driven to a preventive war against the Arab States.'" [25] But if Western leaders were concerned, they were not worried enough to change their positions on Israel's demands. At their final meeting, held several days after Sharett had left Europe, Dulles and Macmillan repeated the general line they had agreed on earlier. Dulles gave Macmillan particulars of the speech Eisenhower was to deliver later that day in Gettysburg and told him: "The President will reaffirm his support of the 1950 Tripartite Declaration [which he believes is] the surest way to prevent Israel from initiating hostilities." [26]

Sharett's public opinion coup probably had very little political significance, since public opinion, which is often no more than media opinion, is superficial and unstable and only seldom produces political turning points. On the other hand, the apparent success in Geneva created an illusion that was destined to lead Israel's Foreign Ministry onto a fruitless and disappointing political path of action for several months. His Geneva discussions with Dulles reinforced Sharett's belief, ultimately proved unfounded, that U.S. arms would be forthcoming if efforts were redoubled on the diplomatic front. Cautious though it was, his interim report to Ben-Gurion stated: "We may possibly get something [i.e., arms] from America." Sharett quoted Dulles in his final report: "If the kinds of weapons [that Israel requests] are defensive, they will be considered even more favorably."[27]

And indeed, at a press conference called by Dulles on October 30, at the conclusion of the Geneva conference, he spoke positively of a defensive arms supply to Israel, stressing the word "defensive." President Eisenhower's declaration of November 9 also included an encouraging hint in the same vein: "We continue to consider requests for arms for purposes of legitimate self-defense, but do not plan to contribute to the arms race."[28]

In retrospect, however, it is clear that American references to an arms supply to Israel were no more than a code word for a refusal in principal to give Israel the quantity and quality of weapons that would permit it to rectify, albeit even slightly, the overturned balance of power. The term "defensive weaponry" was deliberately vague, raising Israeli hopes of tanks and planes, when all the Americans really meant, at the very most, were ground-to-air missiles, antitank guns, and other types of arms that represented an insufficient response to Israel's pressing needs. If the Americans did consider furnishing Israel with arms, they intended to do no more than the minimum, placating U.S. public opinion by providing meager quantities of small arms. Eli Abel, the *New York Times* reporter who had been present at Dulles's press conference in Geneva, told Sharett that although Dulles had said he would consider Israel's arms requests, he had clearly hinted that the ultimate response would be negative. Whatever Israel got, it would be in dribs and drabs.[29]

Sharett was unaware that at their final Geneva meeting, Dulles and Macmillan had reached agreement on the need to continue the Near East Arms Control Commission consultations to supervise arms procurement in the region.[30] As weapons began to stream into Egypt from the Eastern bloc, this agreement could have only worked to prevent France (and perhaps other countries as well) from supplying substantial arms to Israel.

Sharett was also unaware that the two foreign ministers had in addition agreed that Evelyn Shuckburgh, on behalf of the United Kingdom, and Francis Russell, on behalf of the United States, would draw up a statement summarizing the two countries' joint policies in the Middle East. The draft document, approved in principal by Dulles and by Macmillan, reiterated that

> We must avoid being pushed by the Russians into a position of opposition to Arab interests. . . . Our guiding principle is that we should not seem to be moving in to supply Israel with arms on a large scale to offset those supplied by the Iron Curtain. . . . It should be our purpose not to allow a substantial increase in the striking power of the Israel armed forces.[31]

The odds were stacked against Sharett from the very beginning. The dramatic Soviet penetration into the Middle East, against the background of emerging nationalist and anticolonial sentiments in the Arab countries, and the appearance of a nonaligned bloc of nations in the international arena, endangered the American and British position in the region. From their point of view, it was politically illogical to appear to support Israel at a time when the Soviet Union was becoming the defender of Arab nationalism. Eloquence could not change the objective political facts. In France, however, the situation was different.

For Defense Ministry director General Shimon Peres and his aides, the Israeli government's October 3 decision to concentrate on acquiring arms meant direct and immediate action; they had to purchase weapons for the IDF as quickly as possible. "The Czech sale," Peres wrote in his memoirs, "had turned Israel's problems into a sudden drama which could only be dealt with by a thorough-going, immediate and long-range approach."[32] During the previous year France had been the main, albeit not sole, source of arms for Israel. Several transactions that had been approved in principle by the French government had not yet been implemented; the dates now had to be moved up. From the moment he was appointed to his post at the end of 1953, Peres did his best to forge direct ties with influential parties in Paris and with French arms industrialists who were interested in marketing their products— no mean feat in light of the chronic instability of Fourth Republic governments and the traditional reservations of the French Foreign Ministry, which had not yet shaken off the illusion of a strong French influence in the Levant.

Peres concentrated his efforts on the French market for several reasons. First and foremost, of all the Western arms producers, France was the least bound by British and American Near East policies; to some extent, France was even opposed to them. More so than Great Britain and America, France needed clients for its military hardware in order to lower the costs of arming its own forces. Great Britain in particular was assured of the Commonwealth market and of regular customers with whom it had long-standing military ties and agreements, such as Iraq, India, and the Persian Gulf states; France had no such special arrangements with the Arab nations.[33] Second, the French government, and even more so considerable sectors of the French population, were particularly sympathetic to the Jewish people and the State of Israel as a result of shared experiences in World War II. Finally, France was experiencing increasing anti-Arab sentiment, particularly in right-wing circles and in the military establishment, as a consequence of the growing rebellion in Algeria. These sentiments quickly gave rise to the recognition that Israel and France were in fact fighting the same enemy.

Close ties between France and Israel began to form in the summer of 1954, when General Pierre Koenig, the hero of the battle of Bir Hakim in North Africa's Western Desert during World War II and an enthusiastic supporter of Israel, was appointed as France's minister of defense. The ties quickly began to bear fruit as well. In 1955 France agreed to furnish Israel with several scores of medium (155 mm) field artillery pieces, two dozen Ouragan fighter planes, several Nord Atlas transport planes, and a quantity of light arms.[34] The purchase of 30 modern AMX-13 light tanks was already being implemented, and Israel had also been promised 24 Mystère-2 fighter planes, which its air force now wished to replace with the more advanced and efficient Mystère-4s, requiring further approval.[35] Two other transactions were pending: 175 up-to-date tank guns to be mounted on the chassis of old Sherman tanks in Israel, and several hundred bazookas.

In May 1955, as tensions along the borders flared, Shimon Peres flew to Paris again. As usual, he was received warmly by the French defense establishment. Peres wrote in his report that he and his aides were met by "concrete expressions of friendship reflecting common interests wherever we turned . . . there is no doubt that France's interests are, in addition to economic—which is indeed a considerable factor—political as well."[36] Peres submitted a new request to Defense Minister Koenig, including some ultra-modern weapons that were still in the planning stages and had not yet gone into production: 200 SS-10 antitank missiles; 29 Mystère-4 planes; 15 Voutour bomber fighter planes, and 30 AMX-13 tanks (in addition to the 30 already approved). Koenig was not authorized to conclude the transactions without the approval of other ministries, but he promised to support the requests actively and to persuade the other ministers that "Israel should be given more weapons in order for her excellent soldiers to be able to use them properly."[37]

The new proposed transaction was impressive even by French standards. It was now clear that Israel had made a long-term decision in principle to equip its army with French weapons. Peres underscored this in his memo to the French defense minister after their meeting: "The IDF is arming itself more and more with modern French weapons. In light of increasing budgetary needs and in light of the fact that the assimilation of up-to-date arms requires long-range planning—Israel wants to know if it can count on a continuing and stable arms supply from France." In July 1955 Koenig's bureau chief sent a formal letter approving the request in principle and specifying possible delivery dates, subject to duly required approvals.

Thus when the Czech sale was made public, several sizable military transactions were already pending, approved but not yet finalized. Israel was interested in expanding the transactions and speeding up their delivery. The night after the Czech deal was made public, Peres wired Yosef Nahmias, his representative in Paris: "Russian arms sent to Egypt changes our position utterly. . . . The French will doubtless be put under tremendous pressure from the English and the Americans to postpone arms deliveries to us. . . . We are therefore willing to take any risk whatsoever, so long as the planes take off on time."[38] Chief of Staff General Moshe Dayan also sent Colonel Emanuel Nishry, Israel's military attaché in France, a telegram:

> I am very worried about the delays and hold-up of arms from France. I have reason to suspect that France is being subjected to pressure, which will only increase, to cancel and postpone arms supplies to Israel. Please intervene in the matter with French military circles. . . . Also take action to have as yet unsigned contracts immediately signed . . . . early delivery is preferable to perfected technical and security considerations. . . .[39]

Peres decided to go to Paris and exploit the visit of the Israeli prime minister there in order to breach the wall of French bureaucracy.

Many of France's Foreign Ministry officials were diplomats seasoned in Arab countries in France's glory days in the Levant; they still refused to accept the reality of France's loss of influence in the Middle East and consistently rejected the attempts of the French defense establishment to forge ties with Israel. But discipline was lax in the French government at the time, and Shimon Peres was well acquainted with the maze of interministerial and interpersonal conflicts that characterized the Fourth Republic. He knew how to maneuver between the cracks; moreover, the French prime minister sided with Israel's supporters. As Moshe Sharett's meeting with Edgar Faure drew near, he was briefed by Defense Ministry officials on the particulars of Israel's requests. But the detailed briefing was not necessary; Faure surprised Sharett with his positive and energetic response and immediately made direct contact between Peres's staff and General Pierre Billotte, France's new minister of defense who had recently been appointed after Pierre Koenig's resignation (for personal reasons).

The Israelis, who had developed close ties with Koenig, were wary of his replacement; but Edgar Faure's assurance that he was their friend, just as his predecessor had been, proved true from the very first meeting with him. On October 26 Peres and the Israeli ambassador to France, Yacob Tsur, met with Billotte and Jean Crouzier, deputy defense minister in charge of military supplies; the two Frenchmen approved most of the requests, including "accelerated delivery of items included in previous requests, additional deliveries from other special sources, and even provision of weapons from [French] army storage," Tsur wrote in his diary. "When we left the Minister's bureau we were like two people who had suddenly sprouted wings." Nonetheless, Tsur was cautious in his report to Moshe Sharett: "It is not final yet. We will of course be forced to fight for each agreement. But in the end we will get what we want."[40]

And indeed, the elation was premature. The struggle between the French Defense Ministry and the Quai d'Orsay (the French Ministry of Foreign Affairs) continued, and officials of the latter continued to put up hurdles. At the end of October, at a Paris meeting of French ambassadors to the Middle East, it was resolved to try to appease the Arabs, and in particular the Egyptians, if they agreed to halt their support of the Algerian rebels and cease their anti-French propaganda in the "Sauth al Arab" radio broadcasts, the Egyptians' major pan-Arab anticolonial propaganda tool.[41]

In the meantime, a growing realization was taking form among French government and public figures: In order to quell the Algerian rebellion, its Cairo-based center of supplies and support had to be undercut, for which purpose Israel was extremely useful. A minor news item published in one of the Paris papers at the time is more revealing of future French policy than any French diplomatic maneuver; the weekly *France Observateur* quotes French Chief of Staff General Augustin Guillaume as saying "Israel should be encouraged to initiate a preventive war. This will reduce the assistance that the Arab nations are providing the North African rebels."[42]

4
• • •

PREVENTIVE WAR

The dramatic change in the region effected by the Egyptian-Czech arms deal could not have gone unnoticed by Ben-Gurion, a pessimist by nature who was usually quick to sense any danger threatening Israel. Nevertheless, we have no written evidence indicating that he was unduly concerned by it during the first few days after the transaction was announced. Three days after Nasser's speech at the Egyptian army photo exhibit, Ben-Gurion—still only defense minister in Moshe Sharett's transition government—held his weekly briefing with Chief of Staff General Moshe Dayan and Defense Ministry director General Shimon Peres. The Czech arms sale was not on the agenda. Only at the end of long discussions on routine issues did the "Old Man" casually ask, "Could we drop 50-100 paratroops to blow up those planes that are arriving?"[1] Nothing further was said on this occasion.

For two weeks after the announcement, in fact, Ben-Gurion, the man slated once again to be prime minister, was entirely absorbed in the formidable task of forming a coalition government. His mission was complicated by an upheaval in political alignments that had left him to form a coalition with the left-wing Mapam and Ahdut Ha'avodah parties, at the expense of his previous partners from the centrist General Zionists, together with the habitually problematic National Religious Party. Ben-Gurion could be single-minded at times. His preoccupation with the task that lay before him probably was augmented by the fact that he would soon be presenting the new government to the Third Knesset. In all likelihood, he preferred to concentrate on the central issues concerning the country from his new position as prime minister.

But on October 13 Ben-Gurion was suddenly taken ill, and for a short while it was feared he would be unable to pursue his duties. It soon became clear, however, that his ailment was relatively minor and only required two weeks of complete rest. Ben-Gurion probably spent those long days of enforced seclusion considering the Egyptian-Czech arms sale, its implications, and the response that Israel would have to make. This is clear from the first thing he did as soon as his doctors permitted him to resume partial activity from his sickbed: On October 21, less than a week after falling ill, he asked his military secretary, Colonel Nehemia Argov, to recall Moshe Dayan urgently from France where he was vacationing. Argov wired Dayan: "The 'Old Man' rose from his sickbed this morning. His first request was to see you. He wants you to come back immediately." The private meeting took place on October 23 in Ben-Gurion's Jerusalem hotel room; in his memoirs Moshe Dayan relates that Ben-Gurion ordered him to prepare a plan of operations as quickly as possible for the seizure of the Straits of Tiran.[2]

Although Ben-Gurion has been described by one of his biographers as full of fighting spirit at the time, in fact he was beset by doubts. Characteristically, and befitting his position of national leadership, he tried to keep those doubts to himself, and at the end of October and beginning of November he even approved a series of military operations against the Egyptians. Certainly his speech to the Knesset introducing the new cabinet was aggressive and acerbic[3]; but he was less sure of himself than he pretended to be, and Moshe Dayan, keenly sensitive to the "Old Man's" moods, noted that Ben-Gurion "had not yet decided his policy."[4]

The considerations that guided Ben-Gurion and the Israeli general staff in the autumn of 1955 were complex. The first and most pressing was the question of war—that is, what conditions would provoke it and how could it be won. Ben-Gurion and Dayan had long assumed that another encounter with the Arab states was inevitable and that Arab declarations about a "second round" were serious. Until the Czech sale, however, that encounter had not seemed imminent. Since his appointment as chief of staff at the end of December 1953, Dayan had repeatedly averred that the IDF had several years in which to prepare for a decisive battle, preferring a policy of long-range preparations over immediate readiness. The Czech deal turned this view of the situation upside down: If war could be expected within the year, long-range considerations had to give way to increased short-range IDF preparedness. And if war was imminent, then the question of the conditions under which it would be fought became urgent and immediate.

An interrelated consideration was the cost in casualties and physical destruction that the country would have to pay even if the war was ultimately won. Ben-Gurion was plagued by the fear that the new immigrant border settlements established all over Israel only a few years earlier might not withstand an Arab assault; adding to that worry was the expected toll that could be exacted by Soviet-supplied bombers aimed at Israel's urban population.

In March 1955 infiltrators from the Gaza Strip had attacked a recently established immigrant settlement not far west of Beersheba while a wedding was being celebrated, causing one death and several injuries. The next day the entire settlement's population drove to Jerusalem to demonstrate in front of the Knesset. Ben-Gurion was deeply shocked. A few days later he told his chief of staff that he feared that the new immigrants in the border settlements would be the first to run in the event of war.[5] In an address to the Knesset on January 2, 1956, Ben-Gurion praised the new immigrants' ability to stand up to possible attack:

> The settlements' endurance under attack is as important as the strength of the Israeli army. The new immigrants, even those from undeveloped and poverty-ridden lands, have shown their mettle by working hard, building homes and turning arid wasteland into flourishing farms; they will surely also show their mettle by withstanding assaults if, God forbid, war breaks out.[6]

But this was for public consumption; deep in his heart Ben-Gurion's doubts were grave, and privately he had expressed them at a closed session of the IDF High Command: "Right now we have no guarantee that the new immigrants, especially those in the new rural settlements, are capable of withstanding attack."[7]

Ben-Gurion had experienced the London blitz at firsthand and had been horrified at the devastation. He often referred to it and feared similar havoc might be wreaked on Israel's cities. On January 15, 1956, he told U.S. Ambassador Lawson:

> Our real danger is of an air attack. The bombers being sent to him [Nasser] can carry 5 or 6 tons of bombs, can fly as high as 20 km. and as fast as 900 km. per hour. In no time they can bomb our cities and towns, as well as the irrigation installations which are the very foundation of our agriculture.[8]

On another occasion he referred to the coming summer as a possible time of testing:

It will be harder than in 1948. . . . I assume that we will survive it, but at a very high
cost. There will be destruction, in the cities too. There will be bombings, farms laid
waste, but especially a very high cost in human life. . . . The cost will be higher and
more terrible than what we paid in 1948.[9]

There were two obvious conclusions: First, a military engagement had to
take place before the enemy grew strong enough to raise the stakes in terms
of casualties and civilian damage, perhaps even jeopardizing Israel's ability
to win a war in the battlefield. Second, Israel had to strike the first blow;
enemy airfields had to be bombed as soon as hostilities broke out in order to
neutralize the effect of the new planes and to carry the battle deep behind
enemy lines, before the new immigrant settlements could be attacked.

In the early 1950s, the Israeli general staff believed that the circumstances
of the Israeli War of Independence in 1948 had forced the Israeli army to
engage the enemy at the beginning by defensive containment of its attack
initiative, thereby incurring a great deal of attrition. In the future, such circumstances had to be avoided, and GHQ planning called for a first-strike
capability in any coming confrontation. This strategy was especially central
to air force operational planning because Israeli airfields were few in number and very vulnerable, the Arabs had more aircraft, and the Israeli air force
had to be employed as quickly as possible to provide ground support for the
land forces.[10] After reviewing a five-year plan presented at one of Israel's air
bases, Ben-Gurion said at a cabinet meeting at the end of 1953: "I believe
the army's air strike forces should be given preference. As soon as the battle
begins, the air force should destroy the enemy's air power and eliminate his
air strike capability."[11]

All this relates directly to the question of deterrence, usually defined as a
condition in which one country succeeds, for any number of reasons, in
keeping another from attacking it: In other words, *the deterred country* has
come to believe that, under the given circumstances, it has no chance of winning and therefore does not dare to initiate hostilities. The focus in such a
perception is on the deterred side. However, the experience of the last 40
years of conflict in the Middle East suggests that the emphasis should be
shifted onto the deterring nation, making deterrence a condition in which *the
deterring state* believes itself capable of effectively avoiding enemy attack.
Most of the developments in the region came about as the result of changes
in Israel's subjective view of its ability to deter its enemies.[12]

Because of Israel's extreme sensitivity to the question of who would initiate hostilities and deliver the first strike, the subjective dimension of deterrence became central. So long as Israel believed in its deterrent capability
and assumed that the enemy would not dare attack, it could allow itself to

refrain from taking preemptive initiatives. The importance attached at the time to territorial defense—based on a front-line network of armed and fortified civilian settlements—derived from the assumption that the chances of enemy-initiated war in the foreseeable future were slight. Under such circumstances Israel could be satisfied with a minimal defensive capability, just to be on the safe side. The Czech arms deal certainly ate away at Israel's objective deterrence of Egypt, but the major impact was subjective and affected Israel's self-image, severely undermining the country's belief in its ability to deter. When it became a real possibility that the enemy could in the near future take the initiative—that is, when the *deterring state* no longer believed it could deter—the Israeli army could no longer rely on its defensive capability and preferred to take the initiative into its own hands, by striking preemptively before it was too late.

It is thus not surprising that in the autumn of 1955 the IDF command favored preventive war. Moshe Dayan had few doubts as to what needed to be done. On November 10 he wrote a memo to the defense minister regarding the situation along the Egyptian front and recommending, in light of Egypt's actively aggressive policy:

> that action be taken with the aim of (1) undermining the pace of the build-up of the Egyptian army, which, thanks to the Czech sale, will within a few months be ready to operate the new weapons that far outstrip in size and quality anything we have; (2) embarking on an early engagement with the hostile Egyptian regime . . . in order to either topple it or force it to change its policies; (3) reacting sharply and forcefully to Egyptian acts of hostility and violations of the Armistice Agreements.

The chief of staff went on to detail the operational targets and the actions that could secure them: (a) heavy reprisals for Fedayun actions, Egyptian firing on Israeli forces and encroachment onto Israeli territory; (b) guaranteed Israeli control of the Nitzana junction; (c) conquest of the Gaza Strip; (d) seizure of the Straits of Tiran. Despite the fear that "a serious military action on our part will halt (be it ever so temporarily) the French arms supply to Israel," Dayan did not feel that these operations should be postponed.[13]

Three days later he wrote Ben-Gurion again:

> I think we must bring about a major confrontation with the Egyptian army as quickly as possible in order to achieve three goals: (1) to land a serious blow at the Egyptian air force; (2) to gain control of the Rafah and Nitzana junctions; (3) to conquer the Straits of Eilat (Sharm al-Sheikh). I believe that even if chances of getting defensive

arms from the U.S. were good, we shouldn't wait until the end of their deliberations—certainly not if chances are slim.

For the sake of drama Dayan proposed that Yigael Yadin, the IDF's second
chief of staff and renowned chief of operations during the 1948 war, be named
chief of staff in Dayan's place and that General Mordechai Makleff, General
Yigal Allon, and other retired senior commanders be returned to active duty.
He himself, he wrote, wanted the Southern Command.[14] Dayan did not use the
term "preventive war," but that is clearly what he meant. "The confrontation
must not be delayed by so much as one day," he told senior commanders,
"because this Egyptian arms deal may not be a one-time event."[15]

Unlike Dayan, Ben-Gurion did have many hesitations. From the outset he
refused to consider preventive war—that is, an unprovoked frontal attack on
the Egyptian forces in the Sinai. Unfortunately, his diaries from that period
have been lost and our knowledge of the particulars of that October 23 discussion with the chief of staff can be based only on Dayan's evidence and
Ben-Gurion's recollections from much later. In all likelihood Ben-Gurion,
sharply sensitive to international reaction, was well aware that, in 1955, a
small nation like Israel could not expect to be permitted to initiate war
merely because it feared its enemies would one day gain military superiority.
In order to start a preemptive war, the dangers posed had to be much more
palpable, the enemy had to be much more acutely provocative. After World
War II international ethics did not consider a sincere conviction in the
enemy's aggressive intentions as sufficient cause for preemption; subjective
apprehensions were insufficient justification for going to war. There had to
be an imminent threat—not necessarily an actual attack, but at least a concrete danger.

Ben-Gurion was not privy to American and British joint command plans
for military intervention should Israel initiate war, but he did fear such a
possibility. In early December, when the Israeli Cabinet eventually rejected
the option of initiating hostilities, Ben-Gurion felt obliged to explain the
decision to the Israeli army command. Addressing senior officers, he raised
three arguments against preventive war. First, the world, including the
Western powers, would not permit Israel to initiate war except in reaction to
immediate and real danger. If it did, Israel would ultimately find itself totally
isolated in the international arena, bereft of any hope of rearming itself, and
terribly weakened. Second, it was possible that foreign powers, especially

Great Britain, would come running to Egypt's aid to prevent an Israeli victory and to buy Arab friendship. And finally, one war could not prevent further wars. This one would be followed by another, but under much more difficult and trying circumstances for Israel.[16]

During the two months between his illness in mid-October and his address to the High Command in December, Ben-Gurion's rhetoric became more incisive and he grew increasingly entrenched in his opposition to preventive war. But even earlier, at that first meeting with Dayan, Ben-Gurion had refused to consider Israeli-initiated full-scale warfare that was not a direct reaction to outright Egyptian provocation.

The chief of staff's Bureau Diary entry for October 23, the day of Dayan's meeting with Ben-Gurion, contains a summary report of the discussion, which Dayan gave to his deputy, General Haim Laskov, and to the head of Military Intelligence, Colonel Yehoshafat Harkaby[17]: The fundamental solution to Israel's deteriorating security situation was to eliminate Nasser's regime, requiring a decisive full-scale encounter between the Israeli and the Egyptian armies. Nevertheless, the idea of a preventive war was out of the question because it meant a war of aggression initiated by Israel. Despite the urgent need to topple Nasser's regime, Israel could not confront the entire world, which would view it as an aggressor nation in every sense of the term, thereby depriving it of full victory in the war. The British were liable to seize such an historic opportunity to reestablish themselves in the Middle East, bombing the Israeli army columns from their bases in Cyprus; the Soviets were likely to take the opportune moment to entrench their penetration of the region by additional armaments and political support for Egypt, perhaps even sending volunteers to operate the Soviet weapons being stockpiled there; America and France would be immobilized by the U.N. Charter principles against aggression. But a defensive war fought by Israel against Egyptian aggression was a totally different story.

Still reeling from the shock of the Czech sale, and in light of their assessments of Egypt's uncompromising enmity and hostile intentions toward Israel, Ben-Gurion and Dayan longed to strike Nasser a fatal blow and anxiously looked to Egypt to furnish Israel with the provocation necessary to initiate hostilities without earning world condemnation. Could Egypt be irked into attacking Israel before the balance of power was completely redefined? Despite the caution and moderation Nasser had espoused temporarily while the new Soviet weaponry was being assimilated by his army, could he be egged on into defending his newly won prestige and leadership in the Arab world?

The best chances for this to happen lay in the realm of the second set of problems confronting Israel's security establishment, the area of the armistice regime: the day-to-day relations between Israel and Egypt along the borders. In the autumn of 1955, four issues repeatedly flared up: (1) security along the Gaza Strip; (2) infiltration, in particular that of the Fedayun, across the borders; (3) the status of the demilitarized zones around Nitzana and Abu Agheila; and (4) Israeli navigation in the Suez Canal and the Straits of Tiran. Egypt did its utmost to restrict Israel's actions on each of these issues, interpreting the Armistice Agreements minimalistically and reaffirming its claim for a "belligerent" status.[18] Egypt's goal was obvious. Ehud Ya'ari, who investigated infiltration from the Gaza Strip in the early 1950s, writes:

> The political goal of utilizing infiltration to increase violence was no secret: it was intended to keep military tensions high along the Armistice lines to prevent the cease-fire from stabilizing, to exert continual pressure on the young state of Israel, to keep the armed Palestinian struggle from dying—in short, to prevent the *status quo* as fixed in Rhodes through the Armistice Agreements from becoming established and to sabotage further progress in political negotiations.[19]

To use Thomas Schelling's terminology, Egypt retained the "ability to inflict pain" at many points, and the IDF's deterrent capability in terms of total war did not extend to these "pain-inflicting" activities. Israel viewed Egypt's behavior as a serious violation of its own sovereign rights and insisted on its own interpretation of the Armistice Agreements—that they constituted a "*de facto* peace" or at the very least to a state of "non-belligerency."[20]

Early in October, right after the Czech sale was announced, the Israeli-Egyptian border quieted down somewhat, in part due to the relentless efforts of General E.L.M. Burns, U.N. Observer Forces chief of staff, and in part due to Nasser himself, who characteristically eased tensions immediately after taking a dramatic step. But the temporary lull did not solve the fundamental problems, and the blockade of Israeli shipping through and air passage over the Straits of Tiran remained insoluble. No actual confrontation had taken place yet, since Israel had not tested Egypt's renewed blockade. For the moment, however, Israel stopped flying El Al planes overhead en route to South Africa and did not navigate ships to and from the port of Eilat. For the Israeli leaders, the blockade seemed related to recent Egyptian claims to the Negev, Israel's southern desert. Since the 1930s, Ben-Gurion had been arguing that the Negev was vitally important for Israel's future; he pleaded the cause of the Negev and the new town of Eilat almost obsessively. Without the

Negev, he averred, Israel could become another Carthage, which was defeated by the Romans because it had no agricultural hinterland and, like Tel Aviv, was no more than an isolated city along the seashore.

If preventive war was out of the question, Israel could at least insist on its rights and interests in the interim status of neither war nor peace.[21] It could insist on the right of its farmers to tend their fields along the Gaza border without fear of attack from infiltrators, on the right of its guard patrols to move unhindered within Israeli territory, on the right of its citizens to settle and develop the Nitzana area, and on the right of its ships to sail to and from Eilat. If Israel used force to protect these rights, Egypt might be drawn into full-scale warfare.

Ben-Gurion and Dayan believed that insisting on Israel's rights and unequivocally and adamantly subscribing to the armistice agreements might even garner Israel international support despite some limited aggressive actions on its part. In fact, this is what had been happening over the past few months while Israel carried out its policy of reprisals: Despite the anger and criticism these actions elicited, even among Israel's friends, other nations all had to admit that there was an element of justifiable self-defense in them. Since World War II, all acts of aggression had been uniformly condemned by international standards of justice, but Article 51 of the U.N. Charter left room for interpretation of the right to self-defense. Enemy actions that clearly could be viewed as aggressive and provocative (for example, naval blockade or border incursions by irregular troops) could justify actions intended to prevent such acts, even if they themselves were tactically offensive. Limited acts of violence in reaction to Egyptian provocations could thus furnish the fuse by which wide-scale hostilities could ultimately be ignited, leaving the question of blame for aggression ambiguous. Israel could achieve its goal of an early military confrontation with Egypt without being condemned as an aggressor.

To his deputy and the chief of intelligence, Dayan explained how this could be achieved:

> The confrontation must be effected by escalation. Since it is imperative that Israel's actions can be justified in the international arena, she must not do this through any blatant provocation that can be ultimately exposed. . . . But Israel does not even need to provoke; in the current state of conflict between Israel and Egypt, Egypt herself furnishes the provocations night and day. Israel need only stubbornly insist on her rights and retaliate sharply for each act of Egyptian aggression. Such a policy will eventually escalate the tensions to a breaking point. What this effectively means is that we must follow an active and uncompromising policy based juridically and diplomatically on the demand for meticulous and full compliance with the Armistice Agreements and the articles of international law.[22]

Nasser would probably try to avoid a major engagement in the near future, but would be hard-pressed if Israel seriously damaged his prestige, Dayan added. Nasser's self-restraint was not limitless, and at some point he could be expected to lose control and make the kind of response anticipated from a great Arab leader. But should Nasser's self-restraint exceed Israeli estimates and should he not be drawn into full-scale warfare, Israel's policy would at least protect its interests and make some tangible gains, improving its military position before the Egyptian army grew stronger. Israel's full-scale wartime deterrent capability would thus be transferred to back up its interests along the borders, and it would be in a more amenable position when the confrontation initiated by Nasser ensued.

Ben-Gurion's Knesset address ten days later bore out Dayan's interpretation:

> We seek peace, but not suicide. . . . our neighbors have not complied with the Armistice Agreements and continue to wage war against us by other means—economic boycott, blockade, periodic border incursions by murderers and terrorists. . . . The Egyptian Government has violated the basic international law of freedom of navigation in the Suez. . . . It is now trying to block the way for Israel's ships in the Red Sea Gulf. . . . This unilateral war must cease, because it cannot long remain unilateral. The Israeli Government is as willing as ever to faithfully comply with the Armistice Agreements, precisely and in all particulars, in both letter and spirit. But the other side bears this same responsibility. We will not be bound by an agreement violated by the other side. If the borders of the Armistice lines are open to terrorists and assassins, they will not remain closed to defenders and protectors. If our rights are violated by acts of aggression on land or on sea—we reserve the freedom to act to defend them in the most effective way.[23]

The chief of staff translated this political declaration into operational terms: Any harm inflicted on military forces or civilian border settlements would elicit serious and large-scale retaliation; sniper attacks against Israeli observation posts and attacks against Israeli patrols in the Gaza Strip would be answered by occupation of the attacking position, using armor and artillery where tactically needed; Fedayun sabotage and mine-laying or murder would elicit Israeli army raids deep inside the Gaza Strip and attacks on military camps; any Egyptian troops encroaching onto Israeli territory would be attacked. If General Burns could not thin out the Egyptian army concentrations at Abu Agheila, the Israeli army would recapture Nitzana and fortify it. If freedom of navigation was not guaranteed in the Straits of Tiran and the blockade not lifted, Israel would conquer the straits and retain them in order to guarantee free navigation.

Moshe Dayan pinned his hopes on the last issue. He reckoned that Nasser could exercise restraint for all of Israel's challenges but one: conquest of the Straits of Tiran. Night reprisals, IDF entry into Nitzana, or an aggressive policy along the deep furrow that Israel had dug all along the borders of the Gaza Strip in order to demarcate the boundary clearly—these were temporary and transient, and their effects could be mitigated by propaganda. But conquering and retaining Egyptian territory—this was too serious a blow to go unanswered. Thus Dayan perceived the conquest of the Straits of Tiran as the detonator that would set off the general engagement of troops that Israel wanted to trigger.

The only operative order that Ben-Gurion had given his chief of staff at their meeting on October 23 was to arrange for the conquest of Sharm al-Sheikh and the Straits area. Dayan estimated that it would take two months to set up the operation and ordered the IDF to prepare for a general confrontation no later than January 1956.[24] Whether Egypt was drawn into war in reaction to the takeover of the straits or whether it restrained itself and waited until later, a war between Israel and Egypt would certainly be fought sometime in 1956. IDF preparations thus had to be immediate and accelerated. A state of emergency had to be declared, the troops had to be readied for the different missions, operational plans had to be drawn up and updated, and reserve call-up readiness had to be reviewed.

Not six weeks later the Israeli Cabinet would reject the policy of escalation that Ben-Gurion and Dayan had discussed at their October 23 meeting, and Ben-Gurion himself would soon become dubious of its implementation. Not wishing to reveal his hesitancy in public, he continued to articulate a forceful stand on the Straits of Tiran, but Dayan began to sense that Ben-Gurion was not wholeheartedly in favor of the plan. Ben-Gurion probably feared that the international community would not absolve Israel of all blame for the full-scale war that would certainly result from an attack on the straits. Nonetheless, the directives sent that day and in the following days to the various army echelons were vitally important. They created a tremendous momentum of mobilization and preliminary groundwork and planning a full year before the Sinai campaign began. Although the confrontation with Egypt ultimately took place under totally different circumstances, these directives fixed the starting point for the IDF's deployment for that confrontation and initiated the long and arduous process of preparing it for what seemed to be an inevitable war. In retrospect, the conversation in Ben-Gurion's hotel room at the end of October

1955 can be seen as the first signal to start Israeli military preparations and put the actual planning for large-scale warfare into high gear. The history of 1956 is the story of that large-scale preparation and of the vicissitudes that eventually culminated in battle. Twelve months later, when the orders to launch the Sinai campaign were finally issued, the Israeli army was ready for war, its units equipped and trained, its plans laid down to the minutest detail, and its borders fortified.

Within a few hours of the meeting between Ben-Gurion and Dayan, the general staff began to regroup: Nonessential officer training programs were cancelled; any planned but not yet effected changes in command placements were frozen. Colonel Meir Amit was put in charge of reforming the Southern Command, which had been dismantled only a few months earlier for reasons of economy; a new brigade under the command of Colonel Haim Bar-Lev was created for the capture of the straits. On October 26, Dayan ordered a special emergency session of the general staff and issued new instructions. He concluded the meeting by saying that "what this means is that the army must be prepared for war *this year*"[25] (emphasis added).

The realization that force might be used at some time to break the Egyptian blockade of the Straits of Tiran, and the preparatory measures it presumed, had begun to evolve the previous spring. Early in 1955, shortly after Ben-Gurion's return from Sde Boker, the kibbutz in the southern desert where he had spent a temporary retirement during all of 1954, he ordered torpedo boats moved to Eilat: "We cannot cross the Suez by force, our attempts will fail. But we must force our way to Eilat, our troops must be there."[26] Several days later he repeated: "I don't think we can do anything in Suez . . . but Eilat is a different matter; it is an open sea and whoever prevents navigation on the open sea is a pirate; we are ready to fight against pirates."[27] In June several officers from the renowned Givati infantry regiment were sent on a daring reconnaissance mission to check land routes from Eilat to Sharm al-Sheikh. Code-named Yarkon, the mission lasted three days. The navy landed the small unit on the Dahab coast halfway down the eastern coast of the Sinai, and from there the men carried out their reconnaissance on foot, mapping out possible approaches in the rugged wasteland. When the mission was completed, they were airlifted by light planes that had landed and taken off in the rough. The information gathered eventually helped the Ninth Brigade as it proceeded to Sharm al-Sheikh in November 1956.[28]

Now that the green light had been given, preparations to break the naval blockade went into high gear. The operation was code-named Omer and D-Day set for the beginning of January. The regular paratroops, a battalion of reserve paratroopers, and another select infantry regiment that had undergone intensive training in landing operations were placed at Haim Bar-Lev's disposal, and the brigade began to assemble updated information, make detailed plans, and carry out special exercises in preparation for the operation.

The first opportunity to exploit the policy of escalation was not long in coming. On Wednesday, October 26, 1955, the Egyptians launched a surprise attack on a small Israeli guard unit at the southern end of the demilitarized zone of Nitzana. One Israeli soldier was killed, two were wounded, and two were taken prisoner. The Egyptian attack was a retaliation for the abduction three days earlier of a Syrian officer and four enlisted men by an IDF unit in the Golan Heights in the north. Egypt's action was intended to show its solidarity with Syria, with whom it had just concluded a mutual defense treaty and formed a joint Egyptian-Syrian military command.

The Israeli response was swift. On the night of October 27-28 a paratroop battalion attacked the Egyptian border post at Kuntilla, near Eilat. Two Israelis and 10 Egyptians were killed and 29 Egyptians taken prisoner. At dawn the paratroopers returned to Israeli territory, having captured considerable light arms. The Israeli general staff assumed that Nasser would react, and Ben-Gurion instructed the chief of staff: "If the Egyptian response is serious, then our army will take Khan Yunis and Rafah in the Gaza Strip. If the Egyptians employ aircraft, our air force will attack the airfields along the Suez Canal."[29] The IDF called up reserve units, concentrated forces in the south, and prepared to take over Gaza. But despite mounting tensions, Nasser exercised self-restraint. Two small Egyptian detachments tried to assault an Israeli outpost on the Gaza border but were easily repulsed; the battle ended before it began. Egyptian radio inflated the incident, but the Israeli GHQ did not perceive it as connected with the Kuntilla operation and thought it no more than one of many incidents along the Gaza border that occurred during that year.

Another blow was struck on the night of November 2, several hours after Ben-Gurion's bellicose address in the Knesset as he presented the new Cabinet. Several weeks earlier, in the el-Sabha hills not far from where they had recently attacked the Israeli guardpost, the Egyptians had established a new outpost several hundred meters into the Israeli side of the demilitarized zone of Nitzana. Israel's repeated demands that the Egyptians withdraw fell on deaf ears. The U.N. secretary general's recommendation that the border be marked and the forces withdrawn was rejected because Egypt presented counterclaims.[30] Following the policy of meticulously protecting its rights, the Israelis attacked the Egyptian posts. This was the IDF's most extensive operation since the end of the 1948 war. The entire paratroop battalion took part, as well as two other infantry regiments plus armor and artillery units. All the Egyptian outposts in the area were captured, some 70 Egyptian soldiers were killed, and 50 were taken prisoner. A considerable amount of arms were captured as well. Seven Israeli soldiers were killed in the action and 20 were wounded.

Before daybreak Dayan tried to convince the defense minister to keep the Israeli forces in the conquered area, in the hope that this would force Nasser to open a large-scale counterattack and thereby usher in the anticipated escalation. But Ben-Gurion ordered the forces back to Israel before dawn, as was customary in all reprisal operations.

Moshe Dayan's estimate proved correct: Nasser did indeed embark on a large-scale counterattack. The next morning, after long and heavy artillery shelling, an Egyptian infantry regiment attacked the empty outposts that the Israelis had evacuated a few hours earlier. The Egyptian Propaganda Ministry reported that the Egyptians had routed the Israelis from Egyptian soil and claimed 200 IDF casualties, thereby permitting Egypt to acknowledge the deaths of its 70 soldiers and hold a state funeral for the "heroes of the battle of al-Sabha."[31] Thus Nasser managed to take the sting out of the defeat and balance out the tally of "victories."

Ben-Gurion's refusal to accede to Dayan's request to keep the forces in the area revealed a fundamental difference in the approaches of the two men who headed Israel's defense establishment. It turned out that they were not in such close agreement on the policy of escalation as had been thought. The last retaliations after the attack on the Khan Yunis police station two months earlier clearly indicated that Nasser was not being drawn into war in the wake of even large-scale Israeli attacks. In a memo to Ben-Gurion about a week after the al-Sabha operation, Dayan wrote: "There is no sign of the Egyptians responding to our latest actions in Kuntilla and the Nitzana zone. They are clearly in a defensive mode. . . . We can increase tensions here or there, and even provoke a local confrontation of armed forces, but not an extensive Egyptian attack on our forces in Israel."[32] Dayan was willing to step up the provocations, despite the risks of international condemnation and the intervention of Western powers; but Ben-Gurion refrained, and his view prevailed.

Ben-Gurion assiduously read all the telegrams and reports that passed through the Foreign Office communications network and certainly was not unaware of the many hints and even direct warnings that the Americans and British had passed to Israel. He probably also read the report on Abba

Eban's meeting with the U.S. State Department's Francis Russell, who told Eban specifically that the Americans would consider intervention if either side captured territory with the aim of retaining it. Ben-Gurion did not want to test the Americans and refused to permit Israeli troops to be found in Egyptian territory when day broke.

What then was the point of a campaign to capture Sharm al-Sheikh if the conquered area was not retained, at least for a while? Ben-Gurion apparently rationalized that the Egyptian blockade of the Straits of Tiran provided him with sufficient international justification for such a move. He therefore instructed the chief of staff to continue preparations for the campaign. On November 8 he told Dayan, "All preparations must be made as early as possible. What is really important is Eilat; that is our great test. . . . we'll capture the place and then—if we get guarantees that our ships can sail freely, if we get guarantees of free navigation—then we'll leave."[33]

But even on this point Ben-Gurion was not completely convinced. Several days later Dayan informed him that the preparations for the campaign would be concluded by the end of December, but Ben-Gurion told Dayan to "hold up action on Sharm al-Sheikh until the end of January 1956."[34] Israel might get American arms, Ben-Gurion explained, referring to President Eisenhower's declaration of November 9, 1955: "While we continue to consider [Israeli] requests for arms needed for legitimate self-defense, we do not intend to contribute to an arms competition."[35] But it is hard to believe that Ben-Gurion pinned serious hopes on that promise; it is more realistic to assume that the British prime minister's Guildhall address of that same day reinforced Ben-Gurion's fear of British military intervention against Israel, prompting him to postpone the campaign.

The Israeli staff officers were also dissatisfied with the operational logic of the planned campaign. Capturing the Straits of Eilat would obviously provoke full-scale warfare; but in that case Israel would not be entering the war according to the most advantageous order of events and would be forgoing the use of the army's elite corps in the decisive battle. The IDF planning officers wanted to open war by striking a resounding blow at Egyptian airfields at Zero Hour and by a concerted attack of all best available forces against the main Egyptian military concentrations in the north of Sinai. The distant straits in the south, they believed, should be conquered only after air superiority had been achieved and after the central engagement had been won. The plan currently proposed called for the war to be fought the wrong way around, as it were; it risked losing the initiative in the air, forgoing surprise in the central engagement, and engaging in the decisive battle without the paratroops. At the general staff meeting with the defense minister on November 8, Dayan said:

We want to carry out the operation in Rafah first because we're afraid we'll be drawn
into serious war with Egypt. We'll be deploying our best forces in the Red Sea,
weakening ourselves along the Gaza Strip: here they'll be in their own territory,
while our forces are engaged at the other end of the world. If we were in Rafah from
the outset, the situation would be different.[36]

But Dayan was aware of the political dilemma. At least for Ben-Gurion, an
attack on the Straits of Tiran had much stronger political and legal justification than a frontal assault on the Egyptians in the north of Sinai. But so anxious was he to strike at Egypt as early as possible that Dayan was even
willing to risk planning campaigns the wrong way around.

A year later the need to prefer political over operational considerations
would recur, and the paratroop brigade would be shifted away from the decisive battle in order to accomplish a politically vital but strategically marginal mission in the Mitla Pass near the Suez Canal. Planning the Omer
campaign a year earlier clearly helped Moshe Dayan contemplate such a
possibility and even believe in its efficacy. It enabled him eventually to propose that same formula—sending paratroops to an operationally marginal
mission far away from the main force deployment, paving the way for the
entire Sinai campaign.

However, the very assumption that the campaign to conquer the Straits of
Tiran would bring about full-scale warfare ultimately doomed it to rejection.
Although there were good political and moral grounds for attacking the
straits, it was hard to ignore the fact that this mission was no more than a
thinly disguised preventive war. For someone opposed in principle to preventive war, as Ben-Gurion repeatedly affirmed he was, the campaign could
not be justified. A day before he left for the Geneva conference, Moshe
Sharett visited the recuperating Ben-Gurion, who shared his strategic plans
with him. Sharett wrote in his diary that Ben-Gurion opposed an "initiated
war" but wanted to "respond sharply to every instance of Egyptian damage
. . . including the blockade of Eilat." Sharett notes:

What does Ben-Gurion intend? Just to "react" or to provoke war? . . . When he says
that an "initiated war" is impossible, where is the stress, on the first word or the second? . . . Does he not want war or does he indeed strive for war with Egypt on condition that it not be perceived by the world as a war initiated by us but rather imposed
on us?[37]

At the end of November Ben-Gurion asked for Cabinet approval of the plan
to take the Straits of Tiran. It was postponed by a majority achieved by a combination of a few Labor Party members and representatives of smaller coalition parties. Ben-Gurion later angrily accused Sharett of mustering a majority

against him. Several weeks later he even hinted to the general staff that the government had voted against him in the matter of the straits.[38] But he must have been aware of the basic contradiction, and was perhaps even secretly pleased at the Cabinet rejection. At any rate, he did not try to appeal the vote. He had been ambivalent about the campaign from the start; and Sharett's reports from his trip to Geneva, Abba Eban's optimistic cables during the first days of November, Eden's Guildhall speech, and President Eisenhower's declaration of November 9—all these kept him from insisting on the proposal wholeheartedly and tipped the scales against an early military engagement and in favor of waiting for the results of Eban's contacts in Washington.

But Dayan did not give up easily. He bombarded Ben-Gurion with memos in which he reiterated his contention that swift action was vital.[39] He did not believe there were any chances of getting arms from the United States, he wrote, and feared that the opportunity to strike the Egyptians would be lost. On November 17, at their weekly meeting, he again explained the advantages of the early initiation of hostilities to the minister of defense:

> I'll tell you what I think we can gain by war if it starts now. . . . If we take the Straits of Tiran, if we take Rafah, it will give us a better border. And a better border is a priceless weapon, real military strength. It makes a tremendous difference whether they are inside or outside the Gaza Strip. . . . We will have struck a blow to the Egyptian army. One blow cannot solve problems for generations to come, but an army that has been struck is temporarily weakened.[40]

But Ben-Gurion evaded the issue and shifted the conversation to another matter; he did not accede to Dayan's pleas.

Throughout November the Israeli army continued to view the campaign for the straits as a practical plan about to be put into operation. The Intelligence Branch worked hard to get a "test ship" that would leave Djibouti and try to go through the straits; its arrest by the Egyptians would provide the ultimate trigger for activating the campaign. Haim Bar-Lev continued to prepare his brigade, and the GHQ Operations Branch put the final touches on the plans. But the general tension slowly dissipated. At the weekly briefing with the chief of staff on November 17, Ben-Gurion ordered plans for the campaign to continue, but he did not hide his hesitations. He told Dayan:

> English intervention will certainly be immediately forthcoming. I have no doubt whatsoever about it. . . . They will bomb our airfields. . . . They won't bomb Tel Aviv, but they will bomb the airfields, and afterwards we won't get any arms at all. America won't give us any, Italy won't give us any, the Russians won't—where will we get them? . . . At any rate, we will soon know what the American policy is. Over these next few weeks we will know what they have decided, what their policies are regarding the defensive weapons that they are allegedly prepared to give us.[41]

Early in December Ben-Gurion's hesitations peaked. At the weekly briefing on December 1, Dayan pressed Ben-Gurion again to make a decision.
There was a difference between offensive plans and defensive plans, he said;
the IDF had to know in which direction it was going. If the people of Israel
had made up their minds not to initiate a war, "then the army's working
plans must be different from those we would have if we knew that we had to
attack in a month's time." The defense minister wanted to resume discussion
of the question of arms procurement, for which the meeting had initially
been called, but Dayan did not relent: "What happens if it turns out that we
can't get (arms) until May?" "You tell me," Ben-Gurion replied. "You want
me to tell you?" Dayan retorted with slightly more than a trace of bitterness:

> What good will that do? . . . Pretty soon I'll regret that I said anything. There are
> three possibilities: either we get arms, or we lose time, or we gain a victory. But if we
> don't get arms and we lose time until May—we lose the victory. It won't be long
> now before the issue of Eilat slips through our fingers and it won't be long before I
> come to tell you that we can't do it.

Ben-Gurion repeated his doubts:

> There are two serious considerations: that one of the great powers, and I mean Eden's
> Great Britain, might be very pleased at this opportunity . . . [to] play the role of savior
> of the Arab world. . . . the British army or air force will enter the conflict . . . and then
> the assured victory will no longer be so assured. The second danger . . . is that we
> might be branded as aggressors by everyone. That in itself is not terrible. . . . But
> obviously we will not get arms afterwards. . . . There will be a third round and we will
> be isolated in that encounter without any chance of getting weapons. We will be
> branded aggressors and we won't have any weapons.

Finally Ben-Gurion said, "We must very seriously now make defensive
plans." He had already made his decision.[42]

On December 5 Dayan made a final attempt to persuade Ben-Gurion to
approve the campaign. In a memo he sent him on Israeli-Egyptian relations
he wrote:

> I think that our present line of action in this matter [the Straits of Tiran] is wrong and
> will actually lose us freedom of navigation and air traffic in the Straits of Tiran. This
> will leave Eilat no more than a beach on a closed pond. . . . Saying that we will act at
> the time and place of our choice is realistic only when there really are a time and
> place we intend to choose. . . . I don't think that in a few months the time will be
> more propitious for us to take this action. . . . With the Egyptian buildup, in particu-

lar in the air, our chances of success in this campaign will be reduced. . . . Thus I see
our inaction now . . . as tantamount to relinquishing our freedom of navigation and
aviation in the area.

He concluded his memo with a clear warning:

I want to reiterate that if the Egyptians have MiG-15s and we don't have planes of
comparable quality, our chances of successfully taking the Straits of Tiran will drop
considerably. This action is difficult and complicated and vitally dependent on our
freedom of action in the air.[43]

But his pleas and pressures were to no avail. The next day he announced
that purchase of the "test ship" had been abandoned. On December 15 Ben-
Gurion hinted to Dayan that an American diplomat trying his hand at
another peace-making attempt between Israel and Egypt was about to come
to the region, and that he needed a few weeks' grace. But when Dayan asked
him whether there would be a war initiative in the near future, Ben-Gurion
replied, without any evasions, "Right now I have the feeling . . . that for the
next half year we will not be initiating anything serious."[44]

Dayan understood well what had happened. In his formal summation of
the meeting, Ben-Gurion's military secretary had written, "The question of
the campaign will not be decided before next week."[45] But the next day
Dayan ordered the dismantling of the brigade that had been intended to
embark on the straits campaign. Now it was obvious that the policy of escalation that Ben-Gurion had decided on when he was recuperating from his
illness in October and still under the influence of the anxieties created by the
Egyptian-Czech arms deal had been terminated. For the time being the government, and Ben-Gurion himself, followed the line proposed by Moshe
Sharett the day after the Czech sale was announced: to first exhaust all
efforts at procuring weapons in order to regain parity of arms. But before the
turning point in policy became fact, another dramatic event occurred. Dayan
made one last desperate attempt to save the policy of escalation, but by so
doing he assured its final demise.

5
...

OPERATION KINNERET

O n the night of December 11, 1955, the paratroops under the command of Colonel Ariel Sharon attacked the Syrian outposts on the east-northeast bank of the Sea of Galilee. Operation Kinneret, as it was popularly known (from the Hebrew name of the lake), was one of the most daring and brilliant raids ever carried out by the IDF. The attack was three-pronged: One column came from the north, past the complicated mean-derings of the Jordan River, which the autumn rains had turned into a raging torrent surrounded by treacherous swamps. A second column, skirting between the well-fortified Syrian outposts and the Golan Heights abutting the shore of the lake, approached from the south to attack the outposts on the southern sector and the main Syrian outpost at Koursi, a small fishing village. The third detachment landed amphibiously from the lake itself, to attack the linking outposts near Kafr Akeb. The battle was short and fierce; within a few hours the paratroops had taken the entire shore strip and destroyed all the Syrian fortifications. Thirty-seven Syrian soldiers and 12 civilians were killed and some 30 Syrian soldiers were taken prisoner. The IDF lost 6 men, including "Gulliver," one of the most admired paratroop officers.

News of the raid struck Israel's political system like a bolt out of the blue. No one could understand why Ben-Gurion had approved such a large raid, totally out of proportion to the provocations preceding it. True, Syria's mili-tary deployment along the eastern shores of the Sea of Galilee was a long-standing bone of contention between Israel and Syria and repeatedly appeared on the Mixed Armistice Commission agenda. The Syrian positions were emplaced right along the lake shore, in violation of the Armistice Agreement, according to which the demarcation lines were congruent with the international border, which passed ten meters east of the water line. This had been fixed in an internationally recognized agreement signed between the French regime in Syria and the British Mandatory Government of Palestine.[1]

Furthermore, the Syrians repeatedly harassed the Israeli fishermen of Tiberias whenever they tried to approach the northeastern shore, where the choicest fishing in the lake was to be found. On its part, Israel objected to Syrian farmers fishing or drawing water from the lake without getting the same permits issued Israeli citizens by the Israeli authorities. Also involved was the long-standing Syrian demand for the partition of the demilitarized zones, to which Ben-Gurion was vehemently opposed unless the Syrians agreed to make it part of a peace agreement. Thus although in the weeks that preceded the raid local incidents had occasionally cropped up, they were relatively routine events and did not draw any special attention. The large raid was unexpected and viewed by many as unprovoked aggression.[2]

Furthermore, it was no secret in Israeli political circles that the Cabinet had just voted against the aggressive line proposed by Ben-Gurion, and the Cabinet ministers were infuriated by his decision to approve the operation without consulting them. The authority to approve reprisals was not well defined; early in 1955 Ben-Gurion had said to Moshe Dayan: "The procedure is that they [reprisal operations] don't have to be brought before the Government but only before the Defense Minister and the Prime Minister."[3] At the time, Moshe Sharett was prime minister and Ben-Gurion was defense minister; new arrangements had not been instituted since that autumn, when both functions devolved upon one man, David Ben-Gurion. "There was strong objection in the Government to what had happened," Ben-Gurion said after the operation. "The objection was two-fold: procedural as well as substantive."[4]

When Operation Kinneret took place, Foreign Minister Moshe Sharett and his aides were literally knocking on the doors of the American administration on behalf of the Israeli government, which had just decided to concentrate efforts on acquiring defensive weapons. Familiar with Ben-Gurion's tendencies and temperament, Sharett had cabled him at the end of November from New York, pleading that he exercise self-restraint and refrain from authorizing any reprisals:

> Any new large-scale action involving considerable losses and not provoked by any serious incident will shock public opinion and make us look like spiteful provocateurs. . . . Dulles himself will consider it wilful disregard of his requests. . . . It may harm the American arms procurement negotiations which have begun not inauspiciously.[5]

In the first days of December, the U.S. State Department had sent many signals indicating that a response to Israel's requests for arms would be forthcoming. Sharett had met with Dulles a few days before the raid, and Dulles had assured him that he would make every effort to have an answer for him before Sharett left the United States.[6] Quantities and types of weapons were not mentioned, but hopes were high. Thus when word of Operation Kinneret reached Washington, Israeli diplomats were stunned. Sharett wrote in his diary:

> Everything has turned black, the hope of [procuring] armaments has been murdered. I was flabbergasted: I had warned that a military reprisal would destroy [the possibility of] arms grants. . . . again [Israel has created] a blood-thirsty impression of warmongering—no bloodshed preceded the raid, public opinion was not prepared, I was not given any prior warning.[7]

Soon enough Sharett's worse fears were realized: Two days after the operation, the American assistant secretary of state, George Allen, informed Abba Eban that a response on the question of arms procurement was being postponed because of the raid, the timing of which he called "regrettable."[8] Dulles left for a NATO conference without delivering the promised response.

So staggering was the shock at the operation that rumors began to circulate that the army had exceeded the authority mandated it by the defense minister. The left-wing Mapam minister, Mordechai Bentov, publicly stated that "the enlisted men and officers do not always know how to keep their reactions in proportion and we must teach them how. We must particularly educate them against those deleterious and despicable tendencies toward preventive war, where impulse confounds clear thinking."[9] In fact, the authorization for and particulars of the operation had not been recorded anywhere, and Ben-Gurion himself may very well have been surprised by the results. What is clear, however, is that Ben-Gurion did approve the scope of the action and that the chief of staff did not exceed his authority or the mandate given him. Several days after the operation Dayan reminded Ben-Gurion that on the eve of the raid, Dayan had been careful to clarify for the defense minister precisely what was expected: "I said we would clean up the entire coastline, from Ein Gev in the south to the mouth of the Jordan flowing into the lake in the north." Ben-Gurion's silent assent confirmed the truth of Dayan's assertion.[10]

More than any other event, Operation Kinneret reinforced growing popular resentment against what many perceived as undue involvement in political decision making on the part of the IDF command, and first and foremost Moshe Dayan; such involvement was considered totally at odds with the norms of a democratic regime. The public was critical of undue pressure applied by army commanders on political leaders, as well as of disciplinary laxity in taking actions that deviated from—and even violated—the authority granted. Doctor Yoram Peri has correctly noted that the Israeli military elite in the 1950s was ideological in character, and that there is a very high correlation between the viewpoints of senior officers and the political elite, in which Ben-Gurion and the traditional Mapai leadership figured largely. The IDF officer corps had emerged as an integral part of the political leadership.[11]

Moshe Dayan's own political involvement predated his military career. (He was an active member of the Labor Party and even represented it at the 20th Zionist Congress of 1946.) He was more than Ben-Gurion's military advisor and functionary; but his personal loyalty to and unqualified admiration of Ben-Gurion determined his view of the civilian political leadership's undisputed supremacy. In the case of Operation Kinneret, none of the sources reveals even a trace of intention on Dayan's part to break with discipline or make decisions on his own. At the very most a discrepancy was created between the originally intended scope of the operation and the eventual results. Dayan's repeated attempts to persuade Ben-Gurion to reconsider his decision on defense policy represented the legitimate duty of the chief of staff to state his position on the country's security needs.

A thin line separates stating a position—and even attempting to persuade—and exerting undue pressure. In his book on the role of the military in politics, S. E. Finer writes: "Influence . . . can become something not far removed from blackmail, as soon as the military advisers threaten to apply some sanctions should their advice not be followed."[12] When Moshe Sharett, then prime minister, cancelled a reprisal raid scheduled for the night of August 29, 1955, when the forces were already in the field, Dayan submitted his resignation. Situations may arise in which the chief of staff no longer feels capable of bearing responsibility, but Dayan's resignation in this case clearly exceeded the realm of the "legitimate," because it was intended to twist the prime minister's arm. It was not just a matter of conscience; it was tantamount to a political threat. When Ben-Gurion was minister of defense as well as prime minister, however, Dayan was careful not to overstep the bounds of what was reasonable and legitimate in his relations with the political echelon. Time and again he acceded to Ben-Gurion's decisions even when they were in complete opposition to his own judgment and convictions. He did not refrain from expressing his opinion and tried to win the "Old Man" over to his side; but he was always loyal and accepted Ben-Gurion's final decision.

On December 26 Dayan met with newspaper editors and vehemently protested published reports of the army's alleged breach of authority: "I want to say officially that in Operation Kinneret as well as in earlier instances, the standards and scope of action were fixed by the Government [i.e., Ben-Gurion] with full knowledge and complete clarity."[13] Ben-Gurion also found it necessary to come to the army's defense. In the Knesset he vigorously expressed his unswerving belief in the loyalty of its commanders.[14]

The day after the raid Sharett sent a sharply worded and bitter telegram to Ben-Gurion, detailing all the damage he believed the operation had caused: (1) the American response on arms supplies had been postponed; (2) Israel had been severely hampered in its efforts to muster opposition among Britain's parliamentarians to Sir Anthony Eden's Middle East policies; (3) public opinion in the West had been aroused against Israel. He concluded by saying "No time could have been chosen . . . more shockingly at odds with our political and diplomatic efforts on behalf of and under instructions from the Government on vital issues in America and Europe."[15]

In retrospect, it is doubtful if Sharett would have gotten a satisfactory response from the United States on the burning issue of armaments anyway. At the time America's policy was clearly directed at preventing Israel from acquiring counterbalancing quantities of arms. Eisenhower was unequivocal on the point in his memoirs, declaring that the U.S. administration had considered the issue and concluded that providing Israel with arms would only escalate the Mideast arms race; no American weapons would be forthcoming.[16] But Abba Eban claims that

> there was a good and almost assured chance [of procuring weapons] which Operation Kinneret foiled. I have no idea what quantities would have been forthcoming, but we should not belittle the tremendous moral value of any response as far as efforts in other Western capitals are concerned. I fear that whoever consoles himself with the thought that Operation Kinneret did not cost us new weapons is deluding himself and others.[17]

Francis Russell, then engaged on behalf of the State Department in attempting to convince Israel to relinquish parts of the Negev, poured salt on the open wounds when he described Dulles's shocked horror at the raid on Syria just when Israel's arms request was being deliberated. Representatives of the three Western powers meeting at the NATO convention in Paris, Russell relates, all decided that after Operation Kinneret it was impossible to send arms to Israel.[18]

In fact, however, the decisions not to send weapons to Israel had already been taken, one and two months previously. Washington was adamant in its policy of not providing Israel with substantial quantities of arms. Even without Operation Kinneret, America would not have changed that policy.

Moreover, at that point the Americans were very busy preparing another attempt at mediation between Israel and Egypt through the good offices of President Eisenhower's friend Robert Anderson. In all likelihood, the hopes Israel had pinned on a positive American response to its arms requests were illusory. The raid did not so much "murder" the issue of American arms for Israel as provide the U.S. administration with a convenient excuse for reneging on its promise, which it never intended to keep in the first place. Addressing senior army commanders several days after the operation, Ben-Gurion said that the operation "would provide a pretext not to give us arms for those who did not want to give them to us anyway."[19]

Yet it can be contended that Israel should have waited at least a few days before implementing the raid, because there was no special urgency and it was bound to embarrass the foreign minister, who was then in Washington. It would probably have been better to wait and hear just what Dulles meant when he promised an answer before Sharett left the United States, even if that answer was negative or merely evasive. Indeed, Ben-Gurion's reaction to the storm of criticism was weak and unconvincing. Foreign Ministry director General Walter Eytan sent him a sharp complaint for not consulting with ministry officials before approving the raid. Ben-Gurion replied apologetically: "These last days have been troubled ones . . . I really regret that I did not confer and consult with you before the operation."[20] To Abba Eban, however, he replied in a different tone: "If this problem [i.e., public opinion] so hampers us, I doubt our ability to maintain the State, settle the south, safeguard our borders and ensure the lives of our citizens."[21]

Domestically, however, Operation Kinneret proved to be the biggest mistake. The public, and certainly the government, should have been prepared in advance. The raid was greeted with almost universal criticism. At a Knesset Foreign Affairs and Security Committee meeting on December 27, most participants, including members of the coalition, attacked the prime minister. Only Labor Party members came to his defense, although they too found it hard to disguise their displeasure. Not surprisingly, right-wing Herut Party leader Menachem Begin's criticisms came from a different direction: he demanded a preventive war outright and dismissed the value of limited actions. Yizhar Harrari of the Progressive Party, just back from his mission at the U.N. General Assembly, fanned the flames of criticism by describing the shock that gripped the American public. Even Israel Galili of Ahdut Avodah, another coalition partner and generally a supporter of Ben-Gurion's activist policies, deplored the timing.[22]

Ben-Gurion rebutted the criticism as best he could: Considerations of public opinion should guide information campaigns, not the substance of policy-making; the scope of the operation was tactically imperative; the timing would have been even worse if it had been carried out *after* receiving Dulles's answer. But political defeat was inevitable. After the operation the government resolved in its weekly meeting that reprisal operations would henceforth require Cabinet approval.[23] Although the proposal was tabled by the prime minister himself, Ben-Gurion had to recognize that it constituted a reprimand.

What chain of events led to the affair? We have no documented evidence, but we can make a few assumptions.

The Israeli government's decision not to initiate a preventive war and its postponement of Operation Omer to end the blockade at the Straits of Tiran did not explicitly halt the policy of reprisals and other military actions related to day-to-day security problems. Although Ben-Gurion hesitated to follow the policy of escalation to its end, he wholeheartedly approved the strategy of insisting on Israel's rights and believed that Israeli responses to any Arab violation of the Armistice Agreements had to be harsh. The need to strike at Syria was part of the policy of reprisals that he had long supported. Moreover, precisely because he had been obliged to disappoint the army by cancelling the operation in the straits and rejecting preventive war, the "Old Man" may have felt it necessary to authorize reprisals and a hard line on border problems.

Moshe Dayan's considerations were apparently much more far-reaching. He had not intended Operation Kinneret to resolve fishing problems on the Sea of Galilee, but rather to present Egypt's leadership with a challenge. The defense minister's standing directives to the chief of staff at the time did not invalidate the October 23 instructions on intensified Israeli response to any issues under dispute between Israel and the Arab states. Even the straits campaign was not yet formally canceled, merely postponed, and the possibility of Egyptian-initiated full-scale hostilities still appealed to the IDF High Command.

Two months earlier, on October 19, Syria and Egypt had ceremoniously signed a mutual defense pact and set up a joint military command. A central condition called for each country to come to the other's aid in the event of armed aggression. Egypt's commander in chief, Major-General Abdul Hakim Amer, was placed at the head of the joint armed forces. Not quite eight days later Amer was given the chance to prove his credibility. As noted, in reaction to the IDF abduction of five Syrian soldiers in the Golan on October 23, an Egyptian army unit attacked a small Israeli guard unit in the Nitzana zone. The Egyptian media highlighted the offensive because it was important for Nasser to demonstrate Egyptian and Syrian unity for his efforts to convince Jordan to sign the pact as well. General Sir Gerald Templer, chief of the Imperial general staff, was due in Amman shortly in order to persuade Jordan to join the Baghdad Pact—that Western attempt to involve the Mideast nations in Western defense plans—and Nasser was assiduously trying to deter Jordan from the alliance and to bring it into the orbit of Arab states that had rejected dependence on the West.

Against the background of that gesture of Egyptian solidarity with Syria, a large Israeli operation against Syria could be even more effective a provocation than Israel's attacks on Egypt itself. And in any event, a large operation against Syrian forces would have its own advantages, whether or not Nasser reacted: If he did feel obligated to respond, that response might provide the Israelis with a pretext for a large-scale military campaign on the southern front. And if he refrained from responding, he would seriously damage the credibility of Egypt's defense pact with Syria, a pact that had in and of itself provoked Israeli military concern. "I don't care if we don't solve the fishing problem," Dayan told the defense minister at the meeting at which Operation Kinneret was authorized. "The Egyptians are afraid that we'll clash with Syria and then, under the mutual defense treaty, they'll have to do something. They'll have to carry out that first act of aggression."[24]

Dayan's remarks conformed with the policy fixed by Ben-Gurion seven weeks earlier, a policy that had not yet been formally rejected. But matters had not been specifically discussed and these intentions were not entirely clarified. In that sense Operation Kinneret was the last action implemented under the policy of escalation. Its aims went beyond the bounds of the immediate, local issues, and it should be viewed as a final attempt to provoke Nasser to war. From this aspect it indeed ran totally counter to the spirit of recent Israeli government decisions and justly infuriated all members of the government, not just the doves.

In the short run the exercise failed. Nasser responded in word but not in deed; his extravagant diplomatic reactions clearly bespoke his duress. Bound by solidarity to his new ally, he nonetheless was not ready for an intensified confrontation with Israel. On December 15 he sent an urgent cable to the U.N. secretary general in which he stated that "the latest attack on the Syrian forces is unquestionably and positively considered as an aggression against Egypt."[25] Nasser dramatically sent the contents of the cable to the Great Power representatives in Cairo, called a special press conference, gave wide publicity to his meeting with Amer to discuss plans for a military response, and urgently sent the general to Damascus to work out the details of the plans of the joint command. At the emergency press conference he said: "General Amer, the Commander-in-Chief of the Egyptian army, has been instructed to employ the full strength of his forces if Israel takes any further action whatsoever in the future."[26] All these diplomatic and propaganda gestures were intended to make up for the fact that he had no desire whatsoever at this stage to implement his military alliance with Syria. Effectively, then, Nasser was not provoked into action. Ultimately, as well, Operation Kinneret hampered Israel's own diplomatic activity: After an extended debate in the U.N., Israel was severely censured.

In the long run, however, Operation Kinneret was as useful to Israel as it was damaging. Ten months later Syria strictly refrained from intervening in the Sinai campaign, probably in no small measure because the credibility of the alliance with Egypt had been shaken after Operation Kinneret. Moreover, the operation honed and improved the IDF's fighting capabilities. A large force from the regular infantry Golani Brigade took part in the operation, enabling the IDF to give the other forces and units the same kind of battle experience from which the paratroops had benefited, ultimately permitting the daring actions of the Sinai campaign to be planned and implemented.

Operation Kinneret also increased Israel's chances of receiving arms from France. As expected, Ambassador Tsur in Paris was summoned to the Quai d'Orsay the day after the operation and was treated to expressions of "the French Government's deep concern following the Kinneret incident."[27] But Shimon Peres, who was in Paris at the time, has said that at his own meetings with the French prime minister three days later, Edgar Faure reiterated his support for all of Israel's arms requests, never once even mentioning the operation.[28] And French Defense Ministry officials, military personnel, and others involved in French arms production and supply did not try to hide their admiration for the Israeli army's operational capability. "[General] Guillaume was interested in the course of the operation but did not even hint at any concern or dissatisfaction at the incident," wrote the military attaché in Paris in his cabled report on Peres's discussion with the French chief of staff. ". . . [He] did not make his willingness to continue to help us conditional on any terms."[29] Moshe Sharett and Foreign Ministry officials repeatedly argued that if Israel wanted Western arms, it would have to refrain from military actions; but Israel received arms from France in order to act, not in order to refrain from acting. Israel's military capability and pugnaciousness, as demonstrated in Operation Kinneret, were precisely what a few months later enabled the crisis in the weapons balance to be resolved.

In the meantime, however, the impact of the operation was restrictive. The government resolved once more to firmly uphold its previous policy decision to refrain in every way from initiating hostilities and from taking actions liable to bring about war. Diplomatic efforts at arms procurement were given first priority. Thus the turning point in Israel's security policy became a fait accompli. Operation Kinneret and the subsequent Cabinet decision signaled the conclusion of the first phase in Israel's reaction to the Egyptian-Czech arms deal. The policy that Ben-Gurion and Dayan had sought to promote at the end of October, aimed at precipitating an early confrontation, was shelved, and the IDF, which for the last two months had been in full readiness for an all-out offensive, resumed the distasteful defensive posture it had sought to avoid. Moshe Dayan was forced to grit his teeth and bow to the decision: Any war in the foreseeable future would come about through Egyptian initiative; the IDF had to deploy itself defensively. Shortly after Operation Kinneret Dayan had asked Ben-Gurion, "What will the army do from now on?" The "Old Man's" reply was succinct: "From now on the army must be prepared for an Egyptian attack. It must plan how to withstand a possible Egyptian assault in the coming months, in the spring or summer, perhaps even earlier."[30]

On December 16, less than a week after the operation at the Sea of Galilee, Ben-Gurion met with the IDF High Command in order to explain the new line:

> If we weigh all these difficult considerations and we realize that each and every one is a matter of life or death, then the overriding one is to acquire additional arms, improve the army's standing power, and avoid risking a war of aggression that might

end in our military defeat at the hands of a foreign power against whom we cannot stand—and which certainly will end in a moral defeat in the world arena, leaving us alone and isolated internationally. Thus I believe the Government has taken the right stance in deciding that there will be no war initiated by us.[31]

The military was not convinced, but acquiesced. In mid-January the chief of staff addressed the High Command at great length and in much detail with a clear view of moving the army into a new, defensive posture against the possibility of an attack initiated by Egypt.[32] Dayan opened his address with a question: ". . . will there be a war in 1956? . . . and will it be a war initiated by the enemy?" No longer did he speak of an Israeli initiative and no longer did he refer to "escalation." If hostilities indeed began, it would be at Arab and not Israeli instigation. Dayan was not certain that the Egyptians would actually take the initiative. He went into detail enumerating the restraints liable to prevent Nasser from attacking; but it was Dayan's responsibility to prepare the IDF for the worst case: "I don't think that [Nasser's] successes so far—the Egyptian revolution, the expulsion of the British, the elimination of domestic opposition, and the Czech arms deal—are likely to make him less audacious in the future; and we can't assume that he'll miss any opportunity to go to war against Israel."

The balance of power in the wake of the Czech sale bode ill for Israel: "If there should be a confrontation between our armor and Egypt's," Dayan continued, "we will not have the upper hand. We will have to avoid [such] a confrontation . . . [because] quantitatively and qualitatively the enemy's armored power outranks our own." The enemy's armor would have to be repulsed primarily by the Israeli infantry and by territorial defense positions equipped with light arms, at times no more than 100 to 150 meters away—"not an ideal range," Dayan admitted,

but compared to all the other Jewish woes throughout history, I can say that we're not desperate. . . . Our anti-tank mines can tear up the Centurion [tank] tracks, our bazookas can penetrate the enemy tank armor, and we can therefore deploy anti-tank defenses capable of stopping enemy armor. . . . we must prepare for battle under difficult conditions, for . . . aerial inferiority permitting the enemy to bomb our civilian centers, attack airfields as well as our land and sea forces. This is not to say that we won't win; the situation does not preclude victory. But it does demand a supreme effort and the ability to hold fast and endure prolonged civilian and military hardship.

Interspersed throughout his long address were echoes of the previous debate:

In our circumstances, not every peace is constructive and not every war is destructive. A war over our right to divert the Jordan River is a constructive war, and maintaining the peace of Eilat under siege conditions is destructive. . . . unconditional peace means accepting the present situation: with the Jordan flowing into the Dead Sea and not into the Negev, and with Eilat under siege.

Dayan continued the argument, but it was by then academic; the turning point in policy had become fact.

The year 1956 was ushered in with the Israeli army preparing for defensive and holding operations against an anticipated Egyptian strike; it ended, however, quite differently. In Ben-Gurion's address to senior army officers he said, "[This is] the Government's declared position . . . but it is conceivable that events and circumstances might alter it."[33] Circumstances did indeed change that year, from one pole to the other; and, in fact, the war was launched by Israel. Yet that war was not at all a direct continuation of the mood prevalent in Israel in the autumn of 1955: it was not a preventive initiative, born of anxiety for the fate of Israel resulting from the disturbed balance of power. On the contrary, it broke out after a far-reaching improvement in that balance had been achieved. In January of 1956, no one could have guessed that by the end of the year Israel would have solved its dilemma so completely, both acquiring arms and striking at Egypt. Not only were the two goals not inimical to each other, they actually complemented each other, like both sides of the same coin. But these developments were hidden in the future, and in the meantime the army had taken energetic measures for Israel's defense against hostilities initiated by Egypt.

6

■ ■ ■

DEFENSIVE DEPLOYMENT

In the winter of 1956 Israel's military establishment had a complicated mission. The balance of arms had been upset by the Egyptian-Czech arms deal, and it was expected that the Egyptians would sooner or later initiate large-scale hostilities. All Israel's military power had to be mustered and all its manpower mobilized for the anticipated war in order to rectify, however slightly, that upset balance of power. At the same time, the government had resolved not to launch a preventive war; the country had to prepare for the possibility that the next war would begin with an enemy attack and that, at least during the first stages, civilian targets inside the country would be hit. Thus preparations had to be made to absorb the expected Egyptian strike with the least possible civilian casualties and damage. In a broadcast to the army Dayan said:

> . . . We don't have a Czech deal, an American deal or an English deal, and the quantity of weapons we're getting from France doesn't compare with the Egyptian-Czech deal; but there is one nation we can make a "deal" with—Israel. We can make an "Israeli deal." . . . This is the hardest, but also the most promising deal. A supreme effort to increase our strength, a constant striving for improvement, more settlements, becoming better fighters—that is real progress. On this Israeli deal the very essence of the country, the standard of the army and, most of all, the shaping of the people, depends.[1]

The possibility that the army might be forced to fight an Egyptian-initiated war seriously concerned the chief of staff. At a staff meeting early in February 1956 he said:

> The theory [that defense is a stronger battle mode than offense] may be correct in principle, and defense is indeed preferable when your armor and soldiers are well entrenched. But our limited land area, the absence of lines of retreat, the vital importance of safe-guarding the civilian population, and our socio-ethical structure don't allow us to take advantage of this mode. . . . If we had 200 AMX tanks we could permit ourselves the luxury of changing our approach, but to rely on a soldier to fight

tanks with a bazooka, defending the country from a range of 80 meters—that is too
grave a risk.[2]

To the minister of defense Dayan explained:

One of the decisive questions is, who will dance to whose tune? When the Egyptians
are poised to attack with tanks and weapons and . . . we must get ourselves organized
while they've already started to move, i.e., to shift the initiative to our side—it's hard
to contemplate. But if the situation were reversed and, despite all their equipment,
they were not prepared for battle, and we struck first—then they'd be panic-stricken
and couldn't take advantage of all the fire power they had.[3]

These fears crystallized over the winter months as the signals of Egyptian
preparations for an offensive seemed to increase. In mid-February aerial
photographs revealed new Soviet tanks added to the military deployment
that the Egyptians had rapidly erected at Bir Gafgafa in the middle of the
Sinai and columns of new MiGs emplaced on the runways on the airfields
along the Suez Canal. Closer to the Israeli border, in the Abu Agheila area,
the Egyptians had built a training mockup of an Israeli settlement, and early
in March the Sinai Command held large-scale maneuvers, which included
overrunning the Nitzana area and taking Beersheba. Egyptian forces in the
Sinai were augmented to include two armored and six infantry brigades. The
growing self-confidence of the Egyptian leadership was clearly reflected in
their pronouncements. Talking to a group of officers in the Gaza Strip,
Nasser said, "I now speak the language of power."[4] And General Amer
declared, "The Israeli danger does not exist. The Egyptian army can eradi-
cate Israel."[5]

There were those in Israel who believed in the intrinsic advantages of the
defensive strategy and advocated that territorial defense serve as the basis
for all strategic planning. Most prominent among the proponents was
Colonel (Res.) Israel Baer,[6] a well-known military commentator who in
1948 had served as one of the chief operations officers of the newly created
Israel Defense Forces. In 1956 Baer was in the defense minister's bureau,
charged with the task of writing the history of the 1948 Israeli War of
Independence. He also served as the defense minister's occasional advisor.
At the time his newspaper and other articles were cautiously phrased and
very clearly intended not to antagonize his patron, David Ben-Gurion; however, only barely did he manage to hide his dislike for Moshe Dayan and his
disdain for his performance as chief of staff.

Baer was a staunch supporter of defensive strategy by choice. In the winter of 1956 he wanted to turn the concept of defense into a permanent and supreme doctrine: "The strategy [of the State of Israel], like that of the Zionist movement in the past, will always be totally dictated by the need to take a defensive posture, even if tactical—at times operational—actions take on an offensive cast."[7] Baer argued that Israel's War of Independence proved that "defensive gains produce offensive ones, and not vice versa. . . . we could take the offensive only after a stubborn, flexible and dynamic defense had gained us the upper hand." Therefore "the doctrine of 'blitzkrieg'—a swift decisive action, a short-winded gallop—can defeat great armies; certainly a small army should shy away from it."[8]

The debate on doctrine touched on interests as well. If the Israeli army put its trust in the development of its offensive capability, territorial defense would be accorded much lower priority and then considerably reduced security resources would be directed to the agricultural settlements, especially the collective kibbutzim. The central and vital role the kibbutzim had played during the defensive stages of the War of Independence had nurtured in the kibbutz movements a strong belief in their indispensability to national defense. Yosef Tabenkin, who had commanded one of the most aggressive of Israel's brigades during the 1948 war, now wrote:

> We must . . . organize and fortify all of Israel's settlements [and turn them] into fortresses that cannot be taken by the enemy, "hedgehog" outposts along his route of advance for him to break his teeth on, one by one. . . . When the border settlements stand firm, it is not only to defend the lives and property of their inhabitants, but to take a decisive role in the defense of the entire country.[9]

Members and political supporters of the kibbutz movements envisaged the coming war as another version of the first stages of the 1948 war: "[T]he front line of any possible war will crystallize around the settlement areas," wrote one kibbutz member. "[T]he settlements' ability to withstand will be the attacking enemy's weak point: he will not be able to move into the heart of the country so long as our settlements remain behind his lines. . . . The fate of the entire land depends on the settlements' ability to stand firm."[10]

Members of the kibbutz movements associated with the left-wing Mapam Party also joined the debate. Shimon Avidan, renowned for commanding the brigade that contained the Egyptian advance in the battles of May and June 1948, cited from his rich experience:

> The country's topography . . . and the many routes leading into Israel's territory make it imperative that a clear response be given to the question of containing the enemy assault at the first stage. The fact that collective settlements with a specific social character exist . . . gives the State of Israel a precious and powerful tool.[11]

Ethical and psychological arguments were also advanced: "Only by defending our existence when there is no doubt that 'we have no choice' can we educate the nation and the youth to be brave and courageous, loyal and effective fighters."[12] Defense is the best and most effective military-security method because "through it, and through it alone, can each man rise to the highest degree of dedication and sacrifice."[13]

Moshe Dayan disagreed; despite the political decision to refrain from a preventive war, he was not ready to relinquish his strategic principles: "I want to correct a very common misperception," he told a group of writers at the end of January 1956. "[I]t is impossible to win by defense alone. Of course a war can be lost without proper defense, but a war that is defensive only is a lost war. . . . the main point of war is offense, not defense. In our wars against the enemy we must reach his territory."[14] Elsewhere he said, "The lack of [strategic] depth in Israel, where the Gaza Strip border is only 70 kilometers from Tel Aviv, represents a serious danger, because the first 40-50 kilometers which the enemy succeeds in taking by initial surprise will be 50 of the 70 kilometers on the way to Tel Aviv."[15] He was also concerned that the new immigrant settlements might not stand up to an Egyptian armored attack: even in the war of independence not all settlements stood up to attack.

But Dayan had no choice but to accept the government's explicit decision to avoid any belligerent initiative, which meant that the coming war might very well begin with an inevitable albeit short phase of defensive containment; heavy-hearted and anxious, he concluded his directive to the general staff: "We must put up a hard defense and move on to attack at the very first opportunity."[16]

The first conclusion drawn from this mission was that the IDF had to locate additional resources for defense needs without exhausting its offensive capability. Ideas and proposals abounded. One party advocated instituting a third year of compulsory military service, during which the soldiers would put in time on the new immigrant settlements, border villages, and other vital areas. Female parliamentarians from all parties demanded that more women be trained in the use of arms and integrated into vital auxiliary positions in order to free the men for combat posts. The Labor Party Central Committee appointed a special public commission headed by Pinhas Lavon, Histadrut Labor Federation secretary, to work out an emergency program to mobilize the civilian population for the war effort.

For the IDF, however, more immediate and practical solutions were needed to follow the general directive of investing the minimum necessary into a strong defensive posture while channeling most resources to the offensive capability. Investing resources in defense is by its own logic wasteful, since in every anticipated war most fortifications, minefields, and shelters remain unused and do not influence the course of the battles. "We have two kinds of investments," Dayan explained at a general staff meeting, "those that are permanent and those that are transient. If there is no attack, then we will have been very wasteful."[17]

"First and foremost I am interested in mobilizing maximum combat personnel,"[18] Ben-Gurion told Dayan; and Dayan took him very seriously indeed. One of the largest reservoirs of high-quality manpower was concentrated precisely in the cooperative agricultural settlements, both in the territorial defense units and in the framework of Nahal, a special corps that combined military training and agricultural work in preparation for life on the kibbutzim. This entire manpower resource could not be utilized efficiently in the offensive units. The best soldiers were scattered all over hundreds of settlements and attached to territorial defense units, and thousands of the most talented youngsters were on Nahal farms. For any war effort, this represented a waste.

Over the anticipated objections of the politically powerful kibbutz movements, Dayan decided to change this situation. The territorial defense settlements were regrouped into new classifications:

First-Echelon Settlements: Some 150 settlements located right on the borders or along the lines of possible enemy breakthrough. To defend them a company-size force was allocated, drawn from both the local inhabitants and outside reinforcements. They were assigned the best available and highest-standard weaponry.

Second-Echelon Settlements: About 150 settlements located on secondary defense lines. Their defense rested on a platoon-size force drawn from local inhabitants only, the remaining settlers being transferred to other combat units on the basis of their skills and training.

Third-Echelon Settlements: These were now allotted only local reservists aged 39 and over and were issued older weapons that the combat units no longer used.

The new classification made it possible to transfer many younger and better-trained combatants to the assault units and raise their performance level considerably.

Dayan also made the following changes in Nahal:

1. An advanced Nahal training unit became a paratroop battalion and was attached to the paratroop brigade.

2. More Nahal soldiers were sent to officer and combat training courses. Physically unfit soldiers were sent to communications courses.

3. All Nahal reservists who had not previously undergone advanced training were now recalled and sent to various training courses.

Within a short time, Nahal changed from a unit primarily concerned with land settlement and agriculture into an elite combat unit. Not surprisingly, this irked the leaders of the kibbutz movements. They tried to mobilize Knesset members and government ministers into taking action against Dayan's reforms and tried to exert heavy pressure on the prime minister. But Ben-Gurion supported Dayan, and the program was carried out almost entirely.

"We need two things in order to attack," Dayan said. "We need to make sure that we're not killed, and we need what it takes to destroy the enemy's armor. In order not to be killed, we need trenches, and nothing can replace fortifications."[19] If the IDF really had to wait for the enemy to attack first and during the initial stage engage only in hard defensive warfare, then the probable confrontation points had to be fortified, as did the routes along which the enemy could try to break through. But fortifications are expensive, so Dayan decided that only the most vital spots would be fortified, at the lowest possible cost to the IDF budget.

Reclassification of the settlements permitted the army to concentrate its limited resources into the 150 front-line settlements. But to fortify even these settlements, Dayan wanted funds from outside the defense budget. For several weeks he feigned indifference and ignored the question of fortifications, letting the settlers clamor and complain at how the army was neglecting the frontier. Dayan wanted to see how much money and resources the relevant civilian institutions would contribute for fences, trenches, and shelters. Slowly his tactics began to bear fruit. The Histadrut Trade Union Federation and the Jewish Agency's Settlement Department were mobilized into action, and workers from the cities began to volunteer for fortification work in the frontier settlements. Early in February Dayan finally proposed that the army provide materials, professional instruction, and heavy engineering equipment, with the settlements providing labor, either local or urban volunteers. On February 16, the defense minister authorized the fortification of 33 first-echelon settlements by means of the integrated method proposed by the chief of staff. The settlements demanded that the operation be expanded immediately, sparking off a tremendous increase in the number of volunteers and overcoming the Treasury's initial opposition to allocating a special budget for the task.

This was Operation Battlement; Ben-Gurion called together trade union leaders from all over the country and demanded that they generate one million volunteer work days.[20] On March 8 the campaign was launched with a symbolic act widely covered by the media: Led by David Ben-Gurion and Moshe Dayan, all the GHQ officers and enlisted men, together with Defense Ministry employees, set off to fortify Mivtahim, a recently established village near the Gaza border inhabited by new immigrants from Kurdistan. In the chief of staff's Bureau Diary for that day the following entry was made:

> A lot of work got done, and most of the work that should have taken two-three days was finished in one; the main value of the day, however, was in the experience itself and the publicity it generated. Reporters came from all over the world, the glare of flashbulbs competed with the glare of sunshine, and the sound of picks and shovels was drowned out by the noise of movie cameras. With all the spectacle of an "event," the day was still serious, embodying many anxieties as well as many solutions for those anxieties.[21]

As the wave of volunteers grew, and after the Treasury had shown its willingness to allocate funds, the IDF expanded the operation to include all 150 top-priority settlements plus 50 second-echelon ones. Another 100 second-echelon settlements were partially fortified. The campaign reached its climax on May 1; by a unanimous resolution of all the parties in the Histadrut, traditional May Day celebrations and parades were canceled and 40,000 workers mobilized for fortification duty. Operation Battlement turned into an enormous engineering feat, capped off by the army's setting up purely military outposts, digging antitank trenches, and laying mines in sensitive areas where there were no settlements. Within two months the country was wrapped in a solid casing of fortifications, and the settlers' sense of security was greatly enhanced.

As it turned out, the entire operation proved unnecessary; the fortifications were never tested, and the financial and material resources as well as the work days invested were indeed wasted. But it was a paramount demonstration of the volunteer spirit that had taken hold of the entire nation. Over 100,000 people—a considerable percentage of Israel's adult population—took part. Scarcely a family did not have at least one member involved. Operation Battlement expressed the sense of national unity and determination to confront danger, at the same time crystallizing those emotions as well. The widespread public support for the Sinai campaign several months later was nurtured on the mass enthusiasm evoked by Operation Battlement.

The resolution to wait for the enemy to take the initiative and open hostilities lent an immediate urgency to the question of air defense, in particular defense of the airfields and aircraft on the ground. Early in January Dayan held a special meeting on defense against air attack at which it was decided to procure more antiaircraft guns of various sorts and to upgrade the old ones. When spring came the IDF put its antiaircraft deployment into place and entered full war readiness. The air force was also placed on high alert.

Some time earlier, the army had prepared a plan for the construction of underground concrete shelters. Because the shelters were expensive and would take a long time to complete, the Air Force Command undertook emergency measures and, within a few weeks, provided every air force base with temporary fortified hangars made of snail-shape packed-earth walls to protect aircraft from indirect hits. Because there were so few runways available, the old British landing strips, unused for years, were repaired and emergency teams stationed there. By the beginning of July, the air force was prepared to absorb the first strike.

The fear of the new jet bombers that Egypt had acquired made it imperative to upgrade civil defense preparedness as well. As early as December 16, 1955, Ben-Gurion had summoned the interior minister and discussed with him at great length the preparations that local authorities and municipalities would have to make against aerial bombardment. At the end of December Dayan appointed a new Civil Defense commander. Following marathon discussions at GHQ, the Civil Defense was overhauled: The permanent staff was augmented; new bomb shelters were built near schools, kindergartens, bus terminals, and public parks; municipal by-laws obligated homeowners to reinforce apartment house entrances and hallways with sandbags; sirens were refurbished and tested. "In 1940 I saw how the English fought alone, almost without an army and without any weapons, against a vicious and powerful enemy," Ben-Gurion told the Knesset. "[T]he people of Israel will be no less courageous, stalwart and brave than the English."[22]

On April 9 and 10, the general staff held extensive operational discussions on Israel's defense deployment, with the defense minister and all senior officers of the various military branches participating.[23] Ben-Gurion played devil's advocate, posing difficult questions and imagining the worst possible

scenarios of enemy action. All the participants agreed that the most dangerous scenario would be an Egyptian attempt to launch an initial assault from
the Gaza Strip along the coast and on to Tel Aviv, while breaking through
simultaneously from the Nitzana area toward Beersheba and joining up with
Jordanian forces in the Hebron Hills. The settlements lying along these
routes were issued extra weapons and surrounded by deep minefields.
Additional specially trained reservists, veterans of the War of Independence,
were sent to these areas to form a hard core of military manpower.

It was estimated that in the southern sector, the Egyptian army would try
to launch assaults along the Nitzana-Beersheba axis and along the Rafah-
Beersheba axis. Israeli settlements were thin there; only two recently established ones lay along the Nitzana route, and a large, empty expanse of land
ideal for armored maneuvers—and virtually begging to be attacked—
stretched astride the Rafah route. At the end of January, Ben-Gurion ordered
that water lines to these two areas be laid immediately and that additional
settlements be set up. For Dayan the area of Nitzana was particularly vital.
He told Ben-Gurion:

> I don't believe Nasser can attack only on the coast road without trying to take
> Nitzana first, because he'd be laying himself open to the risk of our reaching the sea
> and cutting his forces off from the rear. You can be fairly certain that the Egyptians
> won't launch a major attack on Israel before taking Nitzana. We, on the other hand,
> can set an attack in motion from Nitzana along three or four routes and maneuver our
> forces with a lot of flexibility. . . . So long as we're well-entrenched in Nitzana,
> Nasser can't invade the country.[24]

The decision to set up more settlements in the Nitzana area was problematic. Under the Armistice Agreements, this was a demilitarized zone and
Israel had made assurances that no military units would be stationed there,
although it claimed sovereignty over the area and insisted on its right to set
up civilian settlements. The Egyptians objected, claiming that the Israeli settlements were nothing more than military outposts in civilian guise and
arguing that, by definition, demilitarization precluded any changes at all in
the area. The U.N. attempted to maintain neutrality and prohibited any unilateral actions in the area; in fact, it opposed any Israel settlement activity
without prior coordination.

Nonetheless, in mid-March preparations were completed. On March 19,
after several postponements and despite U.N. pressure, the army raised two
new settlements in the Nitzana area, one at the southern tip of the demilitarized zone and another just outside it, on the road to Beersheba. The barren
landscape came to life, and the audience at the groundbreaking ceremony
was treated to the sight of many soldiers, together with paid and volunteer

laborers drafted especially for the operation, reminiscent of the kind of over-night construction of Jewish villages that had characterized the Palestine of the 1920s and 1930s.[25] Ben-Gurion visited the site a few days after the cere-mony and enthusiastically called on his Cabinet and the delegates to the Zionist Congress then convening in Jerusalem to see with their own eyes how Zionism was being fulfilled: "It is very important that the Congress go there [and see] that the army is also building the country, and how we start from scratch. . . . Come and see what Zionism is!"[26]

Exhilarated, Ben-Gurion decided to further expand settlements in the Nitzana area and close the breach in the area near Rafah. In mid-May 1956 another four outpost settlements were set up: two in the area of Shivta, to fill out defenses along the Nitzana route, and two near the border with Rafah, to close the gap in the west. The Treasury and settlement authorities were very dubious about the economic value of the venture—water was expensive, the land was not fertile, and transportation was difficult—but security consider-ations overrode any economic reservations.

Dayan too had his doubts. If he had to rely on the defense budget, he probably would have set up military outposts rather than civilian settle-ments, which were extravagantly expensive compared to the relatively low cost of temporarily deploying a tank unit on the outskirts of the demilita-rized zone. But since the budget was being borne by the Jewish Agency and government ministries, Dayan was happy enough to solve the security prob-lem this way. Not for the first time in Israel's history did ideological consid-erations mix with purely military-security ones or were actions taken for emotional reasons rather than on the basis of serious inquiry into the actual cost-benefit to the country's military needs.

"We must put up a hard defense and move on to the attack at the very first opportunity," the chief of staff had said. Circumstances indeed forced the IDF to deploy defensively, but Dayan would not let it be at the expense of the army's offensive potential. Thus even at the height of defensive preparations, the GHQ's chief concern was to ready the army for attack and to utilize the bulk of resources for increased offensive combat capability. Because of the deep sense of emergency, the military had access to larger-than-usual budgets and tried to use most of those funds to augment the mobile forces. In 1953, when Dayan was named chief of staff, a plan was prepared to upgrade mili-tary strength by 1960, aimed at increasing IDF battle order up to 14 infantry brigades, three armored brigades, four second-echelon infantry brigades, and various auxiliary units. In January 1956 the IDF was still far from attaining this goal: Three new infantry brigades were only just starting to be organized and no weapons had been found for them yet; the second armored brigade was just beginning to function and still had no tanks; and the IDF as a whole was still short of a great deal of weaponry and equipment. A supreme effort was needed to complete the planned upgrading four years ahead of schedule, and in January the army did not even know if it would be getting the requisite heavy equipment. Only toward summer would relations between Israel and France be advanced enough to ensure receipt of vital arms; in the meantime, GHQ decided to go ahead and make the organizational arrangements for integrating the weapons when they did arrive.

During the spring and summer months of 1956, almost all Israeli reserve units were called up for training. This enhanced defense readiness, since it increased the number of forces ready and available at all times. The main goal, however, was to prepare the units for offensive action. An enormous logistic and organizational effort was invested in raising the combat skills of the entire army as summer approached. The Sinai campaign began about one month after the last of the reserve units had completed its training. Thus the IDF went to war with well-trained and well-motivated reservists, most of whom were still enjoying the benefit of the concentrated training they had just undergone.

Concomitantly the army developed and improved the reserve call-up system through secret as well as public coded announcements. In October of the previous year General Haim Laskov, deputy chief of staff, had written a staff paper that quickly became the basis for planning the order of reserve call-ups for the entire army. The main goal was to cut to a minimum the length of time needed to call up the reserves, to avoid confusion during the call-up itself, and to reduce the mobilizing units' exposure to air attack. Extensive and intensive staff work kept the entire Israeli army busy for several months, from the GHQ down to the smallest units. Deployment was tested; call-up orders were prepared; meeting points were marked; emergency storehouses were built and provisioned; troop and equipment transport was tried out all over the country; instructions were issued for the mobilization of civilian vehicles and their allocation to the military. Maximum troop mobility had to be ensured, and part of the burden fell on civilian automobile owners. During the winter months, however, a major effort was invested in overhauling and servicing hundreds of jeeps, command cars, armored track carriers and other combat vehicles. The de facto embargo on heavy weapons did not include regular vehicles, and Defense Ministry personnel searched every corner of the world for as many as could be had.[27]

The standing army also flexed its muscles. The Southern Command and the Seventh Armored Brigade, which had been dismantled for economic reasons in 1954, were re-formed, and the paratroops were organized within a brigade framework. The combat experience that the paratroops had gained from reprisal operations over the last two years was gradually spreading throughout the entire IDF. Patrols over the borders were stepped up, intended mainly to give the troops real combat experience; at the same time the men learned the terrain and gathered information on the enemy that was vital for the operational and tactical planning that was taking shape at the command levels. From information gathered by the patrols, the Engineer Corps paved access roads in the frontier areas, ensuring maximum flexibility of troop movements and permitting them to penetrate deep into enemy territory rapidly.

"Our victories and our defeats in the minor battles along and across the borders are very important for enhancing security on the frontier, for the Arab evaluation of Israel's strength, and for Israel's belief in her own capability," Dayan wrote in an article distributed to all officers. "Knowing and feeling which army is better—the Israeli or the Arab—depends not only on the pronouncements of the High Command, but also on every outpost, every field commander and, at times, every soldier."[28] Dayan was referring to reprisal operations, but his remarks applied equally to every other operation carried out along and across the borders, and reflected a conscious effort to prepare the army's units for combat.

An atmosphere of emergency and imminent war pervaded Israel during the winter and spring of 1956. The steps taken were the result of a sincerely felt anxiety, but they also inflamed that same anxiety and entrenched the popular feeling, which only a very few would challenge at the time, that Israel was about to go to war. In early April Moshe Sharett participated in an interministerial foreign and security policy meeting at which civilian emergency measures were discussed. In the privacy of his diary Sharett expressed his reservations: "Again I asked myself if putting flesh on the assumption that we are on the brink of war and repeating it incessantly to the public was not liable, by force of inertia, to ultimately contribute to actually bringing war down on our heads."[29]

Sharett's grasp of these dynamics was excellent. The nation's preparation for defensive war naturally increased both the ability to defend the country as well as the readiness to initiate war when the opportunity presented itself.

Many historians have noted that an army's preparation for defense based on an assessment of the enemy's offensive intentions simultaneously creates the potential for its own offensive action, stimulating offensive initiatives.[30] Something similar happened in Israel in 1956. The Israeli army's success in the Suez War cannot be fully understood without taking into account the meticulous preparations for Egyptian attack that had taken place six months earlier. But an enabling condition must be distinguished from a cause: The IDF's preparations for conflict as described in this chapter *facilitated* that conflict when the political conditions required it; they did not *create* the decision to embark on confrontation.

A similar dynamic affected the civilians. The relative ease with which Ben-Gurion succeeded in mobilizing the Israeli people six months later to almost total support of his war initiative can be attributed partly to the atmosphere in which the entire population had been caught up during the previous winter and spring. But a qualification is in order here as well: The people were not manipulated; Ben-Gurion and the IDF Command were genuinely convinced of the existence of a real and immediate danger. Whether Israel was indeed at serious risk remains a moot point—we can never know what would have happened if Israel had not embarked on the Sinai campaign. But the information that Israel had at the time, compounded by the civilian population's emotional atmosphere that winter, created an anxiety that was not irrational, even if irrational factors contributed to its creation. The vast majority of Israelis shared the assessment of imminent danger and the need to avert it.

It is thus no wonder that Moshe Sharett, who thought that "all the cumbersome preparations for the great calamity are nonsense and doomed to evaporate like smoke when no war breaks out," felt "alienated and unneeded, shrouded in a sense of the unreality and insubstantiality of the entire discussion."[31] Soon enough he really did find himself on the outside, and no one, not even his best friends, would come to his defense. Most of the nation and most of the leadership supported Ben-Gurion's assumptions.

7
• • •
"THE ALPHA PLAN"

The Egyptian-Czech arms deal and the challenge it posed to Israel's security in the autumn of 1955 came at the height of an extensive British and American diplomatic effort to resolve the Arab-Israeli conflict. Almost simultaneously, the British and the Americans had concluded that it was in the West's interest to take a daring and far-reaching step that would bring an end to the conflict. The American Republican Party had won the election in the fall of 1952, and the following January General Dwight D. Eisenhower took the oath of office as president of the United States. The new president and his secretary of state, John Foster Dulles, formulated their global policies from a strictly anti-Soviet perspective, seeking to encircle the Soviet Union with a series of Western-oriented military pacts, building a network of military bases all around the Soviet perimeter, facilitating what Dulles referred to as "massive retaliation." Between 1951 and 1954 the Americans had repeatedly attempted to create such a defense pact in the Middle East but had quickly realized that a major obstacle to such efforts was the Israeli-Arab conflict.[1]

Washington viewed Great Britain as the guardian of Western interests in the Middle East,[2] but Dulles was well aware of the difficulties facing the former colonial power in the region. In the spring of 1953, soon after taking office, he embarked on a diplomatic tour of the Middle East.[3] His trip convinced Dulles that the United States could not impose outside defense arrangements on the region but had first and foremost to gain the trust of the local actors. Unlike the Democratic Party, Dulles's Republican Party had no traditional obligations to Israel, and the new secretary of state embarked on a policy that would bring the United States closer to the Arabs, declaring that his government would henceforth be engaged in a more "even-handed" approach to the Middle East. Henry Byroade, assistant secretary of state for Near Eastern Affairs, was more explicit; in a series of addresses and memoranda he accused

Israel of purposely creating tensions along the borders, insisted that it refrain from further efforts to increase immigration and halt the "Zionist process,"[4] and urged it to once and for all integrate into the region as a Middle Eastern nation.

The State Department had never been happy with America's involvement in the creation and development of the State of Israel. Years later, testifying before the U.S. Senate Foreign Affairs Committee, a senior official described the mood of the State Department during the early 1950s: "It was unanimously agreed that the manner in which Israel was created had an unfortunate effect on our relationship with the Arab nations."[5] At that time the State Department felt that Western interests required peace and stability in the Middle East, and that in order to achieve this, Israel had to bow to Arab demands on several issues of principle. At the end of 1950 Moshe Sharett reported to his ministry's department heads that according to George McGhee, a senior Washington official, the United States believed that peace could be achieved in the Middle East only if Israel made concessions to the Arabs.[6]

Dulles's initial approach favored a gradual, step-by-step process, beginning with an agreement on the division of the waters of the Jordan River, which would accustom the Arabs to the idea of cooperating with the Israelis and would ultimately do much to solve the refugee problem. But in 1954 the Western powers were seriously disappointed in their attempts to "organize" the region in Western-oriented pacts, and Dulles realized that more fundamental and comprehensive solutions had to be sought. In the autumn of 1954, after much deliberation, a new policy was crystallized, in cooperation with Great Britain, calling for an "across-the-board approach for the settlement of the Palestine question."[7]

That same autumn, senior British diplomat Sir Evelyn Shuckburgh also set off on a comprehensive tour of the Middle East. Shuckburgh, who had been Sir Anthony Eden's private secretary when the latter was foreign secretary, had recently been appointed to a senior post in the Foreign Office that included responsibility for Middle East affairs. For several years, the bane of British-Egyptian relations had been the controversy over the British bases along the Suez Canal; now that stumbling block no longer existed and England sought to reassert its position in the area. Upon his return from the Middle East, Shuckburgh submitted a detailed memorandum to his superiors on the Israeli-Arab conflict. The memo reflected the United Kingdom's frustration at the erosion of its position of regional prominence and fears of increasing Soviet penetration: ". . . our influence and position in the Arab world are very precarious. . . . time is running against us. I cannot avoid the fear that the Israeli issue is in a fair way losing us the Middle East."[8]

Shuckburgh presumed that certain actors in the Arab world were willing to reach permanent arrangements with Israel and accept the fact of its existence, in exchange for considerable Israeli territorial concessions and allowances in the solution of the refugee problem, provided that such arrangements be based on a just and recognized agreement and not on defeat in war. Shuckburgh referred to "permanent arrangements" and not a full-fledged peace agreement because he did not believe that the Arabs would sign a peace agreement with Israel in the foreseeable future, since Arab public opinion would not quickly come to terms with the idea of complete peace with Israel. He estimated that Israel also had an interest in reaching such arrangements, both for economic reasons and because without them, Communist revolutions in the Arab countries were a distinct possibility, putting Israel at even greater risk in the future. Shuckburgh advocated pressuring Israel into acceding to Arab demands, convinced that only close cooperation with the United States could bring about any movement and that the two countries' common policy had to be based on three principles: (1) pressuring Israel to make tangible concessions; (2) providing it with security guarantees; and (3) ensuring that it understood that the West would not countenance aggressive initiatives. Shuckburgh recommended that Egypt's assistance be enlisted first, because that nation was keenly interested in any arrangement that would enhance its influence in the Arab world.

In an appendix to his memo, Shuckburgh detailed several ideas on how to achieve these ends, including the following:

1. Israel would cede the Negev south of Beersheba to Jordan, creating an unbroken land connection between Egypt and the Arab lands to the East; it would also cede part of the Galilee and would agree to divide the demilitarized zones with Syria and permit Syrians free access to the Sea of Galilee.
2. The number of Palestinian refugees allowed to return to their homes would be increased and the rest would be compensated.
3. The problem of Jerusalem would be resolved by declaring it a neutral and international city.
4. The Arabs would end their economic boycott of Israel but direct contacts would not be normalized in full.
5. Under international supervision, the waters of the Jordan River would be divided.
6. The United States would sign bilateral defense treaties with the regional actors.

On the basis of Shuckburgh's memo, the British prime minister instructed his ambassador in the United States to propose a "new approach" for the Middle East to Dulles and to request the appointment of a joint working party to iron out the details. The British appointee was Shuckburgh and the American was Francis Russell, who had just concluded his post as minister in charge of political affairs at the American Embassy in Tel Aviv. The entire project took place in maximum secrecy and was code-named Alpha.[9]

Great Britain and the United States had different orientations toward Israel. The United Kingdom's temperament, strategic plans, former colonial position in the Middle East in general, and experience during its mandate in Palestine in particular had all led it to a certain amount of disdain and disregard for Israel and a patent preference for the Arabs. An Imperial staff document dated May 1954 makes this clear: "Arab good will is essential to the success of our plans and is more important than that of Israel."[10] The U.S. government, on the other hand, could not ignore either the nation's pro-Israel public opinion or the very active Jewish lobby, and therefore it tended to make more moderate proposals that had a better chance of being accepted by Israel. But at this early stage Shuckburgh and Russell easily reached agreement on a joint recommendation and, at the end of February 1955, submitted the Alpha Plan.[11] The document comprised scores of pages detailing the points raised in Shuckburgh's original memo. For example, there were detailed maps of the proposed division of the demilitarized zones together with an analysis of the type and quality of land discussed, precise maps of the adjustments that needed to be made in the border with Jordan that would permit the Palestinian farmers access to their lands, detailed calculations of the compensation to be paid refugees, and so forth. On the central question of a land bridge between Egypt and Jordan, the plan recommended the creation of two small triangles in the southern Negev, opposite the Kuntilla area, sharing a common apex on the Arava Road. This permitted Israel to retain Eilat and establish free passage to the Red Sea, while creating a land connection between Egypt and Jordan.

An unbroken land bridge between the "African" and the "Asian" Arabs had been discussed in the Arab world since the beginning of the 1950s; the idea of paving a pan-Arab road connecting Morocco and Baghdad intrigued a generation that long advocated the unity of the Arab nation. But it quickly became obvious that Nasser would not settle for the right to "free passage" or even for a pan-Arab road along a narrow corridor under Arab sovereignty.

In the autumn of 1955 he told a Western ambassador in Cairo,

> I do not and will not consent to Israel's existence separating Egypt from the Arab world. Sooner or later, Israel will have to concede the Negev, and we are prepared to go to war for it. Egypt's separation from the rest of the Arab world is a long-standing imperialist plan . . . aimed at turning Egypt into an African country. But I am an Arab and want to stay Arab.[12]

The demand that Israel relinquish the entire Negev south of Beersheba was linked to Nasser's plan to transfer responsibility for the Gaza Strip and for the hundreds of thousands of refugees there to Jordan. Furthermore, he was impelled by the desire to salvage the pride lost in the Egyptian defeat of 1948. Israeli intelligence services reported even more fundamental strategic goals. An American analysis of Egyptian foreign policy early in 1956 that had found its way to the Israeli Foreign Ministry stated, "Nasser needs a land bridge [that will] ensure Israel's isolation and facilitate Egypt's enhanced influence in the Arab world."[13]

The British and the Americans hesitated over the timing of the Alpha Plan's staging. The winter of 1955 saw the establishment of the Baghdad Pact and the Israeli army's raid on Gaza—not the most auspicious atmosphere in which to usher in efforts at mediation. But at the beginning of April Henry Byroade, in the meantime appointed American ambassador in Cairo, proposed the plan to the Egyptian foreign minister, Mahmoud Fawzi, and several days later to Nasser himself. Fawzi's reaction was positive; Nasser was less enthusiastic but did not reject the plan out of hand although, not unexpectedly, he objected vehemently to the idea of the "triangles." He was intrigued by the possibility of transferring the whole of the Negev to Arab sovereignty in exchange for the modest price of eliminating the economic boycott of Israel and perhaps opening the Suez Canal to Israeli-bound shipping. He was not being pressured into making real peace with Israel, since the British themselves had not proposed anything more than certain adjustments to the Armistice Agreements.[14] In a discussion with the British ambassador in Cairo, Fawzi made the Egyptian position unequivocally clear: Egypt was not getting involved in any bargaining; Beersheba was Israel's southernmost border.[15]

The Alpha Plan was doomed to failure because it was based on three mistaken fundamental assumptions about the political and psychological processes that had begun to take shape in the region, even before the conference of Afro-Asian leaders held in Bandong in the spring of 1955, in the wake of which Nasser's foreign policy shifted dramatically.

The first mistaken assumption was that Israel was the major obstacle to Great Britain's restoration of its previous position in the region. The founding of the State of Israel did indeed inject a prominent element of tension into the Middle East and increased Arab enmity toward the Western powers; but more than actively being the cause of the growing tension between the Arabs and the West, Israel gave that tension expression and served as a stage on which it was acted out. The processes of decolonization and the stirrings of nationalism in the Arab world, albeit linked to the Zionist issue, did not take place because of it. Throughout Asia and Africa during the 1950s, Western colonialism was making its inevitable retreat, and, in most places, the process was unrelated to either Zionism or to the Jewish people. The old-guard British diplomats, who had been apprenticed when the British Empire was at its zenith and who now served a Conservative government, found it hard to reconcile themselves to the fact that Great Britain's days of glory in the Middle East were over. But many of the American diplomats, whose own education was predicated on an anticolonialist perception, did understand this process and had reservations about the approach of their London colleagues. One State Department official admitted to his Israeli counterpart that the United States was at a severe disadvantage because of its identification with the Western colonial powers, reminding him that America's world outlook was substantially different from that of the colonial powers. America's support of the Asian nations, he said, was not only tactical: The United States had to find a position midway between the European approach and the Asian one.[16] But early in 1955 the Americans also were incapable of grasping the full impact of the profound historical processes taking place and failed to understand that the nations of Asia and Africa did not make that fine distinction between traditional European imperialism and what would soon be called neo-colonialism, with the United States viewed as its major proponent.

Furthermore, Nasser very effectively exploited the shock precipitated by the Gaza raid; in fact, however, his enmity for the West was more linked to the formation of the Baghdad Pact in which he perceived—and rightly so—a British attempt, with American collusion, at maintaining the United Kingdom's position in the Middle East with the help of "reactionaries" such as Iraq's prime minister, Nuri es-Sa'id, with no consideration for the real desires of the region's inhabitants.[17] The Alpha Plan could not retard the Middle East's decolonialization processes in which Nasser took the lead in 1955.

The second mistaken assumption informing the Alpha Plan was that Nasser could be convinced to reconcile himself to Israel's existence. Shuckburgh and Russell began to promote the Alpha Plan after Egypt had already under-gone a very profound change in its leadership's view of Egypt's historical role in the Arab world. Nasser's renewed enthusiasm for pan-Arabism matured as 1954 drew to a close. By the time the American and British ambassadors tried to "sell" the Alpha Plan to Nasser in the spring of 1955, the Arabization of Egypt had reached its peak; Nasser and his colleagues in the Revolutionary Council based their legitimization on the stage of pan-Arabism. It was hopeless to attempt to reconcile Nasser to Israel's existence, because Israel was becoming a tool by which Nasser could forge Arab unity and pave the way for his leadership of the Arab world.

The third mistaken assumption was that Israel could be persuaded to make substantive concessions. No permanent settlement between Israel and the Arabs was feasible in 1955, because Israel would simply not make any far-reaching territorial, economic, or demographic concessions, certainly not in exchange for arrangements that fell far short of full peace and a final reso-lution of the conflict. Israel's adamant position on these issues found expres-sion in many documents of the day. In December 1955 Ben-Gurion expressed it succinctly in a telegram to Moshe Sharett, who was then hold-ing meetings with members of the American administration in Washington:

> Israel will not consider a peace offer involving any territorial concessions whatso-ever. The neighboring countries have no right to one inch of Israel's land. In peace negotiations we will consider mutually agreed border adjustments to the benefit of both sides. We are ready to make peace for the sake of peace . . . we are willing to meet Nasser in any way, but not on the basis of a plan calling for any part of Israeli territory to be torn away for the benefit of her neighbors.[18]

Nor would the Arabs relinquish their basic hope once again to try their luck in a war culminating in the elimination of the "Zionist invasion."

Today, some 40 years later, the meticulous delineation of the exact borders between Arab Kalkilya and Jewish Kfar Saba in Shuckburgh and Russell's plan and the detailed calculations of financial restitution for the refugees seem pathetic. The naive belief that the important questions were whether to transfer 5,000 acres from one side to the other or whether it was enough to transfer only 4,375 acres, as against the total lack of any chance whatsoever of bringing the two sides to any dialogue on a fundamental conclusion to the conflict, makes the Alpha Plan seem more than slightly ridiculous.

The Alpha Plan missed the boat. Immediately after the initial feelers were sent out, Nasser left for the Afro-Asian conference in Bandong, where the non-aligned nations bloc began to crystallize. The conference participants received him enthusiastically, and Nasser immediately gained the stature of an interna-tional leader. Jean Lacouture describes Nasser's experience in Bandong:

This was not just a trip. This was a flight into the air, a transformation, a metamor-
phosis. Those few days made more of an impression on the Egyptian colonel than
the Baghdad Pact, the Gaza raid, or the arms deal. He discovered new horizons, new
vistas of his country's position in the world, and of his own international prestige.[19]

The dramatic change in Nasser's self-image and his perception of Egypt's
place in the world robbed the Alpha Plan of its very minuscule chance of
being implemented, if it ever had one in the first place. Nasser's evolution
into the charismatic and acknowledged leader of Arab nationalism was well
on its way, but it would take the British and the Americans a full year to
assess correctly the profound transformation that had taken place in the
Middle East. In the meantime, they were hampered by their adherence to a
plan lacking any hope of success and were precluded from exhibiting the
flexibility needed to prevent, or at least slow down, the snowballing negative
processes in the region.

To overcome Nasser's opposition, Shuckburgh suggested to Russell that
the two small triangles in the Kuntilla area be replaced with two larger ones
with one base, along the Gaza Strip border, similar to those proposed in the
1947 Partition Plan.[20] The Americans were not comfortable with the proposal; they did not believe that Israel would be willing to make such far-
reaching concessions. The feelers sent out by the British ambassador in Tel
Aviv were met with a resounding and categorical Israeli "no" to any unilateral territorial concessions.[21] In an impassioned address at the Ramat Gan
stadium that Independence Day, Ben-Gurion declared: "If you want to take
the Negev—you will have to fight. Our army will confront yours."[22] But the
British reckoned that if Nasser accepted their proposals, Israel would be
forced to concede to the combined pressure of England and America, for
both countries would refuse to sell Israel arms or provide it with security
guarantees. Indeed, Russell assured Shuckburgh that the United States
would make no such concessions to Israel unless it agreed to accept the
Alpha Plan.[23]

At the beginning of the summer the Americans became impatient with what
they considered the Alpha Plan's slow progress. In a few months the presidential election campaign would begin and the president would find it difficult to
embark on any measures that American Jewry might interpret as inimical to
Israel's vital interests.[24] Dulles therefore wanted to come out with a public
statement creating an irrevocable obligation to the processes outlined in the

Alpha Plan. In the meantime, a flood of signals was being received that hinted clearly at advanced Egyptian-Soviet negotiations toward a large arms deal, and the State Department urgently sought ways to prevent it or at least soften its harmful impact. Only a vigorous initiative aimed at convincing Egypt that it could hope to achieve major benefits by cooperating with the West could forestall this negative development.[25] Thus after coordinating with the British foreign secretary, Dulles decided to make the Alpha Plan public. On August 26, 1955, he appeared before the venerable New York Council on Foreign Relations and delivered a programmatic address laying out American Middle East policy for the coming months.[26]

Sensitive to the "Jewish vote," Dulles was very careful in his delivery. He refrained from explicitly discussing the specific proposals of the Alpha Plan and the concessions Israel would be forced to make, but he did not succeed in completely taking the sting out. He told his audience that his talk had been preceded by many discussions and consultations with the president—in other words, that the address was a sort of formal public declaration of policy. Three unresolved problems, he said, lay at the root of the growing tensions in the Middle East: the refugee problem, mutual fear and suspicion, and the lack of permanent borders. On the subject of refugees, Dulles made a vague statement that could be interpreted as a pro-Israeli stance: "Resettlement—and to such an extent as may be feasible—repatriation." In any event, he promised American financial aid for both a refugee rehabilitation plan and for financial compensation. Since the Arab governments realized that there was no chance of all the refugees returning to their homes, nothing in Dulles's cautious phrasing was particularly problematic for either side to accept.

America's major contribution, the secretary of state went on, would be in eliminating mutual fear. Dulles ceremoniously announced that the president had authorized him to promise that he would propose that Congress approve valid and binding treaties guaranteeing the new borders agreed upon by the parties. On the territorial issue, one part of Dulles's address worried Israel, namely, the hints about Israel's being asked to concede territory: "The existing lines separating Israel and the Arab States . . . were not designed to be permanent frontiers in every respect." Pointedly hinting at which areas he meant, he added, "The difficulty is increased by the fact that even territory which is barren has acquired a sentimental significance." Ever since the 1949 Lausanne Conference, the Arabs had been demanding that Israel return to the boundaries of the November 29, 1947, Partition Plan, while Israel had insisted that the Armistice Lines were the final borders. The Alpha Plan sought a compromise between the two, with Israel relinquishing only some of the territory beyond the Partition borders. Dulles was not specific; but it was obvious that he meant that Israel would be forced to make several withdrawals from the Armistice Lines to "final and permanent borders."

The day after the address, the government of Great Britain announced its unreserved approval of the principles expressed in the secretary of state's speech. It also affirmed its willingness to cooperate with the American government in providing guarantees anchored in binding treaties for agreed-upon borders and in providing financial assistance toward the resolution of the refugee problem and toward a program of regional rehabilitation.

Arab public reaction to Dulles's speech was overwhelmingly negative: "The Arabs . . . would consent neither to negotiating with Israel, nor to any solution short of the restoration of their territory," Cairo Radio's Sauth al-Arab declared. Popular commentator Ahmad Shawky added, "No solution can ever be found if the right of the legitimate people of Palestine to return to their homes is overlooked and ignored."[27] But in less public forums the Egyptians left the door open. Several weeks before the announcement of the Egyptian-Czech arms deal, Nasser apparently wanted to arouse no more Western antagonism than the upcoming dramatic move would otherwise elicit.[28]

Israel's reaction was ambivalent. Two days before the address the American ambassador in Israel had given Moshe Sharett details of the speech. In his diary Sharett wrote:

> He left me alarmed and frightened. I felt very much like I did on the eve of the 1939 White Paper [in which the British Government more or less reversed its support of Zionism and sought to bring an end to Jewish immigration to Palestine]. Of course there is a world of difference between our position then and now, yet nonetheless, to the extent that we are today also subject to great-power influence, especially that of the United States, so far-ranging a negative step can yet be fatal.[29]

However, Moshe Sharett, who was still prime minister, published a cautious and restrained response. He was very complimentary and praised the speech for its "at once realistic and imaginative" approach to the refugee problem; but insofar as the territorial question was concerned, he was bitterly disappointed: "With all their imperfections, the Armistice Agreements have one valuable advantage—they were made and agreed upon by the parties concerned, whereas the proposal to change the fixed lines seems very problematic." He expressed Israel's position unequivocally: "Israel will refuse to cede any part of her area to satisfy the ambition of any Arab state or for any other purpose."[30]

When news of the Czech sale broke, Dulles's speech seemed to Israel no longer relevant; and indeed, at Sharett's next meeting with the American ambassador, the bulk of their discussion focused on the new situation. Sharett was willing to let the speech pass (although he did comment that it had contained several "ambiguities and contradictions"[31]), as if it no longer had any bearing on a situation that had been upset totally overnight. Nonetheless, the operational aspects of the address, which touched on Israel's requests for security guarantees and for weapons—that is, American's undertaking to Great Britain not to accede to Israeli demands except within the framework of a comprehensive settlement—were still in effect. After the Czech sale was announced, Israel's ambassador, Abba Eban, approached the State Department with a formal request for a guarantee; Dulles responded, "The United States could not guarantee temporary armistice lines."[32] On their part, the Americans in no way regarded their secretary of state's speech as "outdated," and throughout the fall and winter months their Middle East policy followed along the lines enunciated in that speech. It is thus not surprising that in his memoirs Eban sums up that time as "the only period in which America could be justly accused of having left Israel alone to the winds and storms."[33]

News of the Egyptian-Czech deal aggravated worries in the West, particularly in the United Kingdom, about the West's future in the region. Therefore after an initial and spontaneous reaction of anger and a search for immediate and radical solutions, the British Foreign Office resumed its hope of implementing the Alpha Plan. Some two weeks after the Czech sale was announced, Shuckburgh, then the central and moving force in shaping British foreign policy in the Middle East, submitted a basic staff paper to the foreign secretary on a suitable response. Shuckburgh perceived the Soviet move as a brilliant exploitation of the West's fundamental weakness in the region, namely, the existence of Israel as a Western protégé. For Shuckburgh, the real danger was not just to British interests in the Middle East but to the very future of his country and all of Europe. On the assumption that it was possible to contain the fire and bring Nasser back to the West, Shuckburgh made a number of recommendations, including a renewed effort at implementing the Alpha Plan. Bringing peace to the Middle East, he said, was the only honorable way for Britain to extricate itself from its difficulties in the region. In the meantime, the West could not be permitted to indemnify Israel for Egypt's increased military power; such compensation had to remain Israel's quid pro quo for agreeing to the Alpha Plan.[34]

The British prime minister, Sir Anthony Eden, now resolved to take the offensive. On November 9, after the initial rage at Nasser had passed, he delivered a keynote address in the Guildhall, in which he disclosed the main points of the Alpha Plan.[35] To heighten the drama, he said that the project had been painstakingly and meticulously planned down to its smallest detail in utmost secrecy. He starkly described the dangers inherent in the current Middle East situation: ". . . beneath the volcanic crust of those smoldering dangers, lies deeper peril still."

Dulles's address had already hinted at the principles upon which the plan was based, but Eden made them blunter. He also declared his country's willingness to provide guarantees for agreed borders and assured British participation in financing the reparations and rehabilitation of the refugees. He was much more forthright and explicit than Dulles had been on the issue of territorial compromise. The Arabs demanded that Israel return to the boundaries of the 1947 Partition Plan, while the Israelis insisted on the 1949 Armistice Lines: "Between those two positions there is of course a wide gap; but is it so wide that no negotiation is possible to bridge it?" Dulles had only hinted at a compromise; but Eden's intention was clear: The final borders had to be a compromise between the existing condition and the Partition Plan; in other words, Israel had to make substantial withdrawals from areas it presently held. Eden did not stop short of threats: "Let there be no mistake. Were any country to reject counsels of moderation, it would forfeit the sympathy of this, and I believe every other peace-loving nation. Once lost, that sympathy might be hard to regain."

It must be reiterated that the distinctions between Dulles's address and Eden's were matters of style only—Britain was less sensitive to the Jewish and Israeli cause and tended to take more account of the Arabs. As far as the essence of the plan was concerned, however, England and America were in total agreement.

During the first hours after the speech, pandemonium broke out in Cairo and the Egyptian media took England to task. Soon enough, however, Nasser took a more favorable approach, telling Harry Kern, editor of the international edition of *Newsweek,* "This was the first sensible thing I had heard from the West for a long time" and referring elsewhere to "Eden's constructive attitude."[36] The Egyptian media's initially critical tone gave way to a more positive one of acceptance, albeit with some specific reservations concerning the plan's details.

Nasser preferred Eden's speech over Dulles's because the former hinted at much more significant Israeli territorial concessions. But he was cautious; if the mediation efforts failed, the Iraqi premier, Nuri es-Sa'id, could exploit the opportunity to accuse Nasser of having been willing to recognize Israel.[37] Nasser therefore refrained from taking an official stand in the Arab League Political Committee's discussion of the Guildhall speech and qualified his initial positive response by refuting himself.[38] In *Al Gumhurriyah,* Anwar Sadat, one of Nasser's chief aides, quibbled with Eden's proposal that Israel "abandon" some of its lands, claiming that the term "abandon" was reserved for rightful owners and that usurpers could not abandon what they did not rightfully possess.[39]

Israel's reaction was categorically negative. In Jerusalem the Guildhall address elicited a wave of resentment and suspicion against the British. *The Times* summed up Israel's reaction in a headline: "Indignation in Israel. No Middle East Munich!"[40] On November 15 Ben-Gurion gave a brief address at the Knesset intended to clarify that Israel rejected Eden's proposed compromise: Eden's "proposals to lop territory off Israel for her neighbors has no legal, moral or logical grounds and is inconceivable. . . . It is tantamount to awarding a prize for aggression, and the Government of Israel will enter into no negotiations on such terms."[41] Despite the great difference between their respective concepts of Israel's defense and foreign policy, both David Ben-Gurion and Moshe Sharett agreed on this point. Sharett also refused to countenance territorial concessions, with the exception of "small border adjustments" and permitting the Arabs free passage between Egypt and Jordan via an Israeli-retained Negev.[42]

Israel came out firmly against the Guildhall address. In an information briefing to Israeli embassies, Sharett wrote: "England is concerned not with Israel's benefit but with her own position with the Arabs, which she is trying to restore by appeasement at Israel's expense."[43] Shortly before Eden's trip to America to meet President Eisenhower at the end of January 1956, Sharett instructed the Israeli Embassy in Washington to organize an anti-Eden campaign, "obviously masking any sign of the Embassy as the source." This opened up the can of worms that had long plagued Eden, beginning with his 1935 proposal to divide Ethiopia and through the formation of the Arab League and discrimination against Israel in arms procurement.[44]

Only ten days after Eden's Guildhall address, Dulles delivered an official *aide memoire* to Sharett regarding Washington's stance on an Israeli-Egyptian

accommodation that did not differ in the slightest from England's. Nonetheless, because the rhetorical styles of the two speeches were so different,
the Israeli Foreign Ministry at the time believed that there was a substantive
difference between England's position and America's. Israeli diplomats
tended to exaggerate the importance of stylistic nuances in the pronouncements of British and American diplomats and the purported American criticism of Eden's address. In Jerusalem the Foreign Ministry repeated its
instructions to its Washington personnel to try to prevent official American
support of Eden's talk: From Washington Sharett wrote Foreign Ministry
director General Walter Eytan in Jerusalem that if the United States wished
"not to become entangled and dirtied, she would refrain from identifying
[with Eden]."[45] Sharett sent Gideon Raphael, one of his senior aides who
was about to meet with Russell in London, a note stating that it was "important to caution Russell against American identification with Eden."[46] And
Eytan cabled Washington, "We view our prime goal as preventing formal
American support of [Eden's] proposals."[47]

In truth, however, the British and the Americans enjoyed the closest cooperation, and there were no fundamental distinctions between the American
State Department's position and that of the British Foreign Office. In fact,
when Israel's ambassador in London met Eden on November 23, the latter
was holding a report on Sharett's discussions with Dulles the previous day in
Washington.[48] On November 21, at the height of the storm that the Guildhall
address had provoked in Israel, Dulles gave Ambassador Abba Eban a formal memorandum, cautiously worded but clearly expressing agreement with
the British prime minister:

> The U.S. Government believes that a settlement may be possible if the Governments
> concerned accept the approach . . . which involves concessions by Arab States as well
> as by Israel. . . . We believe that it should be recognized that territorial adjustments
> referred to in Secretary Dulles' August 26th speech may have to include concessions
> in the Negev to provide an Arab area joining Egypt with the rest of the Arab world.[49]

In December 1955 American pressure on Israeli diplomats peaked. State
Department officials repeatedly urged Eban, Shiloah, and Sharett himself to
accept the Alpha Plan's demands. Sharett met with Dulles early in
December and submitted a formal memorandum in response to the
American memo of some two weeks earlier. Sharett's document had been
carefully phrased, in full consultation with Ben-Gurion himself. In correct-
ing the draft, Ben-Gurion had been willing to "temporarily put off navigation in the Red Sea . . . if it emerges that there were *substantive* steps being
taken toward peace." But on the central issue he was not willing to budge:

"No territory in the Negev can be ceded, whether or not it is inhabited."[50] But Dulles was just as implacable. In a thoroughgoing discussion with Abba Eban, Dulles told him that the Armistice Lines did not constitute final political and territorial borders but that the American government had no intention of taking Eilat away from Israel or cutting off access to that city. Russell had been working on various plans to find a solution that would satisfy Nasser while ensuring Israel's vital interests in the Negev, and Dulles had always believed that a final settlement might involve adjustments in the border that could result in the loss of some acres for Israel.[51]

Indeed, two days later Russell, chief midwife for the Alpha Plan, gave Reuven Shiloah the full plan, although he did not refer to it by its code name. Russell told the Israeli that the advantages of settling the conflict, for both sides, far outweighed any concessions they would be asked to make. The State Department sincerely believed that Israel and the Arabs were willing to look for a solution, he said, and he urged Shiloah not to lose this opportunity. The key to the solution, he said, lay in satisfying the Arab need for territorial continuity.[52] Several days later Russell reiterated that there was no hope of a settlement without an accommodation in the Negev, such as the proposed triangles, and no negotiations could be undertaken if Nasser could not be assured that he had a chance of reaching some kind of arrangement there that included a land bridge.[53] But Israel rejected the Alpha Plan's territorial concepts out of hand. "We stand by our decision to reject such a solution," Eban said, "even if we are told that there is no other way to reach a settlement."[54]

The Americans, however, seem to have understood that Eden had cooked his own goose, since the bitter opposition his speech had elicited in Israel precluded the possibility of Great Britain serving as an honest broker in any mediation efforts.[55] While Russell and Shuckburgh continued to promote the Alpha Plan, Central Intelligence Agency (CIA) personnel in the Middle East were formulating a new American initiative—dispatching the president's old friend Robert Anderson to the Middle East to undertake a concerted effort at mediation. This plan, at first code-named Chameleon and later renamed Gamma, was based on the recognition that, ultimately, the two sides would have to be brought together for direct talks.

8

. . .

THE PEACE BROKERS:
ROBERT ANDERSON'S MISSION

L ate in 1955, CIA officials suggested that President Eisenhower launch a new Middle East initiative. The proposal may have been motivated by the CIA's assessment that the Alpha Plan had led to a dead end, or it may simply have resulted from the fact that the CIA usually operated independently and along lines parallel to those of the State Department. For whatever reasons, the intelligence agency urged that the United States make another dramatic attempt to mediate between Israel and Egypt toward a permanent settlement or, at the very least, toward a drastic reduction in the tensions that had escalated since the end of 1954. Thus early in 1956 Eisenhower sent his friend Robert Anderson, former assistant secretary of defense (and later secretary of the treasury), to investigate the possibility of direct Egyptian-Israeli talks aimed at ending the conflict.[1]

The mission, like its predecessors, failed, actually increasing Israeli suspicions about Nasser's intentions, reinforcing the Israeli assessment that the true aims of Egypt were not peaceful but belligerent. To understand the circumstances that prompted Anderson's mission and why it failed, we must backtrack and briefly review the development of contacts and attempts at mediation between Israel and Egypt during the preceding years.[2]

Egypt's official position throughout the early 1950s conformed to the usual demands made by all the Arab countries after the Lausanne talks held in the winter of 1949 by the U.N. Conciliation Commission: Israel had to retreat to the 1947 Partition Plan borders, had to allow all the Palestinian refugees who so desired to return to their homes, and had to pay suitable indemnification to the rest for the loss of their property. But even during informal talks at Lausanne, it became obvious that Egypt's major precondition for any settlement with Israel hinged on Israeli withdrawal from the Negev south of Beersheba.[3] Israeli penetration into the Sinai peninsula at the beginning of 1949 still rankled in Egypt's memory, and it feared that Israel would use its foothold in the

Nitzana area once again to penetrate deep into the Sinai. More important, Arab nationalists had long been disturbed by the painful realization that Jewish control of the Negev all the way down to the Gulf of Aqaba created a wedge between the Arabs of Africa and those of Asia.

However, the Egyptians did not preclude occasional, unofficial contacts with the Israelis. Shortly before the revolution in Egypt, for example, Gideon Raphael, the Israeli Foreign Ministry official in charge of Near Eastern affairs, held off-the-record talks with Dr. Mahmud Azmi, one of Egypt's U.N. representatives. Azmi told Raphael that he had been explicitly advised by Cairo that

> the Government of Egypt realizes that continued conflict does not serve Egypt's interests and Egypt has no desire to perpetuate it; nonetheless, no responsible Egyptian politician would dare take the initiative to end it, not because of Egyptian public opinion, which was indifferent to the issue, but in fear of Arab leaders outside Egypt who would be liable to attack him as a traitor.[4]

Soon after the July 1952 officers' revolt in Egypt, Israel had approached the Egyptian chargé d'affaires in Paris and had proposed talks aimed at concluding a peace agreement, or at the very least a preliminary settlement to defuse tensions.[5] But during the period immediately following the revolution, Egypt was careful to refrain from any formal contact with Israel. In February 1953, however, once the revolution had established itself, Nasser's special envoy, Abdul Rahman Saddeq, began more or less regular contacts with Ziamah Divon of the Israeli Foreign Ministry's Near East Department, with whom he was already acquainted.[6] The reports from these talks indicate that Egypt's leaders were then mainly occupied with domestic affairs and with the struggle to oust the British from their bases along the Suez Canal. Understandably, the Egyptians wanted to placate Israel and keep it from intervening and disrupting these efforts. Now and again the Egyptians even toyed with the possibility of using Israel to their own advantage, exploiting the Jewish lobby to gain the support of the American government in Egypt's quarrel against England or for American economic aid.[7] But it was obvious that Egypt was not prepared or capable of reciprocating in kind: "No change can be effected in the political, military and economic enmity between the two countries because of the situation prevailing in Egypt and the Arab world."[8] At the very most, Egypt was willing to consider certain concessions in the passage of Israeli-bound cargo through the Suez Canal (excluding oil and war materiel). At the end of 1953 Elias Sasson, a senior Israeli Foreign Ministry official and Near East expert, summed up his assessment: "Our one and one-half year flirtation with this regime through our Paris channels not only failed to improve the situation, but also to a certain extent misled us and forced us into misleading others as well."[9]

Another question had arisen in the meantime: the division of the Jordan River and its utilization for regional development. In October 1953, acting under unequivocal and outright pressure exerted by the United States, the U.N. Security Council halted Israeli attempts to divert water in the area south of the B'not Ya'acov Bridge north of the Sea of Galilee. The American administration was well aware that Israel would not wait indefinitely for an agreed arrangement and that the resumption of work on the Israeli Jordan River Project would in all likelihood erupt into a general conflagration. After his tour of the Middle East late in 1953, John Foster Dulles was convinced that the solution to the Israeli-Arab conflict lay in a gradual deescalation and that a "technical" agreement on the division of the Jordan would help solve the overall problem. Early in 1954 the president appointed Eric Johnston, a well-known film producer, as special envoy charged with reaching a settlement on the utilization of the Jordan River.[13] Johnston made five trips to the area in 1954 and 1955 and, after exhaustive contacts, succeeded in getting the Israeli and Arab engineers and technical representatives to agree to a plan he had drawn up. In the fall of 1955, however, the Arab League rejected the plan in its entirety for political reasons. The Arabs had been put off by precisely what the Americans were hoping for: that the Jordan River project would bring about practical cooperation between Israel and its neighbors to the north and east and would ease the way to an overall solution to the Arab-Israeli problem.

During Johnston's exhaustive mediation efforts, parallel direct contacts between Israel and Egypt were also continuing. In 1954 informal talks were held between Haim Herzog and Abdul Hamid Ghaleb, the two countries' respective military attachés in Washington,[11] as well as between Gideon Raphael and Dr. Mahmud Azmi. Results were disappointing, however, and Egypt rejected any Israeli overtures for official contact.[12] The situation along the Gaza Strip had deteriorated early that year. Egypt rejected Israel's proposal to meet formally with Mahmoud Riyadh, the Egyptian War Department official in charge of Palestine affairs, and insisted that all contacts be held within the framework of the Mixed Armistice Commission.[13] Toward the end of the year two events further embittered Israeli-Egyptian relations: Egyptian seizure of the Israeli ship *Bat Galim* at the southern end of the

Suez Canal and the exposure of an Israeli spy ring operating in Egypt.[14] Nevertheless, talks between Saddeq and Divon continued, and in addition, several foreign intermediaries tried their hand at reaching a settlement between the two countries. All these contacts indicated that Egypt was indeed ready to soften its position on the refugees, but was adamant in its demand that the Negev be returned to Arab sovereignty.

At the end of 1954 and early in January of 1955, Maurice Auerbach, a Jewish member of the British Parliament, visited Cairo several times on a mission on behalf of the World Jewish Congress and with the blessing of the Israeli government, in an attempt to gain better conditions for the jailed Israeli agents and a stay of execution for those sentenced to death. Auerbach met with some of the highest-ranking officials in the Egyptian regime, including Nasser himself. He reported to the Israelis that Nasser claimed to be interested in peace with Israel but that the time was not ripe and that any steps in this direction would brand him a traitor in Arab eyes.[15] Of all contacts thus far, only Auerbach's mission approached official mediation. The Israeli government authorized him to deliver several practical proposals to Egypt, such as releasing the *Bat Galim,* permitting Israel-bound oil to be shipped through the Suez Canal, halting hostile propaganda, and establishing permanent senior-level contacts between the two countries. Ali Sabri, who met with Auerbach on behalf of Nasser, was for the most part positive; but no practical results were forthcoming.

In the meantime, Divon and Raphael's contacts with Saddeq resumed, including at this stage unofficial, unsigned, and nonbinding messages between Sharett and Nasser as well.[16] Sharett asked Nasser to prove his peaceful intentions with firm actions to reduce tensions, such as gradually opening the Suez Canal to Israeli oil tankers, ceasing anti-Israeli propaganda in the Egyptian media, and holding a formal albeit secret meeting on a senior level. Nasser's response was on the whole negative: Egypt would continue to prohibit oil bound for Israel from being shipped through the Suez Canal; Nasser would not intervene in the trial of the Israeli spies; the *Bat Galim* would not be allowed to continue north; and no senior-level contacts could be initiated for the time being, although contacts with Nasser's authorized envoy Saddeq would continue.

But those talks also were halted after Cairo carried out the death sentences against the two Israeli agents, Moshe Marzuk and Shmuel Azar, and in the wake of the Israeli paratroop raid on Gaza at the end of February 1955. The spring and summer of 1955 saw a further deterioration in relations, and the danger of full-scale war loomed on the horizon. But attempts at mediation continued, and while the American and British ambassadors in Cairo tried to push the Alpha Plan, other efforts in Egypt also increased. The most far-reaching in the fall of 1955 was that of Elmore Jackson, Foreign Affairs secretary of the American Friends Service Committee, which was associated with an American Quaker society.[17] Like Auerbach before him, Jackson tried his hand at shuttle diplomacy, making several trips back and forth between Cairo and Jerusalem. Jackson had been approached originally by Mahmoud Fawzi, the Egyptian foreign minister, and Ahmed Hussein, the Egyptian ambassador to Washington. Were the two of them trying to keep Washington from suspecting the imminent signature of the Soviet arms deal? Or were they perhaps trying to persuade Nasser not to conclude the deal at all? Only the opening of Egyptian archives to public inspection will resolve the mystery. But whatever the reason, Jackson also received the blessings of both the U.S. State Department and the Israeli government.

Jackson was still shuttling between the two capitals when, in the wake of a serious incident on the Gaza border in which an IDF unit captured an Egyptian outpost, Nasser sent Fedayun commando units deep into Israeli territory. The Israeli army was quick to respond; a paratroop unit carried out a reprisal action on the Khan Younis police fortress. Jackson attributed his mission's failure to the IDF operation, but the notes he kept on the negotiations preceding that action make it clear that the two countries' entrenched positions held out little hope of compromise; Nasser demanded that, before anything could be considered, Jackson had to attain Israeli territorial concessions in the Negev. The Israeli army action diverted Jackson from his mission, and he found himself dealing more with questions of how to pacify the borders. Israel's practical proposals to exchange prisoners and to consider substantive questions, such as border adjustments and family unifications, elicited no serious response from Egypt; Israel's proposal that the two countries' leaders meet face to face was rejected out of hand. Nasser reiterated the need to "soothe tempers" before he could make any daring move. Arms negotiations between Egypt and the Soviet Union were doubtless far advanced by then—the transaction may already have been signed—and Nasser needed to gain time and placate the Americans. Ultimately, Jackson achieved nothing, but he remained optimistic and wrote to Ben-Gurion at the conclusion of his mission: "The material out of which a *modus vivendi* and possibly a peaceful settlement can be constructed exists."[18] But his mission could not stop the headlong flight of events.

In November 1955 Canada's foreign minister, Lester Pearson, also met with Nasser, who again reiterated Egypt's traditional positions: Israel must return to the 1947 borders[19]; the refugees had to be given the right to choose between compensation and return; the Johnston plan to divide the Jordan

River had to be postponed until the overall regional political situation improved.[20] At this point mediation proposals from all over the world began to be heard. So many politicians, diplomats, and journalists volunteered to cure all the ills of the Middle East that the Israeli Foreign Ministry was obliged to issue a directive to all its embassies to refrain from encouraging such offers without first consulting with Jerusalem.

The abortive attempt of British MP Colonel Cyril Banks, who came on his own initiative, well exemplifies the dangers of inexperienced peacemaking. At the end of 1955 Banks volunteered to act as go-between for a three-stage plan he had devised. The first stage called for the Armistice lines to be stabilized. Nasser, whose personal charm was great and who radiated sincerity, convinced Banks that he was seriously willing to subscribe to a total cease-fire, contingent on one "small" condition: the evacuation of Kibbutz Ketziot from the demilitarized area of Nitzana. Nasser claimed that the area was vital to Egyptian security because it was on the road to Cairo. Unfamiliar with the history of the dispute in the area, the colonel was convinced that he had pacified the region. When nothing happened, he blamed Israel for intransigence on so minor a point. Israel's Foreign Ministry was obliged to turn to Israel's supporters in Parliament to repair the breach. Afterward the director of the Israeli Foreign Ministry's British desk wrote to Israel's embassy in London: "[Banks's] trip to Cairo and his attempt to mediate directly between us and Nasser caused us no few problems."[21] Only one offer remained on the agenda now—the CIA's Gamma Plan, as Anderson's mission had been code-named, which had been approved by the president and the secretary of state.

On November 26, 1955, the CIA's man in Israel, James Angleton, met with Teddy Kollek, then director general of the prime minister's office. Angleton offered the services of Robert Anderson as mediator.[22] For the Americans this represented the last chance to "save" Nasser from Soviet jaws. Dulles believed it was still possible to limit Soviet involvement in the Middle East to a single arms transaction, keep Egypt from going totally over to the Soviet sphere of influence, and prevent similar transactions with other Arab countries. To compensate the Egyptians, America agreed to help finance construction of the Aswan Dam, assist in marketing its cotton, refrain from joining the Baghdad Pact, provide Nasser with covert aid in his struggle for hegemony in the Arab world, and renew attempts to solve the

Palestinian problem through Anderson's mission.[23] Meeting with Sharett at the end of November, Dulles expressed profound concern in face of the risk of Soviet intervention in the Middle East. The situation was dangerous not only for Israel but for the entire world, he said—the most dangerous event since World War II.[24] Yet at the same time it was clear to the Israelis that the mission was also intended to make it easier for the United States to reject Israel's repeated requests for weaponry. The State Department was still bound by the Alpha Plan and feared that providing Israel with weapons would push Egypt into the Soviet Union's waiting arms.

Uneasy, but left with very little choice, the Israelis acceded to the proposal. In preparation for the expected negotiations and in response to the general pressures that had beset it over the last months, Israel launched a peace initiative of its own. On December 6, 1955, Foreign Minister Moshe Sharett submitted a memo to the secretary of state that included several "concrete suggestions": Israel was prepared to ensure that the borders remain quiet if the Arabs did the same. For the time being, Israel would refrain from taking actions that might exacerbate the situation in the Gulf of Aqaba if serious negotiations were actually entered into. Although Israel suspected that the Egyptian gestures were intended only to gain time in order to absorb the Soviet arms, Israel would accede to Dulles's request and would cooperate in an attempt to reach a settlement. Israel would not consider any settlement that from the outset presumed territorial concessions on its part, but it was willing to meet official representatives of the Egyptian government face to face to discuss all the issues under dispute without any preconditions. Israel agreed to mutually satisfactory border adjustments. It was prepared to permit free air and land passage between the Arab countries on Israeli territory, but refused to relinquish sovereignty. It would place Haifa at Jordan's disposal as a "free port" and would permit Jordanians free passage to that port. Israel would also permit free passage between Egypt and Jordan through the Negev. Israel reiterated its willingness to pay indemnification to the Palestinian refugees as per Dulles's August proposal and to cooperate fully with Eric Johnston's plan to utilize the waters of the Jordan and Yarmuk rivers.

Toward the end of December, with a fanfare of publicity, the Israeli government submitted a formal peace plan along these lines.[25] The staff of Israel's Foreign Ministry and embassy in Washington saw the initiative as a dramatic move that would reflect positively on Israel. The Americans also viewed it as an important step forward and welcomed it warmly. Wilbur Crane Eveland of the CIA, who was made privy to the plan before it was publicized, recalls his meeting with the State Department's Francis Russell at the time and Russell's reaction to the plan. He called it a very encouraging breakthrough in the search for peace from which point negotiations could proceed.[26]

For the White House, Anderson's mission was essentially an attempt to bring senior officials from both sides together, preferably Ben-Gurion and Nasser themselves. The plan called for Anderson to fly between Cairo and Jerusalem in order to set up an agenda for the meeting and delineate the two sides' opening positions. (The Americans did not want to make any overtures of their own.) Nasser agreed to the proposal in a conversation with CIA personnel.[27]

Robert Anderson flew to the Middle East in mid-January 1956, first to Cairo and then, on January 23, to Israel.[28] Nasser insisted that the talks be held in total secrecy. Anderson was meticulous in his report to the Israelis on Egypt's position, which was delivered to him in the course of late-night discussions with Nasser and his colleague Zakaria Mohieddin. As expected, the Egyptians concentrated on the question of territorial contiguity between Egypt and Jordan. The envoy got the impression that "Nasser consistently refuses to consider any arrangement other than Arab sovereignty to ensure contiguity." In other words, Nasser totally precluded the idea of "triangles" as posited in the Alpha Plan and certainly would not countenance the Israeli proposal of free passage through Israeli territory. In his memoirs, Mohamed Hassanein Heikal recalls how Nasser made light of the Alpha idea. Referring to the point at which the triangles met, where an Israeli road to Eilat and an Egyptian road to Jordan were to intersect, Nassar asked what would happen "if one of our soldiers wanted to piss, and did so from the overpass onto some Israelis in the underpass—wouldn't that start a war?"[29]

Nasser also presented the traditional Arab demand on refugees: They had to be given the right to choose between returning to their homes or accepting financial compensation. During the discussions Nasser also raised the issue of the Baghdad Pact, which apparently interested him more than the entire question of relations with Israel. On the contacts with Israel, "Nasser said, and repeated more than once . . . that if the leadership learned that he had undertaken these talks, it was not just a political problem that awaited him but maybe also a bullet." He added that "his people, and in particular the radical forces, were not yet ready for [direct talks]. If word leaked out he would have to claim that it was a lie." The argument was sincere, but the very fact that Nasser tried to maintain total secrecy proved that the conditions for making peace did not exist.

Anderson concluded his Cairo talks report to the Israelis by stressing that the major problem was territorial. To this Ben-Gurion replied, "The main question is whether there is a desire for peace." The Alpha Plan was based on the assumption that, for the foreseeable future, the Arabs would not be willing to sign a full-fledged peace treaty with Israel. Thus the plan centered on secondary issues in the relations, such as the economic boycott and the passage of Israeli-bound cargo through the Suez Canal. Anderson seems not to have pressed Nasser on the question of peace, and Nasser's replies made it clear that he was only considering "concessions" and "arrangements." Ben-Gurion himself was cautious and did not insist on immediate peace; however, he did make two firm demands: a total cease-fire along the Armistice lines and a direct meeting between the parties. "Without direct contact, nothing will happen," he declared.[30] Ben-Gurion rejected the idea of ceding the Negev, insisting that once peace—and with it political and economic cooperation—had been achieved, Israel would no longer be a barrier but rather a bridge. The main question, the Israeli prime minister declared, was: "Does Nasser want peace? . . . If so, is he capable of attaining it?"[31]

Anderson's inclination was to back Israel on the issues of the cease-fire and direct contacts. He knew well that contacts at the highest level were virtually out of the question, but appreciated the changed atmosphere that would ensue from a cease-fire and direct contacts.

Anderson's mission coincided with U.N. Secretary General Dag Hammarskjöld's short tour of the region. Hammarskjöld took the opportunity to initiate negotiations, with the aim of calming the borders and ensuring implementation of the Armistice Agreements on the part of the signatories. Since Anderson also considered a cease-fire essential to the success of his mission, the issues tended to blur. Like Jackson before him, he became bogged down in the process. Because Nasser could make no public declarations, Anderson proposed that the Egyptian and Israeli prime ministers make firm commitments to conform strictly to a cease-fire through simultaneous letters of undertaking to the American president. Ben-Gurion's initial agreement was withdrawn and he insisted on a direct meeting: "If Nasser takes part in person and the entire scope of problems is examined, peace can be achieved within ten days."

Toward the end of the first round of talks, on January 25, the lines along which Anderson's mission could continue became clear: Israel was ready for peace on the basis of the territorial status quo, but if a comprehensive settlement could not be reached, it was willing to settle for partial arrangements that would prevent war. Furthermore, Israel was also prepared to consider border adjustments and the return of refugees, on condition that direct contacts be held, preferably at a senior level and with Nasser's participation. At this point, after having clearly indicated his willingness to stretch out his hand for peace, Ben-Gurion addressed the question of Israel's demands from the United States. To prevent war, weapons had to be provided: "A nation whose very existence is in danger," Ben-Gurion said, "cannot rely on words. . . . we believe it imperative to create facts to safeguard our security."[32] Ben-Gurion limited himself to general statements so that Israel would not be accused of making the success of Anderson's mission contingent on America's meeting Israel's demands. At the end of the first round Anderson told Ben-Gurion that the Israelis were moving much faster and had more formulated ideas about what could be achieved, and that the other side talked only about the existence of possibilities, not how to implement them. Now Anderson set off for Cairo again, where he presented Nasser with Israel's proposals.

On January 31 he returned to Israel. Although Nasser had tried to appear moderate and restrained, their most recent talks contributed nothing to advance Anderson's mission. Nasser proposed that the contacts be continued through American mediators. If there was anything Ben-Gurion wanted to convey to Nasser during the time it took for a direct link to be established, Nasser agreed to have it passed to him by the Americans, word for word, Anderson told Ben-Gurion. But it was obvious that Nasser too realized that this was not an adequate solution.[33]

Nasser promised Anderson that, within a few weeks, clearer and more definitive responses to Israel's proposals would be forthcoming, particularly regarding direct contacts. Ben-Gurion feared that Washington would take advantage of the delay and would put off its own response to Israel's arms request. He therefore insisted to Anderson that America had to supply Israel with weapons immediately, irrespective of the mediation efforts. Anderson returned to the American proposal of providing security guarantees to both sides along the lines set forth in Dulles's August speech, but Ben-Gurion and Sharett both rejected the offer.

Since Anderson was apparently bound by State Department policy and not authorized to make any promises to Israel on weapons or unilateral security agreements, he resumed the matter of direct contacts. "The major stumbling block is arranging a meeting," he said. Israel seemed so keen on direct contacts that Anderson suspected that this was his best card for eliciting Israeli concessions in other areas. Sharett reinforced this impression: "I seriously fear that if the idea of a meeting is dropped, the entire matter will come to nothing. We should strike while the iron is hot; if not—who knows. . . . the situation may be pregnant with another war." For Israel to continue believing in the chances of Anderson's mission, he said, it was imperative "to get some sort of substantive undertaking from Nasser, something that will improve the situation."[34]

After his talks in Israel, Anderson returned to Washington to report to the president.[35] At the same time, Ambassador Eban presented Ben-Gurion's reply to a letter Eisenhower had delivered through Anderson. Summing up Israel's position, Ben-Gurion stressed his country's willingness to begin negotiations without preconditions "with the head of the Egyptian Government or with such responsible representatives as he may designate in order to explore possibilities of a settlement or of progress by stages towards an ultimate peace." Israel preferred talks on a comprehensive peace but was willing, if the other side was, to accept an interim approach to the problem, which would pave the way for peace through partial agreements. However, "if the Egyptian Prime Minister rejects this proposal [direct negotiations], it raises serious doubts about his good will."

The issue of direct talks seems to have become the Israelis' most important card as well. Nasser's insistence on maintaining secrecy and his admitted refusal to report on the meetings to his colleagues in the Egyptian leadership led the Americans to suspect that his intentions of supporting Anderson's mission were not sincere. Ben-Gurion understood that what was important at this stage was the question of who the Americans would hold responsible for the failure of the mission, and thus he made a tremendous effort not to put any obstacles in the way. Nevertheless, in his letter to Eisenhower he once again raised Israel's demand for arms: "And I therefore ask you, Mr. President, on behalf of my Government and my people, not to leave Israel without the chance of a sufficient defense, which only arms from a great power can provide, and to instruct that Israel be provided with the American weapons so crucial for Israel to prevent or repel an attack."[36]

About a month later Anderson returned to the region, again going first to Cairo and then on to Jerusalem, where he arrived on March 9, 1956. In his talks in Cairo he focused on the possibility of a direct meeting between Israeli and Egyptian representatives. Fearful for his personal safety (he mentioned the assassination of King Abdullah four times in one meeting[37]), Nasser rejected the offer and again proposed American mediation. By now it was obvious that the chances of peace were nonexistent because Nasser believed that the Arab world was not ready for it, and perhaps because he himself was not really and truly ready for it.

Egypt and Israel disagreed not only on the details of a possible settlement but also on the basic premises that motivated them to agree to the process in the first place. Israel hoped for direct and formal contacts with Arab leaders, constituting some sort of recognition of Israel's existence and legitimacy. Israel also hoped that if nothing else came of Anderson's mission, it would ultimately be provided with American weapons. Nasser, on the other hand, wanted to gain time and placate the West, perhaps ensuring financial backing for the construction of the Aswan Dam without relying exclusively on the Soviets. He did not welcome the idea of meeting Ben-Gurion face to face, even secretly.

Despite the efforts of the American envoy, who also repeatedly raised substantive issues in his Cairo talks, particularly the questions of territory and the refugees, it was obvious that his mission had foundered. In his last talks in Jerusalem he again proposed "indirect mediation," but Ben-Gurion was now bitter and suspicious: "We cannot just rely on Nasser's statement that he will not attack us. He admits to you that he is not his own master. . . . just as he is not capable of making peace, if he has arms his friends will ask him why he does not destroy Israel. There are powerful factions that will force him into it." Repeating Israel's demand for arms, Ben-Gurion declared that "The only way to prevent war is for Israel to have defensive weapons. . . . that is all it depends on. I don't understand how, seeing the danger, you can morally refuse to give us weapons. . . . If you hope that peace [can be achieved] by all means, continue trying. But only if we feel that we are not in danger of war this summer."[38]

Ben-Gurion was also outspoken on where the blame for the mission's failure should fall: "You did the best you could. The President sent one of the best men he could have chosen—and the situation is what it is: no change for the better; not even the President's intervention could alter it. Nasser says that talking about peace endangers his life. This is a fact with political implications." Moshe Sharett followed suit:

> We had great faith in you. . . . we can now be blamed for having wasted precious time, precious to our national interests, because of an illusion we believed in. If you want to continue, and one day you tell us that there is hope—no one will be happier than us. But your actions are no longer congruent with our view of reality. We cannot but doubt Nasser's sincerity.

Anderson himself was less harsh; he said nothing except that his mission had reached a "procedural dead end," but it was obvious that he understood Israel's position, and perhaps even sympathized with it.[39]

On March 12 Anderson reported to the president. Eisenhower summed up his impressions of the report in his personal diary. He blamed Israel for con-

tributing to the failure of the mission because of intransigence on the territorial issue: "[The Israelis] are completely adamant in their attitude of making no concessions whatsoever in order to obtain peace. Their general slogan
is 'not one inch of ground.'" But Israeli willingness to meet the Egyptians
with no preconditions softened this impression of implacability, and
Eisenhower lay the burden of blame for the failed talks on Nasser: "Nasser
proved to be a complete stumbling block. He is apparently seeking to be
acknowledged as the political leader of the Arab world."[40] The State
Department was also disappointed in Nasser, and Dulles told Henry Cabot
Lodge, U.S. ambassador to the United Nations, that "no hope existed of a
comprehensive Arab-Israeli settlement unless Arab hopes vis-à-vis Israel
are somewhat deflated."[41] Ben-Gurion later summed up the talks: "Anyone
who carefully read the envoy's proposals to Nasser and Nasser's responses
to them could see that although Nasser never replied in the negative, he also
never agreed and it was obvious that he opposed them."

Disappointment in Nasser also undermined the basis for the Alpha Plan.
The Egyptian leader's relations with the United States and the United
Kingdom deteriorated rapidly during the winter of 1956, as Egypt continued
to oppose the Baghdad Pact and the other Western regional defense plans,
and as Britain's position in Jordan became irrevocably weakened by Nasser's
growing incitement and the impact of his leadership. On the other hand,
Nasser's relations with the Soviet Union grew tighter. His political maneuvers
severely tested Dulles's and Eden's abating patience.

The demise of the Alpha Plan was never formally announced, but in April
1956 it had become clear that the death knell had been tolled. At the end of
January 1956, Shuckburgh and Russell had still discussed the plan at the
summit meeting between the British prime minister and the American president, and in February Shuckburgh was still sending memos about it; but he
himself was already tired and had ceased to believe in Nasser's goodwill.
The British even considered toppling the Egyptian regime. CIA representatives met secretly in London at the end of March with George Kennedy
Young, deputy director of MI6, the British secret service, who proposed a
three-stage revolution: a revolt in Syria to neutralize the left-wing forces
aiming for a Syrian-Soviet alliance and to ensure pro-Western Iraq's influence in that country; a revolt in Saudi Arabia and the overthrow of King
Saud; and, finally, the overthrow of Nasser in Egypt.[42]

In a talk with a British diplomat at the end of April, Francis Russell summed up the American view that Nasser's prestige had risen in the wake of the Soviet arms deal. The Americans had hoped, in vain, that Nasser would see this as a chance to resolve his conflict with Israel. Nasser's exaggerated self-confidence had become dangerous.[43] This assessment was a revolutionary turning point in the State Department's position. When the spring harvest began, tensions along the Egyptian-Israeli border once again increased. Attention shifted from the efforts of Western diplomats to those of Dag Hammarskjöld and General Burns on behalf of the United Nations.

✳ ✳ ✳

The Egyptian-Israeli contacts in the 1950s left some observers with the feeling that Israel had missed several opportunities for peace. The Gaza raid, for example, is sometimes blamed for the rupture in contacts between Abdul Rahman Saddeq and Ziamah Divon, and the reprisal action in Khan Younis is credited with disrupting Elmore Jackson's contacts with Nasser. Without going too deeply into this controversy here, we shall make only one general observation: Anderson's talks made it clear that, from the 1948 Israeli War of Independence and until the 1967 Six-Day War, not even the barest conditions necessary for a peace settlement between Israel and the Arab countries existed, not even a de facto state of nonbelligerence. There was very wide consensus in Israel on the absolute refusal to make significant concessions on territory captured in 1948, certainly not on large sections of the Negev that had been allocated to Israel by U.N. resolution on November 29, 1947. Even the moderate and flexible Sharett was in full agreement on this. Nor could Israel agree to permit a very large number of Palestinian refugees to return. On their part, the Arabs were not ready for a true reconciliation in their relations with Israel. At the very most they were perhaps willing to consider stricter adherence to the Armistice Agreements. Nasser's arguments for rejecting meetings with Israeli representatives speak for themselves and express his true vision of the historical situation in which he found himself as potential leader of the Arab world. His rival for that position, the Iraqi premier, Nuri es-Sa'id, may not have been totally objective in his views, but his comments are certainly pertinent. At the end of April 1956 he told the British ambassador to Iraq that he had never believed in the sincerity of Nasser's intentions to reach a settlement with Israel. Nasser's aim, he argued, was to exploit the conflict with Israel in order to present himself as a champion of the Arab cause.[44]

Ya'acov Herzog, who was involved in the various mediation efforts at the time, summed up his own opinion of Nasser: "It is hard to see how, in his attempt to achieve the decisive position in the Arab world as the region's chief spokesman and central representative in the international arena, he could have relinquished the Israeli-Arab problem—if he ever really wanted to give it up."[45] For this reason he never really tried seriously to take advantage of what were for him potentially advantageous offers in the Alpha Plan. Nasser was not even willing to pay the small price demanded of him by the Alpha Plan. In 1956 he was already deeply involved in his life's work: the unification of the Arab world and the unfettering of Arab dependence on the West.

9
...

THE STRUGGLE OVER
THE ARMISTICE AGREEMENTS

By the spring of 1956 the Americans—and even more so the British—had given up any hopes they may have pinned on Nasser and quietly abandoned the Alpha Plan. They tried to formulate a new Mideast policy line but remained steadfast in their views on one issue: All-out war was likely to break out between Israel and its neighbors, and if it did, the gates of the Mideast would be thrown open to Communist penetration, the remaining Western hold on the region would be lost, and Europe's oil supply would be cut off, bringing with it economic paralysis.[1] Word of the Israeli government's December decision to eschew preventive war had reached Western leaders, who were nonetheless concerned that hostilities might break out because of three potentially explosive areas of friction:

1. Israel had never relinquished its right to use the waters of the Jordan River to irrigate its parched southern desert. The possibility of Israel unilaterally resuming work on the Jordan riverbed north of the Sea of Galilee hovered in the air and, at the beginning of 1956, became the focus of attention after Eric Johnston's failed mission. Thinly veiled hints by Israel's leaders raised fears that it might resume the project with the coming of spring.[2]

2. The situation along the Armistice lines, especially the Gaza Strip, continued to be potentially explosive. Although the Egyptians had not sent Fedayun into Israeli territory from their Gaza Strip bases between September 1955 and the end of March 1956, their military attachés in Amman, Damascus, and Beirut were openly involved in operating commando groups along Israel's eastern and northern borders. Nasser repeatedly assured General Burns that his instructions to the Egyptian border troops to hold their fire were still in effect; but the incidents along the Gaza Strip recurred.[3] Nasser also refused to meet Ben-Gurion's demand (conveyed by General Burns) for a public declaration of cease-fire that would also encompass infiltration across the Armistice lines.[4] The shock waves inside the Israeli political community precipitated by Operation

Kinneret temporarily halted the reprisal policy favored by Ben-Gurion and Dayan but did not entirely eliminate it. Presumably, if the Arabs persisted in their belligerent posture, Israel would renew its reprisals, creating a vicious cycle of actions and reactions, ultimately culminating in all-out war.[5] The dismissal of General Sir John Bagot Glubb and most of the British commanders from the Arab Legion early in April raised fears that the Jordanian border was also liable to erupt.

3. The dispute over the demilitarized zone in Nitzana had not been resolved. Moreover, as spring neared and the Straits of Tiran remained blocked to Israeli shipping and air passage, it was obvious that Israel would not wait indefinitely but would sooner or later use force to try and break the blockade.

At the end of January 1956, Dag Hammarskjöld spent several days in the Middle East on his return from a Far East tour; it was his first trip to the region as U.N. secretary general and his first meeting with Ben-Gurion and Nasser.[6] But the visit was too brief and ill-prepared to bear any significant results. Although both Israel and Egypt officially accepted Hammarskjöld's proposals on the demilitarized zone, in fact no real change ensued and tensions continued: Ben-Gurion reiterated his demand for absolute cease-fire, and Nasser his for a separation of forces along the border in the form of a 500-meter retreat of troops along both sides of the line.[7] In early March Israel's right-wing Herut Party again demanded an immediate preventive war.[8] Not unexpectedly, the proposal was defeated; but it served to remind the world that Israeli policy makers had not entirely abandoned the possibility.

In mid-March the British and the Americans decided to involve Hammarskjöld more actively in the urgently needed efforts to stabilize the region. On March 13, 1956, the American and British U.N. representatives told him that they wanted to propose the Security Council appointment of a special "agent-general" to the Middle East, empowered with broad political authorities.[9] Hammarskjöld objected for several reasons, preferring to try his own hand at stabilizing relations between the belligerents on the basis of mutual undertakings to abide strictly by a cease-fire.

Israel and the U.N. had for some time been at loggerheads over the implementation and interpretation of several points of the Armistice Agreements. Some of these questions remained unresolved in the autumn of 1955 and the winter of 1956. U.N. unease increased after March 13, when Israel protested sharply before the Security Council against the Egyptian concentration of forces in the Sinai[10]; on March 26 the Security Council met for extensive deliberations on the Middle East,[11] lasting until April 4 and culminating in unanimous acceptance of the following resolution: "The Security Council . . . requests the Secretary General to undertake, as a matter of urgent concern, a survey of the various aspects of enforcement of and compliance with the four General Armistice Agreements and the Council's resolutions under reference."[12] The resolution also empowered the secretary general to recommend means of reducing tensions, such as removing the forces from the Armistice lines, ensuring total freedom of movement for U.N. observers along the lines, and other local arrangements to prevent frictions. The secretary general was asked to report back to the council within a month's time. Hammarskjöld's mission was not intended to resolve the fundamental problems of the Israeli-Arab conflict, such as belligerency, the Suez blockade, and the general legal status and interpretation of the Armistice Agreements. His mandate was limited to immediate questions on the cease-fire, relations along the borders, and the status of U.N. observers; Hammarskjöld himself tended to interpret his mandate narrowly.

Incidents along the Armistice lines had decreased during the first three months of 1956. Early in February Dayan told his senior officers, "The borders have never been as quiet as now."[13] A month later he briefed the Israeli press: "The settlements in the south claim this is the quietest period they have ever known, with no pilfering or infiltration."[14] But in the middle of the month the situation along the Gaza Strip suddenly deteriorated; whether because the harvest was near or because the Egyptian army's self-confidence had increased, sniper fire and mine-laying were resumed.

While the Security Council deliberated these same issues in New York, tensions along the Gaza Strip reached new heights. From their outposts the Egyptians daily shelled Israeli army patrols and observation posts along the Strip, as well as farmers working in the fields of the civilian border settlements. Under Egyptian army cover, Arab peasants from Gaza stole into Israeli territory to pasture their flocks or pilfer the fields. On April 2 one Israeli soldier was killed and another wounded when an Egyptian unit ambushed an IDF patrol sent to chase off a strayed flock of goats and sheep near Kibbutz Nirim. Dayan issued a firm directive: "Our forces will open heavy fire in response to Egyptian fire."[15] The following day Ben-Gurion authorized the use of artillery where needed. "There is no need for provocations," Dayan told the Southern Command officers, "but when battle is engaged, it must not be lost."[16]

The explosion was not long in coming. On the morning of April 4, an Egyptian ambush attacked an Israeli patrol, this time firing mortar shells. Three Israeli soldiers were killed. The IDF returned heavy but "local" fire. Toward evening the exchange of fire waned, but the next morning the Egyptians again opened fire on Israeli observation posts and patrols along the entire strip. One patrol was pinned down by enemy fire, and the Israeli area commander used artillery in order to rescue the patrol. Firing abated toward noon and ceased by 1 P.M. At 3 P.M, however, the Egyptians suddenly began heavy shelling of two kibbutzim, Ein Hashlosha and Kisufim, and the cycle of violence once again rapidly accelerated.[17] The IDF responded by firing on the Arab village of Abassan and the Egyptian outpost at Ali al-Muntar on the outskirts of Gaza City; in response the Egyptians shelled Kibbutz Nahal Oz. At 4 P.M. Dayan ordered artillery fire aimed at the center of Gaza City. Shells began to fall in the marketplace, hitting homes and the local hospital. When he learned of it, Ben-Gurion ordered shelling of the city itself halted but did authorize continued shelling of military targets. That evening U.N. observers managed to get the two sides to agree to a cease-fire, which went into effect at 6 P.M. Egyptian losses were heavy: more than 50 civilians and servicemen killed and over 100 wounded. Most of the casualties, including women and children, were residents of Gaza, where shells had fallen on a defenseless crowd.[18]

The Gaza Strip had turned into an active military front. The Israeli army and the local kibbutzim readied themselves for more fighting, as it was clear that the Egyptians would be responding all too soon. Sure enough, fighting resumed next morning, but Ben-Gurion acceded to General Burns's pleas to cease firing and temporarily halt Israeli army patrols along the Strip. Dayan was unhappy at the order; he told Ben-Gurion that he would "follow the letter and spirit of the directive, although he disliked it because it did not . . . ensure that the border settlers could harvest their fields or prevent the Arabs from infiltrating from the Gaza Strip to pilfer or pasture their flocks in Israeli fields."[19] Ben-Gurion, however, dictated the orders himself:

> Patrols along the border are halted until further notice. To prevent infiltration for harvesting or pasturing in our fields, ambush parties and observation posts will be maintained at appropriate sites (at least 500 meters from the border), to eliminate infiltrators as soon as they are spotted and to capture their herds alive.[20]

But everyone knew fighting would now continue elsewhere. Nasser unleashed the Fedayun to kill as many Jews as possible, including civilians.

General Burns did not abandon his efforts to smooth things over, but the Fedayun units had already been sent across the lines; even Nasser could no longer control their actions. On April 7 Israeli settlements and roads were attacked at seven spots, with further attacks continuing the following day. The Israeli army took far-reaching emergency measures: Night movement along most roads in the outlying areas was halted; paratroop units were sent to reinforce security at airfields and other sensitive installations; settlements were put on full-scale alert in the framework of territorial defense; some 1,000 ambush parties were positioned along the borders and, using dogs and patrol aircraft, border police units began following Fedayun tracks.

On April 8, Israeli army and police engaged some of the commando units and pushed others back over the borders, in the process killing 11 Fedayun and capturing six. As usual, Egyptian radio reports exaggerated the Fedayun victories. Ahmed Sa'id, Sauth al-Arab's best-known broadcaster, made dramatic calls to Israel:

> Weep, O Israel! Weep as long as you wish. Cry for your future, day and night! Wait for death at any moment, because the Fedayun are everywhere. . . . Today you are fearful and confused and you beg for mercy, but to no avail. . . . The Fedayun have been to you, O Israel, in every settlement, every camp, every road—destroying and sabotaging and spreading terror, confusion and death. Weep, then, weep, Israel . . . because the Fedayun have robbed you of all hope of peace, serenity and stability.[21]

General Burns now concentrated his efforts on restraining Israel from retaliating. But Ben-Gurion had already decided to refrain from reprisals if Fedayun activity ceased; on April 9, at their weekly meeting, he told Dayan that reprisals were not worth the effort: The Fedayun attacks were not particularly damaging and Israeli action would detract from the aggressive image Egypt had acquired in world opinion. Ben-Gurion's decision was also prompted by President Eisenhower's exhortations to exercise restraint; the Israeli defense minister promised the president he would cooperate with the U.N. secretary general, despite his own misgivings about any positive results from Hammarskjöld's mission. For now he was prepared to exercise restraint, he wrote the American president, on condition, of course, that Egyptian actions were halted; "otherwise, not responding would be tantamount to abandoning the residents of Israel to continual terrorism."[22] Dayan concurred with the assessment that defensive measures were sufficient for the time being, even though he usually dismissed them as ineffectual. On April 11 he reviewed the situation for the press and said, ironically, that it was unfortunate that the Fedayun had stopped their actions: "The Jews, like the Gentiles, will be saying that the results of the [defensive] measures against the Fedayun are in our favor. . . . We [are liable to] become accustomed to thinking that we can fight the Fedayun from inside Israeli territory and not in their own bases."[23]

Dag Hammarskjöld landed at Lod Airport on April 10. His main worry that day was that Israel would embark on a large-scale reprisal action if the Fedayun attacks continued. General Burns met him at the airport and told him that Ben-Gurion had agreed to wait 48 hours to see if Nasser had indeed ordered the Fedayun back to their bases and if Egypt would refrain from further aggression. The deadline was due to expire at noon of that day, prompting Hammarskjöld to go straight from the airport to Cairo. He felt the most pressing need was for both sides to consent to isolate Article 2/II of the Israeli-Egyptian Armistice Agreement, which dealt with the cease-fire, from the rest of the controversy and to agree unconditionally to abide by it.

Nasser was forthcoming the next day when he met with Hammarskjöld. The terms of the article to which he had committed himself read, inter alia:

> No element of the land, sea or air military or para-military forces of either Party, including non-regular forces, shall commit any warlike or hostile act against the military or para-military forces of the other Party, or against civilians in territory under the control of that Party; or shall advance or pass over for any purpose whatsoever the Armistice Demarcation Lines . . . and elsewhere shall not violate the international frontier.[24]

The Israeli general staff assessment was that the wave of Fedayun attacks had passed; that same day Dayan rescinded all orders for special defensive measures and recalled most units to routine activity. But that night the Fedayun launched one of their most painful assaults. A terrorist group that had apparently remained in the area, cut off from contact with its command post, got as far as the Sarafend army camp, some 10 kilometers from Tel Aviv. There it attacked a bus on the main road to Jerusalem, wounding several passengers, and opened fire on the camp's gate near the main highway. From there the commandos went to the nearby settlement of Shafrir, where they lobbed hand grenades into a synagogue and riddled it with submachine-gun fire. Forty children were inside, studying; five were killed and twenty wounded, as was the teacher.

The Israeli public was shocked; Sharett called it a "night of horror."[25] At GHQ, Nasser's agreement to comply with the cease-fire was condemned as having been made in bad faith.[26] Feelings ran high in Israel that Nasser had purposely heated up the border during the last days of March and had sent in Fedayun to retaliate for the shelling of Gaza because he was ready for a major confrontation with Israel. That day Dayan said, "Nasser's reply to Hammarskjöld was both impudent and evasive; he is concentrating his army heavily along the border. He is waiting for our reprisal to open real war. He keeps sending Fedayun to provoke us. He seems to have set the whole thing in motion because he has decided to start a war."[27] The Israeli public's mood changed radically: "The atmosphere is that of the eve of war," Sharett wrote in his diary the day after the massacre in Shafrir, "one of despondency and shock. . . . The Cabinet has been called for an extraordinary session tomorrow."[28] Extensive IDF action seemed inevitable, even though it might ignite the entire front. The general staff proposed two options to Ben-Gurion: "Either the paratroops attack the Egyptian armored concentrations in the Sinai and the airfields along the canal, or we attack the Fedayun camps in Gaza and hold them for a day or two. The purpose of either is to position the IDF more favorably for the outbreak of war, which will inevitably erupt as a result of that action."[29]

Ben-Gurion ordered the Israeli army to make preparations for war a few hours after the massacre. The government had not yet made its decision, but it seemed inevitable. In the early hours of the morning, Moshe Dayan convened his staff and issued detailed directives: The reserves were to be called up quietly, the units chosen for reprisal actions were to be concentrated in the launching areas, the Golani infantry brigade was to move south, the air force was to arm its aircraft and prepare for battle, and so on—all the last-minute preparations were to be effected. The next morning Ben-Gurion held an urgent meeting to examine the army's war preparedness. Responding to Dayan's question Ben-Gurion said: "The Government's answer will be affirmative."[30]

The next day, April 13, the Cabinet deliberated at length. The question was not simply whether to authorize the proposed reprisal actions; the government was in fact being asked to rescind its November and December 1955 decisions in principle to refrain from war. The presence of the U.N. secretary general in the region, the reasonable assumption that the Shafrir murders had been committed by commandos sent into the field before Hammarskjöld's arrival and who could not be recalled, and the recognition that a reprisal would probably mean full-scale war—all these convinced Ben-Gurion and the government to wait, despite the provocations. However, the government authorized the defense minister to order the operation implemented if Fedayun activity continued, without bringing the matter for further discussion before the Cabinet.[31]

Fedayun activity halted. Eventually it emerged that the Shafrir incident was part of the first wave of infiltrators and that Nasser had indeed instructed the Fedayun to return to their bases and hold their fire, just as he had told Hammarskjöld. But Ben-Gurion did not know this at the time and exchanged a few angry messages with Hammarskjöld. The White House tried to assuage Israel; President Eisenhower sent Ben-Gurion an urgent message pleading with him not to retaliate and to accept Hammarskjöld's proposals. Three days after Shafrir the crisis had passed, and on April 16 the Israeli government announced its final agreement to abide unconditionally by Article 2/II. On April 19 Hammarskjöld officially notified the press of the bilateral cease-fire arrangements.[32] Once the immediate danger of war had passed, Hammarskjöld could turn to other problems related to the implementation of the Armistice Agreements and the prevention of future tensions. He realized that the situation remained extremely unstable and compared his work to that of a stone mason: "You know that, in building an arch, the construction is not stable until all the stones have been fitted in."[33]

Hammarskjöld also wanted the Jordanian, Syrian, and Lebanese governments to agree unconditionally to honor the cease-fire clause. Syria worried that such consent would tie its hands if Israel decided to resume work on the Jordan riverbed and thus withheld consent pending Israel's undertaking not to do so. But Hammarskjöld's pressure bore fruit. On May 2 he submitted an interim report to the president of the Security Council, announcing that all signatory states to the Armistice Agreements had committed themselves to isolate Article 2/II from the remaining articles and to maintain the cease-fire unconditionally.[34]

Hammarskjöld was now free to consider other unsettled issues between Israel and the U.N.: civilian settlements in the Nitzana area, Israeli restrictions on the movement of U.N. observers in Israeli territory, and Israel's rejection of General Burns's proposal to move its forces 500 meters away from the demarcation lines. At that point Hammarskjöld wanted no more than to stabilize the cease-fire and resolve the immediate issues concerning relations along the Armistice lines, the status of the U.N., and freedom of movement for its personnel. Ben-Gurion confronted him with other issues, such as Arab claims to belligerent rights and the closure of the Suez Canal and the Straits of Tiran to Israeli navigation. The secretary general responded that these questions lay outside his purview and that he could not consider them unless Egypt agreed to discuss them.[35]

The secretary general's self-restraint reveals one of the most fundamental factors that undermined the Armistice Agreements. For over three years Israel had been losing faith in any benefit that the Armistice Agreements might offer it. When it committed itself to uphold them in 1949, Israel assumed that they were only temporary arrangements that soon would be superseded by permanent peace settlements. At the end of 1949 Israel's U.N. representative, Abba Eban, addressed the Security Council and said, "There is an organic link between these agreements and the peace settlement which is now being sought under the auspices of the General Assembly through its Conciliation Commission. . . . the Armistice is envisaged not as an end in itself but as a 'transition to permanent peace.'"[36]

"We all thought that peace was around the corner," Moshe Sharett recalled in an address he made late in 1956 after leaving the Foreign Ministry. "We believed that the Arab world would reconcile itself to the new reality, that it was indeed a question of time, but not a long time, a few years. . . . We all thought that the idea of peace would entrench itself increasingly. This is where our policy suffered its greatest disappointment."[37] During the first year after the Armistice Agreements were signed it seemed that a suitable apparatus for direct meetings between Israel and the Arabs had been created and that time would eventually resolve the conflict. But it was precisely the factor of time, which the Israelis viewed with hope, that made the Arabs apprehensive. The Arabs feared that time and habit would establish the State of Israel as a permanent reality, and thus they repeatedly underscored the temporary and interim nature of the agreements and the temporary and interim nature of the very existence of Israel. Moreover, a wide gulf separated the two sides' perceptions of the concept of "armistice."[38] Israel hoped it would be replaced by formal peace, but was prepared to make the best of the armistice, even permanently, so long as in practice the situation was one of peace. For the Arabs, the armistice was no more than a truce, albeit prolonged, within a permanent and continuous state of war. Many authorities in international law at the time still held the older interpretation of the status of an armistice as a situation that does not cancel the state of war[39]; thus they supported the Arabs' perception.

The main thrust of Israel's energy in the 1950s was devoted to absorbing immigrants, populating the country, and developing the economy. The Arab nations were well aware that if Israel were permitted to succeed in these aims, time would work to their disadvantage and Israel would become a strong and permanent reality in the Middle East. Thus the only way to maintain the Armistice Agreements without losing the whole struggle was to take advantage of the terms of the agreements in order to prevent Israel's development.

Therefore the Syrians repeatedly frustrated Israel's attempts to make use of the waters of the Jordan River, and the Egyptians blockaded the Suez Canal and the Straits of Tiran against Israeli shipping. Therefore the economic boycott was stepped up as well, as was direct or indirect support given to the terrorist infiltrators. After the failed talks at Lausanne in 1949, senior Israeli diplomat Elias Sasson analyzed the three different schools that comprised the Arab position. One approach, he maintained, called for an immediate renewal of the war against Israel and its destruction with no delay. A second view held that military victory over Israel could be ensured only in several years' time, after the Arabs had established their military power and were more prepared. The third school held that:

> the Arab world must, first, try to decrease Israel's territory and limit its Jewish population as much as possible in order to foreclose future territorial expansion . . . and in order to ensure that Israel remain a weak and dependent state. . . . second, to refrain from any cooperation, agreement or recognition of Israel in order to gain time to learn the nature of "this foreign object," as Israel was termed, its racist tendencies and its political aspirations, and to keep it in a state of protracted military tension and general economic and social instability, in the hope that it would simply succumb to its own failure.[40]

The Arab states were too weak to follow the first school of thought, and the second approach involved no specific activity. In fact, the policies of the Arab states during the 1950s and 1960s conform to Sasson's description of the third school of thought: restrictions, attempts at keeping Israel weak, noncooperation, and unrelenting attrition.

Ultimately, a state of neither war nor peace evolved. "Israel will accept this state of affairs," Dayan said, "on condition that there is no war within her boundaries. . . . She is ready to live without peace with the Arab nations, on condition that her way of life is not threatened by active hostility."[41] But so long as they could avoid all-out war, the Arabs were not willing to forgo any chance to restrict or harm Israel. Israel gradually realized that the Armistice Agreements provided the Arabs with a measure of legitimacy and cover for their hostility and concluded that there was little point in remaining loyal to them.

For this reason Ben-Gurion repeatedly stressed to Hammarskjöld the need to uphold the first article of the Armistice Agreements, which stated that the ultimate aim was to promote "the return of permanent peace in Palestine"

and which strictly prohibited the "resort to military force in the settlement of the Palestine question." This was the source of the prohibition against undertaking, planning, or threatening any aggressive action against the other side. To the Knesset Ben-Gurion said, "This first article, which can be found in the preamble to each and every Agreement, is the very heart and soul of all of them. It affirms that the intention of each Armistice Agreement is to restore permanent peace, that is, to achieve an end to the conflict between the adversaries and to bring back peace."[42] Ben-Gurion's recurrent complaint was that Nasser's insistence on Egypt's "belligerent rights" formed the basis for the Egyptian blockade on Israeli navigation in the Suez Canal and the Straits of Tiran and for the hostile Egyptian radio broadcasts castigating and threatening Israel; these acts, Ben-Gurion declared, violated the first article of the agreement and thereby, he felt, its very essence. Thus although Israel was willing to abide by an unconditional cease-fire, it did not consider itself obligated to uphold the other articles so long as Egypt continued to violate the basic premise of the agreement.

Hammarskjöld himself conceded that the Armistice Agreements did not provide for any mechanism to consider violations of Article 1 other than by approaching the Security Council, where the Soviet veto would paralyze any Israeli endeavors. Neither the Mixed Armistice Commission nor any other U.N. body—nor in fact Hammarskjöld's mission in spring 1956—were authorized to deal with this article in depth. On its part, Israel saw no point in discussing any of the matters on Hammarskjöld's agenda so long as the Arabs refused to abide by the spirit of the Armistice Agreements as a whole. On this point Ben-Gurion was intractable and uncompromising. Hence the question of Nitzana remained unresolved. (The IDF even continued preparations to increase settlements in the area.) Hence also Hammarskjöld was only partially satisfied by the accommodations he obtained on the dispute over the Sea of Galilee. But the secretary general was a gifted diplomat; between his skill and the Israeli fear of U.N. censure lest he return to the Security Council with a negative report, the Israeli government found itself obliged to make limited concessions aimed at stabilizing the cease-fire along the borders. Thus despite his previous refusal, and in the face of Dayan's fierce opposition, Ben-Gurion now accepted Nasser's proposal to remove armed forces to points 500 meters away from each side of the Gaza Strip boundary and agreed to U.N. observers' posts being placed along the line.[43] Several days later an agreement was also reached with the Syrians prohibiting Israeli patrol boats from approaching more than 350 meters from the Syrian-held bank of the Sea of Galilee. Syrian farmers were also permitted to draw water from the lake (but not to pump it). Ben-Gurion refused to permit U.N.

observers to set up either a naval patrol on the lake or observation posts in Israeli territory north of it.

Hammarskjöld's success was thus limited indeed; despite all his efforts, he failed to settle the dispute on the Nitzana area and on the deployment of forces in the Negev and Sinai. Nor could he bolster the authority of the U.N. supervisory machinery. Perhaps the most that can be said is that his marathon tour prevented the flare-up of hostilities that had seemed inevitable in the wake of increased tensions along the Gaza Strip and the Fedayun incursions early in April. At the beginning of that month senior Israeli officers had met in the defense minister's bureau in order to examine the IDF's readiness for the war that seemed imminent. Two weeks later a similar meeting was held; the summary written by Ben-Gurion's military secretary makes it clear that things had returned to normal. The topics of the discussion included vacation pay for the families of career soldiers, the question of morning prayers in Israeli army units, the chief of staff's holiday plans, planting trees in Jerusalem's no-man's land, an exhibition at the Sha'ar Hagai entry to Jerusalem, and the like.[44]

Two days later, however, another incident occurred and reminded many in Israel that the U.N. secretary general, gifted and adroit though he was, could do no more than lightly plaster over the cracks that could never be completely mended. The fragile accommodation he had labored for could not resolve the fundamental problems that continued to vex the region. On April 29 Ro'i Rothberg, member and military commander of Kibbutz Nahal Oz, across the border from Gaza City, went to chase away Arab shepherds who had trespassed into the kibbutz fields near the demarcation lines. Several hours later his bullet-ridden and mutilated body was returned from Gaza; the murderers had dragged it over the border so that U.N. observers would think he had been killed after crossing the frontier. Still smarting from the concessions Israel had been forced to make in the talks with Hammarskjöld, Moshe Dayan expressed his bitterness eloquently in the powerful eulogy he delivered the next day at Rothberg's gravesite:

> Yesterday morning Ro'i was murdered. He was bedazzled by the tranquillity of a spring morning and did not see those waiting to ensnare him along the borderline. . . . We must seek vengeance for Ro'i's death, not of the Arabs of Gaza but of ourselves. How could we close our eyes to our fate, to the full cruelty of our generation's destiny? . . . We are a generation of settlers, but without a steel helmet and a cannon's muzzle we can neither plant our trees nor build our homes. Our children are doomed

if we do not dig shelters; without barbed-wire fences and machine guns we cannot pave roads or drill for water. . . . On the other side of the border surges a sea of hatred and vengeance, waiting for the day when serenity dulls our readiness, for the day when we give heed to the ambassadors of plotting hypocrisy calling us to lay down our arms. To us is Ro'i's blood crying out from his broken body. For all those thousand vows we took never again to let our blood be spilt in vain, yesterday once more we were enticed; we listened; we believed. . . . let us not turn aside our eyes lest our hand falter. This is our generation's choice: . . . either to live in readiness, armed and strong and steadfast, or to allow the sword to be dashed from our grasp and our lives cut short.[45]

Ben-Gurion was moved by the eulogy, which was broadcast on the radio, but asked Dayan to eliminate the term "ambassadors of plotting hypocrisy" from the press version; the reference to Hammarskjöld's mission was too blatant.

On a tour of the Egyptian military units in the Gaza Strip on May 13, Gamal Abdul Nasser addressed a group of officers: "Now we will speak in the language of power, because we can feel the strength of our army and our capability; there is no doubt that the Egyptian army will be the strongest in the region, whether Israel wants it or not!"[46] In negotiations with the U.N. secretary general, however, the Israeli government had reiterated its decision of the previous December; Ben-Gurion and his colleagues believed that it was not yet time to go to war and that Israel had no option but to continue its defensive deployment and reinforcement of the IDF's defensive capabilities. Ben-Gurion probably continued to suspect that the British would intervene against Israel if hostilities broke out in the region, although at the time he had no positive knowledge that the British and the Americans both had, throughout that winter, been planning military intervention to halt any Israeli aggressive initiative immediately.[47]

But the events of April reinforced the estimation of the leaders of Israel's security system that sooner or later an all-out confrontation with the increasingly powerful Egyptian army would be inevitable. Ben-Gurion summed up the situation before the Knesset: "It would be a dangerous delusion if we thought that ratifying the agreement to abide by Article 2/II would decrease the main risk . . . the danger of war exists and is getting incrementally greater."[48] Hammarskjöld too did not delude himself that the fundamental problems had been resolved. Sir Brian Urquhart, Hammarskjöld's biographer and one of his senior aides, wrote that Hammarskjöld's "own conclusions from his dealings with the leaders in the area were pessimistic."[49]

Urquhart adds that Hammarskjöld was deeply impressed by Ben-Gurion and, notwithstanding the serious differences between them most of the time, he was very sympathetic to him, whereas his relationship with Nasser was at first cool. Mohamed Hassanein Heikal has a different view: "The two men, the intellectual Swede and the Arab man of action, had little in common. But they liked and trusted one another." Heikal even claims that Hammarskjöld hinted to his Egyptian hosts of tensions that had arisen in his relations with the Israeli leaders and had told the Egyptians, "after visiting Israel I understand your problems better."[50]

Heikal's reminiscences may not always be trustworthy, but in this case the Israelis themselves admitted that relations with the secretary general were tense. Despite the alleged friendship between Hammarskjöld and Ben-Gurion, the latter remained skeptical and suspicious of the secretary general's attitude to Israel. He summed up his impressions in a letter to Abba Eban:

> I constantly felt, as he . . . scrupulously insisted on the rights of the U.N. observers to move freely in Israel, that he saw himself as superior to us. As if the U.N. or the Security Council had a mandate on Israel and he was responsible for carrying it out at his discretion. . . . His words, demands and behavior make it obvious that "this international regime" applies only to Israel. He would not dare make the same demands of Egypt or even Jordan that he allows himself to make of Israel . . . I cannot explain [his] odd behavior, a psychological complex or considerations of career, but he must realize that we are a sovereign state like all states.[51]

Dayan wrote that Ben-Gurion's last meeting with Hammarskjöld on May 2 "ended without any agreement. Ben-Gurion was angry. Hammarskjöld was threatening."[52] Dayan's feeling and Heikal's testimony are reinforced by the report of Great Britain's U.N. representative after his discussion with the secretary general upon the latter's return from the Middle East, in which Hammarskjöld gave vent to much anger at Israel, perhaps even a trace of anti-Semitism:

> Israel, for all outward appearances, had not the makings of a State. It was not really a nation. The motive power came from a few fanatics at the top. . . . the underlying state of mind of the Israeli leadership [is] a combination of an inferiority complex and a fatalistic conviction that violence was their only weapon for survival. This was a very unhealthy, pathological attitude which was far more dangerous than the "madness" of the Arabs. The Israelis were doomed as Oedipus. The Arabs were just plain crazy.[53]

Hammarskjöld was not the first U.N. official to come into conflict with the Israelis. This was, in fact, a recurring pattern throughout the 1950s and 1960s. Most U.N. personnel, particularly the UNTSO observers in the field, eventually concluded that the Israelis were unreasonably stubborn, and most developed negative attitudes toward the Israelis.[54] The description by General Carl von Horn, UNTSO chief of staff in the 1960s, is representative:

> Invariably it was the same story. Nearly all [UNTSO observers] had arrived with the honest intention to help both parties to the Armistice Agreement, but with a conscious sympathy for the people of "poor little Israel." Yet, after two or three years in daily contact with officials, soldiers and private individuals on both sides, there had been a remarkable change in their attitude.[55]

The U.N. tended to support the Arabs in general, and the Egyptians in particular. Heikal explains that "At that time [Hammarskjöld] was nearer to the Egyptian point of view because Nasser was basing his position on the United Nations while the Israelis were ignoring the United Nations."[56] Heikal's assessment was totally correct.

In addition, perhaps influenced by the legacy of the underground that had existed during the British regime in Palestine, Israel was not averse to using a bit of deception in order to sidestep the international organization. For the U.N. officers, most of whom were steeped in Western military tradition, this not only broke the rules of the game but also impugned their fundamental values. Moreover, most U.N. officers preferred to live in areas under Arab control, either because the cost of living was cheaper or because the local Arabs' almost colonial subservience was so much preferable to the aloofness, standoffishness, and outright disdain with which the Israelis treated them.

But the sources for the ongoing tensions between Israel and the U.N. administration went far deeper than issues of character and personality. They included the following:

1. The Israelis saw UNTSO and the other U.N. organs as intruders rather than mediators and peace makers. UNTSO was authorized to do its best to maintain the Armistice Agreements; when Israel lost faith in the agreements and in their power to protect its hoped-for national development, the entire machinery of the U.N. in the region became an intrusive restriction on the Israelis. At the end of the first year of Mixed Armistice Commissions (MAC) activities, Dayan wrote Yigael Yadin, then chief of staff, "We recognize this wall on condition that a door can be found for us in it. If that door is closed, we do not recognize the wall and will break through it."[57] The report sent by UNTSO chief of staff General Vagn Bennike to the Security Council in the fall of 1953 read: "Israel is blatantly impatient with the Armistice Agreements because they have not yet been superseded by a final arrangement. This impatience extends to UNTSO."[58]

Israel's prime concern was the basic question of either war or peace; the U.N. organs in the region had the much more limited task of maintaining quiet along the lines, and the observers' reports generally dealt with border incidents rather than fundamental sources of the conflict and how to resolve it. In a continued state of "belligerency," Israel did not always prefer quiet along the lines, and certainly it was not easily moved to be flexible or to make concessions on local issues so long as the Arabs refused to do so on fundamental ones. As a result, Israel at times exhibited exaggerated punctiliousness and jealously insisted on its sovereignty down to the last centimeter.[59]

Tensions between Israel and UNTSO ran highest on the question of the status of the demilitarized zones; Israel claimed de jure sovereignty over the zones, while the U.N. officials considered themselves to be ultimately responsible for them. At the end of 1949, for instance, the UNTSO chief of staff, General William Riley, issued regulations for the Israeli police in the demilitarized zones. Israel objected vehemently, arguing heatedly that Riley had overstepped his authority; Riley, who was also U.N. chairman of the Syrian-Israeli Mixed Armistice Commission, was forced to rescind the orders.[60]

Thus for Israel the U.N. observer force was at best irrelevant to the vital issues that concerned it; at worst, it was a nuisance. Early in September 1956, at the height of the strained relations between Israel and UNTSO, Ben-Gurion candidly told General Burns that "if the U.N. cannot force . . . the Arabs to live with us in peace, don't bother us with observers who are useless, even if they are well-meaning."[61]

2. Israel did not approve of the presence of U.N. military personnel, a foreign entity not subject to Israeli control, within its borders. Reggie Kidron, one of Israel's representative at the U.N., bluntly presented this objection in a heated discussion with Hammarskjöld:

"None of us will agree to foreign officers wandering along our borders unsupervised. Only eight years ago we got rid of the British army and repulsed the attack by the Arab armies, and now once again we have foreign soldiers wandering around to whom Israeli law does not apply. I am not comparing the U.N. observers to the British army, God forbid; but the public must see it as a certain continuity, a new form of supervision and foreign restriction on our independence and sovereignty."[62]

Von Horn also stressed this difficulty: "Having got rid of the British, the Israeli mind plainly found it hard to stomach another parcel of foreigners, who, in their view, were constantly carping, criticizing and actively obstructing them in their struggle for national survival."[63]

3. Israel had always wanted direct contact with the Arabs, at all levels, which would give it the legitimation it so dearly sought and would imply at least de facto Arab recognition. Israel hoped that direct contacts at low- and middle-echelon levels would eventually lead to discussions at higher levels and facilitate resolution of ongoing problems that cropped up from time to time. U.N. officials were a buffer between Israel and the Arabs and allowed the Arabs to deal with the ongoing problems without granting Israel any kind of recognition and without

having to speak to it directly. Israel thus attempted to ignore UNTSO as much as possible and carry on direct dialogue with the Arabs. The U.N. officials viewed this as sidestepping their authority.

4. The Mixed Armistice Commissions (MACs) included an equal number of representatives from both sides; the chairman of each MAC was an UNTSO official who had the deciding vote. Naturally enough, the U.N. observers (and the Security Council itself) eventually became a kind of judiciary ruling which side had violated the Armistice Agreements. This had become obvious during UNTSO's first year of existence and was noted by Pablo de Azcarate, the man responsible for setting up the observer force during the 1948 truce period: "The Commissions turned into quasi courts making difficult decisions, which exacerbated the situation instead of easing it and finding practical and reasonable solutions."[62]

Israel was irritated by the presence of this foreign authority sitting in judgment on the morality of its actions, and often enough viewed UNTSO decisions as lacking in impartiality. Arab hostilities usually came in the form of infiltration by civilians or irregular forces; in contrast, the IDF reprisals were by definition military acts and the U.N. observers tended to lay the blame on Israel for violations of the Armistice Agreements rather than the Arab states. For instance, even though the number of armed and unarmed civilian infiltrations from Jordan far exceeded the number of Israeli incursions, in most instances the U.N. did not censure Jordan because it did not hold the government of Jordan responsible for the actions of individuals.

Furthermore, the U.N. observers were obligated to take action only when there was unequivocal evidence of violation—amply available in the event of IDF reprisals but much harder to come by in the case of the infiltration of irregulars and civilians. All too often UNTSO officials failed to censure an Arab state because such evidence was lacking even in the face of obvious active or passive responsibility.

Moreover, the dramatic results of IDF reprisals never failed to horrify the U.N., while the individual incursions of unidentified civilian commandos into Israeli territory, even if accompanied by violence, seldom provoked any shock at the Security Council.

5. It became increasingly obvious that the U.N. in general had started to tilt away from support of Israel. In the Security Council the Soviet Union began to exercise an automatic veto whenever a proposal was made that threatened Arab interests.[65] In the 1950s and 1960s in the General Assembly, too, when so many Third World nations gained their independence and joined the international body, Israel's position began to erode in the face of Arab solidarity with the new nations.

6. Western support of Israel was not always matched by voting patterns at the U.N., where internal dynamics and bargaining on other issues often influenced votes on Israel. The tendency to censure Israel in the U.N. despite the more sympathetic stance of most Western governments, and certainly Western public opinion, can also be attributed to the West's enthusiastic commitment to the declared ideology of the

U.N. in its central role as peacekeeper. For most of the diplomats involved, the Armistice Agreements themselves were the international organization's most impressive achievements. When the chairman of the Security Council reported signature of the Armistice Agreements in 1949 he declared, "I consider that this is no ordinary event in the development of world affairs. . . . It is proof of the value and efficacy of this organization."[66] The Armistice Agreements held a special place in the U.N. ethos, and maintaining them at all costs had become an institutional interest. Thus as Israel's initial enthusiasm for the Armistice Agreements cooled, frictions with the U.N. became inevitable.

As early as 1949 Sharett had noted that the U.N. mediation efforts were working to Israel's disadvantage:

> The U.N. representatives' actions had one thing in common: they were not satisfied with an effort to bring the two parties closer together and encourage them to reach an accommodation but instead proposed their own solutions . . . but whenever they did, it was usually to our disadvantage. . . . When these solutions were acceptable to us, this did not pave the way to agreement but rather sabotaged it.[67]

By mid-1954 the mood in Israel was one of disappointment in the U.N. and its organs as, one after another, resolutions were adopted and actions taken inimical to Israel's interests. Soviet veto of a resolution ensuring free passage for Israeli shipping in the Suez Canal, the MACs' refusal to censure Jordan for an attack on an Israeli bus on the road to Eilat, the U.N. secretary general's refusal to convene a special Israeli-Jordanian commission to discuss unresolved issues, General Vagn Bennike's negative stance on the controversy over the Jordan water project—these are only the most striking of many examples. On March 30, 1954, Abba Eban advised Sharett to "completely abandon any thought of further recourse to [the Security Council]."[68] But Israel, greatly dependent on the goodwill of the West in general and the United States in particular, could not afford extreme actions and had to accept the situation, doing what it could to direct its diplomatic course through a hostile sea and fight the currents that often ran counter to her most vital interests.

In 1956 Israel no longer believed that the minor disputes and daily incidents could be solved by the U.N.; it wanted to cut the Gordian knot of the Arab-Israeli conflict with one blow of the sword and force the Arabs once and for all to choose between war and peace, even if it meant general war. The U.N., of course, was inherently opposed to resolving conflicts by force. Thus not only was the U.N. incapable of settling the conflict through mediation, but it actually prevented resolution through direct confrontation.

On May 9 Hammarskjöld submitted a report to the Security Council on his Middle East mission.[69] Naturally enough, he emphasized his main achievement, the unconditional consent of all parties to uphold the cease-fire, and played down the points of disagreement. Moreover, because his mission had been so very limited, the secretary general saw no need to report on Egypt's continued refusal to permit Israeli navigation in the Suez Canal and the Straits of Tiran. Thus the blame for failing to reach agreement on the other points fell, for the most part, on Israel. Hammarskjöld did not refrain from settling accounts with Israel on a number of thorny unresolved issues. For example, in noting how each party had drafted its consent to the unconditional cease-fire, including a reservation on the right to exercise self-defense as defined under Article 51 of the U.N. Charter, he commented that only the Security Council was authorized to determine what conditions justified exercise of that right, hinting at his disapproval of Israeli reprisals. Hammarskjöld declared outright that it was obvious "that reservation for self-defense did not permit acts of retaliation"—clearly directed against Israel's policy of reprisals. Ben-Gurion was most upset by the section of the report on the authority of U.N. organs; Hammarskjöld had written that the Security Council resolutions of August 11, 1949, on the status of the Armistice Agreements, established an "international regime" in Palestine. Israel could never accept such terminology, and it was precisely that point that eventually precipitated a crisis in Israel's relations with Hammarskjöld.

Ben-Gurion had reaped a minor, ambiguous, diplomatic victory on Nitzana. He had succeeded in maneuvering Hammarskjöld into creating a conditional nexus between Egypt's demand that the area of Nitzana be evacuated and Israel's demand that the blockade on Israeli navigation in the Suez Canal be lifted. Since the Egyptians were not willing to accept this condition, Hammarskjöld could not openly criticize Israel for intransigence regarding Nitzana. The Secretary General continued his efforts to resolve these issues even after submission of his final report, but to no avail.[70]

On May 29, 1956, the Security Council opened extensive discussion of Hammarskjöld's report that lasted six sessions and that revealed Israel's inevitably weak bargaining position at the U.N. The preamble to a draft proposal submitted by the British U.N. representative began: "Conscious of the need to create conditions in which a peaceful settlement, on a mutually acceptable basis, of the dispute between the parties could be made. . . ."[71] Ahmed Shukeiri, the talented Arab bloc spokesman, was then Syria's U.N.

representative. He delivered an impassioned objection to the phrase "peaceful settlement, on a mutually acceptable basis, of the dispute between the parties." The delegate from Iran, which was then on the Security Council, suggested the phrase be deleted. Anxious to pass the resolution unanimously, the British succumbed to the joint pressure exerted by the Arabs, Iran, and the Soviet Union, and agreed to eliminate it.

The U.N. ratified the report and empowered Hammarskjöld to continue efforts toward agreement on the unresolved questions.[72] The report condemned Israel roundly albeit indirectly, and Israelis were understandably concerned about continued relations with the international body.

But Israel's worries were one thing; public opinion in the West and among the members of the U.N. diplomatic corps was another. Less than two months later the sky would fall on Western diplomats, but early in June they were in a strange state of euphoria. Hammarskjöld was hero of the day. The British Foreign Office and the American State Department decided to take advantage of his success and the allegedly excellent ties he had made in Cairo and Jerusalem in order to further the peace process, which had been halted after the failures of Alpha and Gamma. At the conclusion of his formal report Hammarskjöld had written, "What has been done may open the door to new fruitful developments."[73] The United States and Great Britain now made their final, pathetic efforts to use Hammarskjöld himself as peace broker.

Political conditions too suddenly seemed more promising than ever. The Egyptians—at least Foreign Minister Mahmoud Fawzi—began to suspect that they had been too hasty in rejecting Robert Anderson's mission and tried to rectify the error. Early in July Fawzi offered the British ambassador in Egypt a new proposition, which seemed to hold out hope for an eventual agreement. The first stage called for an agreed mediator to try to narrow the gulf between the Israeli and Arab positions. Fawzi suggested Hammarskjöld for this role, which was to be played in total secrecy. The next stage would be the formulation, by an international commission, of a compromise to be approved by the U.N. as a resolution binding on all parties. Fawzi suggested that this second stage be left to the American, British, Soviet, Indian, and Pakistani representatives. As a first step, Hammarskjöld should be invited to return to the region as soon as possible.[74]

Great Britain's exhausted Foreign Office officials grasped at the straw held out to them and quickly recommended to their American colleagues that the Egyptians should be encouraged to continue along the lines of Fawzi's initiative. Hammarskjöld seemed the right man for the job, as he was already well versed in the problems and, since he was planning another trip to the Middle East anyway, his presence would not arouse undue attention.[75] Francis Russell, who had brokered the Alpha Plan for America, suspected that the proposal was no more than a last-ditch attempt by Egypt to save its relations with the West from total collapse; but he supported Britain's stance and suggested that the sincerity of the Egyptian offer be carefully examined.[76] The Americans thought the idea should be broached with Hammarskjöld without creating the impression that too many hopes were pinned on it. Hammarskjöld planned his brief visit to the region to renew his ties—especially to mend the rift with Ben-Gurion, which had been provoked by the secretary general's report and by the Security Council discussions early in June[77]—and to bolster the fragile cease-fire agreement he had labored so hard to achieve and which now threatened to come apart at the seams, as well as to look into Fawzi's plan secretly, at Britain's request.[78]

Hammarskjöld arrived in Jerusalem on July 18 and held marathon discussions with Ben-Gurion on a wide range of general philosophical, historical, and economic issues. Although he could point to no real achievements, the secretary general felt he had somewhat regained Israel's trust. After leaving Jerusalem he wrote Ben-Gurion a note in the best of his flowery style: "There may be madness in the pursuit of the stars, and we know that the pursuit will not succeed short of miracles. But it is in itself a miracle when the stars guide our road as to let them cross others, and permit us to experience a deep human contact in matters essential to the very future of man."[79] Ben-Gurion remained skeptical: "Hammarskjöld is a great intellectual, but I don't think his words come really from the heart."[80]

On July 22, after a short stay in Amman, the U.N. secretary general arrived in Cairo. Unfortunately, however, events had preceded him. Two days earlier the Egyptian ambassador to Washington had received Dulles's negative reply for funding of the Aswan Dam, which incensed Nasser and ultimately provoked the Suez crisis. The bombshell of the Suez Canal Company's nationalization had not yet landed, but Egypt's leaders, faced with far more pressing trials now, had little time or patience for Hammarskjöld. Nevertheless, he looked into Fawzi's proposal thoroughly with the Egyptian foreign minister—who had in the meantime become his personal friend—and sent Selwyn Lloyd and Dulles his interpretation and assessment. He was extremely cautious and left no room for undue optimism; however, he indicated that he planned to return to the region in October to begin trying to bridge the gaps.[81] But only two days after

Hammarskjöld sent his message, Nasser nationalized the Suez Canal Company, an act that completely altered all political conditions in the Middle East. At the end of October, Hammarskjöld would be busy with efforts to put out the blaze that made most of the issues related to the mediation efforts thus far irrelevant and outdated.

Years later General Burns wrote his impressions of Hammarskjöld's mission: "Looking back one can see that by the spring of 1956 the currents which were bearing the antagonists in the Mideast towards the whirlpool of war were too strong to be stemmed just by diplomatic intervention or change by simple mediation by third parties, including the United Nations and its agent the Secretary General."[82] Indeed, several days after the nationalization of the canal and after Nasser had threatened Israel in an inflammatory address in Alexandria, Ben-Gurion sharply responded to Hammarskjöld's estimation that the Egyptians remained interested in calming down the region. Writing to the secretary general he mentioned Austin Chamberlain, who had declared in the British Parliament in 1936 that Mussolini was a gentleman and incapable of lying: "Two days after he [Hammarskjöld] sent me the message assuring me that the Egyptian desire to halt tensions was sincere, the Egyptian Mussolini told his people in Alexandria that he would fight Israel until it was wiped off the face of the globe."[83]

While Israel's political leaders were engrossed in mediation efforts of various sorts, and while its army continued to prepare for the possibility of an Egyptian attack in the summer, a revolutionary turn had taken place in total secrecy. On the day of the Fedayun attack on the synagogue in the village of Shafrir, the first 12 French Mystère jets flew directly from France to Israel. This pivotal event, destined to mark the beginning of a change in the entire strategic and political parameters of Israel's activities that summer, took place covertly and unbeknownst to all but a handful of Israel's commanders and senior defense officials. Chapter 10 presents the chain of events in Israel's unceasing attempt to acquire arms, events that also ultimately shaped the nation's basic policy in the coming months.

10
· · ·

THE FAILURE OF ARMS PROCUREMENT
IN THE UNITED STATES

When the Israeli government decided not to embark on a preventive war late in the autumn of 1955, the assumption was that, within a short time, Israel would be able to receive weapons that would restore the balance of arms that had been upset so dramatically by the Egyptian-Czech transaction. "We may be getting American arms," Ben-Gurion had said to Moshe Dayan when he instructed him to put off the campaign for the Straits of Eilat on November 13, 1955.[1] He was referring, first and foremost, to new jet fighter planes and tanks capable of matching the Soviet Stalin-III and T-34 tanks that Egypt had just received. As renewed efforts to procure arms began, Ben-Gurion said, "If we . . . mobilize Jewish and American public opinion to concentrate on the issue of arms—I'm not sure we'll get them, but I'm not giving up in advance."[2] Indeed, the main thrust of Israeli diplomatic activity at the end of 1955 and beginning of 1956 was directed at arms procurement. In nearly every Western capital, Israel's ambassadors repeatedly visited the foreign and defense ministries of their host nations, as well as the bureaus of the heads of state, trying to convince them of Israel's urgent need for weapons. The files of the Israeli foreign minister's bureau are crammed with hundreds of cables and scores of letters and memos hinting at hoped-for imminent supplies of arms, interspersed with anger and disappointment at failed efforts.

In retrospect, two schools of thought and action on the issue of arms procurement seemed to have been at work in Israel. One was adopted primarily by the Foreign Ministry; under Abba Eban's energetic and talented leadership, it concentrated efforts on the American administration. The second was assumed by the Defense Ministry as led by its resourceful director general, Shimon Peres; it concentrated primarily on the French. Each approach seemed to have its own method of action: the Foreign Ministry believed in formal diplomatic contacts; the Defense Ministry's tendency was to initiate direct contacts with arms manufacturers and those influential in the defense establishment, bypassing the official channels of the foreign ministries.

In fact, however, there was no real controversy in principle, merely a difference in the actual circumstances under which the Foreign Ministry officials in America and the Defense Ministry officials in Paris functioned. The premises were different, even contrary, as were the methods and channels of communication that existed in both places. The nature of the presidential administration and the central role played by the secretary of state limited the degree to which Israeli Foreign Ministry officials in America could maneuver. In contrast, the complexities and rivalries that beset the Fourth Republic in France made it easy for Defense Ministry officials, both French and Israeli, to sidestep the obstacles occasionally put in Israel's way by the French Foreign Ministry.[3]

Since the efforts in the United States ultimately failed and those in France bore fruit, Shimon Peres's ingenuity and methods were considered the more successful. This evaluation was not a result of an a priori controversy over conflicting political orientations; it could be made only in retrospect, when the political conditions unfolded and the different circumstances in these countries became clear. From the beginning, Israel did not hesitate to use any source so long as it could supply the required weaponry quickly. Both Foreign Ministry and Defense Ministry officials spared no effort to find any cracks in the bureaucracies through which vital arms could be procured.

In the spring of 1956 it finally became obvious that arms on a substantial scale could be acquired only in France and that the Pentagon warehouses were closed to Israel. But in the first months after the Egyptian-Czech deal became public, the main thrust of political efforts was directed at the U.S. government,[4] for the following reasons:

1. Only two Western nations at the time produced tanks equivalent in quality to the Soviet tanks: the United Kingdom, which produced the Centurion, and the United States, which produced the Patton. Although Great Britain had just supplied several scores of Centurions to Iraq and some to Egypt, the chances that it would also agree to supply them to Israel were very slim. At any rate, the scope of any such transaction could only be very limited.[5]

2. Several countries manufactured modern jet planes on a par with the Soviet MiGs. The French Mystère-4 had just begun to roll off the production lines, England was producing the Hunter, and the Americans

were manufacturing the F-86. In addition, Canada, Australia, and Italy were also producing the American models. Israel's chances of acquiring the British plane were nil,[6] and American agreement was required for any rapid supply of Mystères because the French production line at the time was also engaged in "off-shore procurement." In this system America committed itself to provide arms for NATO allies by underwriting their production costs in Europe. This arrangement entitled the United States to supervise those weapons production lines. Obviously, the Pentagon and the State Department also had to approve any delivery of European-produced American planes to any country.

3. Only America could supply Israel with arms under very favorable financial terms. Smaller suppliers would be much more insistent on cash payment; at the most they might be willing to give Israel short-term credit. News of the Egyptian-Czech arms deal had sent Israel's defense budget soaring, even before any additional weapons were purchased. It had already been swelled by the costs of the defensive deployment and increased training exercises. Another 10 percent had to be invested in preparing the home front for war, and additional sums were allocated by the Jewish Agency, the Jewish National Fund, and the Histadrut Trade Union Federation for different security expenses for civilian settlements and preparing the rural population for an emergency. Total defense expenditures that year tripled. The estimated costs of the minimal quantity of modern weapons would add at least another 50 percent to the annual military budget.[7]

4. Throughout the fall of 1955 and the winter of 1956, the Americans had deluded Israeli diplomats and political leaders into believing that there was a serious possibility that Washington would respond to Israel's requests for heavy arms. In their talks in Geneva at the end of October 1955, John Foster Dulles had told Sharett that the U.S. government would consider Israel's request's for arms "positively," especially its requests for "defensive weapons."[8] Shortly thereafter, on November 9, in a declaration made in Denver, the American president referred to "arms needed for legitimate self-defense,"[9] ostensibly hinting at American willingness to consider supplying Israel with defensive weapons. It was on the basis of this statement that Sharett declared to the Knesset that "We have been promised that our request would be considered positively,"[10] and for Ben-Gurion's assertion to Dayan and Peres that "the President of the United States has undertaken a certain moral commitment, albeit with reservations, to consider positively the supply of arms for purposes of legitimate self-defense."[11]

But archival material makes it clear that the American administration never intended to furnish Israel with the heavy weapons—tanks and planes—

it had requested. Eisenhower's memoirs are unequivocal: "After considerable deliberations we concluded that in the circumstances, a U.S. shipment of arms [to Israel] would only speed the Middle East arms race, therefore we decided against it at the moment."[12] Before the Czech deal was made public, Washington had issued permits for Israel to purchase military equipment for a total of some $3 million. The list included communications equipment, parachutes, spare parts and light arms ammunition; the only "heavy" items were 50 armored half-tracks. Even these procurements were held up for many months and released only in the summer of 1956.[13] At that time the Americans never seriously considered selling Israel jet planes and modern tanks.

So long as the Americans considered the Alpha Plan feasible, they were committed not to furnish arms to Israel by their agreement with the British to exert constant pressure and force Israel to consent to the proposed territorial compromise. At the January 1956 Washington summit meeting between the American president and the British prime minister, the British adamantly insisted that this item in the plan be implemented, and the Americans formally agreed not to provide arms to Israel.[14] The State Department didn't even need British pressure; Dulles himself was convinced that providing arms to Israel would set the entire Arab world against the United States and create an untenable situation in which the Americans were viewed as pro-Israeli and the Soviets as pro-Arab. Dulles believed such a clear-cut dichotomy would put paid to Western influence in the Middle East and jeopardize Middle East oil supplies, threatening the European economy with total collapse. Furthermore, although the secretary of state was well aware that the provision of Soviet arms to Egypt was liable to upset the regional balance of power dangerously, in the winter of 1956 he was still convinced that the balance tilted in Israel's favor and that a decision could be put off without seriously endangering Israel's security. If, in the meantime, the mediation efforts succeeded, the danger of war would also be greatly reduced, as would Israel's need for arms.

But the American government was also eager to camouflage its decision not to provide heavy arms to Israel; the State Department thus tried to fan the last faint embers of hope in Israel. So long as Israel still believed American arms would be forthcoming, it would refrain from resorting to desperate measures and would not embark on a preventive war or resume work on the Jordan River project. And so long as Israel believed there was a chance of getting weapons, the American administration could also put off pressures from Israel's many supporters in Congress and among the American public.

These were the considerations that resulted in all those vague statements by the members of the U.S. administration, whose intent was merely to keep

Israel from learning that a negative decision had already been taken. The American government's problem was not deciding whether to provide Israel with arms, but rather how to go about hiding the decision not to provide them.

On November 16, 1955, encouraged by Dulles's promise to consider moderate requests positively, Israel submitted a formal and detailed requisition for armaments to the American administration. It included 48 F-86 jets and 60 Patton tanks, as well as some 100 more innocuous items. Its composition was calculated to create the impression of "defensive weapons" so that the Americans could respond positively to what were at least clearly nonoffensive items. The Israeli Embassy in Washington appended a document referring to the various declarations made by Eisenhower and Dulles regarding Israel's right to self-defense, and of course Dulles's by-then famous promise to consider such a request "positively," as well as Eisenhower's Denver declaration. To eliminate any doubt, the embassy document stated, "The object of the program in the enclosed Note is not to keep pace with the Soviet reinforcement of Egypt, but rather to strengthen Israel's capacity of legitimate self-defense to a minimal extent compatible with her security."[15]

Obviously, the distinction between defensive weapons and offensive ones was not clear-cut. The Israeli military attaché in Washington reported that the Pentagon also understood "that there is no weaponry which is clearly and innately 'defensive' and that the 'defensive' nature of weapons depends on the intentions of the operator"; the best defense against planes were planes, and the best defense against tanks were more tanks.[16] The recurrent American use of this terminology was intended to distinguish between heavy and crucial arms that could restore the balance of power and those that could not. From this point of view, what Israel really needed was "offensive" weaponry.

Israel's requests were sent on for review by senior Pentagon officials who were asked to look into American military warehouses, set prices, and consider other technical matters; it was obvious, however, that the ultimate decision would be made by the State Department, and that Dulles—and perhaps even Eisenhower himself—held the key. Several weeks later, at the beginning of December, when Moshe Sharett was in the United States, word went out that the technical inquiries had been concluded and a response from the administration seemed imminent. On December 6 Sharett met with the secretary of state himself, ostensibly to consider the American government's new mediation initiative, but also to again broach the issue of arms procurement. Sharett reiterated Israel's concern at the upset balance of power; an *aide memoire* that was officially handed to the secretary of state on this occasion regarding Israel's proposals for a settlement with the Arab countries stated: "Unless prompt steps are taken to reduce this perilous disparity [in arms strength] by providing Israel with additional arms for self-defense . . . there will be an inevitable aggravation of Arab intransigence and of Israeli apprehension."[17] The *aide memoire* clearly hinted at the possibility of an Israeli offensive initiative if its hopes for arms were dashed. In person Sharett added that

> The present calm in Israel is that of tension and great anticipation. The Israeli public believes that the Western powers, and especially the U.S. Administration, are seriously considering her demands for defensive weapons, and we are very fearful of the situation that will develop if the decision is postponed or if the Minister returns empty-handed.[18]

At that meeting Dulles was preoccupied with the peace initiatives and the new Gamma mediation efforts, but he promised that he would try to let Sharett know the American decision before he left the United States in a few days' time. On the night of December 11-12, however, the Israeli army launched Operation Kinneret, providing the State Department with a golden opportunity to put off its response. At the State Department George Allen told Abba Eban that

> the Secretary of State was actively occupied with the problem [of arms] . . . and had even met with Congressional leaders and had hoped for additional talks with Mr. Sharett before Dulles' departure [for a NATO conference in Paris]; in the wake of Israel's action, however, it was no longer possible to make any statement on the matter . . . as he had wished.

Allen asked that Sharett be advised, on behalf of the secretary of state, that "the timing of the action was regrettable and inconvenient for the decision which the Secretary had hoped to discuss with the Minister."[19] Operation Kinneret provided the Americans with a convenient recess of several weeks, until the conclusion of Security Council deliberations on the operation. But senior State Department officials admitted openly that, even without any IDF operation, Dulles's final response would not have been positive; at the most he would have assured Sharett in principle that a response would be forthcoming at a later date, adding specific explanations why the United States could not at this time accede to Israel's requests.[20] The State Department had now freed itself of Israeli pressure for a while, without creating the impression that it was responding negatively and without totally dashing Israeli hopes.

Several days before the Security Council concluded its deliberations on Israel's attack on Syria, Moshe Sharett decided to renew diplomatic activity for arms procurement in America. He sent an emotional and sharply worded letter to the secretary of state:

> With this chapter now drawing to its close, I must renew, with all earnestness at my command . . . the urgent plea . . . for the supply of arms to Israel. . . . Unless something is done without delay to offset the menacing Egyptian superiority, a position will very soon be created in which Colonel Nasser will be undisputed master of the situation, free to attack whenever he chooses. . . . We cannot conceive that the U.S. Government should contemplate with equanimity the development of so ominous a crisis, with all its incalculable consequences.[21]

Security Council deliberations on the Kinneret affair ended on January 20, 1956; the very next day Abba Eban renewed Israel's official request for arms at the State Department. Sharett extended his efforts in a meeting with the American ambassador, Edward Lawson, in Tel Aviv. "The matter of arms is reaching a critical stage," he told him. "[T]he time for a decision has come. We are entitled to know where we stand and what awaits us."[22] But everyone in Washington was now feverishly engaged in preparations for the upcoming summit conference between President Eisenhower and the British prime minister, Sir Anthony Eden, at the end of January. In an urgent meeting that Abba Eban succeeded in arranging with Dulles before the arrival of the British, the secretary of state clarified that the United States government had not yet concluded its review and could not at this stage make a positive response. When Eban expostulated that this new delay would be viewed by his government as a serious blow and would engender one of the most ominous moments in the history of Israel's international relations, Dulles expressed ostensible surprise and shock at the importance of the time factor and the urgency with which the Israelis viewed the situation. But he remained adamant: "He did not reject anything," Eban cabled Sharett, "but he needed time to reach a decision."[23]

As the Eisenhower-Eden summit approached, the Israeli Embassy in Washington sent the State Department an official memo reviewing all of Israel's claims. The document concluded with an emotional appeal: "In this solemn hour of national emergency, the Government of Israel draws the attention of the Government of the USA to the heavy, and perhaps tragic, responsibility which would be involved in the continuous denial of effective weapons of defense to Israel in face of a peril which mounts from week to week."[24]

But all efforts were frustrated. The American and British leaders stood firmly by their negative positions. The statements issued at the conclusion of the summit were familiar to the Israeli diplomats: "We believe that the security of the states in the area cannot rest upon arms alone, but rather upon the international rule of law and upon the establishment of friendly relations among neighbors."[25] The leaders reiterated their call for a compromise along the lines of the Alpha Plan and repeated their contention that only the 1950 Tripartite Declaration could prevent aggression in the region. Eisenhower summed up the resolutions made at the meeting in his diary: "We adhered to the Tripartite pronouncement of May 25, 1950. We agreed that we should meet with the French in order to examine what means we should jointly use to stop a war if it should break out in the region."[26]

These formulations were intended to serve a dual purpose. Since it had been decided not to arm Israel, the 1950 Tripartite Declaration was supposed to replace weapons—that is, it was supposed to provide a sort of guarantee to come to Israeli's defense if it were attacked. It was also intended to deter Israel from any aggressive initiative if the upset balance of power threatened to push the nation to take desperate measures.[27]

In any event, Robert Anderson's second visit to the Middle East was fast approaching. On February 2, 1956, Dulles told Eban that it would be a shame to forfeit a chance for a settlement because of arms, which the United States could easily supply if and when it became obvious that this was the most effective way to stabilize peace. His language remained vague and noncommittal: "If he concluded that there was no chance of a settlement or that it involved a prolonged delay," Eban wrote, "the Secretary of State would examine the possibility of taking steps to provide certain defensive weapons to Israel as well as other security measures."[28]

Meanwhile, public pressure on the administration increased. Most prominent American Jewish leaders joined the effort to press the president and Congress to respond positively to Israel's request for arms. Early in February Philip Klutznick, president of B'nai B'rith, wrote a long and well-reasoned letter to Dulles,[29] mainly stressing the risk that, in the absence of minimal defensive weaponry, any assistance that the Western powers were committed to provide Israel if it were attacked was liable to come too late. He suggested that Dulles's information on Israel's present military capability might be too optimistic and that Israel was liable to succumb to a coordinated Arab strike. At the end of the month Jacob Blaustein, president of the American Jewish Committee, wrote Dulles that he could not understand how providing arms to Israel would provoke an arms race, since such a race already existed and the Egyptians were running far ahead.[30] The significance of Blaustein's letter lay not only in the American Jewish Committee's prestige at the time, but also in the fact that the organization was known to hold positions not necessarily always biased toward Israel and that it represented prominent Jewish Americans whose loyalty to the United States and its interests was unquestionable.

Congress was also uncomfortable with the repeated postponement of a reply; senators and congressmen stepped up their own requests to the secretary of state and to the president for a positive response. But the pressure did not move Dulles, and Henry Byroade's warnings from Cairo and the assessments of most State Department staffers tipped the scales against Israel. "The recent [December 1955] riots in Jordan," Byroade told journalists, "will look like child's play compared to the anti-American uprisings liable to ensue in the Arab states if the United States provides arms to Israel. Furnishing Israel with weapons will push the entire Arab world into the Communist camp."[31]

Dulles pulled out all stops. He formulated detailed arguments proving why at this stage America should not give in to pressure and provide Israel with major weapons systems. In a letter to Republican congressmen who had approached him, he wrote that the United States was obligated to preserve Israel's existence but also obligated to preserve the friendship of the Arab states. Furthermore, he wrote, the American government was well aware that the recent flow of arms to the Arab states could create a dangerous discrepancy in the balance of weapons, to Israel's disadvantage, but he was not convinced that this discrepancy could be reduced by providing more arms to Israel, since Israel had less than 2 million citizens and the Arab countries had tens of millions. Ultimately, the State of Israel could not compete with the Arabs' ability to arm themselves with the aid of the Soviet Union, and thus Israel should rely on other means. The balance of weapons was not the only way to ensure deterrence against attack. The U.N. had enough means to provide security for nations under attack. The 1950 Tripartite Declaration, recently ratified again by the president and the British prime minister, also provided a certain effective deterrence.[32]

On February 24, Dulles appeared before the Senate Foreign Relations Committee and repeated his arguments: "Israel, due to its much smaller size and population, could not win in an arms race against the Arabs, having access to the Soviet bloc. It would seem that Israel's security could be better

assured in the long run through measures other than additional arms in circumstances that might exacerbate the situation."[33] President Eisenhower
endorsed his secretary of state's views and, at a March 7 press conference
declared, "We do not believe that it is possible to assure peace in that area
merely by rushing some arms to a nation that at the most can absorb only
that amount that 1,700,000 people can absorb."[34]

At the end of the month a group of Republican congressmen again
approached Dulles with serious contentions. They told him they objected to
the Republican Party ruining its relations and traditions established over
scores of years. Without the party's victory, they stated, Dulles had no standing or authority as secretary of state; how could he allow himself to endanger
the party? Dulles, who seemed shocked at the force of their attack, asked for
more time, meanwhile promising to review Israel's requisition, support release
of the French planes, and make an announcement that would clarify that the
denial of weapons to date did not perforce imply denial in the future.[35]

Israeli diplomatic efforts reached their peak toward the end of March. In
an urgent meeting between Ben-Gurion and the American ambassador to
Israel, the prime minister bitterly accused the Americans of imposing a kind
of embargo on arms shipments to Israel and extending it to France as well.
To make things crystal clear, Ben-Gurion openly said that if it became desperate, Israel might unilaterally resume work on the Jordan River project,
which would be likely to result in widespread hostilities.[36] Abba Eban and
Reuven Shiloah used unofficial channels of communication to convey to
Dulles the message of just how severe the situation was. Arthur Dean, a
well-known Wall Street lawyer who was Dulles's business partner and
friend, had been holding occasional background meetings with Israeli diplomats, who were well aware that every word spoken at these talks reached the
secretary of state's office. Dean regularly sent Dulles detailed written reports
of his discussions with the Israelis, generally refraining from expressing his
own opinion. But on March 1, immediately after meeting with Eban and
Shiloah, he was alarmed. He phoned the secretary of state's office and left an
urgent message for Dulles: "Eban and Shiloah have reached the end of their
diplomatic rope. They feel that they have failed in their mission and may
well be finished."[37]

Now even Dulles concurred that the Israelis could no longer be put off
and that the delays and obfuscations would have to come to an end. He

wrote Henry Byroade that he did not see how America could continue to reject Israel's requests to purchase arms without proposing a constructive plan with a reasonable chance of success.[38] The next day the president made similar remarks. Herbert Hoover, Dulles's second in command, reported on his March 1 talk with Eisenhower: "The President told me that he was a little worried that perhaps we were being too tough on the Israelis with respect to arms. He had in mind particularly interceptors."[39] Hoover reminded the president that Robert Anderson was in the Middle East, and the president agreed that this was not the right time for any public declarations on arms for Israel.

Meanwhile, the beginnings of a change could be discerned in the American administration's relations with Gamal Abdul Nasser. The Egyptian leader's constant undermining of Western interests in the Middle East, which had reached a new peak when Glubb Pasha had to resign his command of the Arab Legion and which the Western powers attributed to Nasser's manipulations, had already markedly altered the British attitude. They had concluded that a way had to be found to get rid of the Egyptian leader. The State Department under Dulles was less extreme, but the failure of Robert Anderson's mission encouraged them to reconsider their policies. On March 28, 1956, Dulles sent an important memo to President Eisenhower outlining new Near East policy lines[40]: "In view of the negative outcome of our efforts to bring Colonel Nasser to adopt a policy of conciliation towards Israel we should . . . let Colonel Nasser realize that he cannot cooperate as he is doing with the Soviet Union and at the same time enjoy most-favored nation treatment from the United States." But Dulles refrained from extreme steps: "We would want for the time being to avoid any open break which would throw Nasser irrevocably into a Soviet satellite status, and would want to leave Nasser a bridge back to good relations with the West, if he so desires." The actual steps he recommended were thus hesitant and marginal, such as a continued embargo on the supply of arms to Egypt (which was limited anyway), delaying any decision on Egypt's request for oil and grain, and postponing a decision on its request for $40 million from America's economic aid plan. The most important recommendation was that the decision on funding for the Aswan Dam also be delayed for the time being.

The memo includes detailed proposals concerning other Middle East actors, such as increasing support for the Baghdad Pact (without actually joining) and strengthening America's position in Saudi Arabia. Israel is mentioned in reference to the risk that it might start a war: "The United States will seek to dissuade the Israelis from undertaking work at Banot Ya'acob or from taking other precipitate steps which might bring about hostilities and thus endanger the whole Western position in the Near East." The question of weapons was concisely dealt with: "For a further indefinite period the United States will continue to deny export licenses for any major military items to Israel. . . . We would, however, be sympathetic if other Western countries wished to sell limited quantities of defensive arms to Israel." In essence, no real change had taken place in the negative decision of Washington's policy makers regarding direct American provision of heavy armaments to Israel.

The White House and the State Department attached great importance to the "new line."[41] In order to keep the pertinent documentation from reaching too many eyes, the new plan was classified and code-named Omega. In effect, Omega tolled the death knell on Israel's efforts to acquire American weapons. In view of the changes taking place in the region, Dulles and his colleagues were reinforced in their opinion that outright support of Israel would seriously damage Western interests in the Middle East.

Dulles's mood at the time is revealed in many documents; on March 27, 1956, for example, in a personal letter to his friend Arthur Dean, he stressed his view that the West would be severely endangered if it abandoned its policy of not providing obvious and direct aid to Israel: ". . . the whole oil situation and the economic and military dependence thereon of Western Europe and NATO could easily become involved."[42] Revealing the new plan to Senator Walter George, Dulles said, "Control of the Arab states by the Communists would enable the Soviet Union to threaten Western Europe with a cessation of oil, and that, as a blackmail, would be just as effective as if they threatened them with atomic destruction." Without enough oil in the Western hemisphere, Dulles added, "it would mean that the West European industrial complex would grind to a halt and all the progress we have made there through the Marshall Plan and NATO would go down the drain."[43]

Nothing remained but for Dulles to advise Israel of the decision and ward off the inevitable attacks from Congress and from the public. On March 29 he invited Abba Eban to his office and told him that, in the wake of the failure of efforts to move Nasser toward a peaceful settlement, he had decided to embark on a reexamination of American policies in the Middle East. The secretary of state spoke of a turning point in policy toward Egypt, but immediately added that America believed it to be in the interest of the West and of Israel to maintain and strengthen the U.S. government's influence in the Arab world. For this reason he hoped Israel would concentrate its efforts to acquire defensive arms mainly on the European nations from whom it had obtained them in the past. Dulles did not believe it imperative for Israel to obtain its major weapons from the United States. Eban cabled:

> The U.S. Government is very concerned at the possibility that work might be resumed on the Jordan River project. The Secretary of State most seriously requests that we refrain from such action at this dangerous juncture. . . . He hopes that we accede to his request now that the regional policy has begun to change, which might result in a move closer to Israel's position.[44]

As Sharett told Lawson, this was a "shattering blow" for the Israelis, "a most painful and depressing conclusion to the five-month affair."[45] "Everything was overshadowed by the failure of the arms campaign in the United States," Sharett wrote in his diary, "in which I had invested all the pressure and energy of five consecutive months."[46] And in a furious cable to Eban he wrote:

> This is a very disappointing conclusion to the unmatched efforts of five months on all our parts. Dulles has reneged on all those promises that had kept us prisoner of hope; all his talk of having a heavy conscience . . . is no more than hypocrisy. . . . We must really ask whether we can put any faith in what the Secretary of State and his assistants say . . . . See [George] Allen and [make sure] he understands your shock and senses . . . that something has been irrevocably ruined.[47]

On April 3 Ben-Gurion convened an urgent consultation with Moshe Sharett, Moshe Dayan, and Shimon Peres. Dismayed and angered, Ben-Gurion spoke of "low deceit." Moshe Dayan proposed that all lobbying efforts in America cease immediately and that its "good services" in acquiring arms elsewhere be bypassed. He also proposed that the issue of arms procurement be transferred from Foreign Ministry channels to the Defense Ministry.[48] Sharett was furious at the implication that the Foreign Ministry's efforts had been fruitless, but he could not shake off the oppressive sense of failure. No final decisions were made about Foreign vs. Defense Ministry channels, but other proposals by Dayan were approved. Ben-Gurion declared that "further lobbying in the United States was to be halted and that we would not even take advantage of American mediation in acquiring arms in other countries but would instead approach them directly."

The prime minister's resolute decision notwithstanding, Israel's diplomats in Washington continued to urge Dulles to be more active in encouraging other nations to provide Israel with the major items it required. Even in the course of that fateful meeting in which Dulles dashed all Israel's hopes, Abba Eban tried to salvage something, insisting that "the main point was the weaponry, not where it came from." But active and more direct encouragement was needed if America was to move other Western nations to furnish arms to Israel, and the United States had to prove its sincere intentions by immediately releasing at least a few items from the Israeli requisition list. Dulles promised to talk to the Canadian foreign minister, Lester Pearson, and inquire about the possibility of Canada supplying Israel with antitank guns and other military equipment.[49]

Dulles was well aware what his statement meant for Israel. No amount of linguistic acrobatics could disguise the fact that this was a final, decisive rejection of Israel's request, after five months of hopes. He was also well aware that the American administration had to take a series of steps to mitigate pressure from the public while keeping Israel from acting out of desperation. Early in April a plan began to take shape to soften Israeli pressure while maintaining the principle of refraining from directly providing arms to Israel:

1. The United States would quickly release several clearly defensive items that would not represent a change in its basic position.[50]

2. The United States would help create the political climate that would allow Israel to acquire limited amounts of heavy military equipment from another country.

3. The State Department would try to bring a senior Democrat into its confidence in order to separate the issue of the Middle East from domestic partisan politics in the upcoming election campaign.

But these steps did not provide total assurance that war would not break out in the Middle East. Under the 1950 Tripartite Declaration, America felt obligated to come to the aid of the state against whom aggression was perpetrated. To give this undertaking practical validity, on April 6 Dulles proposed to Eisenhower that tanks be loaded on board an American ship to be attached to the Sixth Fleet in the Mediterranean, or that it be permanently anchored at one of the harbors in the region so that the United States could respond quickly in the event of aggression. The scheme was referred to as "arms in escrow."[51]

At the end of April, preparations to station a weapons carrier in the Mediterranean went into the operational planning stage, and early in May the president gave his final approval to their implementation. He even proposed that weapons for the attacked party be supplied by ships flying the American flag, reinforcing the element of deterrence. Dulles suggested that British Foreign Minister Selwyn Lloyd's approval be obtained to station the ship in Cyprus. But the "arms in escrow" were not intended necessarily for Israel's defense; in the spring of 1956 the American administration was more concerned about possible Israeli aggression than Arab aggression. And with the eruption of the Suez crisis, there was no longer any point in the ship's presence in the Mediterranean. Dulles asked the president to recall the ship and cancel the entire scheme.[52]

In May the United States took some more energetic steps toward providing Israel with minor armaments; several weapons supply contracts that Israel was interested in were duly signed. Abba Eban did his best to turn the event into a cause for celebration, so that other potential arms suppliers would be encouraged to follow suit. On May 6 Dulles participated in a NATO foreign ministers conference in Paris and took advantage of the occasion to urge the foreign ministers of Canada, France, and Italy to help Israel acquire weaponry. "This time it's hard to claim that the U.S. Government is evading its responsibility," Eban cited a French diplomat in Washington as saying. "Dulles's statement [at the conference] that the discrepancy [in the balance of power] required rectification came across loud and clear in Paris."[53] But at this stage France needed neither American consent nor American encouragement; Israeli efforts to acquire weapons there would soon take off in new directions of which the American government was not even aware. All attempts to convince the Italians to furnish Israel with upgraded World War II tanks were fruitless; and the negotiations with Canada for F-86 jets kept getting tied up in red tape: Canada was a sovereign nation and was not willing to follow orders from Washington; only after the American government had agreed to send Israel five helicopters, 25 half-tracks, and 110 Browning rifles, and only after repeated petitions did the Canadians finally agree to sell Israel 24 planes on September 21, 1956.[54] For Israel, this was too little and too late. France had opened its gates wide to Israeli arms procurement requests, and the Israeli air force no longer wanted to be confused with different kinds of planes. Moreover, the budgets available for arms supplies were nearly exhausted. Israel thus had to inform the Canadians that it was withdrawing from the transaction.

Thus came to a pathetic end a protracted attempt that had gone on for a year and which, in the final analysis, had been hopeless from the beginning. It is not surprising that Abba Eban wanted to accentuate the positive and prove that the American government had played a not inconsiderable part in Israel's efforts to secure arms in general. In response to a passing remark made by Ben-Gurion, Eban sent an indignant telegram detailing seven events or achievements attained, in his opinion, thanks to American consent and even active intervention. "The total calculation," Eban concluded his cable, "is not entirely positive, but then it is not entirely negative either. . . . the seven facts which I have noted cannot be challenged and have a place in any precise historical reckoning."[55]

Indeed, the total reckoning was not entirely negative and the efforts to secure arms in the United States did ultimately bear an indirect and not inconsiderable advantage. Israel's success in procuring arms from France did not depend on the consent of the American administration, but it is only reasonable to assume that the positive climate created in Washington in the spring of 1956 made it easier for the French to decide to provide Israel with weapons. In retrospect, too, the American attempt was valuable in terms of its impact on American public opinion and, half a year later, even bore fruit in the struggle to hold on to some of the assets achieved in Israel's victory in the Sinai. But in 1956 Israel's major goal was to meet the dangerous challenge posed by the 250 MiGs, 50 jet bombers, and hundreds of modern tanks that Egypt had received from the Soviet Union. The only important question at the time was whether Israel would obtain the minimum number of planes and tanks of similar quality that could meet this challenge. In this respect there is no avoiding the conclusion that the Israeli campaign for arms in the United States was a failure.

But this failure was not the fault of the Israel Foreign Ministry; it was simply inevitable. In later years the American government realized that it could maintain close ties with Israel and guarantee its security while retaining the friendship of Arab nations; but at the time America was the major Western nation protecting Western interests in the region against the Soviet assault on those interests in the Middle East and throughout the Third World. John Foster Dulles and his colleagues feared that the Middle East would fall through their fingers; their fears may not have been justified, but they were nonetheless sincere and profound. Under such circumstances, Israel had no chance of turning the American government into a shield against the dangers that beset it.

The events described in this chapter also make it clear that refraining from military activism in order to secure arms was a mistaken policy. There is indeed a connection between security policy and arms procurement, but that connection is not what certain Israelis in and around the Foreign Ministry had presumed it to be at the time. A great power that wishes to prevent its client state from engaging in an aggressive security policy will not provide that state with the tools with which to engage in such policy. Weapons are made available in order for them to be used. If the intention is not to permit their use, then they will not be provided.

II

■ ■ ■

SUCCESS IN FRANCE

t the end of October 1955, French premier Edgar Faure had promised
Moshe Sharett to facilitate some armament procurements including
two dozen Mystère-4 jet planes. (See Chapter 3.) At the same time, the
French defense minister, General Pierre Billotte, had made certain
undertakings to Israeli ambassador Yacob Tsur and to Shimon Peres to speed
up deliveries, but as Tsur himself said, it was by no means the end of the
chapter, and a long and arduous struggle still lay ahead. After Moshe
Sharett's dramatic meeting in Geneva with the foreign ministers of all four
great powers, Ambassador Tsur returned to Paris and found himself commenting on all manner of delays that had cropped up in implementing the
new purchasing orders. "Our experts have noticed a certain amount of foot-
dragging over the past few weeks, meetings that cannot be scheduled, documents that are being drawn up at a snail's pace."[1] On November 4, 1955, the
meeting at which the agreements were to be signed in Deputy Defense
Minister Jean Crouzier's office ended in great confusion, when it emerged
that the French Defense Ministry's hands were effectively tied. General
Billotte was indeed prepared to send the jets directly from the production
line, but the American NATO off-shore procurement supervisors had
learned of the plans and had sent an urgent protest to the French Foreign
Ministry, which immediately halted the activities.

In the course of the month, ways were found to deliver most of the smaller
items requested by Israel; supplying the Mystère-4 jets, however, met with
obstinate resistance, for four reasons:

1. The French Foreign Ministry officials at the Quai d'Orsay were vehemently opposed to what they viewed as inordinately overt friendship
with Israel. The crisis in the French government at the beginning of the
winter had undermined the authority of the ministers, and the senior civil
servants rushed in to fill the vacuum. It was now the Foreign Ministry

officials whose word was decisive in weapons sales to foreign states, and many of them were laboring under the illusion that France still maintained good ties with the Arab world that should not be jeopardized by too intimate a relationship with Israel.[2] After extensive inquiries with these officials, Tsur's impression was pessimistic: "My last conversations . . . prove that the 'Quai' is adamantly opposed to selling the Mystère for political reasons, mainly not to endanger Egyptian neutrality vis-à-vis Morocco. . . . An obvious pro-Arab breeze is in the air."[3]

2. Both in Faure's government and in the new one formed after the elections early in 1956, several ministers were still undecided on how to respond to the rebellion in Algeria. The group led by Pierre Mendès-France, which still wielded considerable influence, believed it possible to resolve the Algerian issue amicably, including appeasing Nasser into not supporting the Algerian rebels. By that token, massive arms supplies to Israel might push the Egyptian leader off the fence and into a final decision to support the uprising.

3. France still felt bound by the 1950 Tripartite Agreement, whose Near East Arms Control Commission seemed to permit French participation in Western strategic and political planning in the region. The establishment of the Baghdad Pact made the French feel excluded, and they were eager to resume membership in the political "club" of Western powers in the Mideast.

4. The Mystère-4 production line, which had just started to turn out finished planes, was under contract to fill American orders for NATO forces until July 1956. French delivery of jets to Israel before that date required Washington's approval.

Addressing his senior staff on the issue of arms procurement in France, Peres summed up the situation with a Yiddish play on words:

The stimmung [mood] is for Israel, but the opstimmung [decision] is against us. France views Israel as a talented, marvelous, wonderful country that can beat the Arabs. Nobody cares if Israel settles the score with Egypt; but that is only the feeling; it has nothing to do with facts. Facts are determined by very cold calculations.[4]

Throughout November, Israel's representatives shuttled from one office to another, meeting with anyone who had any influence in the French establishment: senior officials, industrialists, generals, ministers. General Pierre Koenig, the former defense minister and an ardent friend of Israel, telephoned the French premier and told him:

We haven't talked to each other since I left the Government, but there is one issue on which I will nevertheless talk with you: Israel. For two years we have been dragging the issue out, and it is a disgrace; this is no way to treat a civilized country. I demand that you conclude the matter because it is a question of honor for France.[5]

General Billotte was also enraged. He had apparently reached a tentative agreement with the American ambassador whereby the United States would approve delivery of the jets to Israel from the offshore procurement quota, but the ambassador's recommendation had been disallowed by Washington and he was prohibited in no uncertain terms from effecting the agreement.[6]

The cables from Paris to Jerusalem alternated between elation and disappointment. Billotte and Crouzier, who felt bound by their promises to the Israelis, exceeded their authority and, on November 10, without obtaining approval from the Foreign Ministry and the other duly empowered authorities, signed a formal contract on behalf of the French government with Shimon Peres for the provision of arms, excluding jets. The principal items in the contract were 60 additional AMX-13 light tanks to be supplied between April and July 1956; 500 bazooka launchers with 10,000 rockets to be supplied beginning in January 1956; 40 "Super" (refurbished) Sherman tanks to be supplied in January; and 1,000 SS-10 antitank guided rockets to be supplied in monthly lots of 50 beginning in December 1955.[7]

The agreement caused an uproar in the French Cabinet and drew ire from the Foreign Ministry officials whose authority had been sidestepped. Foreign Minister Antoine Pinay was deeply hurt and reprimanded the Israeli ambassador severely:

> How could you do such a thing, Mr. Ambassador? How could you engage in negotiations and sign contracts with the Government of France without involving the Foreign Ministry? . . . How could you imagine that a certain Minister whose chair wasn't even warm [i.e., Billotte, whose appointment as defense minister was only a few weeks old] and a certain official who felt superior to everyone [a pointed reference to Crouzier] could obligate the Government of France in a matter as serious as this? Don't you realize that these contracts are not valid without Foreign Ministry approval?[8]

Pinay had acceded to British and American pressure and, at the recent conference of Western foreign ministers, had undertaken to hold off providing arms to Israel.[9] The French defense minister's action was liable to give the impression that Pinay was reneging on his commitments, casting the foreign minister in a very negative light indeed.

Nevertheless, Pinay did not cancel the contract; but when Ambassador Tsur returned to his office, he found a letter on his desk from the Quai's Department of Protocol, reminding him that representatives of foreign nations were prohibited from meeting government ministers without prior coordination with the Foreign Ministry.

The very fact that the agreement had been signed at all was an important achievement in Israel's bid for arms in France; its implementation, however, was not ensured. And in fact, the tanks and rockets contracted for reached

Israel only after a tortuous process of delays, and only after the conditions for a wide-ranging and all-encompassing agreement between France and Israel had already ripened.

In the meantime, however, Edgar Faure's government had fallen on November 28, and the premier took advantage of his constitutional power to duly dismiss the National Assembly; the French nation would go to the polls on January 2, 1956. France was caught up in the whirl of elections, and the government ministers became engrossed in the campaign. The civil service now effectively controlled policy making.

The elections did not hamper the Israeli Embassy staff and the Israeli Defense Ministry mission in Paris in their efforts to procure the jet planes. The Israeli Embassy in Washington was also mobilized to apply pressure on the American State Department to release the planes from the strictures of the offshore procurement arrangement. Now the question arose of who was holding up delivery: French officials insisted that Washington had not yet sent its approval; the Americans claimed the problem lay with the Quai. At the beginning of January Tsur wrote in his diary: "The mess we've gotten ourselves into in this question of French arms deliveries is like a knot that only gets tighter the more you pull the string. Today I looked through the reams of cables that our Embassy had sent to Jerusalem over the past few days and felt like a mountebank."[10]

But underneath the surface profound changes were slowly taking shape. The rebellion in Algeria, which the French government had at first treated as a local and temporary matter, rapidly widened its scope. The French public was panic-stricken and began to demand strong measures. On the day the Faure government fell, the interior minister, Maurice Bourgès-Maunoury, in charge of Algerian affairs and French internal security services, made a short speech to the National Assembly and divulged secret information on the scope of the aid Cairo provided to the Algerian rebels.[11] When France's leaders learned the extent of Nasser's support for the Algerian rebellion, several of them began to reconsider Israel's value to France in its struggle against Nasser. Bourgès-Maunoury, who took an activist position on the Algerian rebellion despite his affiliation with Mendès-France's Radical Party, harbored no doubts that French interests dictated unwavering support of Israel in order to cut Nasser down to size. In an informal talk with Tsur, rising Socialist leader Guy Mollet also expressed full support for Israel.

Destined to become prime minister a month later, Mollet promised that his party would underwrite "any action directed at increasing Israel's security and would advocate a French policy that would openly declare its friendship with Israel."[12]

Even the Quai registered some change. On December 9, the director general, René Massigli, wrote Yacob Tsur and asked him to draw up a new list of arms that Israel wanted from France. Although he reiterated that the planes could be released only after several further inquiries on arrangements with NATO, he officially declared that the French Foreign Ministry had in principle approved the transaction.

Early in December, after the Israeli government's decision to concentrate on arms procurement efforts, Ben-Gurion sent Shimon Peres to Paris once again to try his hand. "You should concentrate on getting 50 Mystères," he told Peres. "[I]f we got that—the entire situation would change, the Czech deal would lose its value and we would return to the *status quo;* and just as we were not afraid of Egypt a year ago, we wouldn't have to be frightened of her now."[13] Peres made no real gains on this trip, but as the French election campaign came to a peak, he managed to establish wide contacts and close ties with many of the people who several weeks later would become France's chief policy makers. A far-reaching changing of the guards was expected after the elections, and Israel feared that most of its long-standing connections in France would become defunct. It was thus imperative to make ties with the "men of tomorrow." The ambassador's hands were tied by protocol, but Shimon Peres had no formal diplomatic status, and he exploited this freedom to its utmost. The new connections he made and the unconventional mode of action he affected proved eminently advantageous when spring came. Peres's task was made easier by the friendships with members of the French government at all levels that Peres's representative in Paris, Yosef Nahmias, had nurtured in the past. Peres has recalled, for example, that he used to operate out of the office of Valery Giscard d'Estaing, later president of France, then economic advisor to Premier Edgar Faure. "Since we became personally acquainted, [Giscard] began working less and less for Edgar Faure and more and more for Israel."[14]

But Operation Kinneret, which took place while Peres was in the French capital, temporarily delayed delivery of items that had been duly authorized and partially delivered. Antoine Pinay, still France's foreign minister, met with the NATO foreign ministers and again committed himself on behalf of the French government to postpone all arms deliveries to Israel until the conclusion of the Security Council deliberations on the operation.[15]

The French reaction to Operation Kinneret was ambivalent. Foreign Ministry officials formally protested to Israel's representatives and publicly condemned the action. But Ambassador Tsur wrote to Abba Eban: "The reaction in general was less sharp than I had feared."[16] Peres, then active in other circles, first and foremost those connected to the French defense establishment, was impressed that the "French did not really care very much about the actual shooting on the Sea of Galilee," but they felt uncomfortable at appearing less pro-Syrian than the British; and considering the stormy reactions in the Middle East, France could not afford to have the Arab world up in arms against it as a result of too blatant a pro-Israeli stance.[17] The day after the operation Peres cabled Dayan from Paris: "My congratulations on the brilliant military achievement. . . . Despite the formal protests, there does not appear to be tremendous grief at the blow dealt Syria. Many people also seem satisfied that the IDF is justifying its reputation. Be strong and take care."[18] And indeed, in contrast to the pro-Arab veneer of official spokesmen, most newspapers in Paris concentrated less on the Foreign Ministry's delicate political considerations than on the drama itself and, in Peres's words, on how the Jews "were reasserting their heroism precisely at Chanukah [commemorating the heroism of the Maccabees] and how our boys were crossing the cold waters of the Jordan." Even outgoing prime minister Edgar Faure reiterated his sympathy for Israel in a private conversation with Peres: "France must help Israel defend herself and must put at her disposal the arms she needs."[19]

The temporary embargo on arms to Israel that the French government had imposed under British and American pressure was short-lived, and even before the Security Council had concluded its deliberations on Operation Kinneret, deliveries were resumed. But the Mystères and the other heavy items agreed upon with Billotte and Crouzier in November—the additional tanks and the SS-10 antitank missiles—were still not being delivered. Peres tried to overcome the American obstacles and suggested "smuggling" a dozen dismantled planes under the noses of the NATO supervisors. Defense Minister Billotte, campaigning outside Paris, tended to agree, and the subject was even raised at a Cabinet session; but most of the experts felt "that nothing could be shipped out without the Quai's signature, and the Quai won't sign on a blatant ruse."[20]

✳ ✳ ✳

The elections resulted in a radical upheaval in French politics. Although Mendès-France's Republican Front (which included the Socialists and the Radicals) received only 188 seats in the National Assembly, Edgar Faure's right-wing bloc, which had won 204 seats, could not form a government. Some of Israel's most stalwart friends left the political stage. Billotte and Marcel Dessault (the industrialist whose firm manufactured the Mystères) lost their seats in the French parliament. At first glance it looked as if Israel's network of contacts in Paris had fallen apart. "We have lost the French elections," Peres quipped bitterly. "Lots of labor has been wasted, and the Right, which more than any other party encouraged friendship with Israel, has suffered a resounding defeat."[21]

After several weeks of negotiations between parties, Socialist leader Guy Mollet succeeded in forming a new coalition government. Christian Pineau, with whom the Israelis were unacquainted, was appointed foreign minister. Maurice Bourgès-Maunoury was appointed defense minister and named as his director-general Abel Thomas, who had in the meantime become Yosef Nahmias's friend. "A new constellation has been created in France," Peres said. "[T]hose on top have fallen and those on the bottom have risen, the stars that shone have become stones, and unknown faces have become the men of tomorrow."[22] But more than mere personnel changes had been effected. Mendès-France stood in the wings of the French government, and most of his group favored decolonization and conciliation with the Muslims. Guy Mollet appointed the aging General George Catroux, known for his liberal tendencies, as governor of Algeria and announced plans to grant Algeria a new constitution giving the Muslims equal rights. But the rebels did not welcome these compromise proposals, and the French and other Europeans who had settled in Algeria—the *pieds noirs*—expressed their rage directly and sharply: Several days after the formation of the government, Guy Mollet visited the French colony and was greeted by a barrage of rotten tomatoes and stinking eggs. He was forced to cancel Catroux's appointment and instead named Robert Lacoste, a Socialist known for his hard line on Algeria. Mollet also announced postponement of the proposed constitution and made any advances in Muslim rights conditional on the cessation of hostilities.

Christian Pineau's expressed views and his initial acts on the Middle East disappointed the Israelis. On February 10, 1956, at their first meeting, Pineau told Ambassador Tsur that he believed "Nasser did not want war, he was overwhelmingly preoccupied with building the Aswan Dam and resolving his economic woes." France did not want to quarrel with Egypt and risk increased Egyptian involvement in North Africa, and thus it was forced to honor its old obligations and provide Egypt with certain amounts of armaments.[23] On February 23 Pineau affirmed that French Middle East policy would be based on the 1950 Tripartite Declaration and on close cooperation with England and the United States. France would not follow a separate policy, he said, and it was interested in friendship with Egypt.[24] These formulas, which were all too familiar to the Israelis, did not bode well.

In contrast, Tsur's first meeting with Defense Minister Bourgès-Maunoury made it abundantly clear that the latter's earlier support of Israel under the previous government was sincere. Bourgès-Maunoury told Tsur that he rejected Pineau's attempt to involve the Americans in the responsibility to arm Israel, and added: "France's obligation is to ensure that Israel not be exposed to attack from her neighbors, and as far as the Arabs are concerned—we cannot win them over anyway. What can they do to hurt France that they have not already done!"[25] "This young Radical leader is undoubtedly one of the greatest exponents of cooperation with Israel," Ambassador Tsur concluded.[26]

Meanwhile, the question of the jets grew increasingly complex. As noted, the French needed American approval to deliver them to Israel. However, the Americans did not want to give the impression that they were allowing Israel to acquire arms, while the French did not want to face Arab protests on their own. The French and the Americans therefore tried to force responsibility onto each other, and the messages that passed from capital to capital were generally couched in vague terminology.

During the last days of the previous government, Henri Roux, deputy director general of the Foreign Ministry, had announced that the long-awaited approval to release the "first dozen" planes had been received from Washington. "A senior State Department official has given the [French] Embassy in Washington its verbal consent"; upon further inquiry, however, it emerged that the approval was not sufficiently clear.[27] A full month elapsed and Ambassador Tsur wrote in his diary:

> [purchasing the Mystère jets] has gotten so bogged down these last few weeks that no one knows if he's coming or going. The French continue to blame Washington for the delay, the Pentagon claims that a positive response has been given to the Embassy in Paris, but the French don't know anything about it, this one and that one give partial answers—in short, a nightmare.[28]

In March the episode was finally resolved. At a press conference on February 27, John Foster Dulles, hoping to defuse internal pressure, revealed that Washington had approved sale of the French jets to Israel. Against the backdrop of the delays and vagaries that had accompanied the affair, and amid reciprocal French and American recriminations, the public disclosure infuriated the French. Henri Roux contended that Dulles was looking to make easy gains in American public opinion at the cost of making the French actually responsible for delivery of the planes. The French also claimed that official approval had not yet reached Paris. Furious, Pineau advised Dulles that France would indeed deliver the jets to Israel, on March 15, irrespective of the receipt of official American approval. Furthermore, he told Tsur, he himself was not averse to the sale of another dozen planes if Bourgès-Maunoury agreed. Pineau even issued a press release announcing that France intended to honor its contract with Israel and was prepared to assume responsibility for it.[29] As France's relations with the Arabs had already been irreparably damaged, Pineau wanted at least to salvage French honor and its amicable ties with Israel. On March 16 France officially informed the United States that it was delivering the planes immediately and would not wait any longer. The Ministry of Defense was given the go-ahead to implement delivery.

To maintain secrecy, the French had initially wanted to dismantle the planes and deliver them in crates. Now that the affair had become public knowledge, this subterfuge was unnecessary, and it was agreed that the planes would be flown over via Italy. The old Mystère engine was just being replaced on the production line, and the planes purchased by Israel had the new Verdun engine. They could thus be flown from France to Israel with only one stopover, but at the risk of reaching their destination on the very last drops of fuel. With tensions along the Gaza Strip increasing, however, and with the cloud of all-out war hanging overhead, the Israeli GHQ and Defense Ministry redoubled pressure on the procurement teams in Paris to send everything as quickly as possible; the risk was taken.

On April 11, 1956, several hours before the Fedayun raid on the Shafrir school, the first three jets landed at the military airport in Hatzor. The defense minister was present with his entourage, which included the French ambassador Pierre-Eugène Gilbert, then considered to be a "comrade in arms." That same evening the chief of staff's bureau chief wrote his impressions of the experience in the Bureau Diary:

> Everyone is in the control tower, making small talk. Nobody can hide the excitement. Ezer Weizman, the Wing Commander, is glued to the radio set, soaking up the reports of the Mystère pilots who are already making their way over the wide blue

sea. Suddenly, in the west, against the setting sun, three tiny dots appear and grow larger with amazing speed. The wings are already visible and even their noise can be heard, and then they are over the field. With a deafening whine they head off into the horizon again. One additional circle and they land with a sharp buzz on the wide runway. Everyone rushes to the dock—there they stand, eagles in the fields of Hatzor, three lovely silver toys shimmering against the black background. On the wings, which stretch back as if the plane is ready to take off at any minute and slice through the air, a blue Star of David shines.[30]

The somewhat romantic description captures the sense of relief felt by all who had labored for so many long months of anticipation and frustration.

The "first dozen" Mystère jets could not have been delivered without the explicit approval of the French Foreign Ministry. But in the meantime, fundamental changes were taking place both in France's political constellation and in French-Israeli relations; from this point on, Israeli arms procurement in France would be effected almost exclusively through direct contact between the two defense ministries, bypassing the French Foreign Ministry.

Few in France at the time could imagine ceding French sovereignty over Algeria. Even Mendès-France, the "great accommodator," declared in the National Assembly that "no French Government or legislature, whatever its tendencies, could give up the principle that Algeria was part of the French Republic."[31] For the French public, the National Assembly, and the political establishment, the Algerian rebellion was no longer marginal; all resources had to be mobilized to assure its swift and utter suppression.

In mid-March the French government announced its policy of "pacification," and Robert Lacoste, who had been granted special emergency powers by the General Assembly, planned a military offensive to suppress the rebellion rapidly. But as Lacoste and his generals began taking measures to quell the revolt, they learned that grave difficulties lay ahead of them, especially in the realm of intelligence.

Since Algeria was considered French territory and an integral part of French sovereignty, the responsible security and intelligence agency was the internal security agency, the DST (Department de Securité Territoriale)—comparable to the FBI or MI5—and not the SDECE (Service de Documentation Extérieure et de Contre-espionage), the French CIA or MI6 counterpart responsible for foreign intelligence. Now, however, it became obvious that the Algerian uprising was not a question of internal security only but rather very much a matter of foreign involvement as well. Arab states, particularly Egypt, Libya, and Tunisia, provided arms as well as training grounds and safe haven for the rebel leadership. The incendiary propaganda beamed into Algeria from neighboring Arab states, especially Egypt's Sauth al-Arab, also inflamed the rebellion. These developments required intelligence sources other than what the DST could provide.

At first Egypt's part in the Algerian revolt was a matter of dispute among French governmental circles and public opinion. Foreign Minister Pineau believed that Nasser could be placated and convinced not to support the rebels. In March, on his way back from a South East Asia Treaty Organization conference in Karachi, Pineau stopped off in Cairo and met with President Nasser; at the end of their discussion Pineau told journalists that Nasser had given him "the word of a soldier" that Algerian fighters were not being trained in his country.[32] But the French public and most National Assembly representatives did not believe Nasser's "word of a soldier," and Pineau's pronouncements were received with snickers. On March 9 Jacques Soustelle, who had until a short time earlier been governor general of Algeria, delivered a fiery address in the National Assembly, referring to the fateful struggle between the Paris-Brazzaville axis, which connected France with its colonies on the African continent, and the Cairo-Casablanca axis, which sought to break this tie. He presented documents proving just how deeply involved Egypt was in encouraging the rebellion. The applause that accompanied his words well expressed the mood in the French Republic.

Now that it was obvious that foreign factors were involved in the rebellion, it became urgent to obtain intelligence information on their actions; the DST, however, could not operate in foreign countries, while the SDECE was incapable of providing the kind of information needed because Middle Eastern intelligence had not been one of its priorities.

Defense Minister Bourgès-Maunoury had been interior minister in Faure's government. As such he was responsible for the DST and aware of its limitations. He sought ways to expand the network and adapt it to the new needs by developing sources of information on the eastern shore of the Mediterranean. Cognizant of the intelligence assistance that Israel could provide France and of the two countries' common interests, he began to forge close ties with Yosef Nahmias, Israel's Defense Ministry representative in France, and eventually with Shimon Peres as well. At their first meeting in the autumn of 1955, Bourgès-Maunoury told Peres that "the tides of the Mediterranean lap the shores of France and Israel with the same regularity."[33] Bourgès-Maunoury's political considerations were reinforced by his personal inclinations; he was prominent in the unofficial "old-boys'" network of anti-Nazi Resistance veterans who had sworn never to allow the events that had led to the fall of France

in 1940 to repeat themselves.[34] The cordiality that grew up between Peres and
Bourgès-Maunoury and his staff was thus predicated on a stable combination
of mutual interests and deep commitments.

When Bourgès-Maunoury was appointed defense minister, he continued
to remain responsible officially, and interested personally, in the Algerian
revolt. His contacts with the Israelis quickly led him to conclude that Israel
could become that lodestone at the other end of the Mediterranean that
France so needed. More than any other minister in Guy Mollet's government, Bourgès-Maunoury believed not only in the importance of the intelligence services that Israel was capable of providing France, but also in the
advantage that France could derive if it strengthened Israel and helped it
become a deterrence against Nasser on the opposite side of the Mediterranean.
Furthermore, since he was in charge of preparing the forces for war in
Algeria, he also had to deal with the increasingly problematic issue of budgets. He was convinced that French arms sales could become a major source
of income that could at least partially balance his ministry's budgets.

In the spring of 1956, the combination of these factors led Bourgès-
Maunoury to conclude that it was in France's clear interest to arm Israel:
"France must fight against Nasser, and Israel is the best weapon France
has."[35] But to implement this goal, Bourgès-Maunoury needed the agreement of a coalition of ministers including the premier and, ultimately, also
the foreign minister. The French and Israelis both understood that arms procurement could be advanced only by sidestepping Foreign Ministry officials
and acting through the authority of other agencies. Ben-Gurion was not
averse to his Defense Ministry taking initiatives alongside those of the
Foreign Ministry,[36] and thus Shimon Peres decided to go ahead. Against the
backdrop of the mid-April crisis on Israel's southern border, Ben-Gurion
once again sent Peres to the French capital, arming him with two letters. One
was for the French prime minister and read, inter alia, "The young Israeli
republic is steadfastly poised against danger; it looks to the veteran French
republic, confident that it will lend it a sympathetic ear." The second letter
was for Bourgès-Maunoury. In it Ben-Gurion had written, "I know well how
deeply interested you are in all that concerns my country's defense problems. . . . Today we need broad and swift action to realign the balance of
power that has been upset so cruelly, in order to foil the Egyptian plots."[37]

In fact, the French security establishment no longer needed Ben-Gurion's
written pep talks. Several days earlier Yosef Nahmias had succeeded in taking a major step without recourse to the Quai d'Orsay. Israel wanted to make
advance payments to the French aviation industry so that production of the
planes intended for Israel could begin even before formal approval of the

transaction; this, however, required a "letter of intent" from the French government. Pineau refused to issue such a letter but Henry Laforest, the air minister, agreed to another arrangement. Nahmias gave the defense minister a "letter of request" in which he specified the requested delivery dates. The aviation minister issued an internal directive, on the basis of this document, ordering the factories to begin production. Nahmias got an "unofficial" copy of the directive to allow him to make the advance payments to the industries.[38] At the end of April Peres and Laforest signed an agreement for the immediate provision of an additional dozen Mystère jets on condition that it was not made known to the French Foreign Ministry.

Israel now sought to expand the scope of transactions considerably, and for this a new approach was needed. Peres had already considered an agreement based on French-Israeli cooperation against Nasser, and therefore proposed that Chief of Staff Moshe Dayan go to France. But Dayan hesitated. "I can see myself clear to come," he wired Peres, "only if it is sure to help and we can sign a suitable agreement . . . if France is ready for this and it is appropriately carried out, that is, by formal invitation of the French Government . . . through [Ambassador] Gilbert here." Ben-Gurion also was not convinced that the time was right for such a step.[39]

In the meantime, the Israeli secret service had obtained information that at first seemed insignificant but that rapidly became vital to France's conduct of the war in Algeria.[40] From its vantage point in the east, Israel could follow the movements of the rebel leaders, the routes of the arms supplies, and the training of the Algerian rebels in the Arab countries. And indeed, as Israel began to deliver its information to France, bit by bit, the French defense establishment, Lacoste, and the prime minister's bureau all recognized the great practical worth that France could derive from expanding ties with Israel.

At the end of May, Shimon Peres found himself in Paris yet again. The Indian government had just cancelled an order for 200 French Mystères, having received a better offer from the Soviets. The French were now even more eager to sell arms to balance their budgets. In his meeting with Bourgès-Maunoury and his staff, Peres for the first time raised the idea of large numbers of tanks and artillery pieces being smuggled secretly on French landing craft to a desolate beach in Israel rather than a port as was usual. It was also suggested that more planes be flown to Israel, disguised as old ones returning from repair and refurbishment in France. The French defense minister liked the idea and immediately ordered the planning of the "French invasion of Israel," as it was thereafter jokingly referred to. Many other persons had to be involved in such an operation, and Peres suggested a secret conference to include Moshe Dayan, himself, and key Israeli intelligence personnel, as well as French Defense Ministry representatives, members of the French intelligence community, and representatives of the governor of Algeria.

Peres and Dayan presented Ben-Gurion with the plans for the "invasion" and the secret conference at the end of May; the latter asked for some time to consider the plan and consult with some of his ministers—he feared French ties with Israel would be endangered if the invasion and the conference became known to certain central figures in the French government, first and foremost the foreign minister, who would be antagonistic. A special envoy was thus sent to make further inquiries: Yehoshafat Harkaby, the IDF's chief of intelligence. Pierre-Eugène Gilbert, France's popular ambassador to Israel, who had been made privy to the secret, gave Harkaby a warm letter of introduction to deliver to Robert Felix, Robert Lacoste's bureau chief and his own personal friend. Meanwhile, though the plan was not yet approved, Dayan summoned a number of his highest-ranking officers and charged them with working out the details of the "invasion," code-named Operation Jonah after the prophet who had been disgorged on the beach by the whale. A desolate stretch of shoreline south of Tel Aviv was chosen as the landing site. The actual operation was entrusted to the major "client," the commander of the Seventh Armored Brigade.[41]

Harkaby met Lacoste on June 5 and proposed the "invasion" and the conference. Lacoste was enthusiastic and said, "You must see Guy Mollet immediately." If Mollet agreed, Lacoste said, he himself would be willing to facilitate transfer of the arms to Israel via Algeria to ensure secrecy. The number of French politicians who became privy to the secret grew, and Harkaby was joined at his meeting with Bourgès-Maunoury by members of Lacoste's staff as well as officials responsible for military supply. It was proposed that the meeting at which the plan was to be finalized be held under the auspices of Pierre Boursicot, head of the SDECE. This would ensure the prime minister's blessing and would permit the French Foreign Ministry officials to be sidestepped once again, inasmuch as Boursicot's agency was constitutionally authorized to engage in covert sales of arms with the sole approval of the prime minister.

Harkaby quickly arranged to meet Boursicot and several of his chief aides, all of whom were eager to put the plan into action soon and who had already begun to work out the details of the proposed conference. On June 6 Harkaby and Nahmias sent a cable to Israel: "The operation looks like it's going to become a reality. . . . We're flying out to you tomorrow on El Al flight 414."[42] Harkaby reported personally to Ben-Gurion. The Israeli prime minister was pleased at the alliance that was about to be formed, a dream he had long held and hoped to see come true. He approved the entire plan and was ready for far-reaching cooperation with the French on the basis of joint and equal political responsibility. "At the side of an ally such as France," he said, "Israel is willing to go to the very end."[43]

On Friday night, June 22, 1956, from a half-deserted military airfield, an Israeli air force transport plane whose markings had been replaced with French ones took off. The plane carried Moshe Dayan, Shimon Peres, and Yehoshafat Harkaby as well as a French intelligence officer who had come to Israel earlier that day in order to navigate the plane to its secret destination, a small airfield not far from Paris. There Yosef Nahmias and Colonel Emanuel Nishry, Israel's military attaché in Paris, waited together with Boursicot's bureau chief and Louis Mangin, Bourgès-Maunoury's friend and advisor. In the small town of Vermars, 15 kilometers south of Paris, Fernand Levin had a summer villa. Levin, a wealthy French Jew known as France's "King of Mineral Water," had lent it to the French secret service without asking too many questions. There, on June 23, at 11:00 A.M., the conference that would end in an agreement tantamount to a French-Israeli treaty opened.[44] Boursicot presided; at his side were all persons involved in the operation: the general in charge of production and supply of war materiel in the Defense Ministry, General Maurice Challe, France's deputy chief of staff, General Birambeau, chief of staff of the forces fighting in Algeria, and Louis Mangin, the defense minister's personal representative.

The first session was intended to define the general aims of the conference and exchange assessments. The purpose, Boursicot said in his opening remarks, was to examine ways to "thwart Nasser's initiatives" (*"faire échec à ses enterprises"*). "The Arab empire Nasser is dreaming about," Dayan said in his opening remarks, "will not arise unless Israel surrenders. So long as Israel exists, he cannot realize his desire."

Three working sessions followed. At the first, intended for a discussion of the issue of weapons procurement, it was decided to fly 72 additional Mystère jets in three equal lots of 24 each, the first by September 1, 1956; the second by December 1; and the third by February 1, 1957.[45] The planes would be flown by Israeli pilots via Brindisi airport in Italy. The "invasion" was also finalized at that session. Three French ships would land on Israeli shores in three cycles of three landing craft each. The ships' decks would hold 120 AMX-13 tanks, 40 "Super" Sherman tanks, 18 105-mm mobile artillery guns, and ammunition and spare parts. All the materiel would come from French military arsenals. The operation would be carried out covertly, at night, beginning at the end of July and continuing through August and September. The entire transaction would cost Israel $80 million; for the sake of secrecy, the French asked for cash.

The second working session was dedicated to joint operations. The French were still not clear what specific operations they wanted to carry out with Israel, nor did the Israelis press them for details; in principle, however, the French had in mind operations against targets related to the Algerian insurgents. Ben-Gurion had instructed the Israeli team to demand "full cooperation in shouldering political responsibility" in all such joint actions, but the French had anticipated him; Boursicot himself declared at the conclusion of the session that "our intention is for joint action, that is, joint preparation, joint responsibility, and joint operation." Dayan was careful not to leave any room for doubt in his own concluding remarks: "On condition that there is full joint responsibility, we are willing to enter into any activities in which you too participate." He was not eager to undertake any unnecessary operation, but he did not want to disappoint French hopes or seem to be wavering in his commitment. At the conclusion of the session it was agreed that the French and Israeli services would exchange liaison officers to work out the details of any operations jointly decided upon and in order to maintain ongoing contact.

The third session dealt with intelligence; it was agreed to exchange information, assessments, and technologies. Here too the technical details were left to the professionals.

The Vermars conference concluded on June 24, to the mutual satisfaction of all parties. The hosts had attained their goals in terms of the diverse interests they represented, while the Israelis had made a historic breakthrough. In the short run, the major result of the conference was the provision of heavy weapons to Israel. Nine months after the Egyptian-Czech arms deal had become known, and after many vicissitudes, Israel had finally been able to obtain the arms it had desired. The Israeli defense establishment believed that the weapons procurement concluded at the Vermars conference provided Israel with the minimal response sufficient to redress the upset balance of power that had thrown the country into turmoil.[46]

The Vermars arms transaction changed Israel's military capability overnight. Large amounts of modern armaments were put at the disposal of the Israeli armed forces. As it turned out, Israel had four months in which to adequately integrate these weapons into its battle order. In the long run, however, the conference's main importance lay in the unsigned pact of cooperation between Israel and France and the deep friendship that would bear fruit in the Suez crisis and long after as well. Nasser nationalized the Suez Canal about one month later; and France and Great Britain began planning a major assault on Egypt. From this point on it was not a few small-scale operations that were under consideration for joint action, but rather the wider engagement of nations fighting a war together.

Had the Suez Canal not been nationalized at the end of July, our story might have ended right here, since Israel had finally found a suitable response to the Egyptian challenge nine months earlier. But as the search for arms to restore the upset balance of weapons ended successfully, a new and totally different episode began: The special relationship between Israel and France forged in Vermars was to add another few dramatic chapters to our story.

After the meeting, Ben-Gurion conferred with Finance Minister Levi Eshkol and new Foreign Minister Golda Meir and endorsed the agreements. "I went over [the material]," he told Peres and Dayan. "[T]here are lots of fantastic and definitely unnecessary items here that are totally useless. But I trust the wisdom of those who were present. Okay, let's get into this. It's a dangerous adventure, but what can we do, that's what our whole existence is like."[47]

Until then, at the behest of the French, Israel's ambassador in France had remained outside the picture, just as the Quai d'Orsay had. But Foreign Minister Pineau, privy to the secret plans, had made broad hints about what was going on to Tsur, who therefore had to be recalled to Israel immediately for a briefing on the agreement between the Israeli and French Defense Ministries. The day he was apprised of the details, Tsur was dining with his friend and mentor Moshe Sharett, who had left the Israeli Foreign Ministry a month earlier and knew nothing at all about what was afoot. Tsur had to maintain confidentiality: "[M]y hands were tied," he wrote in his diary with sincere regret, "and I couldn't tell the man who until a month ago had been my Foreign Minister that the concerted efforts to find arms for Israel which we had directed together for so many months had reached this critical point."[48]

For the sake of secrecy, the Foreign Ministry's formal procurement efforts were continued and even redoubled. From Washington and Ottawa, respectively, Abba Eban and Michael Comay, Israel's ambassador to Canada, continued to try to gain approval for the sale of F-86 jets from Canada, and

Ambassador Tsur continued his petitions and protestations. On June 20 "reliable sources in Paris" "discovered" that since Pineau had not succeeded in persuading Dulles that the United States should share responsibility for arming Israel, France would refrain from providing Israel with arms.[49] In her first press conference as Israel's foreign minister, Golda Meir announced that the Foreign Ministry's future efforts would center on the need for defensive weapons.[50] Several days later Ben-Gurion contradicted the British foreign secretary's contention that Israel had military superiority over Egypt.[51] Israeli leaders had for some time now been making the same kind of declarations; now, however, their purpose was to put up a screen of disinformation.

The atmosphere at Israeli military headquarters, however, had undergone a total transformation. On July 7 Dayan ordered Haim Laskov to freeze all allocations for the IDF's defensive deployment and to immediately prepare a new budget taking the new weapons acquisitions and their absorption into account. All the activities geared toward defense that had been required during the lean months were now canceled, and the bulk of allocations redirected toward paying for the new arms and absorbing them rapidly into the ranks of the Israeli military.

The day after the conclusion of the Vermars conference, the French brought three tank landing craft into Toulon harbor; each could hold 30 tanks and a large amount of ammunition and spare parts. The ships—the *Chelif,* the *Laita,* and the *Odette*—were given Hebrew code names: *Yarkona, Arnona,* and *Yardena.*[52] The first of the three delivery cycles was scheduled for the second half of July, the second for August, and the third for September. For technical reasons the coast south of Tel Aviv was abandoned in favor of the Kishon beach, where a small river flowed into the Gulf of Haifa, and which was closer to the Haifa port installations and services, to the railroad, and to the general roads network. It also afforded greater protection from the elements and was less subject to strong sea currents. The commander of the Seventh Armored Brigade issued the orders for Operation Jonah.

On July 18 Yosef Nahmias sent a cable from Paris: "The first boat sailed at 17:00 on July 17th carrying 30 tanks and a stock of spare parts."[53] Seven days later two Israeli patrol boats left Haifa harbor at dawn for the open sea with 33 tank drivers and a handful of technicians, liaison officers, and naval officers on board. The renowned Israeli author Shabetai Tevet, who was invited to record the historic event, described it[54]:

From beyond the horizon the French landing craft comes into view—a long, ungainly ship with an ugly, clumsy construction, more in the water than out because of the weight of her cargo. A wide piece of sheeting hides her name and number markings from curious eyes. The flags are down. After mutual identification by wireless, the Israelis board the ship. The drivers and mechanics immediately approach the tanks and test them by turning on the ignition. . . . The last orders on the bridge are given and the ship heads for the Gulf of Haifa.

The beach at the Kishon outlet, which had been bare and desolate when the last of daylight ebbed away, becomes a hive of activity as night settles in. From somewhere two heavy-duty tractors appear, a row of heavy trucks grinds to a halt on the road near the banks of the water. The indistinct figures of soldiers wearing black caps run about completing final preparations. . . . Slowly the activity ceases and is replaced by a tense anticipation. . . . At exactly nine o'clock in the evening a small caravan of cars approaches and stops some distance away. A silent group descends to the beach by foot. Ben-Gurion's white plume of hair and Dayan's black eyepatch give them away. . . . Shimon Peres is also there. . . . The only extraneous member of the crew is the poet Nathan Alterman, who was specially invited by Dayan and who would immortalize the event in a poem.[55] The entourage halts a pace away from the shoreline and waits expectantly. . . . Suddenly, silent and hushed, an enormous block of darkness, mountainlike, takes form in front of the group. Another second and the shadow of the leviathan comes into view. A frightful chunk of steel rolls forward, heading straight for the spectators. . . . An ear-splitting screech of steel plates and iron chains breaks the silence—the carrier has come to a halt, its belly hugging the shore. . . . Several muffled orders are heard and the ship's prow slowly stops. . . . Above the raised gangway a short row of white letters is now revealed. The real name of the ship—*Chelif*. . . . A little more and the gangway is lowered . . . to the soft sand and the spectators are treated to the sight of the ship's belly and bowels. In the darkness rent by the lights of dimmed flashlights, the tanks, ranked into avenues, with the muzzles of their guns extending, look like a thick forest. . . . Thirty drivers already seated in their cabs are now starting the engines—and the mood is broken. With a grate of chains and a fearful roar of metal, one after the other the tanks loom out of the belly of the ship onto the gangway, gun turrets momentarily raised as if in a salute, and already sliding down into the loose sand and from there onto the road and into the darkness of the night.

. . . Ben-Gurion and his entourage enter the captain's cabin, shaking hands . . . greeting each other excitedly, and soon all the activity in the bowels of the ship below is over and everyone runs back to shore. At 9:15 P.M. the French boat landed at Kishon beach; at 11:10—less than two hours later—the gangway is raised and heavy metal doors once again conceal the ships' colorful name. With friendly shouts of encouragement exchanged between the Israeli armored personnel and the French sailors, the ship glides slowly into the waves. Slowly it is swallowed by darkness, and disappears. The ship has left behind on Israeli soil 30 modern tanks and a group of grateful Jews. The scene will repeat itself a week later when the "Arnona" arrives, followed by the "Yardena," and then all over again. Israel's salvation has become a reality. The tide is in again.

The success of the armaments procurement efforts in France and their failure in America stemmed from objective circumstances. U.S. policy makers
in 1956 believed that it was in their country's national interest not to supply
Israel with arms, while French policy makers in the spring of 1956 were convinced that arming Israel was congruent with the national interests of their
nation. America was fighting for its position in the Middle East in the face of
growing Soviet influence and feared to increase Arab estrangement from the
West by openly supporting the State of Israel. France, on the other hand, was
fighting to maintain its control of North Africa in the face of increasing
Egyptian and other Arab intervention in Algeria and wanted to find ways to
weaken those states or, at the least, distract them from what was happening in
the Maghreb. Thus the Defense Ministry's methods in France—a somewhat
old-fashioned covert diplomacy—cannot be said to have been preferable to
the Foreign Ministry's method—the pursuit of a modern, overt, and public
foreign policy. Nonetheless, under these special circumstances, those old and
outmoded methods of secret deals still proved useful.

At the end of Chapter 10 we noted the Israeli Foreign Ministry's mistaken
concept of the nature of the connection between Israel's border defense policy and its chances of procuring weapons. Throughout those months of
feverish search for sources of armaments, under constant pressure from the
Americans and British, whose interest was to prevent hostilities from flaring
up in the Middle East, the Foreign Ministry was convinced that Israel had to
"behave itself" and avoid an activist defense policy. For the Foreign
Ministry, Operation Kinneret, the shelling of Gaza, and other such actions
severely jeopardized Israel's efforts to procure arms. The Vermars conference, however, proved precisely the opposite; exhibiting the IDF's fighting
ability and Israel's willingness to follow an active security policy had confirmed the French in their conclusion that Israel could be useful in France's
North African campaign. The French gave Israel arms not for it to avoid
fighting for its interests, but to allow it to become an active military factor in
the service of those security needs that the French estimated were congruent
with their own.

Another important lesson can be learned from Israel's failure to procure
arms in Washington and success in Paris. The question of the influence that
an arms-supplying nation gains in the political decision-making processes of
the recipient nation is complex and cannot be adequately dealt with here.[56]
Suffice it to say what is perhaps obvious but that, in retrospect, was not so
obvious to American policy makers in the winter of 1956: Political influence
in the long run cannot be boosted by withholding arms. A country that wants
to make its influence felt on another nation's decision-making processes

should open its arsenals to that nation. In the autumn of 1955 and the winter of 1956, the "American consideration" was a weighty one in Israel's decision making. But it was short-lived, and when Israel despaired of obtaining aid from Washington, it ended. With the coming of the Suez crisis, it was replaced by the French.

12
■ ■ ■

WAITING IN THE WINGS:
AUGUST–SEPTEMBER 1956[1]

O ver 100,000 Egyptians celebrated the fourth anniversary of the revolution in Alexandria's Independence Square on July 26, 1956. There they heard President Gamal Abdul Nasser, in a rousing address, announce the nationalization of the Suez Canal Company.[2] Nasser's speech marked a turning point not only in Egypt's relations with the West, but also in the Egyptian-Israeli conflict and the Arab-Israeli conflict. The international crisis precipitated by the announcement would determine Nasser's position in the Middle East for better or for worse. If he emerged unscathed, his prestige would soar, as would his ability and desire to confront Israel. If, on the other hand, Nasser lost, Israel might find itself with new opportunities to radically reshuffle its relations with the Arab world. Although its leaders grasped these implications immediately, for the time being Israel could only sit patiently on the sidelines of the main act, especially as its major preoccupation those first weeks after nationalization was to absorb the new French weapons and maintain security along its increasingly tense eastern border. Moreover, the Western powers had resolved to keep their quarrel with Nasser distinct from the long-standing dispute between Israel and Egypt. During the first days of August, the British foreign secretary sent a note to the Cabinet's Egypt Committee saying, "It is essential that our quarrel with Egypt should be isolated as completely as possible from the quarrel of Israel with the Arab states."[3] The stage of political action in the Middle East moved from Gaza and Nitzana to London and Paris. For eight weeks Israel would be pushed to the wings and other players would take center stage.[4]

The canal's nationalization surprised the West, touching a sensitive nerve in Paris and especially London: More than any other institution, the Suez Canal symbolized the glory of European imperialism.[5] With the gradual retreat of Great Britain and France from their colonies in the Far and Near

East and the advent of nuclear weapons, the canal's strategic importance had diminished appreciably. However, it was still vital for Western interests, especially for the oil supply from the Persian Gulf on which the entire West European economy depended.[6] But England and France were less concerned with practical and economic implications than with the issue of prestige and influence that came to the fore in the wake of Nasser's nationalization. The passage of ships through the canal could be well organized and secured under Egyptian management; France and England were more worried lest Nasser's success affect their own positions in the region. Eden writes in his memoirs, "There was no doubt how Nasser's action would be received from Agadir to Karachi."[7] Britain's fear was not Egypt but Iraq and the Persian Gulf, while France feared losing its remaining hold in the Maghreb.

Moreover, the processes of decolonization had left the two former imperial powers with unhealed scars that Nasser's action had once again inflamed. An official British Cabinet document written after the initial anger had passed stated, "The abdication by Britain since the War of her overseas responsibilities is one of the greatest revolutions." Such revolutions are seldom accomplished without a phase of resistance."[8] Nationalization elicited special resistance in the United Kingdom against the background of the symbolic place that the canal had held for 100 years of British policy making. One British commentator noted, "Even so moderate a Conservative as R. A. Butler felt Disraeli, seven Conservative leaders ago, behind his emotions in 1956."[9]

Many of the principal actors in Paris and London were also caught up in the collective experience of their more recent past. World War II, which might have been prevented had Hitler and Mussolini been stopped earlier, preyed on their consciences and clouded their reasoning. The recurrent comparisons of Nasser to Hitler and Mussolini in the documents of those days, the constant reminders of the German army's entry into the Rhineland and Italian aggression in Abyssinia in the 1930s, and the repeated references to "the little dictator from Cairo" who had to be eliminated before it was too late—all these may have been misguided, but they reflected a deep strain of emotional reaction that influenced the political thinking of those holding the reins of power in France and England during the crisis.[10] The chief victim of this syndrome may very well have been England's prime minister, Sir Anthony Eden, himself, renowned for his stand against the appeasement and reconciliation that had characterized British policy in the 1930s. Writing about Eden's resignation from the government at the end of that decade, Winston Churchill openly complimented him: "There seemed one strong young figure standing up against long, dismal and drawling tides of drift and surrender, of wrong measurement and feeble impulses . . . he seemed to me at this moment to embody the life-rope of the British nation, the grand old British race that had done so much for men and which still had so much to give."[11] One of Eden's main motivations during the Suez crisis may have been his strong urge to maintain this image, which he held of himself no less than others did of him. Perhaps the most tragic aspect of the entire episode was that this inordinate sense of moral obligation, which was inappropriate the conditions that then obtained, completely clouded Eden's judgment. To rephrase Santayana, perhaps he who learns too much from history is doomed to be the victim of new errors.

From the beginning of the crisis, it was obvious that the British and French response was very different from the American one. U.S. interest in the Suez Canal was marginal, since the American economy did not depend on the waterway. (However, as its control of the Panama Canal was vital to American interests, the United States had to avoid legal precedents that might put into question its status in the isthmus of Panama.) The major distinction between America as opposed to England and France, however, was a more fundamental one, at the heart of which lay America's inherently anticolonial legacy.

Britain and France wanted to keep their politically preferential positions in the Middle East; the Americans preferred to maintain their relations with the states in the region, which had until recently been under colonial rule, on the basis of mutual economic interests and through indirect political influence, rejecting the outdated forms of government by coercion.[12] In 1953, after Eisenhower's first meeting with Winston Churchill in the former's capacity as American president, he wrote in his diary, "I felt that the last thing the two strongest Western powers should do was to appear before the world as a combination of forces to compel adherence to their announced views."[13] Nonetheless, the Americans felt deeply obligated by their historic alliance with the two great European powers and, despite their disagreements, tried to exhibit solidarity with them. Thus from the outset the United States limited its support of the allies in their clash with Nasser to the legal and technical questions of ensuring free and unrestricted navigation through the canal. The United States clearly maintained reservations regarding the British and French desire to exploit the occasion to resolve the attendant, more fundamental, issues of Nasser's regional prestige. Several analysts have attributed the increasing misunderstandings between the Americans

and the British and French during the course of the crisis to John Foster
Dulles's enigmatic and equivocal style and his evasive personality.[14] A
closer look at the documents of the period, however, indicates that, notwithstanding a certain ambiguity, Dulles's message to the European allies was
forceful throughout. He was consistent in objecting to the resolution of the
crisis by force.

The alarms went off in Washington when several communications arrived
shortly after Nasser's Alexandria speech. The first was a report from the
U.S. chargé d'affaires in London who, in an extraordinary gesture, had been
invited, together with the French ambassador, to an informal meeting of
British ministers, high officials, and chiefs of staff.[15] Next was Eden's
telegram to President Eisenhower advising him that he and his colleagues
were convinced they had to be prepared to use force as a last resort to restore
Nasser to his senses and that the British chiefs of staff had been ordered to
prepare suitable military plans.[16] This was followed by a more detailed
report from special envoy Robert Murphy, sent urgently to London to "hold
the fort" until Dulles arrived, on his informal conversation with old friends
Harold Macmillan and Field Marshal Harold Alexander.[17] From then on,
Eisenhower and Dulles were concerned not with revoking the act of nationalization—which seemed legitimate to them and in any event probably irre-
versible—but rather with how to keep the British and the French from
hotheaded actions.

In the early stages of the crisis, voices were also raised in America—especially in the military establishment—demanding a strong, resolute response
from the United States.[18] But the president and the secretary of state believed
that their mandate from the American people was primarily to keep peace in
the world; from the beginning they perceived their role in the new crisis as
preventing hostilities. Immediately after Dulles returned from a trip to Peru,
and before leaving urgently for London, he met with Eisenhower to coordinate positions. He said, "I had come to the conclusion that, as regrettable as
it might be to see Nasser's prestige enhanced, even temporarily, I did not
believe the situation was one which should be resolved by force." The president concurred and decided that the issue of freedom of passage in the canal
should be kept distinct from that of Nasser's prestige: "Every reasonable
effort should be made to get an acceptable . . . solution to [the] Suez dispute,
but that this issue and question of Nasser and prestige in the Middle East and
North Africa could not wisely be confused."[19]

But America could not ignore the allies' expectations of solidarity. Thus
Eisenhower's letters included several remarks that might have been misunderstood and that convinced them the United States would eventually sup-

port military action or, at least, not oppose it. In retrospect, however, a sentence in Eisenhower's letter, hand-delivered by Dulles to Eden and Mollet, is striking for its patently different connotation: "I have given you my personal conviction, as well as that of my associates, as to the unwisdom even of contemplating the use of military force at this moment."[20]

The British were not initially disturbed by the American reaction, because they themselves needed several weeks to set up a military operation and because they were well aware that public opinion at home and abroad had to be prepared to accept the initiation of hostilities. D-Day was originally set for September 15, 1956—some six weeks after Nasser's proclamation.[21] This would permit the British to play the diplomatic game outlined by Dulles, pleasing the American government and, if not entirely bringing it over to their side, at least preventing active opposition.

In August things went according to British hopes. A joint British-French military staff had been set up in London under the command of British general Sir Charles Keightley and French vice-admiral Pierre Barjot, and feverish planning of what became known as Operation Musketeer got under way.[22] On August 18, England, France, and America convened an international conference in London to forge a united front against nationalization composed of all the countries that used the canal. Invitees included the signatory states of the 1888 Constantinople Convention, on which the administration and supervision of canal procedures was based, as well as nations that shipped considerable cargo through the canal. The conference went as expected: Egypt refused to participate; the Soviets did their best to protect Egypt's interests and frustrate Western intentions; and India's flamboyant representative, Krishna Menon, seasoned the proceedings with his fiery tongue; Selwyn Lloyd, who chaired the proceedings, managed to form a bloc of 18 nations that confirmed a basic demand that canal management be handed over to a new international agency representing the interests of all nations that were the canal's major users.[23] Dulles participated avidly in the proceedings and supported the English and French in their objection to the Egyptian government's unilateral takeover.[24] The conference ended on August 23, resolving to send a delegation headed by the Australian prime minister, Robert Menzies, to Cairo to present President Nasser with the 18 nations' statement.

Nasser's restraint throughout this period was extraordinary. After the headiness of Alexandria he was careful to exhibit moderation; he cancelled the arrest orders issued against canal employees who had left their posts, refrained from stopping French and British ships that insisted on continuing to pay their tolls into the Paris and London accounts of the old company, and proposed an alternate international conference at which either a new international convention would be adopted or the old Constantinople Convention would be ratified. In either case he was ready to assure freedom of passage. He was prepared to go far in his conciliatory proposals, provided that Egypt's sovereignty and right to administer the canal were recognized in principle.

One country not invited to the London conference, despite its direct concern, was Israel.[25] Conveniently enough, the conference organizers had a formal pretext: Israel obviously had never signed the 1888 Constantinople Convention and in fact did not use the canal. Furthermore, as Christian Pineau noted years later, the organizers did not want to give Egypt an expedient excuse for boycotting the conference.[26] A more profound reason for Israel's exclusion, however, was England's concern lest it appear on the same side of the barricades as Israel in its dispute with the major leader of the Arab world. Throughout the crisis, England did its best to deny Israel's involvement and to make Israel's dispute totally distinct from its own.[27] Two days after nationalization the British Foreign Office quietly sent a message to the government of Israel not to intervene in canal affairs in order not to embarrass England.[28] Britain made the same demand of the Americans and especially the French, whom it viewed with suspicion as Israeli allies. Ironically, ultimately only Israel could extricate Eden from the morass he had plunged into.

Those in London charged with planning the military operation were aware that IDF activity on the eastern flank of the battlefield could be operationally advantageous to the allied forces in the canal region; but political considerations overpowered operational ones. A British Foreign Office document on the political background of the operation states, "There would be obvious military advantages if Israel were to engage a part of the Egyptian forces, but such advantages would be offset by the impossibility of securing Egyptian Governmental co-operation after such action."[29] In his memoirs Pineau confirms that at this early phase, "Even though Israel was a victim of aggression, we did not envisage her direct intervention."[30]

Diplomatically too, Israel could have proved beneficial to the British cause; after all, the only evidence supporting the British contention that

Nasser could not be relied on to keep his promise of unrestricted freedom of passage in the canal was his ongoing blockade of Israeli shipping. But the British did not want to play this card, not only because in the past they had tended not to protest until their own interests were at stake, but also—and mainly—because of that profound aversion to anything hinting at collaboration between Israel and England.[31]

For the time being, Israel was not upset by England's adamant objection to its involvement in the Suez crisis, because it needed at least three months to complete integration of the new French arms. The French landing craft that brought the first delivery had reached Kishon beach three days before nationalization, and another eight deliveries were due to arrive, the last one only at the end of September. "Nasser is not coordinating his time-table with us," Ben-Gurion told Moshe Dayan. "[W]e cannot do anything meanwhile except sit tight and conclude the French deal quickly, reinforce our strength, and then, at a later stage, find the right moment to strike."[32] Thus in these early phases of the crisis Israel contented itself with presenting a fundamental demand that its rights be included in any arrangement arrived at ensuring freedom of passage in the Suez.

Shimon Peres was in Paris negotiating further arms procurement when word of the nationalization broke. By then the relations he had developed with the higher echelons of the French Defense Ministry were very close indeed. Despite repeated British warnings, Bourgès-Maunoury and Abel Thomas discussed the canal crisis openly with Peres. Upon returning to Israel, he delivered Bourgès-Maunoury's message to Ben-Gurion: Over British objections, France was interested in involving Israel in at least "planning and advice—and if necessary, in more than that."[33] Furthermore, the French were not ready to give up their newly acquired intelligence assets, and now asked Israel to provide them with up-to-date information on Egyptian military deployment, urgently vital to the French command, as joint military talks were due to open in London within several days. Ben-Gurion's orders were that the French be given the best that Israel had: "This will be our test," he said, "whether we can give the French the information that is first and foremost important to them and not only the information that interests us. If we hide anything that is vital for them, we will be betraying their trust in us."[34] A steady stream of important intelligence items now flowed from Israel to Paris through the new channels set up subsequent to the Vermars conference. The benefit that the French derived now from the Vermars agreement went far beyond their original expectations.

The French were especially eager for Israeli help in aerial reconnaissance, since French bases were far from Egypt and French planes could not photograph over Egyptian territory. Here, as in a few other cases, the French relied totally on the British, whose Canberra planes based in Cyprus could easily do the job. But Eden was afraid of being accused of political insincerity, and thus the British Cabinet put off taking aerial photographs until only a few days before D-Day.[35] Military planning, however, was crucially dependent on up-to-date information. The French thus turned to their ally on the eastern shore of the Mediterranean. Israel's air reconnaissance capability at the time consisted only of old wooden Mosquito planes, which were vulnerable to Egyptian MiGs. Efforts were made to push up delivery of the Vautour planes, but they had not been readied for missions of this sort, and the IDF decided to risk using one specially refurbished Meteor jet alongside the outdated Mosquitoes.

Early in August the French Command made another request of Israel: Having learned that harbors in Cyprus were inadequate for the needs of the operation and that the airfield had a limited capacity, they asked Israel to provide them with technical specifications of its ports and the capacity of its airfields. Without Cyprus, the operation's schedules would be seriously inhibited, as the far-flung ports of Malta and Toulon would have to be relied on. As the British opposed any operational contact with Israel, the French explained that they were planning to use Israeli bases only in the event of an emergency—landing damaged planes or refueling for long-range missions.[36] Ben-Gurion ordered the Dayan to give France all requested information. "We must provide it in good faith," he said. "We must treat them like brothers in everything. Their aid and assistance, as well as our partnership with them, are invaluable and we must cooperate with them totally."[37]

The planned offensive on Egypt soon seemed likely to hamper Israeli arms procurement plans. The French announced that they would have to discontinue deliveries toward the end of August since the landing craft were needed for the planned invasion. But because Israel might be asked to become involved in the battle, the French were no less anxious than were the Israelis to complete the planned weapons procurement schedule; and after only a short hiatus, deliveries were resumed at the beginning of September by regular cargo ships. Now the tanks were unloaded in the dead of night on the docks of the port in Haifa rather than on the desolate beach at Kishon. Maximum security measures were enforced, and the entire operation was completed according to the original schedule. On September 27 the last delivery contracted for under the Vermars agreement arrived in Israel. The tanks now bore the letter "A" for Amilcar—the French code-name for the operation until it was replaced by the name Musketeer—and were brought to Haifa directly from the area where the French troops were assembling for the campaign. Thirty-six Mystère-4A jets also arrived as promised, in two fleets. The explanations of the Israeli air force officers that these were simply planes that had been returned to France for repairs probably did not convince the Brindisi flight supervisors; and in his memoirs Eisenhower wryly noted that the "Mystère fighter bombers for Israel showed a rabbitlike capacity for multiplication."[38]

Now the center of gravity in the effort to reinforce the Israeli military moved back from Paris to Israel. In the army camps, the command headquarters, the workshops and training bases, the race against time began. At Ben-Gurion's suggestion General Haim Laskov was appointed to head the armored corps, which now needed to be reformed. To the new command Laskov took with him his old friend Colonel Meir Zorea, and the two took up their duties energetically.

Not a month after the appointment, a scathing argument erupted between GHQ, headed by Moshe Dayan, and the new commanders. Laskov and Zorea wanted the armored corps to be a separate military arm with wide operational and organizational authority. They also believed that the armor had to be centralized and accessible to the GHQ as a national reserve rather than scattered among many integrated units. Dayan was initially mistrustful of the armor's independent fighting ability and preferred that it serve primarily in an auxiliary capacity for the infantry. The argument was basically one of doctrine,[39] hinging on how the armored corps would be engaged during battle and its status in the general IDF deployment; but it also had a more mundane aspect: allocation of resources and authority. On September 1 a grand symposium was held at GHQ, with the defense minister participating. In his diary Ben-Gurion summed up the argument by saying that "Haim [Laskov] and Zaro [Zorea] demanded that existing personnel be supplemented by 1,100 men, while GHQ was prepared to give only 900."[40] GHQ finally struck a compromise, dismantling one of the two regular infantry brigades and adding one of its battalions to the armored corps. A total of 310 of the 380 tanks Israel had after Vermars were allocated to the armored corps and organized into three armored brigades. The remainder of the tanks were placed in separate armored regiments put at the disposal of the Northern and Central Commands.

The other military branches also redoubled their efforts. In a discussion with air force commanders, Dayan said

> The present political situation requires us to be capable of going to war in the very near future and making the equipment we have operational in a very short period of time. If we are not ready for this, we will not be able to exploit the various political opportunities that might present themselves, and we may be forced to wage war while the efficient and modern tools we have remain unused.[41]

In August and September many of the reserve units were called up and re-assigned to absorb and learn to operate the new weapons. The paratroop brigade was reorganized under the command of Colonel Ariel Sharon; the Southern Command was reshuffled under the command of General Assaf Simhoni; and the IDF as a whole flexed its muscles in anticipation of the coming encounter.

By the beginning of September the failure of the Robert Menzies mission to Cairo was obvious; Menzies had encountered stiff Egyptian resistance.[42] Nasser was cautious and moderate during the talks, but he was not prepared to relinquish the principle of Egypt's sovereignty and its right to manage the canal. He replied to Menzies's memorandum at the conclusion of the talks with his own very detailed and well thought out rebuttal, using the best arguments supplied by his advisors on international law.[43] It effectively rejected the demands of the London conference. In fact, the chances for a settlement had been virtually nil from the beginning. What the British actually wanted was Nasser's submission and retraction of the act of nationalization; Nasser was well aware that any concessions on principles that he made would undermine the tremendous prestige he had earned in the Arab world. Thus he rejected any notion of international supervision of canal management and would not discuss anything with the users of the canal except as an owner bargaining with a client.[44]

The mission was frustrated in another sense as well. The difference, and perhaps conflict, between the French and British approach to the crisis and that of the United States was painfully obvious here too. At first the allies had wanted Dulles himself to participate in the delegation. His very refusal hinted that he was not so anxious to press Nasser to make basic concessions. The American position was further clarified in the course of the talks themselves when the American representative on the delegation, Loy Henderson, began looking for ways to settle and reconcile the issue on the basis of a practical plan of operations. This occurred even though the Menzies delegation had not been empowered by the London conference to undertake any negotiations except for the approval of the conference resolutions.[45]

The mission's failure was a forgone conclusion and did not surprise the British. According to their political timetable, the matter now had to go before the Security Council, where, they assumed, the Soviet veto would effectively block this diplomatic path as well.[46] When this maneuver had been completed, it should be obvious to all that the political possibilities had indeed been exhausted and the military option was unavoidable.

Thus on September 6 the British Cabinet agreed to submit the question of the Suez Canal to the U.N. Security Council.[47] Earlier, on August 22, Eden had proposed that D-Day be pushed off to coincide with the diplomatic procedures, which were progressing slower than originally anticipated.[47] Despite growing opposition at home, Eden was set on beating Nasser and, if necessary, on using Operation Musketeer for that purpose, but he could not do so before he had exhausted the political options.

The French were uneasy about the delay. On September 7 Bourgès-Maunoury announced in the French General Assembly that the French forces had been ready since the beginning of the month and that only political discussions were holding up marching orders.[49] The situation in Paris was the complete converse to that which obtained in London: With the exception of the Communists, the entire French public waited anxiously for the beginning of the military engagement to eliminate Nasser. Christian Pineau was not happy with the British decision to approach the Security Council. Ever since the U.N. had begun to take an anti-French position on Algeria, the popularity of the international organ in France had dropped, and France's politicians viewed the British appeal to the Security Council as just another delay. But the British were insistent, and Pineau was forced to submit.

In the meantime, military preparations were nearing completion. Early in September the chiefs of staff and the Egypt Committee of the British Cabinet discussed the need for a fundamental change in the military concept to allow the forces more flexibility and to shorten the warning time needed from the final decision to initiation of the military action.[50] Instead of a broad engagement of forces to conquer the entire Delta and Cairo, which required bringing forces and supplies from the British Isles, the chiefs of staff now proposed that the first stage consist of the steady bombing of Egyptian air force bases, oil installations, and finally the Egyptian army itself, to minimize opposition to the invading forces and to enable the forces already emplaced in the region to take over the canal zone.[51]

At this point the French began to consider the possibility of involving Israel in Operation Musketeer. The joint military plan called for the French to operate on the eastern side of the Suez Canal, and French planners were concerned with how to prevent the Egyptian forces deployed in the Sinai Peninsula from attacking the French force from the flank. Israel could keep those Egyptians pinned down along its border; and the possibility of Israel's being asked to support the French forces intrigued Admiral Barjot, General Keightley's second in command and the senior French commander in the operation. Bourgès-Maunoury asked him to reexamine the "Israeli option."

In the midst of the IDF's September 1 symposium on the deployment of the armored corps, Ben-Gurion was handed an urgent cable from Yosef Nahmias: ". . . Admiral Barjot wants to invite us to join the battle on D-Day plus seven. He will explain this to the British as a certain weakness in an appropriate area of the front. He wants to invite the Deputy Chief of Staff to a meeting. Bourgès-Maunoury has approved all this."[52] Ben-Gurion authorized the meeting on the spot and after a few inquiries Colonel Meir Amit, effectively deputy chief of staff, who was in Germany, scheduled a meeting with the admiral in Paris for September 7. Ben-Gurion himself wrote the instructions for Amit: "We are ready in principal to help the French in their military campaigns—with all our ability. The use of our air bases and ports, and the participation of our units—if necessary—will be decided in Jerusalem by the Government."[53]

The French, however, had not yet formulated their own ideas on how the Israelis might contribute to the campaign, and it was soon obvious that the meeting was intended as no more than an initial probe and way of obtaining information without demanding or making any commitments. Deputy Chief of Military Intelligence Colonel Yuval Ne'eman reported:

> The meeting was devoted primarily to hearing our assessment of the Egyptian forces. Apparently Barjot called the meeting after consulting with Bourgès-Maunoury. . . . On Israel's active participation he stressed that this was a political problem and wanted to know only if we could allocate sufficient forces to eliminate the Egyptian force on our border. . . . We said we could, taking into account that the Egyptian ranks along our borders had thinned. . . . He wanted to stay in touch and get additional information if necessary and made suitable arrangements.[54]

At this point the French had no reason to suspect that the British had changed their minds about Operation Musketeer, and their approach to Israel was no more than a probe. Nonetheless, the Israelis perceived the meeting as an important signal; two days afterward Dayan ordered all GHQ branches to reexamine their war plans, both for a broad operation in the Sinai and for limited missions, such as conquering the Straits of Tiran or the Gaza Strip.[55]

On September 17 General Dayan convened his staff officers and said, "If war breaks out between the West and Egypt over Suez, Israel may get involved, either at Western invitation or on her own initiative, to exploit the opportunity." Dayan reported Ben-Gurion's directive: "We shall not go to Suez unless we are asked to by the West. Otherwise, the West will be only too glad of the opportunity to demonstrate friendship for the Arabs and will kick us out of there." But Israel's operational goals were mainly the Straits of Tiran and the Gaza Strip. "Here we can strike even if the West does not approve or even opposes it." But the political picture was as yet uncertain. "We don't know the precise nature of the opportunity we'll be given."[56]

War now seemed imminent, though weeks would pass before the French were dismayed enough by Eden's wavering to seriously consider the Israeli option as the critical point on which the entire campaign would hinge. Meanwhile, they were grudgingly dragged along in Dulles's delaying tactics.

Dulles was equally uneasy with the British decision to approach the Security Council. There the United States would have to choose a stand either for or against its allies; doing so would take the risk that the USSR might seem to be the sole defender of the Arab cause. Furthermore, he was aware of the French and British military plans and realized that approaching the U.N. would inevitably lead to military action.[57] Dulles still believed that time would soften the allies' stand[58]; the problem was how to gain more time.

On September 8 he returned from a short vacation with a new plan for establishing SCUA—the Suez Canal Users Association: an attempt to remove the canal from the agenda of high-powered politics by dealing directly and pragmatically with the problems of its administration. Dulles felt the legal base for such an association had to be the concession granted the users under the Constantinople Convention of 1888.[59] Eisenhower expressed his doubts on the plan's practicality, but Dulles told him frankly, "I was not sure either, but I felt we had to keep the initiative and to keep probing along various lines, particularly since there was no chance of getting the British and French not to use force unless they had some alternatives that seemed to have in them some strength of purpose. . . ."[60] Eisenhower thus approved the plan and Dulles presented it to Eden, assuring him that the

United States would participate in the new association.[61] Eden accepted Dulles's plan, but a gulf separated their perceptions of it.

Dulles saw the plan first and foremost as a means to transfer contacts with Egypt onto the practical plane of negotiating the actual operation of the canal. At a September 13 press conference he said, "It is our hope that perhaps practical on-the-spot arrangements for cooperation can be achieved without prejudice to the rights of anyone. This may provide a provisional *de facto* working arrangement until formal agreement can be reached."[62] In contrast, Eden felt that he had been given a tool with which either to force Nasser to surrender or to egg him into closing the canal to Western shipping, thus providing the allies with the pretext they needed for military action. Since Dulles's proposal called for the association to charge users a fee, organize its own navigators, determine the order of passage in the canal, and so forth, Eden believed that Nasser could not accept the terms. Instead he would close the canal to ships operating through the association, paving the way for the use of force against him.[63]

Furthermore, Eden believed, through the plan the Americans would be implicated in the military operation also: Inasmuch as America had promoted the idea of setting up the association, it was only reasonable that it would cooperate with the British and French in implementing their plans when Nasser rejected the new initiative. At the base, the original gap still remained between the British desire to defeat Nasser and bring him to heel and the American desire to resolve only the problem of freedom of passage in the Suez Canal.

On September 12, Eden addressed a special session of Parliament and announced the planned association, adding:

> I must make it clear that if the Egyptian Government would seek to interfere with the operation of the association or refuse to extend to it the essential minimal cooperation, then that Government will once more be in breach of the Convention of 1888. In that event Her Majesty's Government will be free to take such steps as seem to be required either through the UN or by other means for the assertion of their rights.[64]

The next day Dulles called a press conference; in no uncertain terms he clarified that America would not coerce Egypt into accepting the proposed plan: "We do not intend to shoot our way through," he said.[65] Should Egypt prevent SCUA vessels from passing through the canal, the American government would reroute its ships around the Cape of Good Hope. Moreover, what might have been the most effective weapon that the association could wield—refusal to pay tolls—turned out to be unloaded. Dulles agreed to prohibit vessels flying the American flag from paying tolls to Egypt but specified that the same prohibition could not be imposed on American-owned ships navigating under flags of convenience, which in effect represented the vast majority of American shipping through the canal.

The British were utterly dejected at Dulles's announcement. Eden noted bitterly, "It would be hard to imagine a statement more likely to cause allied disunity and disarray."[66] Lloyd wrote, "Mr. Dulles' response is most disappointing. We seem to be further apart than at any time since July 26."[67] The French were tired of Dulles's various maneuverings; Sir Gladwyn Jebb, England's ambassador in Paris, reported to London that Pineau felt that it was a waste of time talking to the Americans and didn't believe they would ever agree to an action that could result in Nasser's defeat.[68] And Pineau wrote in his memoirs, "Dulles' proposal embarrassed us. We could not understand how the 'club' [i.e., SCUA] could administer the canal without prior agreement with Nasser. . . . It is difficult to conceive of a solution more confused than this one."[69]

The plan to set up a users' association was stillborn, and Eden quickly recognized that it had been doomed almost as soon as it was conceived. But he had to play the fruitless game. Once again the nations that used the canal were convened in London for a second conference in order to set up an association, organize its operation, and wait and see what would happen. Eden had no choice, because he still needed a casus belli for opening hostilities.

From the outset, British sensitivity to world public opinion and the constraints of international law, as well as increasing domestic opposition, made it imperative to find a plausible casus belli. In mid-August Selwyn Lloyd had been asked to engage the aid of experts in international law to prepare a document outlining those Egyptian provocations that might justify a military response. The foreign minister told the Cabinet frankly that nationalization of the canal in and of itself did not constitute a casus belli; that would arise only if Nasser interfered with the passage of British warships or attacked them directly, took actions that might endanger British subjects, refused a British ship passage for failing to pay toll fees to Egypt, or occupied the British bases along the canal zone that had remained under the supervision of British civilian contractors since the 1954 evacuation agreement.[70] But Nasser was careful not to provide any such pretext.

Nor could it be said that the Egyptians were incapable of operating the canal properly or that it was blocked, either through negligence or by intent. In mid-September the pilots who had operated under the old regime quit their work, but the Egyptians quickly found replacements and, in the very first week of Egyptian control, proved eminently successful in operating it.

The second London conference opened on September 19 and concluded on September 21. It was a listless affair; most nations sent only their ambassadors already assigned to London, and the British and the French proceeded by rote. The association that was set up lacked any authority or ability to take substantive action. Its founding declarations tolled the death knell for the Western position; Nasser seemed to have emerged victorious from the crisis.

Dulles's ploy to gain time and delay England's military action succeeded beyond his expectations: Operation Musketeer's schedules were put off by a month. But he enjoyed only a pyrrhic victory, because the failure of the proposed users' association severed the last ties between London and Washington and paved the way for an independent Anglo-French action without prior coordination with the United States. Eden wrote in his memoirs, "The American torpedoing of their own plan on the first day of launching it, left no alternative but to use force or acquiesce in Nasser's triumph."[71]

Between Dulles's maneuverings and Eden's foot-dragging, the French had nearly despaired of getting the British to implement Operation Musketeer. They now had two options: provide the British with a new casus belli, or launch the operation on their own, in the hope that the British would soon join them. Naturally enough, they turned their eyes eastward: Did Israel hold the key out of the impasse?

In mid-September Shimon Peres was once again about to leave Israel for talks in Paris. Before his departure he conferred with Moshe Dayan, as he was well aware that his French hosts would ask questions on the possibility of Israel's participation in the Suez campaign. Dayan advised Peres to insist on three conditions: (1) Any initiative had to come from the French and had to be official even if covert, requiring contacts at the very highest level; (2) Israel could not become involved in a quarrel with Britain; (3) Israel would ultimately annex a strip of land along the Rafah-Sharm al-Sheikh line.[72]

On September 18 Shimon Peres and Yosef Nahmias met with Bourgès-Maunoury; Peres sent Ben-Gurion a long and dramatic telegram describing the talk: Bourgès-Maunoury

> discerned a retreat in the British stand on joint military action and he is beginning to doubt if it will ever take place. . . . He himself has concluded that other methods and other partners for war against Nasser should be sought. He believes that the Anglo-Saxon aversion, shared by some at the Quai d'Orsay, to cooperating with Israel in an operation against Nasser is fundamentally exaggerated.

Bourgès-Maunoury claimed that the timetables of the three major Western powers were not identical. There was "a French time-table, which demanded immediate action . . . an English time-table, which preferred political action for another two or three months . . . and an American time-table. . . ." Bourgès-Maunoury asked whether the Israeli timetable was not closer to that of the British; "Israel prefers to choose its partners rather than the time-table," Peres replied.

After the meeting Bourgès-Maunoury sent Ben-Gurion a cable congratulating him on his birthday, adding a cryptic comment: "The problem of Egypt, which is of paramount importance for both our nations, is worsening daily. I am glad we could do something together to protect our mutual interests. For my part, I shall continue to do tomorrow what I did yesterday, taking every occasion to develop active cooperation that will benefit both our nations."[73]

Ben-Gurion replied that same day, thanking the French minister for his good wishes and adding his own loaded comment: "As far as the three time-tables are concerned—the French is in fact more to our taste."[74] Ben-Gurion's reply reached Bourgès-Maunoury several hours before the French Cabinet convened to hear Christian Pineau's report on the second London conference. Pineau, who had returned dismayed and embittered, was now a staunch supporter of the "Israeli option." The French Cabinet resolved to make secret but official overtures to Israel and convene high-ranking talks toward an alliance on military action against Egypt.

Peres returned to Israel on September 25 and met Ben-Gurion and Dayan at a small military airfield. Ben-Gurion was on his way from his home at Kibbutz Sde Boker to a Cabinet meeting, at which a large-scale reprisal operation against Jordan was scheduled to be approved. On the spot he decided to reduce the scope of the reprisal: "What Peres says may be fateful," he wrote in his diary.[75] Immediately after the formal Cabinet meeting he convened his "kitchen Cabinet" of intimate associates plus two ministers from another small coalition party whom he trusted would endorse his policies on this matter. In his diary after the meeting Ben-Gurion wrote:

> I believed that here was our first opportunity to gain an ally. All the fears [expressed by the ministers] are real; but they would also be real if we were alone and Nasser tried to destroy us. We will enter this partnership only if several conditions are met: (1) if France is aware in advance of our limitations in air power and armor; (2) if England actually stands behind France and if [action] is undertaken with the knowledge of the United States; (3) if we get the shoreline of the Straits of Tiran, ensuring

freedom of passage in the Red Sea and to the Indian Ocean, permitting Eilat to really
become a port and the Negev hinterland to develop.[76]

Ben-Gurion decided to send a delegation to Paris headed by Foreign
Minister Golda Meir and including Transportation Minister Moshe Carmel,
Moshe Dayan, and Shimon Peres. The delegates were to meet with French
government representatives and express Israel's fundamental willingness to
enter into the proposed alliance. At the same time they were to learn as much
as possible about the proposal. The delegation was not authorized to conclude
any final and binding obligations; that rested with the Israeli government in
Jerusalem.[77] On September 27 Ben-Gurion gave Golda Meir detailed instructions; most important for him at this stage was the demand that all actions be
simultaneous, and he made that the starting point for his directives:

1. We will not start this action on our own.
2. We will not participate in this action unless England agrees to our participation and guarantees that Jordan and Iraq will not open a second
front against us.
3. We are willing to promise the British that we will not touch Jordan if she
does not interfere, but if we are attacked we shall respond vigorously,
without British intervention and without any complaints against us.
4. It is vital that the action be effected with the knowledge of the United
States. It is imperative that our participation does not harm us in America.
5. We must clarify how different our situation will be in the event of failure; for us failure might mean destruction.
6. The Chief of Staff will make our air, sea and armor limitations clear.
7. Jordan's conquest by another country in the course of the joint operation will entitle us to freedom of action throughout the West Bank of
the Jordan.
8. If the operation is successful we shall demand effective Israeli control
of the shoreline of the Straits of Tiran.
9. We shall propose that the Sinai Peninsula be demilitarized.
10. We shall propose that the new regime in Egypt be required to enter into
peace negotiations with us. In any case, we shall demand freedom of
passage in Suez, if the canal has not been destroyed in the meantime.

Ben-Gurion concluded his instructions in this way:

And perhaps we should also look into what would happen if—and this is very far-
fetched indeed—Russia were to attack us. I think the discussion should begin on a
positive note, stressing our desire to participate and, in general, our willingness to
cooperate with France in all areas and with our appreciation for the help she has provided us since the War of Independence and to this very day.[78]

Shortly before nightfall on Friday, September 28, the contingent took off from a military airfield in an old naval bomber that the French had sent for them.[79] After a short night's rest at the French naval base in Bizerta, Tunisia, the delegation landed at a French air force base in Villacoublay, where they were received by Louis Mangin, General Maurice Challe, and Yosef Nahmias. The Israelis stayed at the palace of Henri IV in St. Germain en Laye on the outskirts of Paris, spending the remainder of Saturday resting and in last-minute consultations. The political picture had still not been clarified. Yosef Nahmias revealed that two days earlier Eden, Selwyn Lloyd, Mollet, and Pineau had met and finally decided to bring the crisis to the Security Council for deliberations. This was to be the last step before the final decision to implement Operation Musketeer, but the French were not convinced of Eden's resoluteness. The Israelis still were uncertain about what the French wanted from them, and thus it was decided to open the talks on Sunday with a request for clarifications.

On Sunday, September 30, at 10:00 A.M. the first formal session of the St. Germain conference was convened.[80] The sessions were held at the home of Louis Mangin in the heart of Montparnasse. The aura of secrecy and patriotic determination was very reminiscent of the glorious days of the French underground during World War II, in which all the French participants of this conference had been actively involved.[81] Christian Pineau chaired the first session, and his opening remarks made it clear that his own expectations were not yet crystallized, that the meeting was in fact intended to explore various options, and that the French could not finalize anything. The Security Council deliberations, Pineau hoped, would be concluded by October 12, at which time he intended "to meet one last time with the British to see finally if they are prepared to join the French in a joint military action against Egypt. But I am not convinced that at the last minute the British Government will be as energetic as we are." Should no action be taken, it would mean a victory for Nasser and a most dangerous situation for both France and Israel. Political, technical, and climatic considerations made it imperative for the operation to be scheduled for mid-October at the very latest. "The minute our joint action with the British is cancelled, there remain only two options: (a) an Israeli operation in which France provides Israel with comprehensive military assistance and later even direct military participation; (b) a joint Israeli-French action against Egypt." Was Israel prepared in principle to embark on a joint action with France if Britain backed out?

As Ben-Gurion had instructed, Golda Meir opened her remarks on a very positive note: "The interests of Israel and of France on the Egyptian problem are totally identical. . . . Israel too believes it impossible to resolve the problem by diplomatic negotiations or peaceful methods. . . . Therefore Israel is prepared to help find a solution, to the extent that she can without risking destruction." But before Meir could provide a final and unequivocal response that would obligate her government, several crucial questions had to be answered: What would be the British position on an Israeli action in Sinai? What would be the British position if other Arab countries intervened? What would happen if Iraq tried to exploit the situation by invading Jordan? And what about the United States? Israel's economy was heavily dependent on the aid provided by American Jewry. Was there not a risk of a general American embargo on Israel? And what about Russia?

> We have no illusions regarding Nasser. . . . We know very well that so long as Nasser is there, the very survival of the State [of Israel] is in jeopardy. We know also that Nasser's victory in the Suez will elevate his standing and that we will be next in line. We are therefore very anxious to find a way to cooperate with you. But we must know if we will be able to fulfil the task that we undertake.

Pineau's response revealed several ideas that the higher ranks of the French government had been considering for some time on Israel's possible role in providing the desired casus belli: "I have no doubt that the British Government will view the [Israeli] operation positively, nor do I doubt that ultimately they will invoke their 1955 agreement with Egypt and reoccupy the canal. They have specifically said so." Did Pineau mean that Israel should fire the first shot? As far as America was concerned, Pineau did not believe the American government "would be able to impose an embargo on Israel before the Presidential elections. . . . you can be sure that Dulles' instinctive reaction will be, as usual . . . not to do anything." But obviously there was no point in asking the Americans in advance. Nor did Pineau think the Soviets would go so far as armed intervention; at the very most they would provide Egypt with equipment and perhaps pilots.

At this point Pineau raised the possibility of Israel participating in the operation even if France and Britain implemented Operation Musketeer, reiterating what Admiral Barjot had told Colonel Amit three weeks earlier:

> If France and Britain go to war together, it will be to everyone's benefit if Israel takes this opportunity to resolve some of her outstanding problems with Egypt. During the first stage of the Anglo-French action, we will be preoccupied with destroying the Egyptian air force and Israel should sit by quietly, if for no other reason than to save her cities from Egyptian bombing. But after a few days, Israel's entry into battle

would be very important. Israel could destroy the Egyptian army stationed between the Gaza Strip and Suez and could occupy the islands of Tiran and Sanafir.

Obviously, the French were not yet sure what role they intended for Israel: they didn't even know who was actually going to fight—the French alone, the French with the Israelis, or the French with the Israelis and the British.

From General Challe's remarks during the discussion, it was clear that France's High Command still considered a joint action with the British vital because Egyptian air bases had to be struck, and that required the British bombers stationed in Cyprus. The French were still hopeful that they could convince the British to join them in the operation, but if Britain hesitated, it would be very convenient for the French if Israel were to open an independent front in the Sinai. This would help them persuade the British to implement the original Musketeer plan while obviating the need for openly entering an alliance with Israel. But things had not yet crystallized sufficiently and this possibility remained hypothetical for the moment. Thus the French saw no point in insisting that Israel make any final commitments. The time was not yet ripe for decisions. Pineau was to leave for the U.N. that very day. He wanted Israel to send a special envoy to New York to maintain contact with him and get firsthand reports as the political picture resolved itself.

Pineau's departure for New York deflated the conference. So long as the political picture remained uncertain, there was little point in going into the particulars of the Israeli-French partnership. The talks in Montparnasse took on an air of unreality. "You must admit that the discussion is now taking place in a void," Bourgès-Maunoury told Shimon Peres frankly during an afternoon conversation intended to examine the strategic aspects of the cooperation. Peres, who was the chief midwife of the conference, was uncomfortable: "I believe that my fellow-delegates were disappointed by this meeting. They believe that either the conference was premature or that we held exaggerated expectations. I fear they credit me with being too optimistic about the possibility of real cooperation with France."[82]

But by the conclusion of the second session, the conference proved to have a very practical side of tremendous importance. Along general lines, Moshe Dayan told the French which missions and land targets Israel would be willing and able to take upon itself. In contrast, the French officers could not say what they were prepared to assume—not because they did not want to, but because they saw no practical way of going to war without the British.

"Our army is large but it is stuck," apologized Bourgès-Maunoury. "We have 400,000 soldiers in Algeria. Our military situation is much more complicated than during the days of Napoleon." But, he said, it was imperative then and there to look into what France could do to prepare the ground, and in particular the Israeli, armed forces for a possible joint operation. Three things needed examination: (1) what the Israeli army was capable of doing in the framework of a joint venture; (2) what supplementary equipment and war materiel the IDF needed; (3) what the Israeli military's logistic deployment was, especially the capacity of its air and naval bases. This would be important if France decided to remove its troops from Cyprus.

A proper assessment, Bourgès-Maunoury suggested, required sending a French military delegation to Israel, headed by General Challe, as quickly as possible; the political decision, after all, would ultimately also be influenced by military possibilities. Soon these inquiries would lead to a new arms transaction destined to increase the Israeli army's armored strength by another 100 tanks and by considerable quantities of other military materiel, in particular transport vehicles, which were later crucial in assuring the swift Israeli victory in the Sinai.

Like Pineau and Challe before him, Bourgès-Maunoury hinted broadly at ideas that the French had been toying with but that would be crystallized only after Challe's visit to Israel. "A *casus belli* is vital for implementing the operation, and Israel's position in this regard is much more convenient." The logical course of action, he intimated, was for Israel to engage battle on its own, thereby providing England and France with the pretext for embarking on war. Israel, however, still insisted on simultaneous action.

The next day Golda Meir met with the French prime minister, Guy Mollet, in an introductory meeting intended to strengthen mutual trust between the two countries. At the same time Moshe Dayan was meeting with General Paul Ely, France's chief of staff, and with the French officers about to leave for Israel with General Challe. Once again Dayan outlined what actions the IDF could take in the Sinai; the French could not respond in kind or indicate what role they could play in any joint venture. In reply to General Ely's question on the aid Israel wanted from France, Dayan was candid: air assistance to destroy Egyptian air power, naval assistance to paralyze the Egyptian navy, and logistical backup, especially in the area of desert mobility. "We don't know the extent of opposition we will encounter from the enemy, but the geographical expanse that we will have to cover, and the extent of resistance that we will encounter from the desert, are very clear indeed," Dayan told his counterpart. Stressing the fact that it was intended only to facilitate the operation and in no way constituted a precondition for cooperation, Dayan also enumerated IDF requests for supplementary equipment: 300 half-tracks, 100 Sherman tanks with modern guns, 50 tank carriers, 300 four-wheel-drive trucks, 1,000 bazookas, a squadron of air transport planes, and more ammunition, fuel, and general equipment. General Ely promised to look into possibilities of supplying the requested materiel from the French army stores, even though most of the equipment was already tied up for the joint effort with England and the commanders in Algeria "were submitting such lists every morning."

The participants continued to exchange operational assessments, but it was obvious that the French were still not ready to go into detail. Yet French thinking seemed to be crystallizing. Again and again the French hinted at their preference for an independent Israeli action that would furnish a casus belli for Great Britain. General Ely could not be entirely unequivocal, and Dayan wanted to eliminate any doubts the general might have regarding his own mandate. "Obviously," he said, "the best help the French can provide the Israeli army is a simultaneous attack against Egyptian targets to keep some of the Egyptian forces pinned down. . . . the main point is simultaneous action."

The St. Germain conference drew to an end. On the evening of October 1, the Israeli delegation took off for Israel—this time in the luxurious plane that President Truman had presented as a gift to General Charles de Gaulle. Also on board were General Challe and a staff of aides from all branches of the French armed forces. Despite having to wait for political developments, the officers began practical preparations for the campaign. But in the meantime the IDF was busy with other matters as well. In the east a new front had erupted. The border with Jordan had been set afire.

13
•••

THE JORDANIAN BORDER FLARES UP

Despite the international outrage and universal condemnation of Israel triggered by the killing of over 60 civilians by IDF forces during a reprisal operation against the Jordanian village of Kibiya in October 1953, the operation was instrumental in creating a prolonged pacification of the Israeli-Jordanian border. The Jordanian army had been taking harsher steps to limit infiltration from Jordan into Israel. General Glubb, commander in chief of the Arab Legion, preferred to avoid unnecessary encounters with the Israeli army and accordingly tried to lower tensions along the border. He was not always successful, however, both because the Legion command could not control everything that went on along the border and because not all the local commanders followed High Command instructions faithfully.[1] Nevertheless, an effective combination of stringent controls along the border and police action in the interior had brought about a significant decrease in the pilfering and killings from Jordanian territory in 1955 and early 1956.

But this situation changed radically in the spring of 1956 with the intensification of pan-Arab nationalism and pro-Nasserism in Jordan, which resulted in the removal of Glubb Pasha and most of the English commanders of the Arab Legion. The Jordanian army's internal discipline grew considerably more lax, as did its ability—and perhaps even desire—to maintain strict control of the extremist factions among the Palestinians on the West Bank of the Jordan River.[2] The Egyptian-Czech arms deal, and even more so the nationalization of the Suez Canal, had sent Nasser's popularity in the Arab world soaring. At the same time it spread unrest throughout the Middle East, including the cities and refugee camps of the Hashemite Kingdom of Jordan. Loyal to his king, General Radi Einab, the Legion's commander after Glubb's dismissal, did his best to follow his predecessor's policies but was soon replaced by Ali Abu-Nuwar, leader of a group of young officers eager to emulate

Nasser and turn Jordan into a nationalistic monarchy or even perhaps a republic. Ali Abu-Nuwar played a double and triple game, walking a tightrope
between formal loyalty to the king and covert promotion of Arab nationalism
that involved him in convoluted conspiracies and counterconspiracies.[3]

Egypt influenced events in Jordan in more direct ways as well. In 1955 and
early 1956, the Egyptian military attaché in Amman, Colonel Salaheddin
Mustafa, was not only active politically but also managed to set up a network of infiltrators whom he sent across the border to Israel upon instructions from the Egyptian intelligence services in Cairo. The purpose was
twofold: to strike at Israel and to provoke it into reprisals that would ultimately undermine the Jordanian regime. After Syria opened its doors to the
Soviets and espoused a pro-Egyptian political orientation, Jordan remained
the only ally of the Hashemite Kingdom of Iraq in its struggle against the
brand of Arab nationalism that Nasser promoted. The United Kingdom had
no direct economic and little military interest in Jordan but viewed King
Hussein's regime as the last support for Nuri es-Sa'id's regime in Iraq,
where the United Kingdom did have economic and strategic interests, of the
very highest sort. Egypt, occupied with the Suez crisis, sought to put a brake
on Jordan's headlong flight into the arms of Iraq. But its distance from the
scene and lack of geographical contiguity limited Egypt's direct intervention. The best card it could play was to rouse and incite the Palestinian
nationalists from within Jordan.

Thus in 1956 Jordan became a main stage for the struggle between the
Egyptian-Saudi bloc and the Hashemite bloc. To buttress the king's position
and in preparation for a general anti-Nasser offensive, which included a plan
for a pro-Iraqi coup in Syria, the British, the Jordanian court, and the authorities in Baghdad considered positioning Iraqi army units in Jordan. An Iraqi
military presence there would underpin the regime, deter Syrian intervention
in Jordan, and indicate to the population on either side of the Jordan River
that its best defense against Israel lay with the Hashemite military alliance
and not with the speeches of Nasser made from the other side of Israel.
Between June 12 and 18 a Jordanian delegation headed by General Ali Abu-
Nuwar conferred with its hosts in Baghdad and concluded an agreement for
the establishment of a joint Iraqi-Jordanian defense committee. For the time
being it was decided to send one Iraqi division to the Jordanian border, ready
to move into Jordan at a moment's notice.

The Hashemite quarrel with Egypt was reflected inside Jordan in the ideo-
logical struggle between the supporters of the regime and the pan-Arabists.
The struggle came to a head in the Jordanian parliament on June 26, 1956.
The king suspected that a coalition was about to be formed against the loyal-

ist government of Jordanian prime minister Said el-Mufti and in favor of terminating the Jordanian-British defense treaty; he therefore dispersed the parliament and scheduled new elections for the end of October.[4] The next four months would give the Jordanian king, the Iraqi prime minister, and the English government time to prepare for the future. But it was not certain who effectively ruled Jordan in the meantime, and those responsible for increasing provocations against Israel could not be readily identified nor their reasons properly analyzed. Two diametrically opposed choices presented themselves in Jordan, with advocates in either camp: an alliance with Iraq based on a pro-Western orientation, or an alliance with Egypt based on the new concept of "positive neutrality" recently enunciated by Nehro, Tito, and Nasser. Had this ideological debate actually penetrated the ranks of the Arab Legion and were the acts of hostility against Israel now a tool in this internal struggle?

Early in July, several days after the Jordanian parliament had been dispersed, the situation along the Israeli-Jordanian border deteriorated even more. On July 9 two Israelis were murdered near Ein Yahav on the main road to Eilat and an Israeli tractor driver was killed by a freshly laid land mine near Afula in the north. On July 14 a young Israeli was murdered by a Jordanian patrol not far from the international airport in Lod, with clear signs that the Arab Legion had a hand in it.[5] And on July 25 a serious incident took plaçe just outside Jerusalem near the main highway to Tel Aviv, as Jordanian National Guardsmen opened fire across the border on Israeli farmers trying to reclaim some land on the Israeli side.[6] Despite a formal nighttime curfew in the villages along the border, and despite the Jordanian National Guard's instructions to open fire on anyone attempting to cross the frontier into Israel, there seemed to be evidence of collusion between the Jordanian military and the irregular infiltrators. It appeared that the Jordanian command was not being strict enough about aggressive initiatives from Jordanian territory. Thus it was hard for Israeli intelligence to pinpoint who and what had escalated the deterioration along the border: Were pro-Nasser factions exploiting the disintegration of the central regime in Amman, or were shadowy figures from high up in the Jordanian government itself pulling the strings? Was it just the Egyptian attaché alone, or did he have allies in the royal palace or Arab Legion headquarters?

The deteriorating situation created a twofold problem for Israel. It had to try to force the Jordanian regime to take effective steps to prevent the violent infiltrations, but in terms of long-term defense requirements, Israel could not permit Iraqi forces to be positioned in Jordan. That might dangerously tip the balance of power along Israel's eastern border and curtail the military maneuverability Israel enjoyed by forcing it to station additional troops permanently in this sensitive sector.

The strategy of reprisals adopted by Israel's security establishment since the early 1950s was intended to cope with the first issue of security along the borders. In this case, however, it stood in direct opposition to the strategy needed to cope with the problem of long-term defense. Increased Jordanian fears of the "Israeli danger" in the wake of intensified reprisals was liable to provide the king and the Iraqis with convincing arguments, and even a convenient international pretext, for positioning Iraqi units in Jordan.[7] But Ben-Gurion and Dayan were not ready to prevent Iraqi penetration at the cost of aggravating Jordanian incursions across the border. If reprisals did trigger an Iraqi penetration, Israel would meet this challenge when the time came. Ben-Gurion had doubted the wisdom of occupying the West Bank at the end of the 1948 war and certainly did not favor such a move now[8]; however, if Iraqi forces entered Jordan, he was prepared to take countermeasures, such as occupying the Hebron Hills or limited parts of the northern suburbs of Jerusalem in order to form an unbroken connection with the Israeli enclave on Mount Scopus.

But an even more fundamental question was at issue. Internal developments in Jordan over the preceding year had provoked fears that the kingdom might succumb entirely to inter-Arab pressures from within and without and from mounting Palestinian nationalism. What measures would Israel have to take if indeed the Hashemite Kingdom collapsed and the race began for the division of the spoils? Those summer months saw Ben-Gurion often engrossed in thoughts concerning this possibility and the dilemma it presented for Israel.[9]

When the Jordanian border had begun to flare up in the summer of 1956, Moshe Dayan had recommended restraint and temperance in order to prevent even the least complication that might jeopardize the flow of French arms. To be on the safe side, however, Ben-Gurion had asked the government for authority to employ the IDF against Jordan if the murders continued.[10] The hostilities from the Jordanian side of the border continued throughout August and early September, until Ben-Gurion felt that the situation had become unbearable. On September 10 an incident occurred that was the final straw that broke the camel's back. Six Israeli students were shot and killed in a desolate area near the border west of Hebron by Jordanian villagers and National Guardsmen. "We must land them a blow tonight that will take away their taste for any more confrontations," Dayan told Ben-Gurion in an urgent consultation.[11] On the night of September 10 Israeli commandos crossed the border and assaulted the er-Rahaweh Jordanian police station in the southern section of the Hebron Hills. Over 20 Jordanian soldiers were killed and the police station blown up.[12] In an unconnected action that same night, Jordanian infiltrators killed three Israeli Druse guarding an oil-drilling installation in the south. On September 13 the Israeli commandos again entered Jordan and took over the Gharandal police station deep inside Jordanian territory, not far from the Nabatean ruins of Petra.[13]

Unfortunately, circumstances in Jordan at the time prevented the reprisal operations from "taking away the taste for any more confrontations." Israel's intention was to force Jordan into choosing one of two options: either escalating the cycle of hostility and risking further and even more painful blows, perhaps full-scale warfare, or cooling down the border. The relative quiet along the Jordanian border in 1954-1955 was proof of the relative utility of the reprisals. But they could be effective only when the Jordanian government was willing and capable of exerting control over its population. When it lost its authority and its ability to prevent hostile initiatives, the reprisals lost their efficacy. Even if King Hussein wanted to curtail the border incursions, domestic intrigues in the higher ranks of the Jordanian regime in the summer of 1956 apparently constrained him from imposing his will on those in the military and civilian population who wanted to keep the border simmering.

Furthermore, the reprisals furnished Hussein with a pretext for carrying through his plan of bringing the Iraqis into Jordan. On September 15, two days after the operation in Gharandal, Hussein flew to Iraq and met with his cousin, King Feisal of Iraq, at Habaniyeh airport to discuss stationing an Iraqi army unit in Jordan. The Arab News Agency announced that the two had reached "an agreement on a joint plan to withstand Israeli aggression."[14] The planned Iraqi military presence was actually intended to prevent a pro-Nasser coup in Jordan and bring home to the population, who feared a general Israeli attack, that only Iraq, and not Nasser, could defend the kingdom. Israeli reprisals served Hussein's purposes well.

At this stage Dayan was eager to reduce tensions along the border. On September 21, he issued an operational order to reduce friction with the enemy to a minimum: "Against the background of the Western-Arab conflict on the Suez and after our reprisals, we must do our best to avoid border incidents. GHQ intends to limit border patrols to the absolute minimum need to protect the settlements, their property and residents."[15]

On September 22, however, Arab Legion soldiers stationed near the Mar Elias Monastery south of Jerusalem suddenly opened machine-gun fire on a group of amateur archeologists visiting a dig in the ruins near Kibbutz Ramat Rachel across the valley from the Jordanian position. Four Israelis were killed and some 20 injured. This was the most serious incident inside Jerusalem in four years. Through the U.N., the Jordanians sent a message that the shooting had been started by a soldier who had gone berserk in the wake of his brother's death in the er-Rahaweh operation. Israel was not convinced by the explanation and would not accede to requests to cooperate in the inquiry into the soldier's alleged mental derangement. In the following two days another two incidents took place. A mother and her daughter were gathering wood not far from their home in a village west of Jerusalem when they were set upon by a group of infiltrators; the daughter was killed. That same day a tractor driver in the fields of a kibbutz near Beit She'an in the north was murdered and his body dragged over the border to disguise the infiltrators' tracks. Ben-Gurion cabled Dayan: "Strong action is needed."[16]

Ben-Gurion and Dayan had originally considered a large-scale operation in the southern part of the Hebron Hills,[17] but Shimon Peres had that day returned from Paris with the invitation to the St. Germain conference. The operation was therefore scaled down, and on the night of September 25 Israeli paratroops attacked the area west of Bethlehem. One commando battalion, commanded by Raphael Eitan (in later years an IDF chief of staff), attacked the Hussan police station and set up roadblocks to the east, while a second one, commanded by Mordechai Gur (who would also rise to the rank of chief of staff in the future), attacked the Jordanian National Guard outpost near the border to open a road for the supply of explosives needed to blow up the police station and allow the first battalion to retreat. The operation succeeded and the missions were fully accomplished, but with greater difficulty than had been anticipated and at a very high cost in human lives. The first battalion penetrated into the area without much difficulty, blew up the police station, and ambushed a convoy of Arab Legion reinforcements attempting to reach the battle site. But the second battalion encountered fierce resistance. Six Israeli soldiers were killed in the course of the battle, and another four died in a road accident during the fighting.[18] Although 40 Jordanians were killed, the Israelis had also lost 10 men, and the taste of victory was bitter. Doubts began to be voiced about the IDF's ability to withstand the accelerating cycle of reprisals, repeatedly asked to take military outposts and engage in hand-to-hand combat with the well-trained regular Jordanian army. Would the cost in human lives become unbearable?

As could have been expected, the Jordanian foreign minister, Auni Bey Abdul-Hadi, rushed to Baghdad the next day and requested immediate military aid. But the Iraqis first wanted to learn if the British were willing to honor their commitment to defend Jordan against Israeli attack, if such attack was provoked by the penetration of Iraqi troops into Jordan. In his diary Ben-Gurion noted an item from an intelligence report stating that Iraq's prime minister Nuri es-Sa'id "does not want to send an army to Jordan if he is not certain that, in the event of an Israeli attack, England will assist the Jordanian and Iraqi forces with a naval blockade, air support, and the supply of ammunition."[19]

Since the beginning of the year, Britain had indeed been considering its undertaking to defend Jordan in the event of Israeli attack. At the end of January 1956 Selwyn Lloyd sent Anthony Eden a memo in which he discussed the implication of that undertaking. There was widespread feeling in the Middle East, Lloyd wrote, that Great Britain does not seriously intend to support the Arab countries if Israel attacks them. This feeling undermines the credibility of British policies in the region in general, and thus Britain must honor its commitments. "Our credit in the Middle East will be irretrievably lost if there is an Israeli attack on an Arab country and H.M. Government takes no early visible action to help the Arabs."[20] The British chiefs of staff had prepared operational plans against Israel. In his memo Lloyd noted that they included the dispatch of British land and air forces to the aid of Jordan, but he added that the Joint Chiefs of Staff had indicated that dispatch of reinforcements to Jordan would first necessitate neutralization of the Israeli air force by bombing its airfields.

General Glubb, who still commanded the Arab Legion at the time, made a far-reaching suggestion, proposing that the Legion be permitted to take advantage of an Israeli assault against any Arab state to attack Israel with British naval and air assistance and to take over those areas that the Alpha Plan had designated for the Arabs.[21] After Glubb's dismissal, the Jordanians announced that they were no longer interested in having British land forces stationed on Jordanian soil. The new British plan, code-named Cordage, was intended to assist Arab forces by attacking Israeli bases from the air, laying a naval siege and attacking Israeli naval bases from the sea.[22] On September 19 the British Cabinet's Egypt Committee deliberated the Jordanian and Iraqi request for clarifications of the British undertaking and empowered the foreign secretary to reassure them that England would honor its commitments to come to Jordan's aid if attacked by Israel.[23]

By the beginning of October the die seemed to have been cast. The Arab press announced the establishment of a joint Jordanian-Iraqi command headed by an Iraqi officer. At the request of the British, the U.S. ambassador in Israel visited Ben-Gurion and delivered formal notice on the imminent entry of Iraqi forces into Jordan. The ambassador spoke of "a token force" that would enter the East Bank and would not cross the Jordan River, adding that the U.S. government supported this step and calling on Israel to refrain from disturbances.[24] In a moment of weakness Ben-Gurion acceded to Ambassador Lawson's request, telling him that "so long as Jordan continued to exist and did not go to war against us, we will not lift a finger." And if Iraq indeed sent only a token force to Jordan and it remained on the East Bank, Israel would not oppose these measures.[25] But upon reflection, Ben-Gurion and Golda Meir began to suspect a plot to divide the spoils subsequent to the collapse of the Jordanian regime. Should that occur, Israel could not sit by quietly. The Israeli Foreign Ministry therefore quickly cabled Washington with added clarifications on Ben-Gurion's consent, now making it conditional on receipt of various guarantees. The meaning was clear: Israel was in fact fundamentally opposed to the emplacement of Iraqi forces in Jordan.[26]

But Ambassador Lawson's notice had been premature. On October 5 it became known that the Baghdad talks had sputtered out in the face of obstacles raised by Jordanian chief of staff Abu-Nuwar, whether for issues of personal prestige or because his true loyalty was to Egypt.[27] The Palestinians in Jordan, and even the officers of the Arab Legion, opposed the Iraqi plan, and Abu-Nuwar threw his weight behind them. The king had no choice but to give in to the combined pressure of the officers and the Palestinians. He decided to approach Nasser, King Saud, and President Shukri Kuwatly of Syria with a request for immediate military aid. This time the Jordanian foreign minister would have to go to Cairo, Riyadh, and Damascus.

✳ ✳ ✳

Escalating tensions along the Jordanian border also aggravated relations between Israel and the U.N. administration, and especially between Ben-Gurion and Dag Hammarskjöld. The quarrel now centered on U.N. demands for the placement of observers at sensitive points along the border, their freedom of movement, and Israel's right to take reprisal actions. In light of the Jordanian hostilities, Israel no longer saw itself bound by its April obligation to Hammarskjöld to unconditionally uphold the cease-fire article of the Armistice Agreements. Israel claimed that complying with the agreement could not be a unilateral obligation imposed on it alone. Citing the right to self-defense as defined in the U.N. Charter, Israel also insisted on its right to take reprisal actions; the U.N., however, did not accept Israel's view and continued to oppose retaliation operations.[28]

Not only Israel and the U.N. were in disagreement over the right to retaliate. The Security Council's adamant denial of a country's right to engage in reprisals did not accurately reflect international customary law, where the issue was unresolved and unsettled. Many international legal experts also disagreed with the Security Council on this issue. George Schwarzenberger, one of the greatest jurists of our time, has said in his discussion of the *status mixtus* between war and peace that, under certain circumstances, a state has the right to engage in retaliatory action: "Once one has transgressed the borderline into 'status mixtus,' it has handed over the choice of patterns [of retaliation] to the state against which such compulsory measures, short of war, are applied."[29]

Small wonder that the dispute between Hammarskjöld and Ben-Gurion also remained unresolved. The U.N. secretary general fell back on the Security Council resolutions, while Ben-Gurion insisted on what he saw as the right of every nation to protect itself and its citizens.

Only a few days after Hammarskjöld returned from his last tour of the Middle East in July, an angry exchange of letters began between him and Ben-Gurion. As the secretary general had promised, he sent Israel's prime minister a detailed report on his talks in Amman and Cairo, in which the Jordanian authorities had promised to take measures to cool down the border; even the Egyptians were interested in curtailing tensions. Therefore, he wrote, he now demanded of Israel as well that it strictly abide by the cease-fire.[30]

In his reply, Ben-Gurion did not hide his disappointment. He retorted that in Cairo Hammarskjöld had not even raised the issue of the Suez and Tiran blockades and challenged his assessment of Egyptian intentions. He compared Hammarskjöld's faith in Egypt to Austin Chamberlain's naive statement in the British Parliament during the Abyssinian crisis, to the effect that

Mussolini was a gentleman and therefore incapable of lying.[31] Hammarskjöld's reply was long and evidently bristling with affront: "Indeed you seem to imply that I permit myself to be fooled." He denied that he was acting out of bias and ended on a positive note: "I hope that [your approach] will provide a basis for a broadened trustful cooperation between your Government and those servants of the United Nations whose only aim in the region is to help in the preservation of peace."[32]

In August and September, however, the tone of the letters became less forgiving. "We have not been able in the last few months to register much of a cooperative attitude from your side in relation to our efforts," Hammarskjöld wrote Ben-Gurion in August.[33] Ben-Gurion bitterly replied, "You understand so much—can you not also understand that, for us, this is a matter of life and death?"[34] Early in September Ben-Gurion bluntly told General Burns:

> I doubt the value of the U.N. observers at all and I don't know if it is worth while going to them with complaints. Condemnations mean nothing to our neighbors, and those who have been murdered, are murdered! . . . If the U.N. cannot force the Arabs to live with us in peace, on the basis of its own Charter, then don't bother us with well-meaning but useless observers.[35]

Hammarskjöld told Israel's U.N. representative, Reggie Kidron, "It is now clear that the Prime Minister does not want to cooperate with the U.N. except in certain matters which can promote Israel's interests."[36]

After the reprisals at er-Rahaweh and Gharandal, Hammarskjöld publicly addressed the Israeli U.N. delegation with the demand for an immediate halt to the burgeoning cycle of violence. In a personal letter to Ben-Gurion he wrote, sadly but unflinchingly, "I am not happy with this continued negotiating by letters where the difference of the laws under which we have to act . . . must be brought out with full clarity, partially outside their general setting. This may create the impression of a widening gulf between us."[37] At this point, fearful that Hammarskjöld's formal report to the Security Council might blame Israel for the failure of the secretary general's efforts to cool down tensions, Abba Eban implored Israel's foreign minister, Golda Meir, "to reach a 'cease-fire' in our relations with Hammarskjöld." He recommended a few concessions, at least in the ongoing quarrel over the status of the U.N. observers: ". . . the main problem is not making a precise evaluation of Hammarskjöld's personality and his feelings on us. . . . we must endeavor rather to achieve clear and effective results."[38]

But events in the field were stronger than any intentions at compromise and reconciliation. Hostilities from across the Jordanian border seethed too strongly for Israel to give up reprisal raids. These raids constituted the main form of its struggle against violent infiltration even though it was the major point of dissension between Israel and the U.N. After the Hussan operation Hammarskjöld gave up trying to persuade Israel by letter. He concluded his correspondence with Ben-Gurion on a bitter note:

> You are convinced that the threat of retaliation has a deterrent effect. I am convinced that it is more of an incitement to individual members of the Arab forces. . . . You are convinced that acts of retaliation will stop further incidents. I am convinced that they will lead to further incidents. You believe that this way of creating respect for Israel will pave the way for sound coexistence, while I believe your policy will push off coexistence with the Arab people. . . . I think the discussion of this question can be considered closed since you, in spite of previous discouraging experiences, have taken the responsibility for large-scale tests of the correctness of your belief.[39]

Ben-Gurion too was tired of the game: "I wrote Hammarskjöld a reply to his last two letters," he wrote in his diary. "I hope that our correspondence ends after this letter."[40] In what was his last letter to the U.N. secretary general, he came very close to denying the validity of the Armistice Agreements: "After these years of violations of these Agreements by the other parties, we could not be expected to regard them as binding on us alone."[41] A few days later Hammarskjöld finally ended the exchange with a last reaction to Ben-Gurion's final letter: "Let that letter be the last word in this phase of our contact."[42]

In that same letter Hammarskjöld tried frankly to explain the main reason for the failure of the dialogue between them. Their points of departure, he wrote, were entirely different, as befitted their different roles and the different responsibilities they bore. It was thus impossible to expect the U.N. secretary general to acknowledge the legitimacy of Israel's acts of reprisal, just as the Israeli prime minister couldn't be expected to relinquish the right to engage in such acts, a right that he viewed as vital to the existence of the state at whose head he stood and for whose citizens' safety and security he was responsible.

The report on his Middle East efforts that Hammarskjöld then submitted to the Security Council was to a great extent an indictment of Israel. Although he accused all parties of failing to comply with their April commitment to eschew cease-fire violations, his resentment at Israel's refusal to cooperate with him was evident. His final verdict seemed balanced: "The Governments of the region . . . failed to carry through the discipline sufficiently firmly to forestall incidents which, step by step, must necessarily undermine the cease-fire." But between the lines it was clear that his criticism was for the most part aimed at Israel.[43]

Ben-Gurion gave back as good as he got. He took the opportunity to settle accounts in a political message to the Knesset. After enumerating one after the other all the attacks on Israeli citizens over the past few months, he said,

> I do not accuse the U.N. representatives of bearing us ill will. But it is obvious that they are ineffectual in forcing our neighbors to honor their promise. The chain of murders continues. We have no choice but to act in self-defense. . . . whoever disqualifies Israel's 'acts of reprisal' also denies Israel the right to self-defense . . . and gives murderers free rein.

Ben-Gurion criticized the U.N. severely:

> The U.N. administration has long exhibited a tendency to turn the Armistice Agreements between ourselves and our neighbors into a unilateral obligation on the part of Israel toward the U.N., thereby effectively absolving the other signatory nations of their obligations towards Israel. . . . UNTSO has a tendency to treat Israel as if it were international territory. . . . We must firmly and clearly tell the world and our neighbors that the Armistice Agreements were signed between ourselves and our Arab neighbors, not between ourselves and the U.N.[44]

Fortunately for Israel, the Suez crisis was preoccupying most of the world at the time and the secretary general's damning report drew little attention. In any event, within only a few days a storm would break that would sweep it from everyone's notice. In it Israel would stand alongside Great Britain and France in a much harsher and more dramatic confrontation with the U.N. Ben-Gurion had suspected Hammarskjöld's true motives and biases. In July the prime minister had written in his diary, "There is reason to believe that Hammarskjöld considers the founding of the State of Israel a political mistake."[45] In mid-October he wrote, "I have gotten hold of Hammarskjöld's letter to Burns of September 19, 1956, in which he reveals himself clearly as an anti-Semite."[46] But Ben-Gurion did not have time to press the issue any further, and the Jordanian border continued to seethe.

✳ ✳ ✳

The abortive Jordanian-Iraqi association and Hussein's decision to hitch up to Nasser's wagon did not halt the border incidents. On the night of October 5 a band of infiltrators ambushed and killed five Israeli laborers on the road from Sodom to Beersheba. Israel's GHQ proposed a large-scale operation against the Jordanian village of Safi south of the Dead Sea, but in light of the contacts with the French, Ben-Gurion wrote Dayan, "I have been considering the Sodom affair for the past two days. . . . I seriously doubt that it is advisable to undertake any action at all this time. . . . I do not think Eden will approve of the Cyprus operation . . . but it is not advisable to provide him with any pretext at all for shirking the operation." Dayan accepted the defense minister's views and after the St. Germain talks even proposed that no raids be carried out until October 20, "unless things go too far."[47] Only two days later, however, they really did go too far. Deep inside Israeli territory, in an orchard near the Tel Aviv–Haifa highway, two laborers were murdered by a band of Jordanian infiltrators.[48] It was obvious that the killers had been well trained. The fact that the victims' ears had been cut off indicated that the infiltrators needed to bring back proof of their "kill," all in all suggesting that an organization was behind it.

On the night of October 10-11, the Israeli army again sent the commandos into action. The target this time was the Kalkiliya police station. Dawn broke over what was the bloodiest and bitterest battle the Israeli forces had fought since the end of the 1948 war. The mission was completed; about 70 Jordanians were killed. But the death of 17 Israeli paratroopers in battle tempered the victory. The target itself had been easily taken after a heavy artillery barrage in the light of large naval searchlights; but the unit sent to block the access routes to the east ended up having to fight. Due to the large number of casualties it suffered, reinforcements were sent to enable its retreat. From the outset Ariel Sharon, who commanded the operation, had wanted to capture the Hirbet Sufin outpost east of Kalkiliya to create convenient access for joining the holding force and to ensure the operation's flanks. But Dayan feared that the fight for the well-fortified outpost would result in a large number of casualties and therefore vetoed that plan. His decision was proved wrong: The IDF forces had to break through the untaken outpost on half-tracks, one of which overturned. More soldiers were injured trying to rescue it, and as the hours passed, the fear grew that the troops would not be retrieved before morning. Dayan ordered war planes into the air, a tank unit called up from the south, and a diversionary attack prepared in the area of Jenin. But the battle ended before dawn and the precautionary measures proved unnecessary.[49]

As the battle raged, King Hussein began to suspect that the Israeli army was planning to enlarge its scope. He turned to his British allies with a demand for intervention. "Our help had been called for and our aircraft were on the point of going up," Eden wrote in his memoirs.[50] The day after Kalkiliya, the British chargé d'affaires in Israel, Peter Westlake, informed

Ben-Gurion that an Iraqi division was about to enter Jordan and that England would help Jordan if Israel intervened.[51] The next day Israel's foreign minister made a formal announcement: ". . . it is clear that the entry of Iraqi units into Jordan is part of a conspiracy to promote Iraq's territorial aspirations and to effect far-reaching changes in the regional *status quo*. . . . The Government of Israel is determined to confront this threat."[52] And on October 15, Ben-Gurion told the Knesset, "There seems to be a new plan afoot to annex Jordan to Iraq. . . . The Government of Israel shall retain her freedom of action if the *status quo* is breached and a foreign military force enters Jordan."[53] War on Israel's eastern borders seemed imminent.

Once again, however, the announcement proved premature. The British Foreign Office informed its ambassador in Tel Aviv that, because of disagreements over the command and for other reasons as well, for the time being the Iraqi division would be stationed near the Jordanian border in the area of the H-3 pumping station along the old Iraqi oil pipeline.[54] But Ben-Gurion remained suspicious of Britain. He was convinced it was plotting serious changes in the region, and he also expected that the forthcoming Jordanian parliamentary elections would bring the current Jordanian regime to an end. Anxious to prevent a pro-Nasser coalition from coming to power, Britain wanted its ally Iraq to have a ruling hand in the disintegrating kingdom. Britain would disregard Israel in these considerations and was unheedful of its vital security needs.[55] Moreover, Ben-Gurion was convinced that Great Britain would not hesitate to take any opportunity to prove its loyalty to the Arabs by blocking, and even harming, Israel.

At this point events in the Jordanian-Iraqi arena intersected with developments in the Egyptian imbroglio. On October 16 Ben-Gurion was informed of the new plan that had emerged from Anglo-French talks held earlier that day: Israel would provide its European allies with a pretext for going to war by unilaterally initiating hostilities against Egypt in the Sinai. Now Ben-Gurion's suspicions of England grew stronger: "I think," he told Dayan, "that the British are plotting to get us entangled with Nasser to facilitate Iraq's conquest of Jordan."[56] Ben-Gurion's fears were concrete enough for him to order immediate preparations for an operation to take over the northern suburbs of Jordanian Jerusalem in order to connect the Israeli enclave on Mount Scopus with the rest of Israeli Jerusalem.

England's ambassador in Tel Aviv recommended that the British Foreign Office take steps to allay Ben-Gurion's suspicions. He conceded that additional efforts were needed to persuade Israel that Britain was acting "in good faith and with no ulterior motives."[57] But the reassurances were useless, and as he departed for the Sèvres conference for discussions of the joint British-French-Israeli operation against Egypt, Ben-Gurion was bursting with resentment and suspicions against Britain. On the eve of the historic meeting, the psychological and political breach between Israel and the United Kingdom was as great as it had ever been since the Israeli air force downed four RAF planes over Sinai in January 1949. Conscious of the complications involved, the Israeli officers wondered if they would end up fighting alongside Great Britain in the Sinai or against it in the northern suburbs of Jerusalem.

The Kalkiliya operation had also increased tensions between America and Israel. The Americans obviously supported the "Iraqi" plan and joined Britain in an attempt to deter Israel from initiating hostilities. On October 15 Eisenhower and Dulles had conferred, and the latter recommended taking a firm stand against Israel. Although the presidential election campaign was in full swing and Eisenhower understood well the impact such a stand could have on the election results, he nonetheless approved Dulles's recommendations

> It would be a shame . . . if the American leadership should make its decisions on any basis other than what was right and other than what was our overall national interest. . . . if any votes were lost as a result of this attitude, that was a situation that would have to be confronted, but any other attitude will not permit us to live with our conscience.[58]

Had Eisenhower made that statement publicly, it might have changed the course of events, for it clearly presaged America's later response to the joint British-French-Israeli action in the Sinai and Suez. Even then Washington's signals were not particularly ambiguous, but the three allies failed to pay enough attention to the American attitude. Thus began the parting of ways between the United States and its allies on the other side of the Atlantic, and events hurtled on along another track entirely.

A troubling malaise enveloped the Israeli Command in the wake of Kalkiliya: Did this operation signal the end of reprisals? Beyond the grief at the loss of life, the raid left heavy doubts in the minds of the IDF commanders on the very value of reprisals and the way they were carried out. The method had been a bone of contention among the Israeli leadership in the early 1950s when they were first implemented. For Ben-Gurion they were first and foremost a means of deterring the Arabs from escalating hostilities. Ben-Gurion had once explained in the Knesset that

> Even penalties for murder which are acceptable all over the world don't stop the
> murders. But without any punishment, all control would be lost, and masses of peo-
> ple would be murdered. Punishment deters. . . . retaliation does not stop attacks
> entirely—but, like any punishment, it deters many. And who knows how many lives
> have been saved thanks to these reprisals.[59]

In contrast, Sharett, who understood that sometimes there was no other
choice and who, as prime minister, had even authorized several, saw the
reprisals first and foremost as a function of the emotional need to release
anger rather than as actions vital to the nation's security needs. Referring to
a General Staff reprisal recommendation, he wrote in his diary:

> I pulled the reins in too tight . . . for the army and the public both. . . . It is clear that
> the murder has brought things to a boil and that the anger must be discharged. This is
> the only logic; there is no other. But I do not believe that the reprisal as such will
> help in terms of security; to the contrary, I am very fearful that it may serve as the
> first blow in a new round of bloodshed on the frontier.[60]

Sharett referred to the paratroopers, privately, as "Israel's tool of collective
revenge."[61]

Dayan's view was firmly opposed to Sharett's. "A reprisal is not an act
of revenge. It is a punishment and deterrence. It is meant to signal that if a
Government does not control its people and does not prevent them from
hurting Israel, Israel's army will wreak havoc in that country."[62] Like Ben-
Gurion, Dayan viewed the reprisals as a means of deterrence. He knew that
it was not the individual raids themselves that deterred but rather their
cumulative effect, which evoked fears that they might escalate into full-
scale warfare. Dayan was led by his conviction that no passive, defensive
method could prevent the infiltrators from their incursions: Israel's borders
were long and porous and could not be hermetically sealed. "It is not difficult for an Arab to stroll around Tel Aviv for a year," he told Ben-Gurion.
"[I]t is not difficult for an Arab to walk into the Knesset today, say that he
wants a meeting with the Minister of Defense or the Prime Minister, take a
card from the information desk, gain entry, shoot, and go home."[63] And in a
special address to officers, which he ordered published in the IDF monthly
review, he said, "We cannot keep every waterpipe from being blown up or
every tree from being uprooted. We cannot prevent laborers from being
murdered in the citrus groves or families from being killed in their sleep.
But we can exact a high price for our blood, one too high for the Arab
Governments to pay."[64]

Dayan also considered the reprisals important in reinforcing general
deterrence.

> Indirectly the reprisal operations serve as a demonstration of the overall Arab-Israeli balance of power. . . . when the Egyptians fail to declare war on Israel in the wake of the Gaza operation, it means . . . that they are not strong enough to beat Israel. . . . Our victories and our defeats in minor battles along and across the border are very important . . . because of their impact on the Arab assessment of Israel's strength—and on Israel's belief in her own strength.[65]

In addition, Dayan believed that these operations served an educational purpose for the Israeli army and helped train and prepare it as a fighting body. The IDF's repeated tactical defeats in the years preceding his appointment as chief of staff, especially in 1953, worried Dayan very much. He saw the main thrust of his task as chief of staff in re-forming the Israeli armed forces into a fighting unit.[66] Any number of measures were needed; reprisals were central.

But all these considerations of course depended on keeping down the costs that the IDF was being asked to pay in the course of the reprisals. The heavy losses in the Hussan and Kalkiliya operations tested the system sorely. The restrictions that the army had imposed on itself since the end of 1953 to engage only in attacking military targets, as well as the experience the Arab Legion seemed to have gained, made the process of slow escalation too expensive and untenable from Israel's point of view. If entire villages could be destroyed, if the armored corps, the artillery and airplanes could be engaged without any limit, if territory could be held on to even after dawn, Dayan argued, then things would be different.

> This situation of neither war nor peace could not continue. We had to force our Arab neighbors to choose between putting an end to the terror against Israel or going to war against us. We could do this in one of two ways: either implementing reprisals during the daylight hours, using planes and armor, or crossing the border and taking key positions and making their return dependent on the cessation of terror.[67]

As they were carried out at that time, Dayan told Ben-Gurion, the reprisals forced the units to engage repeatedly in the hardest stage of warfare, that of breaching the first line of enemy strongholds. Political constraints precluded ever going over to the second stage of benefitting from the success gained in the first stage.[68] During the first half of the 1950s the reprisals were an IDF attempt to develop a limited deterrence tactic in the ambiguous political situation of neither war nor peace that had been created. Kalkiliya proved that it was hard for the Israeli army to maneuver in such a situation. The political situation had to be changed fundamentally so that it was no longer ambiguous—either war or peace. Although the decision to embark on the Sinai campaign was for the most part a function of the relations between Israel and Egypt, the dismay generated by Kalkiliya had a considerable impact on the decision as well as on the military and political planning it entailed. It facilitated the decision makers' resolve to go for broke.

14
∎ ∎ ∎

GENERAL CHALLE'S SCENARIO

The plane that brought Golda Meir and her delegation back to Israel on October 2, 1956, also carried a mission of French general staff officers from all the military branches, headed by General Maurice Challe and Louis Mangin. This delegation was sent by Prime Minister Guy Mollet to ascertain Israel's military capabilities[1] and to determine what weapons and other military equipment Israel needed that France could supply in time for a war initiative. In the course of their two days in the country, the officers were also expected to examine whether Israeli bases could accommodate French troops, should they be stationed in Israel, and whether Israel could furnish logistic aid during the first stages of the joint action, until military supplies arrived from France.[2]

To ensure secrecy, only a small group of senior Israeli staff officers had contact with the French delegation. "We must do everything possible to create trust and cooperation," Dayan instructed the group. "[W]e must be frank and ready to provide any help and full partnership. We must remember that this is our only ally who offers Israel a helping hand in our solitude and duress, and does so not for philanthropic motivations."[3] Relations between the Israeli officers and their guests warmed quickly, and the French were open in their admiration for Israel's daring war plans.[4] On the very first evening of the visit, General Challe cabled Paris and approved the immediate dispatch of the equipment requested by the Israeli delegation during the St. Germain conference. It would be some time before it arrived, and war might break out in the meantime, but Israel would probably need the equipment even after hostilities began.

Golda Meir and the other members of her delegation went straight from the airport to Ben-Gurion's Jerusalem bureau to deliver a detailed report on their Paris talks. That same evening the prime minister assembled an extended group of government ministers for consultation; Ben-Gurion elaborated on the considerations for and against embarking on a military operation with France, putting them in writing in order to clarify things for the ministers and for himself:

> . . . If we are attacked, we must defend ourselves no matter what, without any reservations and with all our strength, because it is a question of life and death. . . . We must not ignore future Arab plots to attack us; the Egyptian tyrant is no doubt biding his time, waiting for the right moment to fall upon Israel and eradicate her. We cannot say "sufficient unto the day is the evil thereof"—it might be too late; we must constantly be on the alert and look for friends wherever we can. . . . Obviously friendship is not one-sided. For this reason we cannot make light of our French friends' plans and proposals. But we must make sure that the profit does not end in loss, and here the loss is not of money but of life, and perhaps of existence itself. . . . I see several serious negatives in the plan, should our friends end up alone with only our help to rely on. (a) There is no assurance . . . that the [Egyptian] tyrant will be eliminated and another Government installed in his place. Obviously, foreign rule in Egypt is out of the question. . . . Nasser can organize guerrillas throughout his country or the neighboring ones and continue the war. And it is very doubtful that our friends can withstand a protracted struggle. . . . We must also not ignore the possibility of "volunteers" from Russia. . . . (b) Without England's participation . . . [the French] must act from inside Israel. This means that we are the initiators. The result: our cities and military installations will be bombed. . . . Our representatives took the correct stand in their talks with our friends—that they must destroy the enemy's air installations during the initial stage, with our army moving in afterwards. . . . (c) Our friends may be correct in saying that the most propitious time is before elections in the United States. . . . [but this is true only] if the English are also involved. . . . There is no guarantee that the U.S. will be as forthcoming with its considerations if our friends act alone, and America's opposition or ill will may cause us much harm. (d) If the English participate, some Arabs may . . . rejoice at the tyrant's downfall and not take serious steps to aid him. This will not be the case if our friends act alone with only our assistance and from within Israel. In that case we may find ourselves— and ourselves alone—facing a united front of all the neighboring states without any guarantee of world support. . . . I believe we must openly and honestly say these things to our friends.[5]

Ben-Gurion's major motivations and concerns are revealed here, helping us understand the decisions he would take in the coming days. Two of his four central considerations impelled him to accede to the French approach. First, he was convinced of Nasser's hostile intentions toward Israel and certain that a military confrontation would sooner or later be unavoidable. It was hard to resist the temptation to confront Nasser under what were very advantageous conditions for Israel. Second, French-Israeli friendship was a political and security asset of the highest order that could not be lightly forfeited or jeopardized. Ben-Gurion believed every effort had to be made to ensure France's interests so that this friendship could be maintained and cultivated.

On the other side of the balance sheet were two major reservations. The first was the prime minister's fear that many lives would be lost in battle and his concern at the amount of destruction Egypt's 50 new jet bombers could do. The second was his concern that a French-Israeli operation in which Great Britain did not participate would entail serious international difficulties. Only ten months earlier the Israeli government's concern for American opposition and possible British military intervention against Israel had led it to forgo the option of a preventive war against Egypt. The United Kingdom's participation in the planned operation thus seemed vital to Ben-Gurion to obviate British hostility, neutralize Washington, and placate some of the Arab states as well. Only when these two problems had been resolved— when British participation in the operation had been guaranteed and the threat of Egyptian bombing of Israeli strategic and civilian targets considerably reduced—only then would Ben-Gurion let the two positive considerations move him to accede to the French request.

Ben-Gurion openly raised his doubts before Maurice Challe and Louis Mangin; they could not allay his fears, as they too were not convinced that the French-Israeli plan could be implemented before Britain's active participation was guaranteed.

Doubts notwithstanding, the possibility of a joint enterprise now became very real. The St. Germain discussions and the talks with the French delegation in Israel made it obvious to Dayan that full-scale preparations for war had to begin immediately, as tremendous efforts had to be expended in order for Israel to perform its role in any plan that might be concluded. With Ben-Gurion's approval Dayan summoned the Israeli High Command to his bureau on October 3 and shared the secret with his generals, effectively putting the Israeli army on the alert for war: On some date after October 20, Israel might open full-scale hostilities against the Egyptian army in the Sinai. This possibility required taking immediate steps: Information on enemy deployment had to be updated; all operational planning had to be reexamined and battle orders adjusted in light of the new equipment and recent developments in the forces' deployment; equipment and ammunition had to be moved to staging positions near the front; battle gear had to be issued to all units, which had to be readied for war; regular army units and reserve units on active duty had to be placed on full alert; the civilian home front had to be prepared to absorb bombing from the air. "The knowledge that war had to be prepared for was like an electric current," Dayan wrote in his memoirs. "[T]hose present at the meeting were already heart and soul on the battlefront. The highest echelons of the Israeli army sat around the table. ... They knew what that order meant, but not only were they not deterred by this mission, they were even eager to perform it."[6]

At this point the question of secrecy became urgent, as any leaks could jeopardize the entire operation. Dayan ordered his staff to keep their own staffs and subordinates unapprised of the full plans; directives to the lower ranks would be limited to no more than what should actually be implemented by them, with no unnecessary explanations. The high state of alert could be accounted for by the increasing tensions along the Jordanian border and the threat of the Iraqi army's entry into Jordan.

As it turned out, the assumption that Israel and France would have to embark on the operation without Great Britain proved wrong; yet the general staff's activities subsequent to the French delegation's visit was not wasted, as the alert gave the Israeli army 27 days in which to ready itself for battle. Furthermore, during the few days of the French officers' stay in Israel, all the fine points of the plans were gone into, which facilitated the absorption of the French air force in Israel, the necessary coordination between the Israeli and French navies, and the close cooperation between the two staffs that eventually materialized during the campaign itself. Moreover, the French delegation gave the go-ahead to a new arms procurement transaction whose scope ultimately exceeded even what was agreed on at Vermars. In the next three weeks the Israeli army would receive another 100 "Super" Sherman tanks and other vital war materiel and transport equipment that would enable it to execute the central moves of the campaign in the Sinai desert.

General Challe's mission also provided the French with the opportunity to observe the IDF's preparations and capabilities from close up. Colonel Jean Simon of the French land forces submitted an enthusiastic report on the IDF's fighting ability to his superiors; and the French were persuaded that Israel could carry its share in any joint plan against Nasser.[7] "The greatest utility of the delegation," Dayan summed up, "is that before its arrival in Israel, the French army only had a pro-Israeli *theory;* now that theory had a solid base. Now they have a clearer picture of the makeup of the IDF and are completely convinced that it is worth supporting."[8]

This conviction in the IDF's capability had political ramifications as well. After his visit General Challe was reassured that a way could be found to overcome the major obstacle to a joint French, British, and Israeli operation: Israel's objection to opening the war alone. Dayan reiterated the importance of Israel's D-Day attack being carried out simultaneously with a French attack on another front. But now it became clear to Challe that Israel could stand firm during the first hours on its own: "In the report I submitted to my Government," he wrote in his memoirs, "I affirmed that Israel's army, which was small but well-trained and well-equipped and could grow five times stronger within a short period of time, was capable of confronting the Egyptian forces alone."[9] Less than two weeks after General Challe's visit to Israel, his new familiarity with the Israeli army would provide him with the key to the plan he would propose to Great Britain, a plan that eventually led to the Sèvres agreement for British, French, and Israeli cooperation in the campaign against Nasser.

For the next two weeks the major political developments would be taking place far from Israel, at U.N. headquarters in New York. As expected, Nasser rejected the second London conference's proposals for SCUA to set fees, appoint pilots, and invest the profits from the Suez Canal into its development; he remained opposed to granting the association any real authority to manage the canal or supervise its day-to-day operation. It now seemed that the diplomatic course had been exhausted. All that remained was to bring the issue up for deliberation before the Security Council. Formally, the British wanted the Security Council to force Nasser to accept effective international supervision of the canal's management.[10] They realized that this was unlikely, but Sir Anthony Eden felt obligated to exhaust all political avenues before taking military action, because of the British domestic opposition's obdurate and uncompromising demand that the issue be brought before the U.N.[11]

The deliberations in New York lasted from October 5 until October 14, at which point Dag Hammarskjöld entered the picture. In an effort to find a formula for a settlement, he summoned French foreign minister Christian Pineau, British foreign secretary Selwyn Lloyd, and Egyptian foreign minister Mahmoud Fawzi to his bureau for marathon *in camera* talks.[12] Fawzi endeavored to present a moderate Egyptian position, without compromising the principle of Egypt's supreme authority for managing the canal:[13] He was willing to recognize SCUA as an entity that had to be negotiated with in regard to navigation conditions in the canal; he was willing to reach an agreement on fees and how much Egypt would have to invest toward maintenance and further development of the canal; he was even willing to consent to compulsory arbitration to settle disputes.[14] But in essence he would make no concessions on the question of Egypt's right to manage the canal, and his practical proposals remained vague and noncommittal.

Hammarskjöld summed up the points on which the parties seemed to have agreed and issued a document stipulating six principles for operating the canal:

1. All parties would be assured freedom of navigation through the canal at all times.
2. Egyptian sovereignty over the canal would be honored.
3. Canal management would be kept separate from the policies followed by the user nations.
4. Fees would be determined jointly by the Egyptian Government and the users.
5. Appropriate sums would be allocated from canal profits for its development.
6. Disputes between users and the canal management would be submitted for arbitration.[15]

Pineau and Lloyd could not object to these principles, which closely followed the resolutions of the London conferences and even included fundamental recognition of SCUA; but they considered them insufficient, as they omitted the major points: users' participation in the actual management of the canal and international supervision. The six principles were thus brought before the Security Council, with an addition demanding that the Egyptian government accept the London conference's endorsed principles and agree to SCUA's active participation in the canal's management.[16] The proposed resolution was split into two parts; the six principles were approved unanimously, but the Soviet Union vetoed the addition.

With the Security Council's approval of the six principles and despite the failure of the British and the French to introduce the additional provisions, the crisis seemed to be well on the way to being resolved; all that remained were some details that could be ironed out in further negotiations. Hammarskjöld wanted to take advantage of the momentum created in his "private" talks with the three foreign ministers and proposed another meeting in Geneva at the end of the month. Eisenhower said optimistically: "A very great crisis is behind us."[17] And even Selwyn Lloyd believed the crisis could be resolved by negotiations.[18]

But Christian Pineau and Anthony Eden were less optimistic. For them, the Security Council deliberations had failed, inasmuch as they did not give them what they wanted. Brian Urquhart, Hammarskjöld's biographer, writes that the six principles were intended to convert the users' organization into a working body that would cooperate with Egypt rather than defy it.[19] But here lay the very heart of the problem; Eden and Mollet did not want to find ways to cooperate with Nasser: They wanted to humble him and chasten him. Above all else they wanted to deflate the enormous prestige Nasser enjoyed in the Arab world and elsewhere in the Third World in the wake of the act of nationalizing the canal. They aspired for something that would prove beyond a shadow of a doubt, for all the world to see, that Nasser had in effect renounced nationalization. From the Security Council deliberations, it seemed that Nasser was likely to emerge with the upper hand, and that was something to which Eden and the French could not agree.

A day after deliberations at the U.N. opened, General Yehoshafat Harkaby, head of Israeli military intelligence, went to New York, as requested by Pineau at the St. Germain conference. "The situation at the Security Council is terrible," Pineau told him. "Fawzi won't budge and Selwyn Lloyd is weaker than ever. . . . The French and Israeli military plans should therefore be carried on."[20] A few days later Pineau's assessment had not changed; he saw little real hope of an operation initiated by the French and British, but believed that if Israel and France took the initiative, Great Britain would join in, basing itself on the article in the 1954 agreement that allowed the British to reoccupy the bases along the Suez in time of war. Harkaby's major task in New York had in fact ended, as it was clear that the ultimate political decisions would be taken in Paris and London and not New York. His secondary task—meeting Allen Dulles, the CIA head and brother of the U.S. secretary of state, and sending out feelers about a U.S. reaction to the possibility of an Israeli attack on Egypt—had to be abandoned, as Dulles was in the Far East; Harkaby saw no point in staying: War was approaching, and urgent intelligence duties awaited him in Tel Aviv.

In the meantime, Yosef Nahmias had organized the massive new arms procurement effort in Paris. The French had placed at Israel's disposal three commercial cargo ships drafted for the war. On October 13 they left the port of Toulon one after another. They were bound for Haifa carrying 100 "Super" Sherman tanks, 200 half-tracks, 300 four-wheel-drive trucks, 20 tank carriers, 20 jet refueling tankers, 10 extricating tanks, 10 bulldozing tanks, 5 tow trucks, and large amounts of ammunition, airplane fuel, and other items. Everything reached Haifa between October 20 and the day the war actually broke out, October 29. (Some of the equipment came straight to the staging grounds a few hours before H-Hour.)

In Tel Aviv the general staff updated operational plans: The operation was renamed Kadesh, after a biblical site and one of the important stops during the Israelites' wanderings in the desert. The plans called for the IDF to attack along two main axes and to execute one diversionary action; the fighting would be left mainly to the armored regiments, the paratroop brigade, and the regular infantry brigade. At H-Hour the paratroops would effect an integrated amphibious landing and air-dropped attack on el-Arish, the main Egyptian base. A division commanded by General Haim Laskov, including a new armored brigade and the Golani infantry brigade, would simultaneously attack Rafah and thrust westward to join up with the paratroops in the el-Arish area. Another division, commanded by Colonel Yehuda Wallach, comprising the veteran armored brigade and two reserve infantry brigades, would break through from the Nitzana area toward Isma'ilia, flanking the Abu-Agheila-Umm Kataff area. The Ninth Brigade, a newly mechanized reserve unit, would execute a diversionary move along the Qal'at-a-Nahel-Temed axis. Once the paratroops had completed their mission in el-Arish, they would again effect an amphibious landing and air-drop to occupy the Sharm al-Sheikh and Tiran Straits area. It was assumed at GHQ that the forces would get as far as the al-Arish line by the end of the second day and would reach the canal in four or five days.[21]

In addition to the large el-Arish jump, Dayan proposed that one or two paratroop platoons be dropped deep into enemy territory at H-Hour in order to harass supply and reinforcement lines along the major axes and confuse the Egyptians.[22] The assumption was that, within 48 hours at the most, armor units could link up with these paratroopers and get them out. Although Dayan's proposal was marginal to the campaign plans, this insignificant "addendum" in fact served as the key to the plan that eventually facilitated Israeli-British-French cooperation.

On October 7 a decisive operational conference was held in the war room; the chief of staff approved the plans and, on October 9, a "Command Group" was held at GHQ. Dayan instructed operational orders to be brought down to lower levels and more detailed planning commenced immediately:

> Our goal is to bring about the collapse of the enemy's deployment as quickly as possible and to gain complete control of the Sinai peninsula. We are interested in capturing enemy arms and equipment, not in inflicting enemy casualties. Our units must advance steadily until their missions are completed and must not remain behind to mop up isolated enemy positions.

Now actual preparations began in earnest, but Dayan ordered no more than the usual complement of reserve units drafted into duty in order to maintain secrecy and to ensure total surprise.[23]

General Challe met with the French foreign minister in New York and brought him up to date. Pineau told the general, "The plan is to be carried out. Nothing remains but to persuade the British."[24] General Challe now set to work on this task. Accompanied by Minister Albert Gazier, standing in for Pineau in his absence, Challe left for Great Britain on October 14 and met with Anthony Eden at his country home in Chequers, acquainting him for the first time explicitly and fully with what came to be known as "Challe's scenario." General Challe's close observation of the Israeli army and its operational capabilities now bore fruit. He proposed that Israel be persuaded to open a general offensive in the Sinai peninsula. In reaction, France and Great Britain would issue an ultimatum to Israel and Egypt, demanding that the belligerent forces retreat ten miles from either side of the Suez Canal and permit French and English forces to occupy positions along the canal in order to ensure navigation. If Egypt did not acquiesce to the ultimatum—as it probably would not—the allies would, after 72 hours, begin air bombardment on the basis of the Musketeer plans. This scenario had one tremendous advantage: It provided Eden, who was desperate for an opportunity to strike at Nasser, with the casus belli he so needed.

Growing opposition to the campaign within England made such a casus belli imperative. Domestic British dissension over the issue increased and made itself felt throughout society, up to the government itself. In mid-month Sir Walter Monckton, secretary of defense, resigned, officially for health reasons, but his reservations over the prime minister's approach were well known.[25] Anthony Nutting, minister of state for foreign affairs, also found it more and more difficult to toe the party line with a clear conscience.[26]

It is thus no wonder that Eden saw "Challe's scenario" as a great boon and was hard put to hide his enthusiasm for the stratagem. If Israel attacked the Egyptians in the Sinai and approached the canal, the United Kingdom would be able to demand that British troops return to the bases it had evacuated only a few months earlier, even though the Anglo-Egyptian agreement explicitly excluded an Israeli-Egyptian military confrontation from the list of eventualities that entitled Great Britain to return. It was obvious that only one strict condition had to be insisted on: Israel's initiative could in no way involve any prior agreement whatsoever in which Britain had a part. Great Britain had to be "surprised" so that the Arabs would view British intervention mainly as an attempt to halt Israeli aggression. Not even indirect coordination could be countenanced, because for Eden, Nasser's defeat was a necessary step toward rehabilitating Britain's position in the Middle East, and cooperation with the hated Zionists against an Arab state would be tantamount to destroying this very position.

Now it remained to be seen if Israel would agree to the proposed scenario under these conditions. On October 15 Bourgès-Maunoury sent General Challe and his friend Mangin to Yosef Nahmias to report on the talks at Chequers. Knowing that Israel was vehemently opposed to initiating the operation unilaterally, the two tried to soften the scenario as best they could without deviating too far from the truth.[27] But the major difficulty remained: Would Israel agree to take the role of a detonator? Would Ben-Gurion agree to open fire in the Sinai to allow the British to play the role of the policeman coming to separate the two scufflers?

That day General Meir Amit met with Paul Ely, chief of staff of the French army. Amit had come to Paris to make some sense out of the talks of October 12-13 considering operational plans for the joint Israeli-French venture. Challe's new plan made it impossible for the French officer to discuss the option of a joint French-Israeli operation seriously; to the IDF officers in Paris, who at this stage knew absolutely nothing about Challe's plan, the French seemed utterly confused. Meir Amit came to straighten things out, but his own discussions with Ely exacerbated the sense of confusion, as the French general also now discounted the possibility of a French-Israeli operation. In light of Challe's scenario, about which Amit knew nothing, he claimed at this point that the only possible alternative was an independent Israeli attack to precede the Anglo-French campaign.

But General Amit had come to Paris armed with precise instructions not to deviate from the fundamental Israeli demand for simultaneous action. Dayan had been unequivocal in his directives to the general: "Israel is not moving her ground forces until the French ground forces have set foot on Egyptian soil." And in a handwritten note Ben-Gurion added, "D-Day for the ground forces must definitely be simultaneous."[28] Although Bourgès-Maunoury had ordered contacts to be maintained and the Israeli option still discussed, the French officer was planning on the basis of Challe's scenario, while the bewildered Amit stuck by his own instructions. Here the talks inexorably reached a dead end.[29]

The stalled talks now made it clear that only discussions at the highest political level could resolve the problem. Shimon Peres reached the same conclusion. With great trepidation he brought Ben-Gurion Nahmias's cable describing Challe's scenario. Ben-Gurion's reaction was unmitigated and furious—the proposal was unthinkable, a fine example of the "best of British hypocrisy," Peres noted; "[Ben-Gurion thought that it showed the British] desire to hurt Israel more than their determination to destroy the Egyptian dictator."[30]

Ben-Gurion's first impulse was to slam the door on the entire episode, but after some reflection he decided to leave a narrow crack open and cabled Nahmias:

> We are prepared to cooperate with France and England according to alternative A [an Anglo-French operation with indirect Israeli cooperation]. We are willing to also consider the plans for a joint action with France alone, on condition that England does not interfere. We do not accept the proposal for France and England to separate between the two belligerents.[31]

In the meantime, Anthony Eden had recalled Selwyn Lloyd from New York. On October 16, after an informal talk with a small circle of British ministers who were in favor of the war initiative, both men left for Paris to meet Guy Mollet and Christian Pineau at Hotel Matignon, the official residence of the French prime minister.[32]

At first the British deluded themselves into thinking it was possible to embark on the operation based on a unilateral Israeli initiative apparently unsupported by any early allied coordination. The French claimed Ben-Gurion could be persuaded to execute the Israeli part of the plan despite this total distance Britain insisted on maintaining between itself and Israel. Israel demanded a simultaneous assault because it feared that otherwise, the international community would lay full blame at its feet and would impose sanctions against it, the French explained; therefore they had to assure Israel that the allies would stand by their commitments and would go into battle as quickly as possible. To convince the Israelis, the French wanted something in writing. Ultimately Mollet and Pineau did manage to get a cautiously worded, two-paragraph document out of Eden, hinting at a fundamental British obligation to fulfill its part in Challe's scenario. The document was not addressed to any particular recipient and included two brief paragraphs:

> 1. In the event of any threat of hostilities in the neighbourhood of the canal the French and British Governments would call the belligerents to halt and to withdraw from the immediate vicinity of the canal. If both agreed, no action would follow. If one or both refused, Anglo-French Forces would intervene to ensure the free passage of the canal.
> 2. In the event of hostilities developing between Egypt and Israel, Her Majesty's Government would not come to the assistance of Egypt

because Egypt is in breach of a Security Council Resolution and has moreover repudiated Western aid under the Tripartite Declaration. Different consideration would of course apply with Jordan, with whom Her Majesty's Government have, in addition to their obligation under the Tripartite Declaration, a firm treaty.

The French immediately gave a copy of the British undertaking to Yosef Nahmias so that he could pass it on to Ben-Gurion; they also told him that the British had agreed to sign another document that would specify the political arrangements to be fixed after the war. The document would take Israel's demands into consideration.[33]

The French believed that what they had managed to achieve at the meeting in Hotel Matignon was the most that the British would be prepared to concede for the time being; now they had to convince Ben-Gurion to give the orders for the IDF to play its role in the plan as formulated thus far. The French probably realized that the ties that had developed between the two countries, and Israel's increasing reliance on France for armaments, made Israel particularly eager to comply with France's wishes; but the signals Israel was sending throughout that week did not portend an easy fight.

That evening, after Eden and Lloyd had returned to London, Pineau and Bourgès-Maunoury met with Nahmias and at length described the talks that had just ended, expressing their opinion that only one possibility remained: an Anglo-French action *in the wake of* an "independent" Israeli action. They obviously wanted to pressure Israel into accepting the proposal agreed on at Hotel Matignon. "If Israel refuses the only proposal on the table," they told Nahmias, "she will be assuming responsibility for having missed an historic opportunity to overthrew Nasser's regime."[34]

Word of the Hotel Matignon talks reached Israel that afternoon, and Ben-Gurion again cabled Nahmias: "Regarding the arrival of the English and French representatives in Paris, you must immediately contact the French and ask them if the meeting can be a three-way one. . . . You must make a supreme effort to contact them and immediately send a reply home."[35] The request was not practical. This telegram crossed with Nahmias's cable stating that General Challe had delivered a formal invitation from Guy Mollet to Ben-Gurion to come to Paris secretly and urgently in order to find a solution satisfactory to all parties.[36]

The next day, October 17, Ben-Gurion summoned Peres, Dayan, and his senior ministers, Levi Eshkol and Golda Meir, to his bureau to discuss the new situation. All favored a meeting at the highest rank. Peres cabled Nahmias that Ben-Gurion was ready to come to Paris; just to be on the safe side he added, "The British idea of an Israeli assault and a British separation of belligerents is out of the question. But if Guy Mollet thinks it necessary, the repudiation of this proposal notwithstanding, then Ben-Gurion is prepared to come to Paris."[37]

At midnight on Thursday, October 18, 1956, Guy Mollet's answer arrived: He repeated his invitation to Ben-Gurion, despite all reservations. Shortly thereafter the Israeli prime minister's reply was sent out: He would indeed arrive with a small contingent on Sunday, October 21. Dayan knew that Ben-Gurion feared that the Egyptians would bomb Israeli cities if Israel opened fire first. To enable Ben-Gurion to agree to the proposal, if he wanted to, Dayan had the commander of the Israeli air force prepare a background paper outlining Israel's requests from France in order to reinforce its air defenses.

On October 19 Ben-Gurion conferred once more with Peres and Dayan; but everything had already been analyzed and scrutinized many times over and little remained to be added. Despite the "Old Man's" doubts, spirits were high and the participants felt that they were on the brink of a historic event. Ben-Gurion gave free rein to his imagination and spoke of a major reshuffling in the Middle East.[38]

On Sunday morning, October 21, the luxurious airplane that General de Gaulle had received from President Truman landed at the military airfield in Hazor, bringing General Challe and his confidant, Louis Mangin, to Israel. Their intentions were clear: They wanted to try to persuade the Israelis even before the discussions in Paris began.[39] In a brief meeting, Dayan clarified Israel's position: "We are not opposed to a joint operation, but under no circumstances will we agree to an operation in which one party acts and the other two pretend to chase him away. We are ready to talk, but only about real partnership." Challe tried persuasion: "The English will come into this only if they can be seen as intermediaries. . . . No one will be fooled, but the British insist on this charade. . . . And Israel will have signed documents from the British Government and will always be able to prove that it was staged from beginning to end." "Shakespeare may have been a great playwright," Dayan replied cynically, "but I doubt if Eden is as talented." On a much more serious note he added, "It is inconceivable that Egypt [be permitted to] bomb Tel Aviv and Haifa and destroy our civilian population, while our 'partners'' aircraft carriers wait off shore until the play has been enacted."[40]

On the way to the airfield for his trip to Paris, Ben-Gurion shook General Challe's hand warmly but told him with bitter humor, "If you plan to offer us the British proposal, then the only advantage of my trip to France will be that I get to make the acquaintance of your Prime Minister." But once he was inside the airplane, Ben-Gurion began consulting the Bible and ancient Greek geographers for sources substantiating the antiquity of Jewish rights to the southern part of the Sinai peninsula. Several days earlier he had already found a reference in Procopius mentioning the existence of a Jewish kingdom in "Yotvat," which, Ben-Gurion said, had been identified by several geographers as the island of Tiran.[41]

15
...

"COLLUSION": THE SÈVRES CONFERENCE

The French had decided to hold the clandestine meetings in the villa of the Bonnier de la Chapelle family in Sèvres, an affluent suburb of Paris. The family had been closely connected with the French Underground during World War II; the only son, Fernand, was an 18-year-old student when he was executed by the Vichy government for murdering Admiral Darlan on orders of the Resistance. Lieutenant-Colonel Mordechai Bar-On, who served as secretary for the Israeli delegation, has written in his record: "It was easy to sense in this house the thousands of minuscule threads that connected the former members of the underground whose past now held them in the bonds of *noblesse oblige,* and committed them to a devoted activism in the service of their country."[1] "One of these days," Abel Thomas, the French Defense Ministry director general, said to Ben-Gurion in a conversation at the conference, "the Sèvres conference will become known. It is up to us whether it becomes known as a second Yalta or as the Munich of the Middle East."[2] One of the weightiest of the French considerations was their powerful desire to rid themselves of the legacy of Munich and the Vichy surrender, which the Bonnier de la Chapelle home symbolized for them.[3]

The first session convened on the afternoon of October 22. The French participants included Premier Guy Mollet, Foreign Minister Christian Pineau, Defense Minister Bourgès-Maunoury, and a handful of aides; Israeli participants included David Ben-Gurion, Moshe Dayan, Shimon Peres, and several aides. This was an introductory session intended to pave the way for the decisive meeting with the British scheduled for that evening and which the Israelis had learned of only upon their arrival in Paris. Ben-Gurion opened his remarks with what he himself referred to as a "fantastic" plan to reorganize the Middle East. There was no need to rush, he said; better to discuss things with the Americans and take advantage of Western readiness to overthrow Nasser's regime as well as the anticipated collapse of the Jordanian regime in order to redraw regional borders. What was necessary was an explicit, "on-the-table" treaty among all the interested parties in order to stabilize the Middle East and secure it for Western as well as for Israel's interests.[4] Ben-Gurion's "fantastic" opening gambit reflected his tendency to think big and envisage far-ranging historical processes, as well as the reigning atmosphere in the Middle East triggered by Iraqi plans to encourage the overthrow of the Syrian government and send military forces into Jordan. But Ben-Gurion also had a tactical motivation: He wanted to embark on discussions with the French from a vantage point that did not totally discount their proposals, even if he did not yet accept them. He wanted to counter the pettiness of the scenario to which the British had agreed with an imaginative and more wide-ranging one. Under the terms proposed by the British, Ben-Gurion wanted to stress, Israel was not keen on the entire enterprise. The campaign could be considered only after the plans had been adjusted to its own interests, and only after Israel's gains from the plan had been clarified and carefully spelled out. Israel was not happy at providing a limited service that did not entitle it to a share in mapping out the future of the region.

But Ben-Gurion's ploy quickly fell victim to the political and military reality that prescribed French policy. Ben-Gurion's proposal called for postponing the campaign for several months, but the French military forces had been on the alert for many weeks and could not wait until Ben-Gurion's "fantastic" vision was translated into action. And at that stage the French were convinced that only Challe's scenario could secure British participation in the venture. They believed that there was no room for any alternative plans. "The proposed principle," Pineau said at that preliminary meeting, "is the only one likely to result in active cooperation on the part of all the parties." "Time is working against the West," Guy Mollet said. "[P]ostponing Challe's plan today is tantamount to cancelling it entirely." Bourgès-Maunoury, directly responsible for the armed forces, simply said that "France has already reached the limit of her war mobilization capabilities. . . . If we do not engage forces immediately, discipline will collapse. . . . In three months the political and military situation may have other advantages, but by then France will be out of the game." Even Ben-Gurion's request "to formulate a political plan that Eisenhower would not oppose or would at least tacitly accept by remaining silent" was rejected in the French eagerness to begin the operation.

The French made several tentative suggestions to "improve" the scenario in order to allay Israeli fears without departing from its principles: the time span during which Israel would be forced to wait for allied military intervention could be reduced; French air and naval forces could be put at Israel's disposal to defend it from enemy air bombardment; Israel would not be required actually to reach the banks of the canal in order to claim that its forces were approaching it—"there won't be any reporters around." But Ben-Gurion continued to attack the "British proposal" sharply. Pineau's summary of the discussion sounded a tired note: "We are both of the same opinion, but British agreement is lacking. . . . it took us a long time to move Great Britain from a total lack of comprehension to a partial grasp of the issue. It is an illusion to think that we can now move them to total understanding."[5] At the last minute a slight crack appeared in Ben-Gurion's apparently impenetrable objection, as he permitted Moshe Dayan to make his own "private" proposal: "Israel will initiate war towards the evening of D-Day with a foray deep into Egyptian territory and come close to the Suez Canal. England and France will make their political maneuvers and engage their forces at daybreak the day after D-Day."

Behind the proposal lay the idea of Israel opening hostilities with a kind of large-scale but limited operation and not a full-scale offensive; that way, if the British changed their minds at the last minute, Israel could retreat and walk away from the affair, claiming it had done no more than embark on an extensive reprisal raid. Egypt would be confused during the first hours of fighting and would not know whether Israel's intentions were to go to war or effect a limited operation and would not engage all its forces, perhaps even refraining from bombing Israel's urban centers. Dayan's proposal was intended more to allay Ben-Gurion's fears than to reconcile the French. The "Old Man" did not give the slightest hint that this proposal was acceptable; but the French probably realized that he had at least not rejected it out of hand.

That evening the representatives of Her Majesty's government came to the villa in Sèvres: Foreign Secretary Selwyn Lloyd and his private secretary, Donald Logan. The meeting between Ben-Gurion and Lloyd gave all appearances of a fiasco. The two leading actors differed in more than just personality and style. In his memoirs Dayan recorded his impression of the British foreign secretary: "He may have been a sociable and pleasant man; but if he was, he succeeded in hiding it this time. He could not have been more antagonistic. Everything about him shouted repugnance—at the place, the company, and the content of the issues he was forced to deal with."[6] Lloyd's description was equally unflattering: "Ben-Gurion himself seemed to be in a

rather aggressive mood, indicating or implying that the Israelis had no reason to believe in anything that a British minister might say."[7]

Selwyn Lloyd opened his remarks by saying that a "compromise on Suez
could be achieved within a week," but Britain was prepared to honor its undertakings as agreed at the Hotel Matignon six days earlier. Israel had to launch a
full-scale military offensive in Sinai, actually threatening the canal, without
any sign that Britain had initiated the operation or was in any way involved in
coordinating it. The British position on Jordan also remained unchanged:
Britain was obligated to act under its defense treaty with the Hashemite
Kingdom, which it would enforce if Israel attacked Jordan. That same day the
Jordanian election results were announced; although Suleiman el-Nabulsi's
government would only assume power in a few days' time, it was already clear
that the pro-Nasser forces had achieved a majority in the Jordanian parliament
and that the plans for Iraqi troops to enter Jordanian territory would be shelved.
Nevertheless, the British hung on to their old formulas.

Enraged, sullen, and stubborn, Ben-Gurion again stated his unequivocal
position:

> My reaction to the plan is negative and final. Israel is not prepared to declare war on
> Egypt. Israel does not want to be labeled an aggressor, nor does she want ultimatums
> hurled at her to leave the canal zone. Israel will not initiate a war with Egypt. Not
> today and not at a later stage. If we are attacked—we will defend ourselves. Even if
> we are forced to stand alone against the Egyptians, we will overpower them. We may
> suffer heavy losses, but ultimately . . . we will prevail. In 1948 we had no airplanes,
> we stood alone, and we won.

But despite his implacable opening position, Ben-Gurion himself now
presented the proposal Dayan had made several hours before:

> Israel can engage in a reprisal raid against Egypt. Israeli forces can cross the border
> in the evening on D-Day and carry out a limited operation. That night the British and
> French Governments could meet and issue a demand to the belligerent forces that
> they clear the canal. Israel will comply, but because she never really intended to get
> as far as the canal, the demand will be meaningless for her. If the Egyptians do not
> accept the Anglo-French demand, the allied air forces will begin bombing Egypt's
> airfields on the morning after D-Day.

Ben-Gurion concluded by proposing that the French supplement Israel's air
defenses with French pilots and aircraft—a proposal to which the French
had already consented.

Lloyd apparently did not comprehend the full implications of the new
proposal and the possibilities it presented. Therefore he rejected it out of
hand; he insisted that Israel had to implement "a real act of war" that would

directly endanger the Suez Canal and justify allied intervention. A sufficient period of time was also necessary to permit the diplomatic moves to take place at a reasonable pace. Lloyd was adamant even in his objections to the proposal that the French air force use bases in Cyprus in order to provide Israel with an air umbrella—"the whole world would realize that this was collusion between England, France and Israel." He was, however, prepared to ignore any actions that the French air force might take from bases inside Israel. As the night drew to a close, the discussion reached a dead end. The gap between the Israeli and British positions seemed unbridgeable.

But the French had not given up. They discerned the fundamental movement that had taken place in the Israeli position and believed that the gaps between the Israeli proposal and Lloyd's demands ultimately could be bridged, as the major obstacle had already been overcome: Israel had agreed to open war "at her own initiative" and without the simultaneous participation of its partners; everything else was just a question of details, they believed. Since Selwyn Lloyd did not share the French perception, it was decided to send Pineau to meet with Anthony Eden the very next day in order to make clear just what Israel's concessions meant.

The next day Lloyd reported to Eden that the talks had reached a dead end. Meeting with the Cabinet, Eden informed the assembled group, "From secret conversations which had been held in Paris with representatives of the Israeli Government, it now appeared that the Israelis would not alone launch a full-scale attack against Egypt." But the British prime minister decided to postpone his decision until Pineau's arrival in order to hear France's final position.[8]

The second day of talks at Sèvres was peculiar indeed; on the surface, the ball was in the British court and no progress could be made until Pineau returned from London with Britain's answer. In fact, however, the decisive move was made that very day, in Paris, by the Israelis themselves. Before Pineau left for London late that afternoon, he asked for the precise terminology of Israel's new proposal and inquired just how flexible the Israelis would be. Flexibility would increase his chances of persuading the British prime minister, whom he would be meeting in a few hours, to accept the new proposal.

No formal discussions were held between the Israelis and the French that day, but several casual meetings did take place. A tempest had erupted that morning in the French National Assembly in the wake of the capture of the Algerian rebel leader Muhammed Ben-Bella and his colleagues. This had been preceded by the interception of the Egyptian ship *Athos,* which was caught carrying weapons to the Algerian rebels. The parties on the right blamed the government for failing to quell the Algerian rebellion and proposed a no-confidence vote. The French ministers were thus busy most of the day with parliamentary maneuverings. Yet Bourgès-Maunoury and Pineau succeeded in getting away for an informal chat with Ben-Gurion. To reassure him about Britain's commitment, Pineau revealed that he and Bourgès-Maunoury had spoken with the French president, René Coty, who had, as required by the French Constitution, approved the provision of a formal undertaking toward Israel to the effect that France would honor its commitment and would not back out at the last minute. Bourgès-Maunoury reiterated the importance with which France viewed Israel's compliance with its requests; he also reassured Ben-Gurion and declared that France would increase the air and naval defense it would furnish Israel during the first days of the campaign, but appended a hinted threat:

> Over the past two months of my contacts with Israel I have told you only the truth and you can therefore accept my words in all sincerity. I do not believe that in the foreseeable future France will have another opportunity for a joint operation if action is not taken now. . . . I must reiterate and assure you that in the future too, France will not cease to aid you to the best of her ability; however, it is doubtful if we will be able to help you as we could have done now, that is to say, by means of the joint operation we are proposing today.

The friendliness of the tone notwithstanding, the intention was obviously to put pressure on Ben-Gurion, and he probably felt it very clearly.

Major progress toward a resolution, however, took place in the discussions held by the Israeli representatives themselves. Dayan had spent the morning trying to find an operative plan that would bridge the gap between his proposal and Lloyd's demands. Scanning the map of the Sinai peninsula, he recalled the addendum he had proposed to his staff at the beginning of the month: parachuting several platoons of paratroopers behind Egyptian lines in order to harass and disrupt the supply lines. He kept coming back to that same narrow mountain pass in which he had proposed to parachute one of those small detachments, and a new plan crystallized in his mind. In the course of Ben-Gurion's consultations with Peres and Dayan after lunch, Dayan made his proposal: On D-Day, as daylight faded, a battalion of paratroopers would be dropped near the Mitla Pass some 40 kilometers from the city of Suez at the southern end of the canal. Simultaneously, two other battalions of the Paratroop Brigade would overrun several border posts and break through to the west, along the Kuntila-Temed-Kal'at e-Nachal axis, in order to join up with the first battalion as quickly as possible. The paratroops either would provide armored reinforcements, antitank guns, and supplies, or, if necessary, would get the first battalion out and back to the Israeli lines. The other IDF forces would remain inactive until the allied bombings began. No battles would take place other than those needed to safeguard the paratroopers, nor would the air force be engaged except for the same purpose. Thirty-six hours later, the Anglo-French air forces would begin systematically destroying the Egyptian air force. Only then would the other IDF formations set out to take the Sinai peninsula and reach the Straits of Tiran.

The new plan, Dayan said, met the British demands to effect a "real act of war," since dropping a battalion of paratroopers in the vicinity of the canal and sending a full armored brigade 200 kilometers into Egyptian territory could hardly be considered a minor incursion. Further, it also met the British demand that the action be seen to endanger the Suez, inasmuch as the Mitla Pass—at least on the map—looked very close to the canal. In addition, it permitted Israel to accede to the British demand for an interval during which the diplomatic process could be engaged without unduly risking Egyptian bombing of Israeli cities, since the other Israeli forces would not be entering battle until the allies had begun to destroy the Egyptian air force. And even if the Egyptians responded earlier with aerial bombardment, Israel would have received French assistance in defending its skies and coastline. At the same time, the advantages of the original plan remained: If the British backed out at the last moment, Israel could present the action as an enlarged reprisal raid, and the Egyptians would be uncertain of Israel's intentions during the first hours of fighting. An additional and important advantage to this plan, Dayan concluded, was that because the parachute drop would be taking place in a desolate area and because IDF action during the first 36 hours would be limited, there was a reasonable chance that Israeli losses would not be excessive.[9]

As was his wont, Ben-Gurion asked many questions and played devil's advocate; but it was obvious that Dayan's plan helped him overcome some of his hesitations. Thus without taking a position on the plan, he allowed Dayan to give Pineau an outline of the proposal before the latter left for London. By now the details of the scenario were no longer important; Ben-Gurion had to decide on a much more fundamental question—whether to lead Israel to war at all. He did not have to wait for the British response to the particulars of the plan but had to make his own decision before Pineau returned. After consulting with Dayan and Peres, he retired to his room "to think things through."[10]

Ben-Gurion's tentative approval allowed Dayan to provide Pineau with a written draft of the Israeli proposal, should Ben-Gurion decide to accept the fundamental premise of the Challe scenario. Pineau realized that the Israelis no longer needed to have pressure applied, since Dayan's new plan was enough to meet his needs in London. Dayan's draft would undergo several alterations, but would ultimately form the basis of the document that became known as the Sèvres Protocol. At this stage it included eight points:

1. Israel would not open full-scale war but would initiate an operation representing an actual threat to the Suez Canal and that would look like a "real act of war."
2. The French and British demand that Egypt and Israel withdraw their forces from the canal zone would not constitute an ultimatum but rather an "appeal." The formulation of the appeal to Israel would differ in language from that sent to Egypt, and Israel would not be condemned as an aggressor.
3. France and the United Kingdom undertook to engage their forces against the Egyptian air and ground forces no later than 36 hours after the beginning of the Israeli action.
4. The appeal to Egypt would include a demand that Egypt cease hostile acts against Israel. The allies would intervene even if Egypt agreed to retreat from the canal zone but refused to cease hostile acts against Israel.
5. Israel would accede to the allied demand to cease fire only if the Egyptians did so as well.
6. During the waiting period before Britain and France engaged their forces, two French fighter squadrons would land in Israel and two French battleships would be deployed along Israel's coastline to reinforce its urban and shore defenses. The French would also send pilots to man the Israeli Mystères whose crews had not yet completed their training.
7. Great Britain undertook to refrain from providing any assistance to Jordan or Iraq if either attacked Israel. Israel itself undertook not to initiate an attack on Jordan.
8. Israel affirmed its intention to retain its forces in all areas east of the el-Arish-Abu Agheila-Kal'at e-Nachal-Sharm al-Sheikh line for permanent annexation. Great Britain and France undertook to support these Israeli plans or, at least, not to oppose them.

Provided with this document, Pineau left for London. We have no precise information on the events there on the evening of October 23, 1956; the testimony of the participants is vague.[11] At any rate, Pineau seems to have succeeded in convincing Eden that the Israeli offer satisfied the minimum demands required to put Operation Musketeer into action. Late that night Pineau returned from London bearing a document to which the British had agreed and that was no more than a slight adaptation of Dayan's draft. The next day Her Majesty's representatives would be going to Paris to finalize plans.

That evening the Israeli delegation found itself in the midst of general confusion over Ben-Gurion's ultimate decision. Later in the evening, when the "Old Man" had retired to his room to make his final calculations, Dayan called the Israeli team to report on developments. Not even he knew Ben-Gurion's real views. "The 'Old Man' has let me make my proposal to the French and watch their reaction, even though he himself is cool towards it," he told his colleagues. "Maybe the 'Old Man' wants to appear calm and collected among all the noisy hot-heads. . . . If it's only a ploy, he's being very clever."[12] Mordechai Bar-On recorded his own impressions of the mood of the Israelis that night: "When Dayan and Peres left Ben-Gurion that evening, they were still consumed with trepidation about the decision being made by their leader." Ben-Gurion's enigmatic style prevented his aides from second-guessing him, but they felt that by asking all his questions and airing all his doubts in the course of their discussions, he was looking for arguments to underpin his own tendency to reject the proposal—at least, most of the considerations he raised seemed to indicate that. But when they met him late the next morning, Ben-Gurion's smile made it clear that he had decided positively. With obvious emotion Bar-On recorded his own impression:

> Ben-Gurion looked like someone who had recovered from a long and painful illness. He had obviously stayed up much of that night. He looked like . . . one of those heroes of antiquity who had dedicated the last night before battle to a vigil, praying and taking counsel with themselves and their gods, but who, upon rising worn and exhausted, are clad with strength and zeal. . . . Stretched as taut as strings on the point of breaking, the "Younger Ones" waited for the "Old Man's" words—had he made his decision? As soon as Ben-Gurion opened his mouth, even to make a casual remark, the sense of relief was obvious. The positive answer shone forth from his countenance.[13]

During the night Ben-Gurion had prepared another 20 or so written questions, but they constituted directives for action rather than stumbling blocks. The morning meeting drew to a close but Ben-Gurion had not yet made his decision explicit. The "Old Man" had a style of his own; at the end of the discussion he noted offhandedly, "We will have to draw up a protocol of the negotiations to be signed by us all and which will be binding on the parties." And before the group dispersed he remarked, as if looking at a distant vision: "I keep wondering how a Jewish state could have existed in Yotvat without a drop of water; life cannot exist without water. Didn't the Children of Israel harass Moses because they wanted to drink water?"[14]

Formal discussions resumed in the afternoon of October 24th. Pineau reported on his talks in London: After the British had realized that Israel consented to open hostilities in the Sinai at "her initiative," they agreed to the proposal whereby Israel would undertake a "large-scale reprisal operation" that would appear to threaten the canal. Great Britain agreed to shorten the interval until allied bombing began to no more than 36 hours, consented to replace the word "ultimatum" with the word "appeal," to couch the appeal to Israel differently from the Egyptian one, and to make Israel's agreement to a cease-fire contingent upon Egyptian agreement. Eden even acquiesced to French planes being stationed in Israel, on condition that they were painted in Israeli air force colors. D-Day was set for Monday, October 29, at 5 P.M. Israeli time.

While Pineau was making his report, two British representatives came to the villa: Donald Logan, who had also participated in the talks two days earlier, and Patrick Dean, a senior Foreign Office official who was chairman of the British Intelligence Services Committee.

Dayan's and Eden's drafts were for the most part agreed to by both the Israelis and the British. One point, however, remained in dispute: referring to Israel's territorial demands, which had appeared in Dayan's draft but had been omitted from Eden's. Ben-Gurion knew that the United Kingdom and France could not officially approve the retention of territory occupied by Israel, but it was important for him that they be aware of Israel's intentions. He therefore demanded that the final document mention the Israeli demand to retain the Straits of Tiran: "France and England had a positive interest in the Suez," he said. "[T]he Straits of Tiran are Israel's Suez Canal. . . . We intend to capture the straits, and we intend to remain there and thus ensure freedom of navigation to Eilat." The British agreed to include a paragraph in the final document in which Israel declared its intention to retain the Straits of Tiran, without any mention of the French or British reaction to it.

Finally, the British delegates asked whether Israel intended to declare war formally. Even at this late stage they apparently feared that the world would not view the Israeli operation as a real act of war, depriving them of the necessary casus belli for military intervention. Ben-Gurion made it clear that the existing state of relations between Israel and Egypt precluded this necessity.

"We will not make any declaration—we will simply strike," Dayan had said. But to allay British fears, Ben-Gurion promised that the public Israeli announcement of the operation would stress that IDF forces were near the canal and that the blockade of Israeli shipping in the canal would figure prominently in Israel's explanations of its motivation.

Now the protocol was finally formulated along the lines of the revised drafts, and at 7 P.M. the parties sat down unceremoniously to sign. Ben-Gurion, Christian Pineau, and Patrick Dean signed on behalf of their respective governments. All the signatures required final approval of the several governments, but for Ben-Gurion and his aides the issue was concluded. The "Old Man" did not hide his excitement: "When he received his copy of that fateful document, he held it between his fingers gingerly, as if it were more precious than gold, and then slipped it deep into his vest pocket."[15] Dayan, who would from now bear the brunt of the burden, cabled Meir Amit, his second in command: "Good chances Operation 'Kadesh' will begin soon. Call up Zaro [i.e., armored] units immediately. Assure secrecy of mobilization. Immediately initiate a diversion in the direction of Jordan concerning Iraq's troops. We take off tonight, arrive tomorrow morning."[16] Shortly thereafter Dayan boarded the plane. With nothing to do but wait for the landing, he drew a caricature depicting John Bull and Marianna making way for "little Israel" and gesturing "After you . . ."[17]

When Logan and Dean returned to London and showed Eden the protocol, the prime minister was furious. Although he had never said as much, it seems that Eden did not think that the Sèvres talks would end in signed documents of any sort. Patrick Dean was a veteran of the foreign service and punctilious about diplomatic procedures, in which negotiations were customarily concluded with signed protocols; he had not been party to all the confidential details of the talks and had signed the protocol in all innocence, as a matter of routine. In a rage, Eden destroyed his copy of the protocol and ordered Logan and Dean to return to Paris immediately to try to destroy the other copies as well.[18] But by then Ben-Gurion's copy was hidden deep in his vest pocket, somewhere in the sky on the way to Israel. He would keep the document secret until the day of his death and would not part with it at any price.

What became known in Britain as the "Sèvres collusion" provoked impassioned reactions throughout the British government and the public. But had there in fact been any collusion?

Most wartime alliances involve secret agreements, disinformation, and even deception of a common enemy. Not in every case are such plots and stratagems deemed "collusion"—certainly not when the deception is aimed against a common enemy as part of the war effort itself, with the ultimate goal of defeating that enemy. This, however, was not the case in the protocol signed in Sèvres. The overwhelming domestic British condemnation of the Sèvres alliance stemmed mainly from the fact that the deception was aimed at the citizens of the United Kingdom. It was therefore perceived as base and fundamentally negative in Britain, not because of the actual war plans, but because of Anthony Eden's persistent attempt to hide its existence from the British public and from the entire world through half-truths and even outright lies.[19] France and Israel were tainted by association, although their collusion in the deception was not motivated by their own interests.

For the most part, the French and Israeli public identified with the goals of the war. Egypt had given Israel no end of casus belli over the past years, insisting as it did on maintaining a state of belligerency despite the Armistice Agreements. Israel thus believed it had the moral right to decide when and where to resume hostilities—in any case, that was the way the Israeli public saw things. In December 1955 Ben-Gurion had addressed senior Israeli army officers and counted off the reasons for the government's decision to refrain from a preventive war, but he never questioned Israel's fundamental moral right to embark on war against Egypt, a country that stubbornly insisted on belligerent rights.[20] Thus the Israeli leadership did not perceive the triple alliance as an immoral act to be condemned; the clandestine nature of the alliance was dictated by operative circumstances—a perfectly reasonable state of affairs. In a rather flowery turn of phrase, Shimon Peres expressed the Israeli view: "We were witness to our nations joining together to destroy evil, to wage war against a battle-hungry and arrogant dictator. There was no sense of conspiracy; it was a decision taken to defend ourselves before our enemy rose up to slay us."[21] In France too a war against Nasser was viewed as justified because of his support of the Algerian rebels; and once the triple alliance had played out its role in the war itself, keeping it a secret seemed pointless.

But things were different in Great Britain. The British leadership wanted to keep the alliance a secret even after the actual needs of the war no longer required it, because they still feared for Great Britain's position in the Arab world and because the opposition at home was so incensed. Even to themselves, Anthony Eden and Selwyn Lloyd persisted in the charade that they had had no part in encouraging Israel to attack Egypt. On October 23, after Lloyd returned from Sèvres, he sent an urgent message to Christian Pineau:

"In light of what happened last night, it must be made clear that the United Kingdom makes no demand on the Government of Israel to undertake any action whatsoever. We only wanted to clarify what our reactions would be if certain events were to take place."[22] Lloyd was obviously trying to rewrite history while making it. The Sèvres talks had alarmed him, as it finally dawned on him that he was indeed involved in collusion and sought to dissociate himself from it. On October 24 Eden, who had already agreed to the Israeli proposal, addressed the Cabinet and made a bland announcement in order to maintain the illusion that things were happening of their own accord and that Israel was taking action in the Sinai without prior coordination with England: "It now seems . . . that the Israelis are after all advancing their military preparations with the aim of attacking Egypt."[23]

Furthermore, once the United Kingdom and France presented Israel and Egypt with the ultimatums, it would be obvious to all that Britain, France, and Israel had contrived a plot; but even then Eden denied any contact with Israel when he addressed Parliament: ". . . to say—and this is what I want to repeat to the House—that Her Majesty's Government were engaged in some dishonorable conspiracy is completely untrue, and I most emphatically deny it. . . . It is quite wrong to state that Israel was incited to this action by Her Majesty's Government. There was no prior agreement between us about it."[24] Word of the alliance leaked out almost immediately after the Sinai campaign. Christian Pineau and Moshe Dayan both referred to it openly in their memoirs published 20 years later. But until his death, Eden could not admit that he had indeed lied to Parliament.

What took place during the three days at Sèvres that caused Ben-Gurion to change his mind? When he left for France he had been adamant: The British scenario was unacceptable. But when he returned to Israel he carried with him an agreement that he had signed, based on that same scenario. The details had been adjusted and made more palatable—the interval during which Israel would have to wait for British and French forces to act was shortened from 72 to 36 hours; Israel would initiate hostilities within the framework of a limited engagement; and the French would reinforce Israel's air and coastline defenses. Nevertheless, at the foundation of the Sèvres agreement lay the scenario that General Challe had proposed to Anthony Eden at Chequers: Israel was to open hostilities against Egypt at its own initiative; accept an "ultimatum" demanding that it cease hostilities; wait 36 hours during which time the entire force of Egypt's war potential might be set in motion against it—and all this while keeping the existence of the agreement secret from the international community. Great Britain would be allowed to continue to act as if Sèvres did not exist.

Four things combined at Sèvres to change Ben-Gurion's perception of the situation and tip the scales toward a positive decision:[25]

1. Even before his departure for Paris, Ben-Gurion knew that his decision would have an enormous impact on future relations between Israel and France. But only when he sat face to face with the leaders of France did he realize just how anxious they were for the proposed alliance to be formed and with what importance they viewed the campaign. The ultimate failure in Suez and the French retreat from Algeria six years later under de Gaulle might make the contemporary observer wonder at their eagerness; but France of 1956 was convinced that the rebellion in Algeria could be contained and harbored the belief that "French Algeria" could continue to exist. If Ben-Gurion ignored this, the newly forged ties between his country and France were likely to suffer.

2. The new operational plan put forward by Moshe Dayan during the Sèvres conference held out a reasonable chance of overcoming three major anxieties that troubled Ben-Gurion as he contemplated an attack on Egypt: retaliatory Egyptian bombing of Israel's urban centers, excessive battlefield casualties, and Britain's backing out of the venture at the last moment, either because of international pressure or internal dissension, leaving Israel alone in the field. Dayan's proposal to embark on what could be interpreted as no more than a large-scale retaliation operation rather than full-scale attack made immediate Egyptian bombing less likely, cut down the number of potential battlefield casualties, and left Israel in a politically more tenable position should Britain indeed back out of the alliance.

3. The face-to-face meeting with senior British officials and the signature of the representatives of Her Majesty's government on the Sèvres Protocol removed one of the major impediments to Ben-Gurion's agreement to Challe's scenario. Ben-Gurion harbored a long-standing bitterness against what he thought of as British perfidy and suspected a plot to restore the United Kingdom's place in the Middle East at Israel's expense. The meeting between Ben-Gurion and Selwyn Lloyd at Sèvres had been a disaster. But a British signature on the Sèvres Protocol provided Israel with a bond against British duplicity. Try as they might to pretend nothing had happened at Sèvres, Eden and his colleagues could not deny that a pact had in fact been entered into between Britain and Israel. The Sèvres Protocol gave Ben-Gurion a kind of "mortgage": Britain would in all conscience remain indebted to Israel. Moreover, Ben-Gurion wanted to meet the British ministers face to face just as eagerly as Eden wanted to prevent such a meeting. On behalf of his country, Ben-Gurion felt degraded by the British attempt to induce Israel to enter into a war on Britain's side without public acknowledgment. His meeting with the British foreign secretary did much to make up for the slight.

4. The act of signing the Sèvres Protocol was tantamount to creating a military pact among France, Israel, and Great Britain. This eliminated one of the major considerations that had prompted the Israeli government to forgo the option of a preventive war the previous autumn—fear of international outrage at the Israeli initiative. Ben-Gurion believed that the Sèvres alliance would obviate a great deal of international pressure. In addition, as the Israeli prime minister told his French colleagues during his opening remarks, he hoped the alliance would be public and open, unlike the kind of arrangement originally suggested in the Challe scenario. Among other reasons, Ben-Gurion had objected to the scenario just because the British wanted to keep it hidden. But now he correctly assessed that, the British interest in secrecy notwithstanding, the international community ultimately would not be fooled and would realize that an alliance had indeed been forged against Nasser. Indeed, Eden's misguided belief that he could maintain the pretense of noninvolvement in Israel's Sinai initiative was dashed as soon as the fighting broke out.

These are the factors that tipped the scales in favor of Ben-Gurion's positive decision; but underneath it all was one fundamental assumption that Ben-Gurion shared with most of the Israeli leadership in 1956: the inevitability of a confrontation between Israel and Nasser's Egypt. It was in Israel's interest to ensure that it took place at a time and under conditions most favorable to it. The night he made his decision, the "Old Man" wrote in his diary, ". . . it seems to me that this action must be taken. This is a unique opportunity, when two not insignificant powers try to eliminate Nasser, so that we need not stand alone against him as he gains power and conquers all the Arab lands."[26]

16
• • •
OPERATION KADESH: POLITICAL DIMENSIONS

Because their authors were unfamiliar with the secret political considerations that shaped the operational planning and decisions, most military studies of the Sinai campaign have misinterpreted some of its
main military moves by explaining them through military logic only.
Several writers have perceived the IDF paratroop drop in the Mitla area and
the maneuvers of the Israeli armor in central Sinai as brilliant examples of
Liddell-Hart's doctrine of the indirect approach strategy, attributing the
rapid disintegration of the Egyptian ranks in the northern part of the Sinai to
the IDF penetration deep into Egypt's southern flank.[1]

Indeed, since the last days of the 1948 war, when Israeli forces had penetrated deep into the Sinai Desert, all subsequent GHQ operational planners
were convinced that any war with Egypt would require that same kind of
flanking strategy, with rapid penetration into the middle of the peninsula at
the very start of battle.[2] During the Sinai campaign itself the field commanders followed the same line of reasoning in their more detailed planning. Yet
in the overall plans, as they eventually emerged from the drafting boards of
GHQ Operations Branch, the Sinai campaign was a splendid example of the
total subordination of military planning to political exigencies. In order to
satisfy political demands, Dayan was forced to make far-reaching changes in
the original plans, affecting timetables, allocation of forces, and fixing targets—changes that went *counter* to purely military reasoning.

By the time Dayan reached his bureau straight from the airport on
Thursday, October 25, reserve mobilization was in full swing. The chief of
staff's most urgent task was to coordinate and adapt operational plans to the

political dictates of the Sèvres Protocol. As soon as he returned, he summoned General Meir Amit and a small group of officers who had been made privy to the clandestine political moves and told them the details of the protocol. He later explained the new guidelines for reshaping the operational plans:[3]

1. Actions taken by the IDF on behalf of the allies were to be kept strictly distinct from those taken in order to achieve the aims of the State of Israel.

2. Wherever possible, actions would be deferred until the point of allied military intervention. For the first 36 hours the Israeli armed forces would be acting alone, and only those operations dictated by the Sèvres Protocol or moves vital for the security of the forces in the field would be carried out. At this stage, fighting was not to be extended needlessly.

3. After allied intervention, any land targets Israel wanted to seize were to be quickly taken, first and foremost the Straits of Tiran.

4. Secrecy was imperative, second in importance only to victory on the battlefield.

The new directives obliged far-reaching deviations from the original plans confirmed less than three weeks earlier:

1. The paratroops, the elite IDF brigade, would not be carrying out the two central missions of the campaign—conquest of el-Arish and capture of Sharm al-Sheikh—but would instead effect a mission of paramount political importance but minimal military significance. The planned air drop and sea landing of troops to take el-Arish was scratched; fighting would begin by air drop near the Mitla Pass, far from the major battle arenas.

2. Instead of the air force destroying enemy air power at H-Hour, as per IDF doctrine, its role when fighting broke out would be limited to defending Israeli air space and providing air cover and logistic support for the paratroops.

3. The armored corps would not be activated at H-Hour but only at a second stage, 36 hours later.

4. Sharm al-Sheikh, the main Israeli territorial target of the entire operation, would be taken by the mobile reserve Ninth Brigade, which would steal its way to the target area through the rugged terrain along the eastern coast of the Sinai peninsula.

These changes conflicted with everything the IDF had tried to inculcate into its ranks for several years and were utterly at odds with the aggressive fighting spirit that Moshe Dayan himself had tried to nurture in the Israeli armed forces since his appointment as chief of staff. Asking the Israeli army to delay activating its full striking power was not only psychologically difficult, it conflicted with the IDF's three basic principles of warfare: initiative, speed, and surprise. The commanders of the Israeli air force had repeatedly told their pilots that their main mission would be to destroy the Egyptian air force as quickly as possible. Now they were relegated to minor roles only. At the most, they would be carrying out support missions for the ground forces. If the enemy was daring, they might be lucky enough to take part in a few dogfights in Israeli air space or over the Sinai. The armored corps would be forced to restrain its forces at the staging line and lose the advantage of initiative and surprise. The paratroops had always expected to be sent on the most crucial missions; now they were charged with taking a "theatrical" role—politically central but militarily marginal. Only three weeks earlier, upon his return from St. Germain, Dayan reiterated his demand to his senior commanders for a daring, aggressive, and rapid action. Now the same man who had repeatedly used phrases such as "galloping steeds" and "charging forward" had to ask his army to walk a tightrope and engage in a battle that diplomacy had dictated would be marked by caution, waiting, and operational minimalism.[4]

The most important challenge was secrecy. Dayan insisted that the circle of people familiar with the entire political background remain restricted.

> Everyone will know only those details vital for carrying out his mission, even if he does not understand the overall situation. . . . Political events will require surprising orders, in contradiction to all plans made to date, and at times even contrary to military logic. [Therefore] all levels of command are ordered to carry out their superiors' orders faithfully and strictly.[5]

Israel's army commanders thus would be forced to act against military logic and to carry out decisions whose meaning they could not grasp. That evening, after the Operations Branch had redrafted battle plans according to the new directives, the chief of staff called the entire Israeli High Command together and gave them up-to-date orders. In this broad forum Dayan was not free to explain the background to the changes and made only a general statement: "This time secrecy is not a function of field security only but also of political problems of the highest order. There is no objective need for everyone to know everything."[6]

The Sèvres Protocol required the approval of all three governments. On the evening of October 25, Yosef Nahmias cabled from Paris that Guy Mollet had just sent Ben-Gurion a letter "on behalf of his Government approving the conclusions of the talks as they had been recorded in the Protocol." In the meantime, Eden continued his pretenses. While asking his government to approve the moves agreed at Sèvres, he still believed he could avoid any semblance of direct contact with Israel. Instead of abiding by the agreed procedure of sending his Government's approval directly to the two other partners, he sent Mollet a letter advising him that the British government had received word of the talks that had taken place in Paris: "[We] confirm that in the situation envisaged [we] shall take the action desired. This is in accordance with the declaration enclosed with my communication of October 21st."[7]

Unaware of any message of October 21 from Eden, the Israelis were puzzled by the communiqué. Nahmias assumed it referred to a British commitment to implement Operation Musketeer if Israel opened hostilities in the Sinai. However, none of the contemporary documentation mentions a British undertaking other than what was included in the October 16 note drafted at Hotel Matignon. Eden was apparently referring to Selwyn Lloyd's message to Christian Pineau a few hours after his encounter in Sèvres, in which he reiterated that the English government was not asking Israel to take any action in Sinai but, should it take action on its own initiative, England would keep its commitment under the Musketeer plan. At the time Pineau did not show the Israelis this letter, lest it enrage Ben-Gurion and scotch any chances of success that the conference might hold out.

Since the Israelis did not understand what Eden was referring to, Ben-Gurion asked for a specific and clear undertaking—although with the Sèvres Protocol signed, Eden's cautious games could not release him from this obligation, and his own formulations made it quite clear that Eden was not looking for a way out and was determined to go to war. Ben-Gurion did not want to complicate the issue unduly; he cabled Nahmias: "(a) Want to know from Guy Mollet or Pineau if the English Government approves the Sèvres conclusions of October 24th. (b) If the Sèvres conclusions are approved by the two Governments, they are approved by the Israeli Government as well."[8]

Eden too may have had some misgivings about his overly cautious approach; that same day the British ambassador to Israel delivered a direct message from Eden to Ben-Gurion: "Eden is aware that Ben-Gurion suspects the English and does not believe that Eden is convinced of the need to eliminate Nasser. Eden therefore wants to reassure Ben-Gurion emphatically and most personally that there are no grounds for his suspicions and that [Eden's] negative attitude to Nasser remains unchanged."[9] Ben-Gurion was amused by the situation and was somewhat at a loss: How should he relate to the ambassador, who did not know the first thing about the clandestine events and could not understand the purpose of his own mission? He noted in his diary, "[I told him] that I had no permission to speak with him about what I knew." When the ambassador proposed continuing the conversation, Ben-Gurion told him, "Next week will be better than this week," and the ambassador was "taken aback."[10]

A telegram from Paris finally confirming the alliance arrived the next morning: "Pineau formally notifies you that both France and England have approved the Sèvres conclusions. He has therefore noted the approval of the Israeli Government and has so informed the British Government."[11]

On Friday, October 26, reserve mobilization was at its height and could no longer be disguised.

> The chauffeurs from the foreign embassies were mobilized, the hotels were emptied of employees, most of the taxicabs disappeared from the streets of the large cities, here and there stores closed when their owners were called up, transport services became bogged down when buses were removed from public service, hundreds of Israelis with . . . backpacks could be seen every morning . . . rushing to their units' assembly points.[12]

Embassies and foreign correspondents reported on the Israeli army's call-up for war. All eyes, however, were turned to the eastern front, where continued tensions along the Jordanian border made it seem likely that a blowup was about to take place. The IDF did its best to reinforce this misleading impression. The British government, fearful that its untoward indifference to events in Israel might give away its real intentions, quickly and formally demanded that the Israeli ambassador in London explain the meaning of the extensive mobilization and cautioned Israel against hasty actions against Jordan.[13] At Britain's request France did the same, but not before Yosef Nahmias had been given a suitable explanation for the French "protest."[14]

In Washington, on the other hand, concern was genuine that Israel was about to attack Jordan. The Americans had noticed the gap widening between themselves and the French and British since the conclusion of the Security Council talks in the middle of the month, but the idea of a triple alliance between Israel and America's closest allies in the West was too far-fetched to be contemplated. On Saturday, October 27, Edward Lawson asked to meet urgently with Ben-Gurion and gave him a personal letter from Eisenhower:

> I must frankly express my concern at reports of heavy mobilization on your side, a move which I fear will only increase the tension which you indicate you would like to see reduced. . . . I renew the plea . . . that there be no forcible initiatives on the part

of your Government which would endanger the peace and the growing friendship
between our two countries.[15]

The next day, Sunday, after the Israeli government had approved the war
plans, reserve mobilization was formally announced, "for the safety and security of the borders and the frontier settlements."[16] The American ambassador
again urgently met with Ben-Gurion and brought another message from the
president. This time Eisenhower did not plead but hinted very broadly at possible American steps that might be taken on the basis of the 1950 Tripartite
Agreement if Israel embarked on aggressive actions. Ben-Gurion did not treat
the U.S. president's message lightly, but by now it was too late to halt the
"scenario." He probably viewed Eisenhower's letter as the natural response of
a superpower and did not foresee the tremendous pressures that the United
States would bring to bear on him once the fighting started.

In the meantime, the French troops that would be taking part in Israel's
defensive deployment began to arrive. The French air force vanguard had
already arrived on October 22. A small airfield in the center of Israel was
turned into a French base. The interception squadrons were positioned in the
military section of Lod International Airport and at an Israeli air force base
in the north. The French set up a small command group alongside the Israeli
air force command in order to coordinate effective supervision of their units
and flights. Naval and ground forces officers also began to arrive, one after
the other. By Monday morning, October 29, a tight network of command
posts and coordinating offices was already functioning. At French request,
and over vigorous British objections, two senior IDF officers were sent to
stay at Admiral Barjot's command post in Cyprus. On the night of October
28 a large fleet of French transport planes landed, bringing hundreds of soldiers and the equipment needed to operate the French interceptors, scheduled to arrive the morning of D-Day. When the planes arrived, their tricolor
was replaced with Israel's blue-and-white Star of David insignia; by afternoon they were patrolling the skies of Israel.

Ben-Gurion's concern for Israel's air defense was sincere, and he believed
its reinforcement was essential. Moshe Dayan and the Israeli air force chief,
General Dan Tolkovsky, felt his concern exaggerated, but since the deployment of the French air force in Israel also had political value, they did not try
to dissuade Ben-Gurion. Ultimately, other than the considerable assistance
provided by French transport planes in parachuting troops and war supplies

at the Mitla Pass once the battles began, the French presence in Israel was superfluous. The Egyptians did not even try to send planes over Israel; only one Egyptian aircraft passed fleetingly into Israeli air space on the night of October 31, dropping two "blind" bombs—one hit an uninhabited hillside and the other demolished the tractor shed at a kibbutz. Once the battles began to gather momentum in the Sinai and the allies began to bomb Egyptian targets, the French command allowed its pilots in Israel to integrate into Israeli interception missions over Sinai—a role Eden officially protested.[17]

On Monday, October 29, the commanders of the French navy's small fleet assigned to patrol Israel's coastline met with Dayan. The French ships were part of the integrated Anglo-French fleet and subordinate to the supreme command in Cyprus. The French did not want to irk the British commander and therefore asked Dayan to submit a request for naval assistance. Any written proof of a relationship between Israel and the allies was desirable for Israel, and thus Dayan willingly wrote out a formal request.[18] But the French naval assistance—two destroyers and one cruiser—ultimately was also unnecessary. One French destroyer took part in the assault on the Egyptian destroyer *Ibrahim al-Awal,* and, at Dayan's request, the cruiser *George Laique* participated in the shelling of Rafah's fortifications before Laskov's division stormed it. The Egyptian destroyer would have fallen into Israeli hands without French help, and the bombardment of Rafah did little good, perhaps even provoking Egyptian alert earlier than anticipated.

Although the French forces at Israel's disposal may not have provided any great operational advantage, their integration into IDF ranks was impressive. In the course of the operation some 3,000 French soldiers were stationed in Israel. Their rapid integration can be understood only in light of the preparations made after the visit of General Challe's entourage three weeks earlier and because of the strong motivations of the French, who were happy to assist "brave little Israel" and of the Israelis, who were more than happy to realize an international military pact. "The significance of the direct operational assistance provided by the French army to Israel's campaign in the Sinai," the chief of staff's bureau chief summed up, "was mainly political, because in deeds and actions it certified the alliance forged between Israel and France."[19]

On the last days before D-Day, several decisions with political implications still remained to be taken: for example, whether to impose a blackout on Israel's cities and towns on the night of D-Day in order to protect them from Egyptian bombing. If a blackout were declared, the Egyptians might conclude that Israel was planning full-scale war; but Israel wanted to reserve the option of withdrawing during the first hours of battle and claiming that the paratroop drop was only a reprisal raid. Dayan brought the matter to the defense minister for a decision. "I don't think the Egyptians will do anything that night," Ben-Gurion told Dayan. "[A]nd it is not good to make a domestic fuss and risk the impression of war for the outside."[20] Nonetheless, preparations were made for last-minute imposition of a blackout if it should become necessary.

Another problem was the policy to be followed by the Central and Northern commands during the battles in the south. The major object was to avoid opening additional fronts. The Syrians and the Jordanians had signed defense treaties with the Egyptians, but the general staff believed that if the Israeli army was careful not to provoke them, they would not be anxious to jeopardize themselves. As it turned out, once the battle began the Syrians did make a lot of noise and even falsely reported shellings and bombings carried out by their troops. In fact, however, the border along the Golan Heights was quieter than ever before, and even the flagrant entry of Israeli troops into some of the demilitarized zones failed to elicit any reaction. The Syrians may very well have been paying Nasser back for talking but not acting when Israel attacked the Syrian forces in Operation Kinneret the previous December.

The situation was more sensitive along the Jordanian border. There the Israeli army was ready to attack Arab Legion positions north of Jerusalem and link up with the besieged Mount Scopus enclave, and even conquer the Old City, if the Jordanians dared risk war. Manpower in the Central Command was beefed up considerably for this purpose, but the Jordanian front also remained quiet. Except for some Fedayun bands roaming between Gaza and the Jordanian border that had to be taken care of, the Central Command troops remained inactive.

On Sunday, October 28, the chief of staff visited the Southern Command to verify that his orders were being carried out precisely. It had been suggested that, once the paratroop brigade linked up with the battalion dropped near the Mitla Pass, it should proceed west to the Suez Canal. Dayan dismissed the idea sharply: "It is not worth sacrificing even one man for such a mission. In any event, the IDF will not be able to reach the canal, so that the 40 kilometers separating the Mitla Pass and the canal are immaterial." The paratroop brigade eventually would be directed south, not west, to assist in the final assault on Sharm al-Sheikh. Dayan also stressed again that during the first day the armored corps was not to move across the border unless the reserve battalion's attack failed on the Qusseimah border position, which was considered vital in order to open an alternative axis to support the para-troops in the Mitla.[21]

On Monday, October 29, during the last hours before H-Hour, there was nothing left to do except draft the army spokesman's formal announcement, which would be delivered to the media immediately after the parachute drop. This was no easy task; it had to be dramatic enough to facilitate British activation of the "scenario," yet cautious enough not to elicit an exaggerated Egyptian reaction while keeping the Egyptians in the dark about actual IDF intentions. Every word was crucial, because news of events on the field might reach the Egyptian leadership only several hours later, whereas the IDF spokesman's announcement could evoke a premature reaction. Moshe Dayan and the chief of Army Intelligence considered the matter at length and even brought a draft to Ben-Gurion for approval.

At 4:00 P.M. on October 29, the following entry was recorded in the chief of staff's Bureau Diary:

> The paratroops will be dropped in about an hour's time at the Mitla and we will have crossed the Rubicon. The tensions of the last few days are dissipating at GHQ, and were it not for the noise of office furniture being moved to the secret command post, this historic Monday could be one of the most tranquil days in the Chief of Staff's Bureau. There is nothing left to do, all the plans have been made and agreed on, the units are already moving toward the staging lines. If things have been done well, they will fare well; if we have made mistakes, then we will pay for them. There is no point in thinking about it now. Tomorrow at dawn, when the battle has begun to rage and the changed conditions present new problems, our brains will still have time to be exercised making the appropriate decisions to direct the decisive effort of thousands of soldiers to cut the Gordian knot. Today there is not even that helpless tension you feel in a night raid command post before the troops reach the fences and the night is shattered by the sound of a thousand thunderbolts. From here the war looks distant and somewhat theoretical. There, on the air field at Ekron, near the French Dakotas, the hearts of the paratroopers are doubtless pounding much harder than ours are here.[22]

At 5:00 P.M. the paratroop battalion was dropped several kilometers east of the Mitla Pass; within half an hour the men were already marching toward Colonel Parker's Monument at the eastern entrance to the pass.[23] On the 7:00 P.M. news report a Voice of Israel radio announcer read the IDF spokesman's communiqué: "IDF forces entered and struck at Fedayun units in Ras el-Naqeb and Kuntila and captured positions west of the Nahel cross-roads near the Suez Canal. The action was provoked by Egyptian military strikes on Israeli land and sea transport, aimed at wreaking havoc and disturbing the peace and tranquillity of Israeli citizens."[24] That same hour the British and French military attachés were summoned to meet with the chief of Israeli Intelligence Services, who brought them up to date on the details of Israeli army actions.

Not 24 hours later it became obvious that despite Dayan's precautions and efforts to prevent the fighting in the Sinai from spreading too rapidly, a serious gap had developed between GHQ orders and troop behavior in the field. The mishaps of Operation Kadesh were less indicative of lack of discipline than the inevitable result of the dissonance between the special political requirements of the operation and the spirit that the chief of staff himself had tried to inculcate into the Israeli armed forces. For three years Moshe Dayan had been urging speed and aggressiveness and had demanded of his commanders "not to look back," "not to worry about the supply lines," "to move forward," and "to penetrate in depth." Dayan's doctrine had become part of the consciousness of the commanders at all ranks and levels. Now that same chief of staff had to contain his troops at the starting post and make them toe the line. Forced by diplomatic constraints, they now had to wage a cautious and restrained war. At the field levels the commanders were unaware of the precise political background and could not understand why Dayan had suddenly done an about-face, reining in his "chargers." A strong surge seemed to well up from below and quickly put paid to GHQ's cautious plans.

Although the greatest deviation from accepted IDF doctrine affected the air force, no problems arose there. The highest air force echelons had already had several weeks in which to become accustomed to the possibility that most of the work of destroying the Egyptian air force would be carried out by the British and the French. Furthermore, activation of the entire air force lay directly with the control center at GHQ, and the stringent order not to proceed west of the Suez Canal was unchallengeable. As Colonel Ezer Weizman, then a wing commander, recalled, "the Suez Canal was our Yalu River. . . . It could not be crossed. . . . We were free to do as we wished in the Sinai, but Heaven forfend if we cross the canal!" Their frustration notwithstanding, the Israeli pilots abided strictly by that directive. "The order not to cross the canal clipped our wings," Weizman wrote. "We pleaded with [Dan Tolkovsky] for permission to pound the Egyptian planes in their air fields. . . . We could get there, destroy [them] and get back. We could do it!"[25] Israeli air force pilots carried out interception missions in the Sinai, and a few even got to take part in some dogfights; but most of the air force's strike capability was not tested.

The mishaps that did occur took place among the ground forces. Everything went well until dawn of Tuesday, October 30. The paratroops had been dropped and had reached their targets according to plan and had begun to dig in. The rest of the Paratroop Brigade captured Kuntila on the border and began moving west rapidly. The Ninth Infantry Brigade took Ras el-Naqeb near Eilat, and the Fourth Infantry Brigade, which had begun its assault on Qusseimah with a considerable delay because of difficulties in moving toward the target, took the little desert village shortly before dawn. At that point the first problem arose. At daybreak it became obvious that Egyptian forces were still holding the western outskirts of Qusseimah. Southern Command chief General Assaf Simhoni worried that the reserve infantry brigade would not be able to complete the operation and, against GHQ orders, instructed the Seventh Armored Brigade to move in.

Late that morning Moshe Dayan reached the forward command post near the Egyptian border in the Nitzana area. There he discovered to his dismay that, although Qusseimah had been taken before the armored forces had arrived, the tanks had moved west and made their first contact with Egyptian units on the perimeter of the main Egyptian deployment at Umm-Katef. An entire armored brigade had already penetrated and was spreading into the desert—a clear breach of discipline. "I had a serious row with the Southern Command Chief yesterday," Dayan wrote in his memoirs.

> He sent in the Seventh Armored Brigade before schedule, despite specific orders that the armored corps not begin action before October 31st. The Command Chief said that he was not prepared to rely on "someone" [British and French forces] going into action and sees no justification in delaying our attack by 48 hours. He views GHQ directives on this issue as political and military errors for which we would pay dearly.[26]

Furious, Moshe Dayan continued westward and joined up with the armored brigade commander. "The brigade was already deployed some 40 kilometers inside Sinai, while the plan called for it to be 40 kilometers inside Israel," Dayan wrote. "By now we cannot prevent the armored corps' movement into the Sinai from triggering Egyptian reactions prematurely. We should thus make the most we can of it."[27] The chief of staff accordingly sent the armored brigade farther west at full speed toward the central Sinai road leading to Isma'iliyah. By noon it had gone through the Daykah pass and dug in on the central road west of Abu Agheila.

The second mishap occurred the next day. Previous plans called for the paratroops to be dropped west of the Mitla Pass, but as last-minute air reconnaissance photos showed tents set up nearby, the drop site was moved to the eastern approaches of the pass. When brigade commander Colonel Ariel Sharon reached Parker's Monument, he saw that his unit's topographical deployment was unsatisfactory. Sharon's natural tendencies always to move forward, and his ignorance of the entire political background leading up to the drop on that particular site, led him to push his troops west and enter the pass against GHQ orders. Taking advantage of permission he secured from the deputy chief of the Southern Command to patrol westward, Sharon sent in a large contingent. These soldiers encountered heavy resistance from the Egyptians, who had meanwhile taken up positions on both sides of the pass. These positions now had to be taken if the Israelis were to extricate the contingent, trapped inside the pass. Lieutenant-Colonel Aharon Davidi, one of the brigade commanders, legitimately called the battle of the Mitla "a glorious fight": "I do not recall a similar instance in which a relatively small unit entered so perfect a trap yet managed to overcome the would-be trappers in a bitter fight that lasted for hours, inflicting enemy losses ten times greater than its own."[28] It was, nevertheless, a needless battle that added nothing to the IDF's general effort in the Sinai.

Moshe Dayan, the spiritual father of the battle ethos that motivated General Simhoni and Colonel Sharon to push their men forward, was perhaps more aware than anyone else of the positive aspects of these mishaps. Nine years after the Sinai campaign he explained why he had not taken disciplinary action against the paratroop commander and the command chief: ·

> My major criticism had always been directed at soldiers who did not make the supreme effort to keep up their share in battle . . . and not at officers and enlisted men who took on more than what duty demanded. I'm not saying it's always desirable; at times it can precipitate disaster. But such outbursts, which reveal great courage and bravery, are a tremendous asset for the IDF. We have to hold on to this vigorous and ebullient tradition.[29]

In his memoirs he wrote, "It is better to fight with chargers that have to be restrained than lazy oxen that have to be urged on."[30]

Wednesday, October 31, saw the fiercest fighting of the entire campaign. At dawn several units of the Seventh Armored Brigade prepared to attack the Egyptian strongholds around the Ruwafa Dam near Abu Agheila, while others farther west made contact with some Egyptian tanks that had passed the canal going east the day before. The paratroops were poised to penetrate into the Mitla. The Tenth Infantry Brigade had taken the outlying Egyptian positions east of the main Egyptian entrenchments on the central axis and was preparing for the decisive battle at umm-Kataf. At dawn General Haim Laskov's division entered battle and began fighting for the Rafah outposts on the northern axis near the coastal road. Except for the units that were intended to take the Gaza Strip and the Straits of Tiran, all IDF forces were engaged and in the heat of battle.

At daybreak that same day, when Nasser had rejected the allies' ultimatum, which had just expired, British and French military intervention seemed imminent. The Egyptian High Command ordered a general retreat of all its forces in Sinai. Nasser believed that Britain, France, and Israel had plotted to trap the Egyptian army in the Sinai, and he was anxious to save his troops while he still could.[31] Moreover, because the allies threatened to invade the canal zone, he preferred to concentrate his forces for the battle against the invaders from the north and not against the IDF in the east. But by the time the order was issued, the Israeli air force had full control of all transportation routes in the peninsula and its armor was already in positions behind the Egyptian main lines. Thus Nasser's order spread chaos among the Egyptians, and in most sectors the retreat became a rout. Thousands were taken prisoner, many were scattered in the desert, and only two brigades out of the three divisions defending Sinai managed to cross back over the canal more or less intact. The entire Egyptian deployment in Sinai disintegrated. With the exception of the forces in umm-Kataf, which managed to hold out for two more days, and the forces around Sharm al-Sheikh, which had not yet been attacked, the Egyptian army stopped fighting an organized war.

Thus far the "scenario" went according to plan. On the evening of Monday, October 29, London and Paris "learned" that Israeli army forces had been parachuted into an area "not far from the Suez Canal." The next morning Mollet and Pineau went to London. That afternoon, after an urgent consultation, Israel and Egypt were given a note demanding that they immediately cease hostilities and permit Anglo-French forces to deploy along the Suez Canal to safeguard navigation. The belligerents were given 12 hours to respond. The British Parliament was in the midst of a stormy session precipitated by Eden's announcement that the government had decided to take the military route if either side failed to accede to the ultimatum.[32] As expected, Nasser rejected the ultimatum, and the background was set for the bombings to begin at dawn on Wednesday, as agreed in Sèvres.[33]

But Wednesday morning dawned quietly over the canal. Anxiety in Israel grew as GHQ officers and intelligence personnel waited out the hours that passed without a sign of allied bombardment. Early that afternoon a cable arrived from Yosef Nahmias explaining that, despite urgent pleas from the French, the British had decided to put off the bombing until the evening. The previous day, British Canberra bombers on patrol had drawn heavy antiair-craft fire and Egyptian intercepting aircraft had been particularly daring and aggressive. The British air force thus preferred not to begin an action at dawn and leave itself open to Egyptian counterattack all day long. The High Command in Cyprus had decided to begin bombing only at twilight, but Eden promised to send the Royal Air Force in earlier if vital Israeli targets were attacked before then.[34]

Ill and bedridden, Ben-Gurion was furious at Great Britain, "that tired old whore,"[35] for violating clearly defined and signed agreements without so much as an apology. He was enraged that Britain dared risk the lives of Israeli citizens for the tactical considerations of field commanders. Ben-Gurion wanted the paratroops brought back from the Mitla before they engaged in any heavier battles that they could not be extricated from easily; only after considerable efforts did Dayan manage to convince the "Old Man" that such a move was liable to put paid to the entire campaign. Shimon Peres cabled Nahmias: "Our forces have also encountered the Egyptian strength which Eden has just discovered, putting several of our units in a tight spot. We view the delay in implementing the operation as serious sabotage. We emphatically demand that immediate orders be given to begin bombing."[36] Several hours passed between cables and, toward evening, the British and the French finally began bombing Egyptian air force bases. Operation Musketeer had started, and Israel breathed a sigh of relief.

Meanwhile, dramatic developments were taking place at U.N. headquarters in New York. During the first hours Israel was alone, facing not only the threat of Egyptian bombing, but also the political pressure brought to bear on it by the entire international community, especially the United States. Word of the Israeli army's entry into Sinai reached President Eisenhower on October 29 when he was en route to deliver a campaign speech in Richmond, Virginia. Only two weeks earlier Eisenhower had told the secretary of state that the American leadership should base its decision making only on American interests and that under no circumstances would he permit the upcoming elections to interfere with his considerations. True to his word, the president canceled his Richmond speech and quickly returned to the White House; that same day he ordered an urgent consultation of State Department, CIA, and Pentagon personnel.

Eisenhower's personal aide, Brigadier General Andrew J. Goodpastor, took notes at the meeting and recorded that the president had taken an active role, setting the pace of the discussion. He had obviously set his mind on upholding America's commitment to the 1950 Tripartite Agreement, to which he referred at least six times, making remarks such as "We must make good our pledges," "We must move to help Egypt at once in order to honor our commitments," "We are prepared to redeem our pledge."[37] Eisenhower was also miffed at the Israeli refusal to heed his personal pleas to refrain from hostilities in his message to Ben-Gurion when word of wide-scale mobilization of Israeli reserves had reached him.[38]

The meeting ended in a decision to call for an immediate session of the Security Council and demand that Israel cease fire at once and retreat to its borders.[39] Dulles instructed U.N. Ambassador Henry Cabot Lodge to be adamant: "No domestic factors ought to stand in our way of taking a firm position against the Israeli aggression."[40]

On Tuesday, October 30, at 11:00 A.M., the Security Council convened in New York to consider steps to halt Israel's military action in Egypt.[41] Lodge proposed a resolution calling for an immediate Israeli cease-fire and general retreat.[42] At that very minute, however, Sir Anthony Eden was advising the British Parliament of the Anglo-French ultimatum to Israel and Egypt. This startling news immediately raised suspicions in New York that the Israeli assault had somehow been coordinated in advance with France and the United Kingdom. In a telephone conversation with Senator William F. Knowland of California, Dulles said, "The evidence is that the Israelis were used as a decoy."[43] Now that France and Britain were also indicted, and attention drawn primarily to them, political pressure on Israel abated somewhat. Abba Eban wrote, "We who had that morning come in as the sole accused, proud and sure of our right but nonetheless alone against eleven judges, went out reassured, hand in hand with two of those self-same judges."[44]

On Wednesday, October 31, a dramatic turn of events took place in the Security Council: The French and British representatives vetoed the American proposal, eliminating any remaining doubts about joint British, French, and Israeli orchestration of the events in Sinai. Shortly after the vote Dulles told Senator Walter George, chairman of the Senate Foreign Relations Committee, "They are more or less conniving in an attack against Egypt and are using that as a prearranged pretext. . . . It is almost certain that Britain and France are working in collusion with the Israelis."[45]

But that very day a way was found to circumvent the Security Council. The Yugoslav representative tabled a proposal for an emergency session of the General Assembly on the basis of the "Uniting for Peace" procedure that had been initiated during the Korean War. This was intended to bypass the Security Council when one of its permanent members vetoed a motion and stalled action. Being a procedural proposal, no veto could be cast; it was therefore passed, and the next day the drama moved to the General Assembly.

On Thursday, November 1, an overwhelming majority of the General Assembly vote called on the parties—including France and Great Britain, which had by then begun bombing Egyptian air fields—to cease fire immediately and demanded that Israel retreat to the Armistice lines. All U.N. member states were called on to refrain from sending arms to the region. The General Assembly would remain in session until the crisis had passed.[46]

At this point Dag Hammarskjöld entered the picture. At the conclusion of Security Council deliberations, before the issue was transferred to the General Assembly, the U.N. secretary general had dramatically hinted to the council members that he would resign if the U.N.'s efforts failed. Now, in the crucible of the General Assembly, Hammarskjöld became a central figure. "He appeared as the embodiment of the U.N.'s highest values," Eban wrote. "[H]e turned into a kind of martyr. Almost ritualistically, nearly all the representatives felt themselves bound to make expressions of loyalty and personal esteem to him. For many this was a desperate sign of . . . holding on to the U.N. as the ultimate hope for attaining peace."[47]

But another figure was about to emerge in the General Assembly. On Saturday, November 3, the Canadian foreign minister, Lester Pearson, proposed the establishment of an international force to supervise the cease-fire and remain in the area evacuated by the belligerents retreating according to U.N. resolution.[48] Two days later the General Assembly voted to establish the U.N. Emergency Force (UNEF) and placed it under the command of General E.L.M. Burns, up to that point chief of staff of the U.N. Observers Force in Jerusalem.[49]

✻   ✻   ✻

The call for a cease-fire started a race against time. Israel would shortly be forced to comply with the U.N. resolution, but before then the conquest of the Sinai peninsula had to be completed. On November 1, in the evening, the first units of the Israeli armored corps reached the "stopping line" ten miles east of the canal, beyond which the Sèvres Protocol prohibited the Israeli army from going. At the same time, the paratroops began moving south from the Mitla area to take the western coast of the peninsula, from Ras a-Sudar through Abu Rudeis down to a-Tur and Sharm al-Sheikh. By Friday fighting had stopped throughout the peninsula, with the exception of the southern tip. On Saturday, November 3, the IDF had already begun moving some of its reserve units back north.[50]

Only the conquest of Sharm al-Sheikh and the opening of the Straits of Tiran remained. The Ninth Mechanized Brigade had been ordered to move south on Friday morning after a delay of 24 hours. Even though the French and British had been pounding the Egyptian air force since Wednesday evening, no one knew precisely how badly hurt it was. Dayan did not want the Ninth Brigade to become bogged down in treacherous desert routes, open to Egyptian air attack. He may also have misjudged the time needed for the units to complete their operation. Indeed, only on Sunday, November 4, were the Egyptian outposts in Ras Nasrani at the straits taken; Sharm al-Sheikh itself was not captured until November 5.

On Saturday, November 3, Dag Hammarskjöld demanded that Israel, Great Britain, and France provide an unequivocal response to the General Assembly's call for a cease-fire. If the IDF were to complete the conquest of Sharm al-Sheikh, diplomatic pressure had to be reduced. Thus Abba Eban replied that Israel would agree to a cease-fire if Egypt agreed, and on the condition that Egypt ended the state of belligerency in its relations with Israel.[51] But the British and French also needed more time, as their assault forces were still three days away from Egyptian shores; they therefore told Hammarskjöld that their governments would accede to the cease-fire provided that Egypt agreed to the presence of Anglo-French forces along the canal until the U.N. Emergency Force was organized, and provided that this force was stationed in Egypt until all parties could agree on a satisfactory arrangement for control of the Suez Canal.

Clearly, the response was insufficient for the U.N.; Christian Pineau and General Challe therefore left for London that very day and pleaded with the British to step up the assault by dropping troops into Egypt 36 hours before the amphibious force landed along Egypt's coastline. But the British command in Cyprus was hesitant to expose the paratroops to Egyptian armor. The French therefore proposed that the Israeli forces located not far from the canal provide tactical cover for the allied paratroops. Admiral Barjot urgently sent the French liaison officer for Israel to find out from Dayan if the Israelis would consider an operation on the eastern bank of the canal and an assault on Kantara. Dayan consulted with Ben-Gurion; Israel was indeed willing to help France, and also wanted to ensure the physical presence of

Anglo-French forces on the ground before the U.N. steamroller could enforce a cease-fire. Thus shortly before midnight on November 3, Israel sent a positive reply to French headquarters in Cyprus. But the British commanders refused to listen; the French could do whatever they wanted inside Israel, but no Israeli soldier was to go beyond the agreed "stop line."

The news did not particularly upset Israeli army GHQ. Though they were anxious to see the allied forces finally touch Egyptian soil, the Israeli commanders were not keen to sacrifice the lives of their soldiers on the altar of what they considered British caprice. "Ben-Gurion does not want to get bogged down in the international morass of the canal," Dayan explained to his staff. "[W]e are not partners on the Suez issue, we have enough problems without it, and there's no point being in a coalition on an issue that the whole world is involved in and opposed to. Israel will see to the Sinai; someone else will see to the canal."[52] The French pressure finally took effect, and Eden sent his defense minister to Cyprus to push the British commanders into action. The parachute drop was advanced by 24 hours and scheduled for Monday, November 5.[53]

By the afternoon of Sunday, November 4, the Ninth Brigade was poised to attack the Sharm al-Sheikh outposts and conclude the battle at dawn on Monday. That same day Hammarskjöld reported to the General Assembly that the United Kingdom, France, and Israel had not complied with the call for a cease-fire.[54] The Israeli U.N. delegation felt extremely pressured. At Abba Eban's suggestion, Golda Meir approached the French and British ambassadors in Israel and asked if their governments objected to Israel announcing that it accepted the cease-fire order. Inasmuch as the Sinai campaign had been planned and coordinated through Defense Ministry rather than Foreign Ministry channels in all three countries, and since the three foreign services were not privy to the details nor aware of the exact implications of Israel's question, the two ambassadors replied that their respective governments would not object. At the conclusion of Sunday's General Assembly session, shortly after midnight on Saturday (7:00 A.M. Israeli time), Abba Eban announced that Israel was prepared to accept an immediate cease-fire on condition that Egypt responded in kind. No objections were raised by the IDF, which assumed that several hours would pass before the cease-fire went into effect, by which time Sharm al-Sheikh would be taken.

Eban's announcement, however, was greeted with furor in Paris. If the Israeli army ceased firing before the Anglo-French ground forces reached

Egypt, what justification remained for the operation? Abel Thomas urgently telephoned his friend Shimon Peres: Eban's U.N. announcement had to be rescinded immediately. Peres replied that Israel had fulfilled all its obligations and if the British had chosen to fritter away their operation, that was their problem. Thomas pleaded with Peres to find some formula that would save the situation,[55] and Bourgès-Maunoury was alerted to lend his weight. Nahmias cabled:

> Bourgès-Maunoury says that the French Government has heard from London that we have agreed to the U.N. Secretary General's request for a cease-fire. He asked me to inform you that the French Government views this as an extraordinary act on our part and asks whether we know that this fundamentally alters the entire situation. He requests an immediate reply, in the hope that the news is mistaken and was maliciously spread by our enemies. Please respond immediately so that it arrives before Mollet's trip to London tonight.[56]

From his sickbed Ben-Gurion consulted with his aides and advisors. Eden had already been looking for a way to untangle himself and cancel the landing; the Israeli announcement could be a convenient pretext for just that. Since that left France on its own, and the party most seriously injured by Israel's acceptance of the cease-fire, Ben-Gurion decided to accede to France's pleas and instructed Abba Eban to rescind his U.N. statement. Late Sunday night Eban publicly declared that he had been misunderstood; his intention had not been to announce Israel's compliance with the cease-fire call but merely to describe the actual situation on the battlefield.[57] In any event, time was running out. On Monday morning, November 5, the British paratroops jumped and conquered the Gamil airfield west of Port Said, and the French paratroops took the bridges south of the city. Now Eban was free to notify the U.N. of Israel's unconditional compliance with the cease-fire. That same morning the Ninth Brigade also overran the last of the Egyptian outposts in Sharm al-Sheikh, and the vanguard of paratroopers arrived from the northwest and joined up with the forces that had just completed their mission. On the chief of staff's desk lay a telegram from Colonel Avraham Yaffe, commander of the Ninth Mechanized Brigade: "Sharm al-Sheikh is in our hands. It's over, thank God."[58]

On Tuesday, November 6, the allied landing forces finally touched the shores of Port Said and captured the town. The paratroops dropped a day earlier continued south, but when they reached al-Cap, a few kilometers north of Kantara, the order to halt reached them.[59] Britain and France were forced to announce compliance with the U.N.'s cease-fire order and bring their forces to a standstill. A day earlier, on November 5, the Soviet Union, partially relieved of its preoccupation with the Hungarian revolt, had begun to apply pressure, requesting that the Security Council convene and proposing a resolution calling for U.N. military assistance for Egypt.[60] The resolution was defeated, but the next morning the Soviet premier, Nikolai Bulganin, cabled Great Britain, France, and Israel and hinted broadly that the Soviet Union would intervene with missiles if they failed to comply immediately with the General Assembly's call for a cease-fire.[61]

America was applying heavy economic pressures on the British government, threatening to undermine the British pound sterling. Domestic pressure was also mounting; the Labour Party organized mass demonstrations in London, with crowds calling for "Law not war!" and urging "Eden must go!" Serious rifts emerged within the ranks of the Conservative Party. Newspapers and even the BBC were openly critical of Eden's government. Pressed on all sides, and urged by his colleagues, Eden called the fighting to a halt.[62]

Operation Musketeer failed; the Anglo-French forces did not complete their missions. One of the main reasons for the failure was British insistence on maintaining the pretense of no prior collusion in Israel's attack on Egypt. Operation Musketeer as redrafted in September was based on massive bombing of Egyptian air force bases and other strategic targets and on the subsequent landing of ground forces that would then take the entire canal zone. The ground forces were to leave from bases in Malta and Toulon, at least six days away from the landing beaches at Port Said. Since the British were obstinate about maintaining the pretense of no prior coordination with Israel, they could not begin to dispatch the landing fleet before the ultimatum to Egypt and Israel had run out. Thus the allied ground forces arrived eight days after the Israeli paratroops had landed in the Mitla Pass, by which time international pressure was so great that the operation had to be terminated just as it reached its peak. Operation Musketeer's failure did not affect the Israeli army in the course of its own battles, but it had a great impact on the political constellation that emerged after the fighting ended.

The cable Bulganin had sent Ben-Gurion was less subtle than the ones sent to London and Paris:

The Soviet Government has already expressed its definite condemnation of the armed aggression by Israel, as well as by Britain and France against Egypt. . . . Disregarding this, the Government of Israel, acting as a tool of foreign imperialist Powers, continues the foolhardy adventure challenging all the peoples of the East who are waging a struggle against colonialism. . . . The Government of Israel is playing with the fate of peace, with the fate of its own people, in a criminal and irresponsible manner. It is sowing hatred for the State of Israel among the peoples of the East, which cannot but affect the future of Israel and which will place a question upon the very existence of Israel as a state. . . . Taking into consideration the situation that has arisen, the Soviet Government has passed a decision to advise its Ambassador in Tel Aviv to leave Israel and immediately go to Moscow. We hope that the Government of Israel will duly understand and appreciate our warning. (signed) N. Bulganin.[63]

Ben-Gurion was not immune to a fear of Soviet missiles, but it seems that he recognized the seriousness of the Soviet threat only later. The IDF's victory and success in the Sinai apparently filled him with euphoria for several hours. At a meeting that evening he playfully considered the question of a suitable Hebrew name for Sharm al-Sheikh. Someone proposed *Sha'arei Eilat* (the Gates of Eilat), but Ben-Gurion protested that gates could be closed as well as opened; perhaps then *Mevo Eilat* (the Eilat Approaches)— always to stay open? The eventual consensus was an allegedly historic name: *Mifratz Shlomo* (the Gulf of Solomon).[64]

That morning a victory parade was held in Sharm al-Sheikh to mark the end of the war. Moshe Dayan read Ben-Gurion's telegram to the forces:

To the soldiers and commanders of the Ninth Brigade—you have been given a unique and historic privilege—you have brought to a successful conclusion the greatest and most glorious campaign in the history of our people and one of the most wonderful operations in the history of all nations. . . . With tremendous drive the combined IDF armed forces have stretched out a hand to King Solomon who developed Eilat as the first Israeli port three thousand years ago. . . . Eilat will again be a Hebrew port in the south and the Red Sea straits will be open to Israeli navigation and Yotvat, known as Tiran, which until 1,400 years ago was an independent Hebrew state, will again become part of the Third Commonwealth of Israel. Congratulations to the victorious IDF.[65]

The next morning, Wednesday, November 7, Ben-Gurion addressed the Knesset in a what may be described as a victory speech.[66] He began on a note that well expressed the general public atmosphere and his own mood: "The drama at Mount Sinai, which has been reaffirmed recently by the courageous force of the Israeli army, is also a focal point not only for the consolidation of the State's security and internal tranquillity, but also for our external relations on the world scene." He was careful not to be specific about the future, but it was obvious what his intentions were: So long as there was no full peace, Israel would retain at least some of the territory taken in the campaign:

> The Armistice Agreement with Egypt is dead and buried and cannot be restored to life. . . . In consequence, the Armistice Lines between Egypt and Israel have no more validity. . . . We do not wish our relations with Egypt to continue in the present anarchic state and we are ready to enter into negotiations for a stable peace, cooperation and good neighborly relations. . . . On no account will Israel agree to the stationing of a foreign force, no matter how it is called, in its territories or in any of the area occupied by it. . . .[67]

He concluded his emotional address on a calmer note: "We will meet the future with courage, wisdom, the awareness of our just cause and our strength, without ignoring our natural and inevitable ties to the family of nations in the world." Not a day later, Ben-Gurion would be forced to see just how much strength and wisdom he and his colleagues needed in order to hold on to at least some of the gains of the campaign that he had so glorified to the army and the Knesset and to see just how very oppressive those "natural and inevitable ties" really were.

17
· · ·

WITHDRAWAL

The Israeli U.N. ambassador's announcement of November 5 of Israel's compliance with the cease-fire order was not enough for the General Assembly. The resolutions of November 1 and November 4 called not only for a cease-fire but also for a complete withdrawal of all forces from the territories taken during battle. The Israeli forces were expected to retreat beyond the 1949 Armistice Lines. On the night of November 7, after the cease-fire went into effect, another General Assembly majority vote demanded "immediate withdrawal."[1]

Several times before hostilities had even begun, Ben-Gurion had wondered about Israel's chances of retaining any territory it might take in the Sinai. On October 28, when he recommended going to war to his government, he had said, "I do not know what the outcome in the Sinai will be. . . . I can imagine that power will be brought to bear to force us to leave the Sinai peninsula. . . . and I fear America most of all. America is capable of forcing us to withdraw. She doesn't need to send an army for that purpose. She has other effective means which are powerful enough."[2]

But now that the Israeli army held the entire peninsula, Ben-Gurion tended to believe that Israel could hold on to at least some of the fruits of its military victory. The allusions in his Knesset address, to the effect that Israel would insist on retaining the entire Sinai peninsula, the cradle of its civilization and religion, were out of character; and other than those brief hours of euphoria, Ben-Gurion never deluded himself that Israel could hold on to the entire territory. But for several weeks he did believe that some of it could be held for at least a while, in particular the strategically vital Straits of Tiran and the Gaza Strip. In the Knesset he had been unequivocal: The 1949 Armistice Agreement and Armistice Lines had been finally laid to rest and were no longer valid; the demand to withdraw IDF forces beyond those lines was thus fundamentally unacceptable.

But indeed such powerful political and psychological pressure was brought to bear on Ben-Gurion immediately after his Knesset address that within 24 hours he was forced to instruct Abba Eban to announce Israel's compliance in principle with the resolution on withdrawal too. The only reservation that Abba Eban and Ya'acov Herzog, Ben-Gurion's political aide, managed to include in the announcement at the last minute was that Israel's withdrawal would be linked to the deployment of the U.N. force: "The Government of Israel will willingly withdraw its forces from Egypt immediately upon the conclusion of satisfactory arrangements with the U.N. in connection with the international force."[3] This reservation could not ultimately prevent total IDF withdrawal from all conquered territories, but it allowed Israel to bargain stubbornly and at length about the pace of withdrawal, about the functions of the U.N. force and its authorities, and especially about the political guarantees Israel would receive in exchange for withdrawal. The bargaining did not result in any formal, contractual changes, but it effectively created a totally new situation that would obtain in Israeli-Egyptian relations for the next ten years.

On November 8, however, all this was still unclear. The announcement of compliance with the order to withdraw simply expressed Israel's painful, total surrender to international pressure. What induced Ben-Gurion and the Israeli government to make this dramatic move? Had Bulganin's threats taken hold? Or was it the American government's implacability that precipitated the move? There is no one unequivocal answer, as we can neither fully analyze nor even document the tidal wave of pressures that beset the prime minister's bureau that morning nor precisely weigh Ben-Gurion's own considerations. Years later he admitted that the Soviet threats had left their impression on him—"the fear was real," he told a group of senior army officers.[4] Nonetheless the sum total of available evidence indicates that although Soviet pressure did constitute a weighty consideration for the Israeli leadership, its main effect was indirect, through the panic that seized the Western capitals.

Upon receiving Bulganin's telegram, Ben-Gurion sent Golda Meir and Shimon Peres to Paris to clarify just how serious the Soviet threats were. In the French capital the two Israelis met with Pineau, who seemed very worried indeed: French intelligence had apparently received word that Soviet troops had entered northern Syria, provoking great anxiety in Paris.

"M. Pineau sadly told us that France would stand by Israel 'no matter what,'" Peres wrote. "She would share military resources, but the superior strength of the Russians should not be ignored. They have missiles and unconventional weapons, and we should draw our conclusions accordingly."[5] French fears as expressed in Pineau's discussions with Meir and Peres doubtless weakened Ben-Gurion's resolve.

But the main effect of the Soviet missile threat came through the U.S. government's fears of Soviet intervention in the crisis as reflected in the mounting American pressure on Israel to withdraw. When fighting broke out, and especially when the British and French roles became obvious, the main concern of American policy makers was that the Communists would exploit the situation and take over the Middle East, winning for good the grateful loyalty of the Third World in general and the Arab states in particular. More than anything else, Washington feared that the Soviet Union might succeed in maneuvering the United States into taking a stand alongside the aggressors, vilified together with them for the colonialist campaign. Indeed, the concern was not groundless; in his memoirs Nikita Khrushchev relates that Bulganin had sent Eisenhower a letter proposing a joint Soviet-American action against the aggressors,[6] consulting first with veteran Soviet diplomat Vyacheslav Molotov. Asked whether he thought the Americans would accept the proposal, Molotov replied, "Of course not, but this way we will force them to refuse, we will reveal the hypocrisy of their declarations condemning the attack on Egypt."[7]

During the first 24 hours of the crisis President Eisenhower stressed the moral arguments; later, however, the overriding motivation—mistrust of the Soviet maneuvers—became apparent. In a meeting of the National Security Council on November 1, Eisenhower and Dulles repeatedly reiterated that "If we were not now prepared to assert our leadership in this cause, leadership would certainly be seized by the Soviet Union . . . [and] all of these newly independent countries will turn from us to the USSR. We will be looked upon as forever tied to British and French colonialist policies."[8]

American fears were great while the Soviet Union was still preoccupied in suppressing the Hungarian revolt; they skyrocketed once the revolution had been quelled. The Soviet invocation of the Security Council on November 5, the proposal to Eisenhower for a joint U.S.-USSR use of force in defense of Egypt, and Bulganin's threatening cables of November 6 to Eden, Mollet, and Ben-Gurion clearly signaled to the White House that the weeklong Soviet hesitation caused by its East European distraction had ended, and the Soviet Union had finally decided to plunge into the Middle East crisis, exploiting it to the fullest.

Like the French, the American State Department panicked at rumors of Soviet presence in Syria, among other reasons because of the messages sent by the U.S. ambassador in Moscow warning against the danger of Soviet military intervention.[9] Word of Soviet submarines sighted in the eastern Mediterranean fanned rumors, as did the passage of Soviet warships through the Straits of Gibraltar and the high-altitude downing of a British Canberra bomber over Syrian territory, which triggered conjectures that it was downed by Soviet pilots. News also began to arrive of "volunteers" being drafted in the Soviet Union, China, and Indonesia. Whether the Americans contributed to the campaign of fear, they themselves undoubtedly were afraid of Soviet intervention and worried that it would force the United States to take a stand alongside its allies, nullifying any political advantage they might have gained by their quick reactions at the outset against the invasion of Egypt. Eisenhower ordered an increased military alert but pressured his people to urge Hammarskjöld to station the U.N. force in Egypt as quickly as possible. Once this force had arrived, any Soviet intervention would have to be viewed as inimical to U.N. interests. Hammarskjöld himself considered the U.N. force to be a vital barrier against Soviet intervention.[10] But many days would pass before the international force became operational, and in the meantime Hammarskjöld and the Americans were aware that only an immediate British, French, and Israeli declaration of intent to withdraw from the conquered territories would eliminate the cause for unilateral Soviet intervention.

Ben-Gurion's Knesset speech on November 7 worried both Washington and the U.N. His blunt reference to the demise of the Armistice Agreements, his opposition to the stationing of an international force in any area under Israeli control, and his hints that Sinai was not in fact "Egyptian soil"—all these were interpreted as Israel's rejection of the demand to withdraw.[11] A few hours after the speech the American president sent Ben-Gurion an urgent telegram drafted courteously but unequivocally: "Statements attributed to your Government to the effect that Israel does not intend to withdraw from Egyptian territory . . . have been called to my attention. . . . Any such decision by the Government of Israel would seriously undermine the urgent efforts being made by the United Nations to restore peace in the Middle East." The telegram concluded with a clear threat: "It would be a matter of the greatest regret to all my countrymen if Israeli policy on a matter of such grave concern to the world should in any way impair the friendly cooperation between our two countries."[12] Lest any doubts remained, Herbert Hoover, filling in for the secretary of state, told Abba Eban: "We both have evidence that the Soviets are exploiting the situation in a way that might endanger world peace. . . . Israel's refusal to withdraw will be interpreted as contempt for American public opinion and will inevitably lead to grave measures, such as ending public and private aid, imposing U.N. sanctions and, finally, expulsion from the U.N."[13]

That day, hemmed in from all sides by the pressures of an atmosphere of acute crisis, Abba Eban sent off a series of urgent telegrams and phone calls to Jerusalem that clearly reflected his severe misgivings, imploring Ben-Gurion to accept the General Assembly's verdict. In his diary Ben-Gurion wrote, "Eban called me, transfixed by fear. His cables are also spreading alarm. Everyone seems to have been panic-stricken by Russia."[14] That afternoon Hammarskjöld took Eban out of a General Assembly session and demanded that he inform him officially whether Israel was prepared to pull its forces back.[15] Shortly thereafter Eban cabled Jerusalem, analyzing the situation bluntly:

> The Soviet Union is threatening that if the armies do not get out she will intervene with force the way the British and French did last week. The United States is taking this threat seriously and insists that the international force enter and disregard any external or internal pressure, because the Americans believe that the issue concerns world peace and defense against atomic war. . . .
>
> If we refuse to permit the U.N. force to enter, we may very well find ourselves fighting against it. Which means confronting all the great powers. . . . I see great danger of losing all the tremendous advantages we have already gained and which we still can gain in the wake of our military victory.[16]

In yet another cable Eban wrote Ben-Gurion: "The general feeling is that issues on which world peace hangs are in your hands."[17] And Nahum Goldman, president of the World Zionist Organization and a leader in the campaign to gain American Jewry's support for Israel, cabled that "If an open rift develops between Israel and the U.S. Administration on this point, I see no possibility of gaining American Jewry's support, either politically or financially."[18]

Despite the plethora of cables, Eban was afraid that his government did not actually comprehend just how serious the dangers were. He wanted to send Reuven Shiloah to Jerusalem to explain the situation in person. But this was unnecessary; Ben-Gurion's bureau and everyone present there at the time was not spared the panic that had taken hold.[19] "A nightmarish day," the "Old Man" wrote in his diary on November 8.

> [F]rom Rome, from Paris and from Washington: talk of a fleet of Soviet planes and "volunteers" for Syria, of a promise to bomb Israel. . . . Much of it may be exaggeration, but Bulganin's message to me—a letter that could have been written by Hitler—and the pandemonium of Russian tanks running loose in Hungary are evidence of what these communist Nazis are capable of.[20]

Late that evening, after two urgent Cabinet sessions, Ben-Gurion gave in and cabled Eban instructions to announce Israel's compliance with the order to withdraw. Moshe Dayan, who was present, recalled that Ben-Gurion "was very pale and as enraged as a wounded lion."[21] In a national broadcast shortly after midnight, Ben-Gurion announced Israel's acceptance of the demand to withdraw. To his people and to the Israeli army combatants he could only give a few words of consolation: "There is no power on earth that can nullify your great victory. . . . Israel after the Sinai Campaign will no longer be the Israel of before this great campaign."[22] Ben-Gurion tried to sound optimistic and encouraging, but his voice choked, revealing to most listeners his true feelings of disappointment and pain.

Israel's announcement was received with relief in Washington and at U.N. headquarters in New York. Hammarskjöld told Eban that this most welcome decision would benefit the people of Israel for generations to come.[23] Eisenhower cabled Ben-Gurion: "This decision will be widely welcomed not only by the United States but by all the nations which are struggling to restore peace and security for all nations in the Middle East."[24] For Israel, the announcement was the first step in a long, exhausting struggle beset by one disappointment after another. Despite his agreement in principle to withdraw, at this point Ben-Gurion still hoped that Israel might be able to retain two vital strategic areas: Sharm al-Sheikh and the Gaza Strip. For this purpose it was imperative to gain time. Tempers had to be calmed at the U.N., and a comprehensive effort had to be launched to persuade the world, and in particular the American public, to support Israel's demands. "Time is of the essence in our political struggle," Ben-Gurion told senior IDF officers. "We need time for the world to consider the issue calmly, not hysterically, not panic-stricken, but lucidly."[25]

Israel also needed time to create facts on the ground. For the opening of the straits to Israeli shipping to become a solid fact, Ben-Gurion dispatched three old naval frigates from the Mediterranean to Eilat though the Cape of Good Hope. Israeli Treasury officials quickly consulted with petroleum and ocean transport experts in order to formulate a plan for an oil pipeline to be laid between the Red Sea and the port of Ashkelon on the Mediterranean, making Eilat not only Israel's main oil supply port but also Europe's, replacing the Suez Canal, which was now in capricious Egyptian hands.

It was taking longer than expected to set up the U.N. Emergency Force (UNEF); and inasmuch as its first task was to facilitate the withdrawal of the Anglo-French forces from the canal, Israel could enjoy several weeks before the UNEF commander could move his force to the Sinai Peninsula.

The proposal to establish a special U.N. task force to guarantee the cease-fire and the withdrawal of invading forces was raised by the Canadian Foreign Minister, Lester Pearson, on November 1, shortly before the General Assembly emergency session convened.[26] It was not a new idea and seems to have been inspired by General E.L.M. Burns, the Canadian chief of staff of UNTSO, who had long been frustrated by the fact that the observers he commanded lacked authority and actual power.[27] But Pearson's original concern was not primarily to ensure the welfare of the U.N. observers, but to provide Anthony Eden with a lifeline to obviate the need for actual military intervention. He submitted the proposal on November 3, when the allied forces were still far from Egyptian shores and the operation could still be cancelled. He writes, "I brought up the possibility of an emergency UN force . . . to provide a substitute for British-French intervention, thus giving them a good reason to withdraw from their own stated objective of restoring peace."[28]

Hammarskjöld was initially cool to Pearson's proposal because it smacked of enforced Egyptian acceptance of the U.N. force to safeguard navigation in the canal, thus to a certain extent constituting international supervision. This is indeed how Eden at first understood the proposal. Before officially bringing it to the emergency session of the U.N., Pearson had consulted hurriedly with Britain's U.N. representative. He had been advised that Eden was about to inform Parliament of his agreement in principle to an arrangement of this sort and would be adding that "police action must be there to separate the belligerents. If the U.N. were then willing to take over the physical task of maintaining the peace, no one would be better pleased than we."[29] Anthony Eden seems to have seen the new proposal as an occasion to realize his desire for international supervision of the canal without needing to get entangled with occupying forces and military government. It was precisely for that reason, however, that Hammarskjöld thought

Nasser would reject the proposal. But it quickly became clear that Egypt's leader did not reject the idea, as it did not specifically call for UNEF to stay in the canal zone as a supervising force for an extended period. Nasser saw the proposal as a way of preventing or halting the allied landing without relinquishing Egyptian sovereignty over the canal.

At this stage the resolution was vague enough for all parties to agree to its implementation; no reference was made to the makeup of the force, the duration of its presence, the precise area of its deployment, or its powers and responsibilities. Egypt was not opposed in principle; the British tended to accept it; the Americans saw it as the only defense against Soviet intervention; it could be implemented within a reasonable period of time; and several countries already announced their readiness to put their troops at the U.N.'s disposal: All these considerations turned the secretary general into an avid supporter of the proposal who now strongly advocated its rapid implementation. British U.N. Ambassador Pierson Dixon has described Hammarskjöld's enthusiasm: "He was clearly fascinated by the sudden emergence of a new U.N. Command . . . he has visions of building up a U.N. police force under his command. A sort of peace brigade to put out world fires under the general direction of the head of the world organization."[30]

On November 3 the General Assembly passed the following resolution: "The General Assembly . . . requests, as a matter of priority, the Secretary General to submit to it within 48 hours a plan for the setting up, with the consent of the nations concerned, of an emergency international U.N. force to secure and supervise the cessation of hostilities. . . ."[31] Two days later Hammarskjöld submitted a short interim report to the General Assembly, which instructed him to immediately take those administrative steps required to implement the resolution.[32] It also approved the appointment of General E.L.M. Burns to command the force and empowered him to draw on the existing observer force in order to immediately set up the necessary staff to supervise the establishment of UNEF.

❉ ❉ ❉

Lester Pearson was not successful in halting Operation Musketeer; the British and the French did not call off the landing. UNEF's main duty from this point on would therefore be to ensure the withdrawal of the allied forces from Egyptian territory and afterward to move on to the Sinai.

Britain initially had hoped that the U.N. would agree to its troops—which were in the area anyway—becoming part of the new force, permitting them to implement their original objective: ensuring international supervision of the canal.[33] But British hopes were quickly dashed; under no circumstances would Hammarskjöld countenance prizes being awarded for aggression: "The U.N. could never condone what it virtually condemned."[34] The U.N. was obdurate: The British and French forces had to withdraw from the canal.

But for a while the U.N. Secretariat, which was busy organizing the new force, did not push Britain and France to announce a final evacuation date for their troops. The United States, however, feared intervention on the part of "volunteers" from the Soviet bloc and exerted considerable pressure on the secretary general to speed up UNEF's deployment to prevent the creation of a military vacuum that could be filled by undesirable forces. But the Americans, like Hammarskjöld and his staff, realized that it was imperative that an effective and efficient U.N. force take over the evacuated areas. Thus they were willing to wait until UNEF had organized itself and was suitably prepared to take up its duties.

By the end of November, however, UNEF was taking form and pressure was finally mounting on Britain and France to announce the timing for the evacuation of their troops. The canal was blocked and no oil moved through it to Europe. Iraqi oil for Europe had also stopped flowing through the pipeline to the Mediterranean coastline because the Egyptians had persuaded Syrian intelligence to blow up the pumping stations in Syria. Europe was on the brink of an industrial and economic disaster, but Nasser adamantly refused to clear the canal until the Anglo-French forces had left; and the United States refused to implement emergency plans for an alternative oil supply to Europe. America also blocked British efforts to save the pound sterling by prohibiting Britain from drawing on its balances with the International Monetary Fund. The situation at the beginning of December had become untenable, and the British Cabinet, headed temporarily by R. A. Butler, voted to concede and announce the immediate withdrawal of Anglo-French forces.

The British and the French pulled their forces out of the Port Said area on December 22. Egyptian troops followed fast on the heels of UNEF, and the Egyptian authorities immediately demanded that the U.N. force leave the city with all due speed and move on to the Sinai. British and French expectations that UNEF would remain in the canal zone and thereby grant it some kind of international status evaporated.

From the outset, Israel had been wary of the very idea of a U.N. force. In his November 7 address to the Knesset, Ben-Gurion stressed that "Under no terms will Israel consent to foreign forces, whatever they may be called, stationed within her borders or in one of the territories held by her."[35] This principle was also included in the Israeli Government's November 11 decision formulating Israel's requirements in exchange for IDF withdrawal from Sinai: (1) the Egyptian army would not return to the Sinai peninsula; (2) the international force would remain in the canal zone; (3) the Armistice Agreements would be annulled and negotiations toward a stable peace undertaken between Israel and Egypt; (4) the Straits of Tiran and the coastal strip connecting them with Eilat would remain in Israeli hands.[36]

But it was early yet. Hammarskjöld was busy with UNEF's organization, the evacuation of the Anglo-French forces, and the clearing of the canal. He had not yet found it necessary to contend with Israel's position. Nor was Israel eager to present its demands to Hammarskjöld before it had been able to gain Western support for them.

On November 20 Hammarskjöld was to submit a report to the General Assembly on his contacts with Egypt and on the deliberations of the U.N. Advisory Committee, which was set up to guide and monitor UNEF's deployment and activity; the day before he had met with Golda Meir and asked several questions regarding the Israeli plan of withdrawal. Meir managed to avoid any firm commitments for the time being, commenting that a fundamental discussion on the entire issue was needed.[37] Hammarskjöld did not press Israel at this point and even implored Abba Eban to make sure that Israel's withdrawal from Gaza not be too rapid, as he was all too aware of the risks implicit in a hasty Israeli withdrawal without a U.N. presence.[38]

Israel's demands had not yet been actually put to the test; however, Hammarskjöld's report of November 20th to the General Assembly on the U.N. force made it clear that the first two of Israel's four demands would not even be considered. Hammarskjöld did not intend to prevent the Egyptian army from regaining sovereign Egyptian territory and actually considered the main thrust of UNEF's duties in the Sinai peninsula, not along the canal.[39]

Israel's New York and Washington delegations took advantage of the respite until the Anglo-French troops evacuated Egypt and the U.N. force prepared itself to enter the Sinai peninsula to try to persuade the West, and especially the United States, that its claims were just. The efforts proved fruitless; the American administration, whose influence in the U.N. was likely to be decisive, adamantly refused to get involved and repeatedly referred Israel to Hammarskjöld, reiterating that it was not willing to take any initiative outside the U.N. framework and that "the U.N. must settle the crisis."[40] In that setting the U.N. secretary general, who tried to hide his resentment against Israel behind a thick curtain of cold and uncompromising legalisms, saw himself as the representative of the majority of the General Assembly, whose members, from the outset, showed no special enthusiasm for Israel's interests.[41]

The British government could not be a particularly strong bulwark of support for Israel. Adhering even at this stage to the "scenario," the British time and again repeated that their intervention in the canal had been provoked by their demand for Israeli withdrawal. With its last ounce of strength, the United Kingdom tried to salvage what remained of its Middle Eastern assets. Anthony Eden told Albert Gazier, France's acting foreign minister, that Britain had to oppose Israel's remaining in the Gaza Strip and certainly in the rest of the Sinai peninsula. He was obviously intimidated by Arab threats and was particularly concerned about losing the remaining sources of oil, such as Kuwait. British Cabinet discussions and diplomatic communiqués were reminiscent of the tone used in the days of the defunct Alpha Plan, but now they evoked Israel's disdain rather than anger. When Richard Crossman, a veteran hand in Near Eastern affairs, visited Ben-Gurion in mid-December 1956, the Israeli prime minister reminded his guest that, several years earlier, Israel offered to join the British Commonwealth. "Well," Ben-Gurion said, "the offer is withdrawn."[42] The sarcasm expressed not only contempt for British behavior throughout the crisis, but also the realization that Great Britain had ceased to be an international actor with whom to reckon seriously.

Israel's only prop was France, which had also lost considerable footing as a world power and whose ability to deter the Soviet Union was minimal; but its loyalty to Israel remained unswerving and in many areas its capabilities remained significant. The French public enthusiastically supported Israel and considered the Israeli military victory in the Sinai a kind of compensation for the disaster of Port Said—France, after all, had contributed to that victory. In mid-January 1957, when relations between Israel and the U.N. secretary general reached a nadir, Pineau met with Dulles and tried to persuade him to back Israel's demands, noting that France was concerned about the pressure being exerted on Israel to leave Sinai and Gaza without receiving any guarantees for its security, its freedom of navigation in the straits, and the cessation of Fedayun raids.[43] On January 19, only France joined

Israel in voting against the U.N. proposal demanding Israel's unconditional withdrawal. "Unlike England, France has not yet shed her skin," Ambassador Tsur wrote. "She loyally guards our interests, demands guarantees and rejects unconditional withdrawal."[44]

Political pressure on Israel mounted as soon as UNEF had become an operative force. On November 28 Hammarskjöld finally found time for the first of nearly a dozen "in-depth and thoroughgoing" discussions with Israel's delegates on the withdrawal and the attendant problems. Now was the time for Israel to put forward its conditions and demands. But the very first meeting made it clear that these demands would not be addressed seriously; the Israeli delegation could do no more than haggle over the pace and schedule of withdrawal. Whenever Abba Eban, Israel's ambassador to the U.N. and to the United States, raised fundamental issues, the U.N. secretary general responded with ambiguous statements; at this stage Eban could report to Jerusalem only that "the discussion on the Gulf and Gaza has been postponed to a later stage; meanwhile, we're just sitting here."[45] Hammarskjöld used a clever tactic: He would press Israel only on what had to be implemented at any given point, threatening that failure to comply would result in his submitting a negative report to the General Assembly, which would probably sway the already hostile organ to adopt resolutions detrimental to Israel. The basic problems regarding later stages were postponed repeatedly and in the meantime remained in a state of calculated ambiguity. This tactic deprived Israel of the chance to exploit the early stages of withdrawal to obtain guarantees and settlements regarding the later stages of the process. Slowly but surely, Israel was being forced to concede all its positions, without the secretary general having to compensate it for these concessions. Israel had hoped to avoid a return to the status quo; Hammarskjöld, on the other hand, adhered to the principle that aggression should not be rewarded and therefore the status quo ante had to be reinstated before any new arrangements could be discussed. In this nearly three-month war of nerves between the secretary general and the Israeli U.N. delegates, it was the secretary general who had the upper hand, backed as he was by a resounding majority of the General Assembly and unchallenged by the U.S. government, which would not side with Israel.

✻　✻　✻

At his first discussion with the Israelis on November 28, Hammarskjöld asked only to be informed of Israel's consent to withdraw forces from the immediate vicinity of the canal. The meeting was held just when word arrived that the British and French would, within a few days, announce the implementation of their own troop withdrawal. Abba Eban wanted to gain a tactical advantage; two days before Selwyn Lloyd stood up in Parliament and announced the withdrawal of the Anglo-French troops, Eban announced Israel's withdrawal to a position 50 kilometers east of the Suez Canal.[46]

With this announcement began a process that lasted some six weeks, as Israel, step by inexorable step, retreated from the entire Sinai peninsula except the Gaza Strip and Sharm al-Sheikh. Ben-Gurion's policy at this stage was to slow down withdrawal as much as possible: "Whenever pressure increases," he told Dayan, "we will declare a further withdrawal [and in the meantime] gain some time."[47] The delaying tactic was intended to permit enough time for a large-scale campaign to be mounted throughout the Western world, and especially in the United States, in an attempt to gain public approbation for Israel's claims to Sharm al-Sheikh and Gaza.

Detailed negotiations on the pace of withdrawal and coordination between the Israeli army and UNEF were transferred to the generals. At the el-Arish airport on December 6, Moshe Dayan held his first meeting with General Burns in the latter's new capacity as UNEF commander. With the exception of a Yugoslav reconnaissance unit that had just arrived in the region, most of Burns's force was still tied up in the Port Said area; he was therefore not anxious for the IDF to speed up withdrawal yet. However, although Burns did not pressure Israel, it became obvious in the course of the discussion that the U.N. had no intention of keeping the Egyptians out of Sinai. Now Burns told Dayan that the presence of Egyptian forces east of the canal did not depend on him, though he himself would have preferred the Egyptians to stay west of the canal.[48] This put paid to any ideas Israel may have entertained of formally demilitarizing the Sinai in the course of the evacuation process through some explicit arrangements. Demilitarization would now depend solely on the desire and policy of Egypt itself. The strict limits of UNEF's authority in areas where Egyptian sovereignty could not be challenged became crystal clear on December 22, when the British and the French withdrew from the area of Port Said and the UNEF had to leave the canal zone immediately thereafter.

The UNEF's movement east into the area vacated by the Israelis brought it up against the "scorched earth" that the IDF had left behind. All roads, military buildings, and installations, as well as the railroad lines, had been utterly destroyed and great tracts of land had been mined, hindering the U.N. force's progress. In a formal communiqué Hammarskjöld urgently demanded of Abba Eban that the demolition cease promptly;[49] Eban replied that the base of aggression in Sinai had jeopardized Israel's existence as well as world peace and that the Israelis had therefore done whatever was necessary to ensure that it would never recur. But Eban could not hold out against Hammarskjöld for long. Dayan had also tried to maneuver his way out of supplying Burns with requested maps of the minefields: "Handing over the minefield maps is not a technical issue. The question is whether UNEF will be moving with the Egyptian forces. If so, handing over information on the mines is different from handing it over if the U.N. forces advance on their own."[50] Although Burns did not deny that some Egyptian forces had already entered Sinai, it was obvious that the UNEF was not advancing together with them, and Dayan was therefore forced to order the maps delivered; but he refused to dismantle the mines that had already been lain.

The Israeli government decided at this stage to set the pace of withdrawal at 25 kilometers per week. It also decided to continue its efforts to link the IDF withdrawal from Sinai with a solution of the fundamental problems, despite the fact that the U.N. secretary general refused to deliberate on the problems before Israel had actually withdrawn. Israel therefore decided that the army would halt at the el-Arish line and would withdraw no farther until its demands on the disputed issues had been met. "We plan to stop at the el-Arish line and declare that we will not continue to withdraw until we receive outright guarantees," Ya'acov Herzog cabled Eban on December 10.[51] When Hammarskjöld learned what Israel's planned rate of withdrawal was, he was enraged; his military advisor, the Finnish general Mertulla, calculated that it would be four to six weeks before the Armistice lines were reached.[52] At Hammarskjöld's instructions, General Burns wrote Dayan on December 20 that the proposed pace was too slow and was unacceptable to the U.N. Secretariat.[53]

Once the Anglo-French troops concluded their withdrawal from Egyptian soil on December 22, Hammarskjöld could pour all his energy and efforts into pushing Israel to withdraw. He insisted to Eban that the pace be quickened; he had no choice, Hammarskjöld declared, but to consider Dayan's proposed rate of withdrawal as a fundamental change in the situation, equivalent to a deadlock, obligating him to report on this development to the General Assembly.[54] Ben-Gurion took the risk and did not increase the pace. In another few days the General Assembly would recess for Christmas, and, he believed, Hammarskjöld would not bother the members with something as minor as 25 kilometers. He knew pressure would be renewed in January, but until then there would be another 50 kilometers before the IDF reached el-Arish, and Israel would have gained another two weeks.[55] Ben-Gurion wrote Foreign Minister Golda Meir, who had joined her ambassador in New York, that a serious confrontation with the secretary general could soon be expected and that "the key to our ability to stand firm depends on the American position. All efforts must be made to win over the Secretary of State and the White House."[56] He knew that the U.N. could not accept the Israeli position; thus he pinned his hopes on American intervention in the imminent crisis.

But the Americans were not yet about to intervene in Hammarskjöld's efforts. In the last weeks of 1956 the State Department was preoccupied with problems concerning the reconstruction of the shaken Atlantic alliance. In addition, Britain's loss of influence in the Middle East and the danger of Soviet penetration into the political vacuum that had been created made it imperative for the United States to assume direct responsibility for safeguarding the pro-Western regimes in the region. As 1957 neared, this approach crystallized into the "Eisenhower Doctrine," calling for America to curry favor with the Arab states. America's new regional policy eliminated any possibility of helping Israel achieve even some of its political aims in the wake of its military successes. American public opinion and many congressmen, however, tended to side with Israel and supported several of its demands. The only way for the administration to maneuver in this complex situation was to leave the question of Israeli withdrawal to the U.N. secretary general and give him unequivocal support.

At his first press conference after major surgery, Dulles spoke on a wide range of issues. U.N. activity was at a fever pitch, and Israel was desperately trying to hold on to the gains it had achieved in battle; but the American secretary of state touched only briefly on the issue, saying that the American government adhered to the policies it had fixed a year and a half earlier in his famous speech of August 26, 1955.[57] Dulles met with Golda Meir on December 30 and spoke at length, from a "historical" perspective, about the future of the State of Israel in its hostile surroundings; but to the practical questions that Meir raised, he replied that these issues had to be negotiated with the U.N. secretary general, whom the United States government supported; the secretary of state was not authorized to make any arrangements with Israel behind Hammarskjöld's back.[58]

The only direct intervention the State Department was willing to make was intended to support Hammarskjöld's basic stance. On December 31 the U.S. ambassador to Israel, Edward Lawson, delivered an official *aide memoire* to the Israeli government outlining the legal status of the Armistice Agreements, which Israel claimed had expired. The *aide memoire* stated the American administration's position: No party to the agreements was entitled to annul them unilaterally, since they were based on Security Council resolutions. At any rate, the American administration believed that "clearly in the best interests of all signatories the General Armistice Agreements should be upheld in their integrity so as to facilitate transition toward Israel-Arab peace."[59]

Eban summed up the American government's position for Jerusalem: "If we could only get Hammarskjöld out of the picture . . . but the American Government is implacable in its decision to work through him. . . . I cannot imagine that the American Government would agree to bypass him and view itself as the official address for guarantees and undertakings."[60]

Despite the Christmas holidays, the U.N. secretary general and his advisors kept up their pressure on the Israelis. Abba Eban passed the pressure on to Israel through the scores of cables he dispatched from the U.N., castigating his government for intending to halt at the el-Arish line. "Our presence at the el-Arish line under these circumstances," he wrote to Ben-Gurion on December 20, "will be met with extreme opposition by our enemies, as well as by those concerned for the security of the region and the world and our own security."[61]

Early in January 1957 the delaying tactics reached the end of the road. "The respite has ended," Eban wrote on January 6.

> It is becoming increasingly obvious that our retention of the Sinai is weakening rather than strengthening our position in the fateful struggle for freedom of navigation in the Gulf and for Gaza. . . . All of us here believe that we have reached a situation in which an unequivocal announcement of the completion of the evacuation of Sinai [i.e., the entire peninsula excluding Sharm al-Sheikh and the Gaza Strip] is imperative if we want to hear the faintest echo in the world in favor of our insistence on freedom of navigation and Egypt's non-return to Gaza.[62]

On January 7 the Israeli army took up positions on a line from el-Arish southward. At first Dayan tried to hold on to the town of a-Tur on the western shores of the peninsula, which was vital for the water supply to Sharm al-Sheikh; but under U.N. pressure he was forced to give up this little fishing village on the coast of the Gulf of Suez. About a week later he was forced to concede the capital of the Sinai as well. On January 8 Ya'acov Herzog informed Eban of Ben-Gurion's decision to withdraw another 25 kilometers and relinquish el-Arish.[63]

On the morning of January 15, 1957, Moshe Dayan went to el-Arish in order to be present during the last minutes of Israeli army control of the city. Replying to the journalists who asked why he had come, Dayan said that "IDF commanders must taste everything . . . the bitter as well as the sweet."[64]

Now the final struggle began for Sharm al-Sheikh and the Gaza Strip. In addition, Dayan insisted on an IDF presence in a 25-kilometer-wide strip along the Gulf of Eilat and in a small bulge west of the international border at the Rafah junction at the southern tip of the Gaza Strip. But on December 31 the Israeli government made a decision that hinted at things to come: "Our goal in Sharm al-Sheikh is to ensure freedom of navigation . . . and our army shall remain there until freedom of navigation is effectively and totally ensured."[65] Thus Israel had in principle accepted the need to withdraw from Sharm al-Sheikh as well; from here on, the struggle would consist of trying to make that withdrawal contingent on suitable "arrangements and guarantees." As far as Gaza was concerned, the earlier decision remained in effect: The government decided to oppose return of the Egyptian forces and the entry of U.N. military forces into the Gaza Strip because Gaza was not unequivocally subject to Egyptian sovereignty and because Egypt's right to retain it derived from the Armistice Agreements, which Ben-Gurion no longer recognized.

From the beginning Abba Eban had realized that Israel would not be able to remain in Sharm al-Sheikh or the Gaza Strip, viewing the Israeli government's decision to stay there as no more than a ploy aimed at eventual "arrangements and guarantees." "If we think that we will be able to avoid leaving the Sinai . . . without incurring serious risks, we are mistaken," he had said at the beginning of the diplomatic struggle. "If we gain freedom of navigation in the gulf and perhaps also in the canal, can keep Egypt from returning to Gaza and can ensure against renewed Egyptian military deployment in the Sinai, this will be a not inconsiderable victory—but that, in my opinion, is the maximum."[66]

Toward the end of December, when the U.N. began to pressure Israel on Sharm al-Sheikh and the Gaza Strip, Eban also began to pressure policy makers in Jerusalem. Here too he effectively passed the U.N. pressures on to Israel. As the year drew to a close, he sent a barrage of reports to Jerusalem detailing his meetings with Hammarskjöld and volunteering his own assessments and opinions. Herzog stepped into the breach and tried to convey something of the atmosphere in Jerusalem to New York; but Eban's outstanding rhetorical and polemic talents, and his front-line diplomatic position, relegated Herzog's efforts to that of second fiddle. Eban's pressure was an influential factor in the Israeli government's decision of December 31 that effectively conceded Israel's ultimate withdrawal from Sharm al-Sheikh.

Furthermore, Eban was extremely pessimistic even on Israel's chances of receiving formal guarantees and assurances in exchange for withdrawal and believed that it would be forced to settle for informal arrangements. "There is a chance for *de facto* freedom of passage in the gulf, serious restrictions on Egypt's ability to reestablish a military presence in the Sinai, and the non-return of Egyptian forces to Gaza," he wrote Ben-Gurion on December 10; under such security conditions, "we will have to plan our steps for the future."[67] As it turns out, the situation created after Israel's withdrawal from Sharm al-Sheikh and the Gaza Strip, which would be in effect along Israel's Egyptian border for the next ten years, proved Eban correct; but this does not absolve the historian from asking whether the ambassador's pessimism did not contribute to the creation of that situation itself and if Eban did not exceed his mandate by pressuring his government so strongly. Be that as it may, by mid-January of 1957, the stage was set for the last act of the drama.

18
...

DIFFICULT DECISION

I

On January 22, 1957, the Israeli army dug in near the international border. Israel's withdrawal from Sharm al-Sheikh and the Gaza Strip had now become a burning issue at the U.N., and a head-on collision with the secretary general and the General Assembly was inevitable. Dag Hammarskjöld had lost patience. The earlier frustrations of his contacts with Israel in the spring and summer were also reflected in his current attitude toward Israel's representatives, but the crisis was not rooted in his prejudices or suppressed dislike but rather in the total lack of room for any compromise between the official stances, which the secretary general felt obliged to uphold by virtue of his position, and Israel's desires and perceptions. By the beginning of January 1957, Israel's minimal hopes had been clarified and the points of disagreement between itself and the U.N. had grown sharp.[1]

The U.N. attitude was premised on the principle of denying an aggressor any political or geographical gains. Israel thus had to withdraw unconditionally from Sharm al-Sheikh and the Gaza Strip. Any changes in the status quo could be considered only after such withdrawal. Israel, however, did not perceive the Sinai campaign as an act of aggression but rather as one of self-defense. Further, its bitter experience during the spring and summer when Hammarskjöld had tried to improve the conditions under which the Armistice Agreements were carried out eliminated virtually any hope for changes after withdrawal. Israel insisted on obtaining guarantees that the status quo ante bellum would be altered before agreeing to final withdrawal.

Aware of Israel's profound fears of Egyptian aggression, Hammarskjöld did his best to obtain informal "understandings" and "agreements" from the Egyptians that the old belligerency would not be reinstated and that new and better relations would prevail in the future along the demarcation lines; this, however, meant that Israel had to rely on Egypt's goodwill. The secretary general eventually did persuade Mahmoud Fawzi and President Nasser to refrain from exercising Egypt's sovereign "rights" in full. Israel then was forced to accept the de facto state of affairs that had been created and, indeed, to rely on the goodwill of Egypt's leader; but in January of 1957, Ben-Gurion's consent to such an informal arrangement could not be foreseen.

Israel insisted on the fulfillment of three basic conditions to ensure that its previous security problems along the Israeli-Egyptian border would not recur:

1. Egyptian military deployment in the Sinai would not be resumed, resulting in the effective demilitarization of the entire peninsula or at least the areas closer to the Israeli border.
2. The blockade against Israeli shipping in the Straits of Tiran would not be renewed. To meet this demand, the Egyptian army could not be allowed to return to Sharm al-Sheikh or, alternatively, Israel had to be provided with effective international guarantees.
3. Fedayun incursions and other hostile actions on the part of regular and irregular forces from the Gaza Strip had to cease. For this purpose, the Egyptian army could not be permitted to return to the Gaza Strip and the IDF had to be allowed to supervise security in the area.

From its inception, the U.N. based itself on the principle of national sovereignty. Even if he had wanted to, Hammarskjöld could not have considered any arrangement in the Sinai and Sharm al-Sheikh without Egyptian consent, because Egyptian sovereignty in these areas was not in question. But the likelihood of Egypt agreeing to any formal restrictions on its sovereignty was negligible. As far as the Gaza Strip was concerned, Hammarskjöld could only fall back on the 1949 Armistice Agreements granting Egypt a kind of quasi-sovereignty there. Thus here, too, the secretary general could do nothing without Egyptian consent.

In his Knesset victory address, Ben-Gurion proclaimed the Armistice Agreement dead, and he stubbornly refused to retreat from this position. He believed that Egypt had violated the very spirit of the agreement by insisting on its belligerent rights. Hammarskjöld rejected Ben-Gurion's stance out of hand. As U.N. secretary general he could make an accommodation between Israel and Egypt only on the sole agreed juridical basis actually in effect and sanctioned by the U.N. Eliminating this basis would leave a legal vacuum whose chances of being filled by any other agreement were at this stage nonexistent. To no avail, Ben-Gurion repeated his contention that no accommodation with Egypt was needed and that Egypt was obligated to refrain from belligerency by virtue of its membership in the U.N.[2]

Israel argued that UNEF's presence in the area did not require Egyptian consent. The U.N. force had to remain in place so long as Egypt insisted on its belligerent rights against Israel, and its removal could be effected only by a Security Council resolution or by a two-thirds majority vote of the General Assembly. In fact, however, the UNEF was established in November 1956 by a General Assembly resolution that made the force's presence in the region specifically contingent on Egypt's consent.

Such were the fundamental disparities between Hammarskjöld's political constraints and Israel's expectations and wishes in early January 1957. Even if the secretary general's attitude to Israel was more favorable, he would have been constrained from meeting even some of its demands. Israel's chances of persuading the General Assembly to change its own attitude were, of course, nil. It therefore now looked to Washington in the hope that America, together with a coalition of friendly states, would take steps outside the U.N. framework. But the United States was not prepared to go this far. The collision course was paved in advance, and the imminent crisis approached inexorably.

Abba Eban did his best to prevent or at least delay the confrontation. He implored Ben-Gurion to refrain from any "explosive" proclamations[3] and delivered five questions to Hammarskjöld for clarification, in the hope that the phrasing of the responses would make Israel's position in the General Assembly more tenable.[4] But Eban's questions and his delaying tactics only made Hammarskjöld more intractable. On January 5 the secretary general formally provided Eban with his replies in a rigid and uncompromising memo:[5]

1. Hammarskjöld repeated the U.N. resolutions citing Israel's rights to freedom of navigation in the Suez Canal, but was not at present prepared to look for ways of enforcing them.

2. He would not consider the question of the Fedayun incursions until Israel had reconfirmed its acceptance of the Armistice Agreements.

3. He did indeed believe that the Straits of Tiran should be open to all, but he saw no way to negotiate on this matter if negotiations started not from a status quo ante but from the situation obtaining as a result of Israel's military action.

This dry, legalistic document signaled to Israel that it had no hope of obtaining anything from the secretary general, who did not even try to dispel the sense of stalemate in his style.

The Israeli government also reiterated its position. On January 13 it took a series of decisions:[6]

1. Israel would not leave the Straits of Tiran until its freedom of navigation there was assured.

2. Israel demanded real guarantees for freedom of navigation in the Suez Canal.

3. Israel would retain the Gaza Strip, set up an independent administration for the inhabitants, and be responsible for security through its own police force. Israel opposed handing over security in the Gaza Strip to a U.N. force.

4. The U.N. had to declare Sinai, or at least its eastern part, demilitarized.

Ben-Gurion realized that the government decisions represented a direct challenge to the U.N. General Assembly and knew that the moment of truth was approaching. A week earlier he had told Dayan, "There is almost no doubt that the U.N. will impose sanctions against us. Even America will 'explode' at our decision and impose a full economic and financial embargo on us." But he was prepared for the blow and told Finance Minister Levi Eshkol to consider the continued Israeli presence in the Straits of Tiran and Gaza Strip as "the economic development goal for 1957. . . . Isn't it a highly worthwhile investment?"[7] To Eban he wrote, "We will not leave Gaza and Sharm al-Sheikh . . . even if the U.S. imposes sanctions. A nation that is not willing to suffer in a struggle for its fundamental rights cannot exist."[8]

On January 17, after the Christmas holiday and a recess of about three weeks, the General Assembly resumed deliberations on the issue. A group of Afro-Asian states submitted a draft resolution condemning Israel for not having completed its withdrawal and demanding that the secretary general submit another report to the General Assembly on Israel's stand in five days' time. Seventy-two countries voted in favor of the resolution, several abstained, and only Israel and France voted against it. On January 20 Hammarskjöld met with Eban for talks that quickly deteriorated into an acrimonious argument. On January 22 the Israeli government decided to prepare the country for a state of emergency.[9] For a short while Ben-Gurion surfaced once more as a fiery leader who inflamed his followers to acts of heroism based on a strong sense of self-righteousness, ready to meet all challenges.

In New York Abba Eban and Golda Meir prepared a memo for the General Assembly, to clarify once and for all Israel's "fundamental position."[10] Ben-Gurion, however, seems not to have relied completely on his two representatives to convince the General Assembly of the firmness of the Israeli decision. From the Knesset, using his best debating style, but with great restraint and caution, Ben-Gurion settled the score with the United Nations:

Israel would not evacuate the Straits of Tiran unless Israeli navigation was guaranteed by specific and valid treaties; Israel would not leave the Gaza Strip and rejected both the stationing of the UNEF there and the return of the area to Egyptian control.[11]

The tone was moderate, but the address was clearly meant to challenge the General Assembly, scheduled to convene in New York the next day, January 24. That day Eban again met with Hammarskjöld, who did not hide his disappointment at the Israeli memo. Under the circumstances he saw no point in continuing the discussion, he said, and had no choice but to report to the General Assembly on Israel's refusal to withdraw. He was approaching the U.N. deliberations, he said, "with dark foreboding."[12] As anticipated, the secretary general's report of January 24, 1957, was harsh: "The U.N. cannot condone a change of the *status juris* resulting from military action contrary to the provisions of the Charter."[13]

The debate on Hammarskjöld's report was long and acrimonious. Some of Israel's friends, especially the Canadian Foreign Minister, Lester Pearson, proposed resolutions that at least partially met Israel's demands, and American delegate Henry Cabot Lodge tried his hand at convoluted formulations.[14] But fear of the Afro-Asian bloc led by India's fiery Krishna Menon overrode and, on February 2, a resolution—the sixth on the issue—was adopted calling for Israel's immediate and unconditional withdrawal. Another resolution passed by a majority did acknowledge the need to take measures after withdrawal to ensure progress toward the creation of peaceful conditions in the region, but the phrasing was uninspired and noncommittal, and Israel could not accept it. The next step, Israel knew, would be to demand that sanctions be imposed on it. Thus all its efforts had to be aimed at persuading the Western nations, and chiefly the United States, to come to Israel's aid to— if not actually to prevent the sanctions, at least to refrain from participating in them. The Israeli representatives in the American capital, however, had a difficult task before them.

On February 3 President Eisenhower sent Ben-Gurion a cordial but uncompromising letter. The American government demanded that the Israeli government comply with the U.N. General Assembly resolutions: "The essential first step must be the completion of the withdrawal of Israel forces behind the Armistice Line. It is my earnest hope that this withdrawal will be completed without further delay. . . . Israel should not continue to ignore U.N. resolutions." Eisenhower did not balk at overt threats: "Such continued

ignoring . . . would almost surely lead to the invoking of further U.N. procedures which would seriously disturb relations between Israel and . . . the
U.S."[15] Dulles had tried to evade journalists' questions but had to admit that
"If there was action in the way of sanctions we would of course have to give
them very serious consideration."[16]

King Saud of Saudi Arabia was visiting Washington at the time. He
brought with him a memo drafted in Cairo on January 15, 1957, signed by
Egypt, Syria, Jordan, and Saudi Arabia, that demanded unconditional Israeli
withdrawal.[17] Rumors in Washington had it that "the American Government
had promised Saud to firmly stand on its demand [that Israel] evacuate Gaza
and Sharm al-Sheikh,"[18] since the goodwill of the Arabs, especially the Saudi
monarch, was a prerequisite for the success of the Eisenhower Doctrine,
which then held center stage in congressional and Cabinet discussions.

But Ben-Gurion remained firm. Eisenhower's allusions to U.N. sanctions
enraged him. He told Ya'acov Herzog to write and tell the president "to shell
us. . . . He has atomic weapons; why doesn't he use them against us? Let
them impose their sanctions."[19] Moshe Dayan, who had come to visit the ail-
ing prime minister, recalled that he was "adamant, with a kind of bitter stub-
bornness like someone convinced of his just cause and who knows he has
been wronged."[20] Ben-Gurion's reply to Eisenhower was sharp: "Is it conceivable that the United States, the land of freedom, equality and human
rights, should support such discrimination? . . . Our people will never accept
it, no matter what sacrifice it may entail."[21] He appended a succinct note to
Golda Meir: "Our position must be made firm and clear to whoever we talk
to. With no linguistic juggling."[22]

It was not easy for the American administration to consider sanctions on
Israel, because it would elicit strong opposition among important congressional leaders. Dulles was caught on the horns of a dilemma: If the United
States failed to support an Afro-Asian proposal, America would lose whatever political gains it had made during the whole Suez crisis. If it supported
the proposal, President Eisenhower could anticipate a head-on collision with
Congress. Time was running out; Hammarskjöld was increasingly impatient
and made it clear that he no longer believed Israel could be persuaded to
withdraw without the real threat of sanctions. Dulles therefore decided to
intervene personally, before it was too late and the United States had to
choose between these two difficult options. He proposed a kind of compromise: Israel would withdraw with no preconditions, and the U.S. government

on its part would guarantee that it would take steps that would eventually ensure Israel's interests.

On February 11 Dulles gave Eban a memo containing the American proposal.[23] He could make no promises about the Gaza Strip. At the very most it could be hoped, but not guaranteed, that the UNEF and the Egyptians could reach some kind of accord that would facilitate a pacification of the region. However, the United States was willing to take a more positive initiative regarding the Straits of Tiran. There, too, Israel had to withdraw unconditionally, but the American government was willing to declare that it viewed the straits as an international waterway and even to persuade other nations to make similar declarations. Furthermore, the United States was willing to influence ships carrying the American flag to demonstrate this freedom of passage. Finally, America was prepared to bring its powers of persuasion to bear and try to have the UNEF permanently stationed in Gaza and in the Straits of Tiran.

For Abba Eban, the American memo seemed to be a breakthrough. The next day he wired Ben-Gurion enthusiastically: ". . . we seem to be nearing the fulfillment of the vision you have personally championed with such special fervor: Israel's doorway into the vastness of the Red Sea through Eilat opened and American cooperation in guaranteeing this national and international advantage secured."[24] He also estimated that "the issue of sanctions is tottering under the pressure of the Senate and the press." But Ben-Gurion was less enthusiastic and replied that

> The memo contains the desire for a positive resolution, but what is actually proposed is not positive and we cannot agree to it. There are no guarantees for Israeli shipping. . . . We shall not return to the Armistice Agreement under any circumstances. . . . In Gaza we will agree to the evacuation of our army on two conditions: that the Egyptians do not return, and that Israel be a partner to an administration set up jointly with the U.N. . . . we cannot budge from this position even if sanctions are imposed.

But Eban, who viewed the proposals as an important achievement, was afraid that the Israeli government's intransigence would sink the American initiative. He therefore bombarded Ben-Gurion with a barrage of cables—interpretations, "secret" information, imprecations, and entreaties. The details could indeed be bargained for, but, he implored, it was imperative that the American government be given a fundamentally positive response.

> They are asking us to make a basic decision. . . . We cannot reject this plan without losing the advantage we hold in public opinion as well as our first opportunity to attain an American security guarantee on a vital Israeli interest. . . . What hangs in the balance is something far more important than a quarrel with Hammarskjöld, and

that is our relationship with the Government and people of the United States and the chance for a growing partnership instead of the dangerous division that has existed for months.

Reuven Shiloah, his deputy, followed suit: "The President is convinced of our just cause and has tipped the scales in our favor, but our friends caution us that he is nearing the end of his tether; they are warning us not to pull too hard against the ropes."

To avoid a confrontation with the United States, Ben-Gurion acceded to his ambassador's pleas and agreed to view Dulles's memo as an opening for further negotiations between Israel and the United States. On February 14 the Israeli government convened and drafted its response to the State Department memo. In principle, Israel accepted the U.S. approach to the straits issue but, fearful that the Egyptians might return before a peace treaty was signed, Israel proposed that the UNEF be formally positioned in the straits until peace with Egypt was attained or, alternatively, that Israel be guaranteed freedom of navigation in a formal accord. Discussion should be opened with the American government immediately in order to achieve an agreed solution to the problem.[25]

Dulles's chagrin at the Israeli government's reply was obvious; Israel had misread the essence of the American initiative, he told Eban. The United States had not intended to make any new proposals that did not conform to the U.N. resolutions, but only thought that if Israel were made aware of the U.S. government's attitude to the problems, it would be easier for it to implement the U.N. resolution. The American administration had no authority to replace the U.N. secretary general and his negotiations conducted on behalf of the General Assembly. Israel was obviously not satisfied with "clarifications" but was in fact demanding "a bilateral agreement"; that, Dulles told him, was impossible. Frankly, the secretary of state told Eban, tensions between America and Israel at this time would cause internal friction. The American government wanted to avoid any such complications and was therefore trying to find a solution. But as there was a limit to what the American government could do, Dulles urged Eban to keep in mind the strictures on America's political capabilities and to settle for an American declaration of intent. Time was running out at the U.N.; only one day remained before the General Assembly would meet for final deliberations on sanctions against Israel. Dulles therefore wanted Israel to reconsider the issue and reply as quickly as possible.[26]

Characteristically, Eban's message to Ben-Gurion was impassioned: "As far as the press and our own friends are concerned, we stepped beyond the limit." Dulles was ready to consider Israeli points on the precise wording, he wrote, but his initiative is a final position "representing the outside limit of his willingness to help." If Israel did not accept his offer, the approach would be abandoned and the issue would revert to the U.N.[27]

Still Ben-Gurion was adamant. On February 16 he wrote a personal cable to Eban: "I think the issue will go back to the General Assembly. I can't predict what will happen there, although I do not expect salvation and consolation. . . . But in my opinion—and to the best of my knowledge it is shared by everyone in Israel—we cannot move from these two positions."[28] Ben-Gurion was ready for the head-on collision in the General Assembly in a few days' time.

The American president's patience was also not unlimited. After meeting with Dulles at his vacation home in Thomasville, Virginia, Eisenhower decided to cut his holiday short, return to Washington, and face Congress and the American public. Dulles convinced him that if the United States took one more step toward meeting the Israeli demands, all the Arab states would be up in arms. "It would spell the failure of the 'Eisenhower Doctrine' even before it got under way."[29] Eisenhower was resolute to take action and not wait for an Afro-Asian initiative, and on February 17 he published a declaration: The American memo of February 11 provided Israel with the best guarantees it could expect without detriment to anyone else.[30]

Dulles's press conference of February 19 was equally disappointing for Israel. The secretary of state evaded a barrage of questions and remained for the most part vague and ambiguous. His few clear statements, however, made it obvious that the United States had not obtained, and had not even tried to obtain, any assurances whatsoever from the Egyptian government. The entire proposal, in fact, was based on a pious belief in the changing of the international atmosphere with regard to positive compliance with the terms of international law.

On February 20 Eisenhower summoned congressional leaders from both parties to the White House and tried to convince them that economic pressure had to be applied in order to force Israel to withdraw; most of the congressmen, however, did not share the president's view and refused to support him publicly.[31] Disappointed, Eisenhower turned to the American public and addressed the nation that same evening on radio and television. In oblique albeit clear terms he announced that the United States would support the U.N. resolution calling for sanctions on Israel: "The U.N. must not fail. I believe that in the interest of peace the U.N. has no choice but to exert pressure upon Israel to comply with the withdrawal resolutions."[32]

Eban wrote that the president's announcement had done its job and that considerable segments of public opinion now viewed Israel as a nay-saying nation seeking self-justification. The address was a declaration of war. It was inconceivable that the United States would retreat from a position that the president himself had so dramatically enunciated. Ben-Gurion understood this and wrote in his diary, "I fear that after this speech any mutual understanding is impossible."[33]

American Jewry took up Israel's cause with a vengeance. The incursion into Sinai had at first embarrassed Jewish leaders; addressing the Conference of Presidents of Major Jewish Organizations on October 30, Reuven Shiloah found himself at a loss trying to overcome his audience's reservations. But the Jewish leaders quickly recovered their equanimity and began coming out in support of Israel's demands. The Jewish lobby at the time was steered by the Zionist organizations, and through the Conference of Presidents, the embassy also managed to recruit such non-Zionist organizations to its side as the B'nai B'rith Anti-Defamation League, the American Jewish Congress, and the major synagogue affiliations.[34]

By the beginning of February, when the dissension between Israel and the American administration was growing acrimonious, every single Jewish organization, with the exception of the avowedly anti-Zionist American Council for Judaism, had joined ranks with Israel. On February 7 the three major religious streams met in an emergency session in New York—a rare phenomenon in and of itself—and called for all American Jews to protest the threatened sanctions against Israel.[35]

The actions of the Jewish organizations significantly influenced the positions of the American Senate and of the press. Non-Jewish politicians of the first rank, including Republican presidential backers, came out in support of Israel's demands. The impact of the Jewish pressure on Congress was especially important because the imposition of an embargo on private aid to Israel, involving steps such as cancelling the tax exemption on charitable contributions, required legislation. To be sure, the direct confrontation between the Israeli government and the president placed the Jews in a very delicate position, since at the time they were still very sensitive to accusations of double loyalty. The public at large tended to view the president's stance as an expression of "national American interests," and therefore Jewish support of Israel's position was liable to be interpreted as lack of national loyalty, or at any rate as preference of particular over general interest. But the fact that many of the congressional leaders, and a considerable share of the press, also opposed the policy of sanctions made it easier for the Jews and legitimized their struggle.

The impact on the Senate and the media of a united front of American Jewry worried the White House; at the very height of the crisis, Dulles took the unprecedented step of inviting eight prominent Jewish leaders, chosen at his discretion, to a "background discussion." "There was a well-grounded fear that this discussion would be used . . . to break up the Jewish front," Shiloah wrote Herzog. To be on the safe side, the Conference of Presidents empowered their president, Philip Klutznick, who was also B'nai B'rith president, to make it clear to Dulles that the Jews were totally united on the question of Israel. The conference also sent a letter to President Eisenhower formally supporting Israel's demands and scheduled mass rallies all over the United States, including one in Madison Square Garden in New York City on February 25. Many non-Jews also participated in the rally, and cables in support of Israel were received from many senators; particularly moving was the telegram sent by Eleanor Roosevelt, the widow of the late President Franklin Delano Roosevelt.[36]

When it was obvious that Israel's relations with the United States had reached a crisis point, Ben-Gurion recalled Abba Eban to Jerusalem and let him present his arguments to an emergency session of the Cabinet convened on the night of February 21. Despite his eloquence, however, Eban did not sway the Israeli government, which then and there ratified its earlier decisions.[37] The next day Ben-Gurion addressed the Knesset in one of his most aggressive speeches:

> We are not obligated to say "Amen" to everything that the Government of the United States does. . . . We shall not cease our efforts to convince the American Administration and the American people of our probity and just cause. . . . But if disaster strikes and members of the international community take a hand, directly or indirectly, in the schemes which the Arab leaders and their allies are plotting against Israel . . . we will not bow to the verdict but will oppose it with all our moral strength.[38]

But despite the government's decision and his firm public stance, Ben-Gurion now realized that he had no choice but to satisfy the U.S. government and comply with some of its proposals. He sent Eban back to Washington with a softened version of Israel's position in which he agreed to Israel's retreat from Sharm al-Sheikh in exchange for informal guarantees. Ben-Gurion would not move on the Gaza Strip question, but here too he made some mollifying gestures, proposing that the U.N. send a commission of inquiry to study the issue and make new proposals for a permanent settlement.

What induced this fundamental change in Ben-Gurion's stand? Far from the public eye, the pressure had begun to make itself felt. Abba Eban and the other Israeli delegates to the U.N. relentlessly urged him to concede. Shiloah reported a friendly informal conversation between Dulles and the Israelis shortly after he had returned from Thomasville: "If we give in and leave Gaza and the Straits," Shiloah wrote, "the U.S. and all of humanity would owe Israel a great debt which he believes would be rewarded."[39] The statement was informal and unofficial, but probably made an impression on the Israelis in Washington as well in Jerusalem.

Abba Eban did not hesitate to enlist his not inconsiderable polemic skills when he wanted his points to sink home, using the same eloquence on his superiors as he did at the U.N. and in Washington. Many of his arguments were very persuasive and probably left their impression on Ben-Gurion. Indeed, although Eisenhower's promises had no formal validity and were not even properly stated in public, nevertheless, Eban insisted, they had considerable moral and political value. Eban repeatedly urged that the American proposal concerning navigation in the Straits of Tiran was invaluable and could not be rejected out of hand: "There can be freedom of navigation without our presence in Sharm al-Sheikh, and we can be in Sharm al-Sheikh without enjoying freedom of navigation." Ben-Gurion too saw no promising future in an Israeli presence in the straits in opposition to U.N. resolutions. "We need an exit to the Red Sea for no reason other than our ties with Asia and Africa," Eban claimed, "and no Asiatic country will maintain commercial ties with us through Eilat so long as we remain on Egyptian soil." As far as Gaza was concerned, even Ben-Gurion balked at the idea of assuming full responsibility for the hundreds of thousands of residents and Palestinian refugees that were packed together in the confines of the narrow strip.

It was America's unyielding position that seems to have ultimately produced the turn-about in Ben-Gurion's thinking. Washington's disapprobation of the Israeli war initiative in Sinai had been no secret from the very beginning, but Ben-Gurion was surprised at the resolute stance taken by the American president during the U.N. deliberations. "An extraordinary thing has happened," Ben-Gurion told senior IDF officers once the crisis had ended. "[H]ere is a President who is totally inactive in Presidential matters and who spends his time playing bridge or golf. In the morning he reads a little sheet of paper that his secretaries give him about what's going on in the world—and of all things, he picks this issue to get completely involved in!"[40]

Ben-Gurion had misread the American reaction to the British-French-Israeli initiative, but he could hardly be blamed, not only because he had repeatedly referred to the need to consult with the United States before the campaign, but mainly because no one could really have foreseen the extent to which America was prepared to take a stand against its own allies. The Suez War and the allies' failure had a tremendous impact on U.S. policy in the Middle East, as America now had to shoulder the entire burden of defending Western interests in the region. This shift in U.S. Middle East policy began to emerge in December 1956 and January 1957. The regional competition between the two major superpowers that had become keener in the wake of the war, America's fear of losing its newly won central position in Middle Eastern affairs, the gradual formulation of the Eisenhower Doctrine, and the American administration's desire to ensure regional support for that doctrine—these factors impelled the United States to toughen its stance toward Israel.

When Ben-Gurion realized that the United States could not be moved by persuasion, nor by an adamant Israeli counterposition, nor by the pressure of the public opinion, and was even prepared to support the proposal to impose sanctions on Israel, he understood that he had no choice but to be more flexible.

II

On February 25, one day before the U.N. General Assembly resumed deliberations on Israeli withdrawal, it became clear that Dulles was also not enthusiastic about the anticipated confrontation and preferred a way out. That day Abba Eban returned to Washington with Ben-Gurion's new complicated formula, which he presented to the secretary of state during a midnight consultation at Dulles's home. Dulles's response was encouraging; he seemed prepared to accept Ben-Gurion's response as a positive reply in principle.[41] A compromise was finally reached in the course of the next few days on the issue of the Straits of Tiran: Israel would declare unilateral withdrawal from Sharm al-Sheikh, but it would also state that it reserved its right to defend free passage of its ships through the straits under Article 51 of the U.N. Charter.[42] The United States would also submit a declaration to the General Assembly, announcing that it viewed the straits as an international waterway and noting Israel's declaration regarding its right to self-defense. It was understood that the United States and other nations would take appropriate action to implement freedom of passage in the straits.

Ben-Gurion was fundamentally in favor of the formula. The negotiations on the question of Gaza, however, had reached an impasse. Several hours after the midnight conversation with Dulles on February 24, it became clear that Eban had either overstepped his mandate or had not understood the limits of his instructions. Ben-Gurion's proposal called for a U.N. commission to

examine the issues of a civil administration in the Gaza Strip. Eban presumed this meant the withdrawal of the IDF, to be replaced by the UNEF,
because "it is inconceivable that a U.N. commission of inquiry operate in
Gaza while our army is there and we refuse to countenance UNEF's entry."[43]
Herzog informed Eban of his mistake by phone: The Israeli government had
not yet agreed to relinquish direct military control of the Gaza Strip. The
government had proposed that a U.N. commission look into the complex of
issues relating to civil administration only; it had not agreed to the entry of
the U.N. forces. Herzog instructed Eban to apologize for the misunderstand-
ing and clarify the actual position of the government of Israel.[44]

The General Assembly convened that same day, and Hammarskjöld asked
Eban for Israel's final response before submitting his report to the General
Assembly.[45] Characteristically, Hammarskjöld was unbendingly legalistic;
and Eban made good use of this stance in order to retreat from the mistaken
impression he had given regarding the Israeli position on the Gaza Strip.
Because Hammarskjöld showed no flexibility on Gaza, Eban proposed to
Dulles that the question of the Straits of Tiran, on which almost full under-
standing had been achieved between Israel and the United States, be kept
separate from the issue of the Gaza Strip. He proposed that Israel inform the
General Assembly of its willingness to withdraw from Sharm al-Sheikh
only, thereby preventing a vote on the resolution to impose sanctions.
Deliberations on the Gaza Strip would continue at a later stage.

But Dulles informed Eban that he would not separate the issues and proposed that "efforts continue to resolve all the problems." The secretary of
state did not sound pessimistic and apparently was not particularly upset by
Eban's recanting of his earlier agreement. The fact that the Israeli government had already softened its position considerably may have led him to
believe that he could ultimately overcome the last of its reservations. But
perhaps his optimism stemmed from a new source, a new ray of hope: Those
who had drawn Israel into the misadventure would also extricate it. That
morning, he told Eban, he and Eisenhower had met with Guy Mollet and
Christian Pineau, and they had made a proposal that all four men believed
was likely to result in a solution. He proposed a meeting with Pineau to hear
his proposal.[46]

Toward the end of February, France's prime minister, Guy Mollet, and
foreign minister, Christian Pineau, had come to America to patch up their

country's relations with the United States. The French had been following
Israel's struggle at the U.N. with sympathy and concern. The crisis, however, placed France in a serious dilemma. The French felt morally obligated
to help Israel to realize those goals for which it had subscribed to the Sèvres
Protocol. At the end of January, Pineau informed Hammarskjöld that
"France would not recognize any General Assembly resolution imposing
sanctions on Israel. . . . the French Government was determined to provide
Israel with all the help needed to meet her just demands."[47] But at the same
time, the French were also seriously concerned with the possibility of having
to cast their vote against an overwhelming majority at the General
Assembly, since that vote would exacerbate their relations with the Arabs,
with the Third World, and perhaps even with the United States.

France was now urgently trying to restore relations with the Arab world,
from whom it received most of the oil that fed its economy. French leaders
had repeatedly stressed to the Israelis that France did not want to "burn all
her bridges with the Arabs."[48] In addition, France was probably under a good
deal of pressure from the other European states, all of whom were laboring
under a severe oil shortage because of the blockage of the Suez Canal and all
of whom feared that Nasser would refuse to clear the canal so long as Israel
did not retreat from the last of its positions in the Sinai and the Gaza Strip.
France thus had good reasons for bringing the crisis to a rapid conclusion.

Throughout the struggle, Eban was careful to keep Pineau and France's
ambassador in Washington, Hervé Alphand, well-apprised of his contacts
with the Americans and with Hammarskjöld. Pineau was thus aware of the
understandings that had been achieved regarding Sharm al-Sheikh and
apparently believed similar accords could be reached on the future of the
Gaza Strip. The proposal attributed to Pineau may very well have been
Dulles's idea in the first place, but the secretary of state realized that if it
came from Pineau, the Israelis were more likely to accept it.

Mollet and Pineau met with Eban on February 27 and proposed the following: Instead of bringing the issue to a vote at the General Assembly,
Israel would take the initiative and announce its withdrawal from Gaza, on
the assumption that the UNEF would be deployed in the Gaza Strip for a
transitional period and would assume full responsibility for its military and
civilian supervision. Israel would declare that it hoped that the transitional
period would extend until a peace accord was reached with Egypt; should
Egypt not agree to a peace settlement and should the situation once again
deteriorate, Israel would have the right to self-defense under Article 51 of
the U.N. Charter. Israel's declaration would be followed by that of the U.S.
government, and any other interested government, to the effect that Israel's

announcement had been noted and that it was to be hoped that the role of the U.N. force would continue until peace was achieved.[49]

To this proposal Abba Eban added the verbal interpretation that the French had given him:

> The plan follows the logic of the American proposal concerning the issue of the straits, i.e., the international nature of the straits and of the Gaza Strip is dictated by unilateral Great Power declaration . . . guaranteeing that the U.N. does not leave, and therefore that the Egyptians do not enter. This creates a situation whereby the U.N.'s evacuation would carry with it the risk of war.[50]

Unlike Sharm al-Sheikh, the Gaza Strip was not sovereign Egyptian territory, and the Egyptian right to rule there derived from the Armistice Agreements. While it was impossible to prevent the Egyptians from returning to Sharm al-Sheikh if they so desired, the Americans, and perhaps even Hammarskjöld himself, and certainly Eban and the French hoped that it would be possible to prevent them from returning to the Strip.

In the meantime, after exhausting negotiations, U.N. legal advisor Constantine Stavropoulos managed to obtain Egypt's agreement on the UNEF's status in Egypt. Among other things, Egypt agreed that it would not eject the UNEF from Egyptian territory without asking the secretary general to bring the issue before a special supervisory commission made up of General Assembly members participating in the U.N. force; the commission would be entitled to bring the matter before the U.N. General Assembly for deliberation.[51] Unfortunately, this mechanism was not precisely defined and left room for various interpretations. Abba Eban cabled Jerusalem with his own version: "UNEF cannot be removed from the straits without the advisory commission informing us and the General Assembly and [without] the opportunity to appeal. The United States will oppose removal of UNEF until active belligerency has ceased."[52] Eban's interpretation was incorrect and groundless: Egypt was indeed obligated to turn to the secretary general, and the secretary general was indeed obligated to approach the advisory commission; however, the commission was not *obligated* to turn to the General Assembly, but only *permitted* to do so. And indeed, in 1967 the U.N. force was ordered to leave Sharm al-Sheikh and the Gaza Strip without the issue being brought before either the General Assembly or the Security Council. In 1957, however, Eban's misinterpretation allowed the Israeli government to concur with his claim that "there was no difference between this arrangement and the permanent emplacement of UNEF" and facilitated its acceptance of Pineau's proposal.

There was no time for further inquiries by the evening of February 26; the General Assembly had been in session for three days, and if Israel did not quickly announce the withdrawal of its forces, sanctions would be imposed. Israel had to announce withdrawal from both Sharm al-Sheikh and the Gaza Strip, inasmuch as the Americans were not prepared to separate the two issues. Thus if Israel failed to accept Pineau's proposal on the Gaza Strip, the agreement that had been reached with the United States on Sharm al-Sheikh would be lost. "It is imperative . . . to give Dulles and Pineau a fundamentally positive response to the plan today," Golda Meir cabled Ben-Gurion. "There is no chance of reaching a more favorable arrangement. If we don't hold on to a proposal which comes from the French, we will be totally isolated."[53]

Ben-Gurion and his emissaries in the United States swallowed the bait and accepted the French proposal without investigating it sufficiently. Late at night on February 28, Ya'acov Herzog cabled Eban: "The Government agrees in principle to Pineau's proposal, on the assumption that it means that, until peace [is achieved], only U.N. forces remain in the Gaza Strip and the Egyptians do not return, neither in the form of the army nor the police nor an administration nor any other form, directly or indirectly."[54] The appended reservation was illusory, since it should have been obvious that no one could guarantee that the Egyptians would not return to the Strip.

On the morning of March 1, before Abba Eban left for New York for the decisive session of the General Assembly at which Golda Meir was to announce Israel's final withdrawal from Sharm al-Sheikh and the Gaza Strip, Eban met with Dulles for one last meeting to reiterate that the Egyptians would not return to the Gaza Strip in any manner "directly or indirectly." But Dulles made it clear that the United States' abilities and authorities were restricted: "We want a full international regime without Egypt," Eban reported on Dulles's cautious undertaking; ". . . the plan is aimed at preventing a military or civilian return of the Egyptians to the Gaza Strip, but the United States is not omnipotent. . . . I cannot swear to its full success, but I do undertake to make a supreme effort to ensure this. . . ." The American government's constrictions were thus obvious; nevertheless, hoping that the Egyptians would not want to return to the Gaza Strip, Dulles ceremoniously told the Israelis that they had scored a great political coup: there was an almost 100 percent chance of the Gulf of Eilat being opened as an international waterway, and Egyptian rule in Gaza had ended.[55]

Hammarskjöld knew that it was impossible to guarantee that the Egyptians would not come back to Gaza. When Alphand and Pineau showed him their proposal, he told them frankly that it was based on impossible assumptions, but kept his comment a private one, lest it disrupt the French efforts. His biographer writes, ". . . it would be irresponsible [of Hammarskjöld] to protect himself publicly at the risk of wrecking the slender chance the Washington talks provided of getting around a difficult corner in an atmosphere of studied vagueness."[56]

The U.N. secretary general had reasons of his own for not apprising the Israelis of their misperception; but why did their friends the French stay silent? And Eban himself—did he not realize that the Americans had no authority to guarantee that the Egyptians would not resume the occupation of Gaza? In retrospect, it is difficult to avoid the conclusion that the French actions contained an element of illusion, even deception. But was it not also self-deception on the part of the Israelis? Thirty years later it is difficult indeed to discern the fine lines between the motivations of actors constrained by last-minute pressures as the clock was about to strike 12, but several guesses can be made. Did Pineau think that the Israelis needed to make an honorable exit that should be provided even at the cost of a bit of deception? Did Abba Eban think that Israel had no choice but to withdraw anyway and no hope of achieving any real guarantees and therefore had to acquiesce in the maneuver? Was Ben-Gurion tired of fighting and looking for a way out and hence not fastidious in examining the proposal?

Ben-Gurion's motivations are partly revealed in his diary, where he recorded his conversation with Dayan on the day the decision was made to withdraw: "We are utterly convinced that France may also turn away from us, putting us in danger of not getting any more arms," he told Dayan. Dayan disagreed and claimed that Israel had enough weapons to last the coming year; but Ben-Gurion replied that Israel's arsenal was sufficient "in the context of current reality, not in the context of a reality liable to be created if we reject the Pineau-U.S. proposal and if sanctions are applied against us and we are left without a single friend."[57]

Ben-Gurion mustered additional arguments in the discussion he felt obliged to hold with the disappointed IDF commanding officers on March 1, the day Golda Meir addressed the General Assembly. He was positive that the Straits of Tiran would remain open to Israeli shipping, whereas Israel's continued control of Gaza was liable to be a "terrible disaster" because "we can't kill 100 Arab terrorists every day." He did not try to delude the officers: "We may have to fight again. If we do, we won't have the entire U.N. behind us, but there will be enough countries [who would support us] to enable us to fight under better conditions." Ben-Gurion did not delude himself about public reaction either:

There won't be any dancing in the streets tomorrow; I can imagine the disappointment . . . in the army. But I am sure that in another six months . . . ships will be coming, and oil tankers will be sailing, a railroad will be begun; American, French,
English, Italian and Ethiopian ships will be coming, things will be looking up. . . .
Then it will be obvious that this fateful decision was a better one.[58]

In fact, Gaza did revert to Egyptian rule, but Ben-Gurion's predictions
came true. A new status quo in the Straits of Tiran and the Gaza Strip was
consolidated, and 11 years later, when Nasser tried to turn the clock back,
Israel's contention that this constituted a casus belli was supported by many
Western nations, including the United States. But for a while, some more
bitter disappointments still awaited Ben-Gurion.

Before Golda Meir made the announcement of Israeli withdrawal, she and
Abba Eban showed the text to Pineau and to the Americans. Dulles, however, did not show the Israelis the text of the announcement to be made by
the American ambassador to the U.N. He claimed that the final version was
not yet prepared but assured the Israelis that it would follow the principles
agreed on. In any case, he said, Lodge would declare that America considered Israel's announcement "reasonable and legitimate."[59] This was soon to
become the source of grave misunderstandings, almost provoking Israel into
rescinding its announcement of withdrawal. Under last-minute pressures,
Eban and Meir seem not to have paid heed to the possible discrepancies
between the Israeli and American declarations and failed to insist on seeing
the American text before it was made public. Eban mistakenly believed that
American acceptance of Golda Meir's declaration meant that their own
would not differ from it. The mistake became obvious all too quickly.

At the opening session of the General Assembly on the afternoon of
March 1, in an atmosphere of tense anticipation, the Israeli foreign minister
stepped up to the podium and announced that Israel had decided to comply
with the U.N. Resolution of February 2, 1957, and would withdraw its
forces from Sharm al-Sheikh and the Gaza Strip. As agreed, Golda Meir
then detailed the expectations and assumptions on the basis of which Israel
had agreed to withdraw, including its retention of the right to self-defense
under Article 51 of the U.N. Charter if its freedom of navigation in the
Straits of Tiran was hampered or if Egypt resumed hostilities in the Gaza
Strip.[60] The second scheduled speaker was the American ambassador to the
U.N., Henry Cabot Lodge; but here a bitter surprise awaited the Israelis.

The contacts among Eban, Dulles, and Pineau had sparked fears among Arab delegates who began to suspect that America and France would give Israel assurances that were not compatible with the American undertaking to keep Israel from enjoying any political gains from its aggressive action in the Sinai. In order to dispel these worries, and apparently also under pressure from the U.N. secretary general, the American ambassador embellished his announcement with a few comments that had not been previously agreed upon with the Israelis and that effectively altered the entire tenor of the American declaration. Lodge expressed American approbation of the consensus reached on the Straits of Tiran, supported the permanent emplacement of the UNEF, and enunciated American insistence on the need for the U.N. secretary general to approach the General Assembly before responding to Egyptian demands to evacuate the UNEF from Egyptian territory. On the issue of the Gaza Strip, however, Lodge deviated from the expected script: He quoted a passage from Hammarskjöld's report of January 24 that included specific statements regarding Egyptian rights in the Gaza Strip and referred to the Armistice Agreements as the basis for any continued treatment of the issue.[61]

Henry Cabot Lodge's change of course was not incidental, and the Israelis found it hard to believe that it was strictly his own doing. And indeed, as Lodge was delivering his address, Dulles was meeting with Arab ambassadors in his office in Washington, formally advising them that the Israeli withdrawal was not contingent upon any assurances or concessions on the part of the American administration.[62] As a matter of fact, Dulles's statement to the Arabs reiterated only what was well known and agreed upon: The United States had not committed itself to any *formal* undertakings vis-à-vis Israel. But to the Israelis his announcement, which was made public that very day, represented a reneging on *informal* understandings.

In her autobiography Golda Meir wrote: "Perhaps not everyone at the U.N. that day understood what Cabot Lodge was saying, but we understood it very well. . . . There was nothing I could do or say. I just sat there biting my lip, not even able to look at the handsome Mr. Cabot Lodge. . . . It was not one of the finest moments of my life."[63] Pineau tried to soothe the Israelis and told Eban, "The main thing is not the wording and points of U.N. etiquette but rather the reality, namely, that France and the United States have agreed to ensure freedom of navigation in the Straits and to set up an international regime in Gaza."[64] But in Jerusalem the feeling was that America had betrayed Israel. "We shall have to make it clear that we have been deceived," Ya'acov Herzog cabled Eban. Ben-Gurion's immediate tendency was to publicly rescind the withdrawal announcement, but Herzog convinced him to wait. At the first Israeli Cabinet meeting ever convened on a Sabbath, the government decided to demand that America provide "clear notice that Egypt would not return to the Gaza Strip." Ben-Gurion also instructed Dayan to put off his meeting with General Burns, which had been scheduled to coordinate the details of the withdrawal.

But meanwhile the Americans had already taken a few steps to placate the Israelis. In reaction to Abba Eban's telephone protest to the State Department immediately after Lodge's address, Dulles called him in for urgent discussions: "He's worried at my being worried," Eban reported to Jerusalem. The secretary of state was willing to exchange letters with the Israeli government if it so requested, "but in the meantime [he wishes to inform] the Prime Minister that they are well aware that they approved the text [of Golda Meir's address] and insist on their intention to recognize it officially." The next morning Eisenhower sent a reassuring cable to Ben-Gurion, reiterating the American obligation in principle. Golda Meir's address referred to Israeli hopes and expectations, which the United States also supported, the president wrote, and, immediately after the withdrawal, steps would be taken to create stabler and calmer conditions that would be more conducive to the welfare of the entire region. "I believe that it is reasonable to entertain such hopes and expectations and I want you to know that the U.S. . . . will seek that such hopes prove not to be in vain."[65]

As he had done often in the last few months, Eban turned to Ben-Gurion with a plea, this time to ratify the announcement made at the U.N. by Golda Meir. In an emotional cable he wrote that "Eisenhower's identification with the assumptions in the Foreign Minister's address yesterday is far more important than whether or not Cabot Lodge worded his address as we wanted him to." He recalled Israel's achievements in the most recent political struggle and said, "In your place I would stand before the nation and history with pride and with a sense of victory and enumerate these achievements as the bountiful harvest of our having successfully stood alongside you, inspired by your tenacity and the force of your welcome judgment." Eban concluded by urging Ben-Gurion to proceed "fearlessly in the same course taken in the Foreign Minister's address and reaping . . . all the attendant benefits, within Israel and outside her."[66]

Ben-Gurion scarcely needed Eban's urgings at this point, since he could hardly afford to undo what had been accepted in prolonged discussions with the Americans, and after French intervention, simply because of a few unfortunate turns of phrase on the part of Henry Cabot Lodge. It was too late to rescind the withdrawal. Eban was eventually proved correct in his estimation, but at the beginning of March his eloquence could not mitigate the sense of abject failure that Ben-Gurion doubtless felt.

On March 3 Ben-Gurion cabled Golda Meir and Eban that "the Government tends to accept the verdict," but he wanted to soften the blow by receiving "written clarification from the Secretary of State regarding our right to self-defense in the matter of Gaza."[67] But Dulles told Eban that "it was very hard for him to obligate himself for anything that he did not want made public," and proposed that Israel settle for verbal clarifications and the president's most recent communiqué. The Israeli Cabinet met the next day, March 4; by a majority vote, it decided in favor of withdrawal. Afterward Herzog cabled New York: "The die is cast; an hour ago the Prime Minister instructed Dayan to request a meeting with Burns today."[68]

Moshe Dayan and General Burns did meet that day, at the airport in Lod, where it was decided that the UNEF would enter Gaza in the evening hours of March 6 and would enter Sharm al-Sheikh on March 8. After the meeting Dayan reported to Ben-Gurion. The chief of staff's Bureau Diary records that "Ben-Gurion looked like a man who had risen from a long and difficult illness—tired, exhausted, but already over the worst . . . Dayan was stern and was careful not to belittle the problems nor hide his own frustration." For several months relations between the two men had been tense; Ben-Gurion was preoccupied with the political struggle at the U.N. and met with Dayan and Shimon Peres only sporadically. He may very well have been avoiding Dayan, who did not hide his criticism of the measures taken. Dayan was bitter; his bureau chief wrote that "the tension seemed to be taking its toll on Dayan. It's hard for him to take a stance so completely opposed to Ben-Gurion's own. His attempts to justify and understand Ben-Gurion's steps have not been successful. . . . Moshe believes that Ben-Gurion's agreement to withdraw was the result of weakness and not of far-sighted policy." But the die had been cast, and Dayan could only carry out the decision faithfully.[69]

The Foreign Ministry continued its efforts to flesh out the American promises. At U.N. headquarters, rumors began to circulate that Hammarskjöld was planning to have the Gaza Strip revert to Egyptian control within two weeks. The rumors prompted Golda Meir to write Dulles on March 6 that "If the U.N. does not implement full military and administrative supervision [of the Strip], the situation is liable to rapidly get out of control."[70] Dayan knew the foreign minister's veiled threat was no more than a bluff, and in the consultation called by Ben-Gurion he had only one question: How would the government vote if reliable information were received that the Egyptians would be coming back to Gaza? "The answers were most evasive, no one gave a categorical and clear-cut response, and Ben-Gurion was silent."[71] Any further delay was pointless; in the evening hours of March 6, General Burns's troops entered the Gaza Strip. As was his wont, Moshe Dayan was there, ready to swallow the bitter pill; two days later he went to Sharm al-Sheikh and found a large number of senior Israeli officers who, like him, had come to say farewell to the beautiful spot that more than any other site symbolized the victory of the Sinai campaign, the fruits of which the Israelis had just been forced to relinquish.

Apparently Hammarskjöld hoped that the UNEF would be able to manage the Strip's affairs on its own, at least for a while: General Burns wrote in his memoirs, "The assumption was that UNEF would be responsible for administration for the time needed to complete negotiations with the Egyptians on final arrangements."[72] But things worked out differently. As soon as the U.N. force entered the Strip, Egyptian agitators began to incite the inhabitants to condemn the U.N. administration and demand Egypt's return. The UNEF's Scandinavian battalion was forced to use tear gas and even opened fire, injuring a local Arab in the course of stormy demonstrations. The demonstrators tried to raise the Egyptian flag on U.N. headquarters and carried banners reading "Egypt is our mother" and "We shall never be separated from Egypt." Five days later the U.N. assistant secretary general, Ralph Bunche, went to Gaza. When he realized that the U.N. force could not control the area under the conditions that had been created, he proposed a "nominal Egyptian presence." But the Egyptians were not satisfied with that; in the course of Bunche's shuttling between Gaza and Egypt, they informed him that, in light of the unrest in Gaza, they were appointing a "Governor General" who would be assuming responsibility in two days. When asked if the UNEF would oppose the governor general's entry, Bunche and Burns replied that "the U.N. force does not have the authority to prevent the return of the Egyptians."[73]

Israel Foreign Ministry officials were incensed and did what they could to prevent the move at the last minute. The foreign minister told the American ambassador in Israel:

> Who would have believed that the dire predictions would come true with such dizzying speed. . . . We will not be able to tolerate a situation in which the Egyptians

return to Gaza in any form whatsoever, and if the situation deteriorates, we will have no choice but to exercise our right to self-defense. . . . If war breaks out, responsibility will lie with the U.N. Secretary General. Israel will not be prey to Nasser's pressure and the Secretary General's deceptions.[74]

In New York, Abba Eban also tried to prevent the Egyptian return, but his efforts were in vain, as were Bunche's pleas with Nasser to wait until Hammarskjöld reached the region. On March 14, as evening fell, General Muhammad abd al-Latif of Egypt entered Gaza and took up the reins of power.

General abd al-Latif arrived with a limited administrative staff; in fact, no Egyptian military forces entered Gaza. The Americans noted it and Dulles's deputy, Christian Herter, said, "We do not believe that the presence of the Egyptian personnel [as opposed to military forces] in the area in which Egypt has administrative rights under agreements, grants Israel any cause for action."[75]

The Israeli Foreign Ministry remained unplacated and continued its efforts to undo what had been done. Immediately after abd al-Latif entered Gaza, the Israeli Foreign Ministry spokesman issued an exceptionally biting statement,[76] and Golda Meir embarked on a series of dramatic visits to Washington, New York, and Paris, where she vented her anger at Dulles and Hammarskjöld before her French friends. Hammarskjöld admitted that the appointment of an Egyptian governor for Gaza "was a hasty and disappointing move."[77] Guy Mollet was furious. "It is hard for him to accept the fact that Eisenhower and Dulles cheated them." Bourgès-Maunoury promised that "if Israel is forced to take action, France would place at Israel's disposal . . . what limited means she has."[78] But Dulles said, "It's still too early to assume that our hopes won't come true. For the time being there is no foundation for assuming that the Gaza Strip would again serve as a base for the Fedayun and that Israeli shipping will be disturbed." And he pleaded with Israel "to have patience for a while longer and not to conclude that the game is lost."[79]

Nothing came of the Foreign Ministry efforts, and Golda Meir returned empty-handed. Only military action could undo what had been done, but Ben-Gurion would not even consider that option. On the day General abd al-Latif entered Gaza, Ben-Gurion told Dayan that "he had no intention of responding to the Egyptian entry into Gaza with military action even if they came with an army. . . . Even if the Egyptians used Fedayun, we will not take over the Strip."[80] During the entire struggle, Ben-Gurion had been ambivalent on retaining the Gaza Strip, where control of the overcrowded and hostile Palestinian population was extremely problematic. After Israel's withdrawal, he certainly believed that retaking the territory was out of the question, "first and foremost because I do not believe it is in Israel's interest to control Gaza."[81]

In April 1955, some two years before the events related in this chapter, Ben-Gurion had proposed to the Cabinet that the Gaza Strip be taken in reprisal for the Fedayun attacks, which had culminated in the murder of a young woman helping the immigrants in a village near the Gaza border. Ben-Gurion's view of Gaza's place in Israel's security policy had changed considerably since then. The Israeli army's control of the Gaza Strip in the months following the Suez war probably convinced him that control of Gaza was indeed a liability and not an asset.

Moshe Dayan was not unsympathetic toward the "Old Man's" position on this point, even when he believed that the conquest of Gaza was strategically important. On September 17, 1956, when he briefed his officers for the first time on the goals of the coming war, he said:

> Gone are the days when a Government dominated the people; today it's the population that dictates its wishes to the Government. This makes it vitally important for a state to consider the question of the relative size of any minority that it can allow itself to "swallow." . . . The addition of large numbers of Arabs to the country would be our undoing and would constitute a tremendous danger to Israeli democracy, progress, culture, internal regime and, ultimately, its future. . . . Even in the Gaza Strip, a situation can be created which would dwarf any current troubles we might face there, posing enormous economic, political and security problems if we conquer it with all the refugees there. . . . The next generation will ask us, "What kind of fools were you to trade a border that could be held by two infantry companies for this can of worms? Why didn't you hold on to the splendid border you had at the end of the War of Independence, with the Gaza Strip and its barren sands and its 300,000 Arabs outside of Israel instead of inside?"[82]

The new situation created after the Sinai campaign provided some assurance that the Gaza Strip would not pose the same risks to Israel's security and that the border incidents that had plagued it before the war would not recur. Since Dayan was already ambivalent about the wisdom of holding Gaza before its conquest, he did not find it hard to accept Ben-Gurion's orders after his forces withdrew.

Some time later it emerged that Dulles was right in his assessment and that the game was not lost at all. Nasser did manage to regain formal sovereignty over the Sinai and the right to control the Gaza Strip, but the strategic conditions in the region had undergone a radical change.

In fact, for ten years Nasser did not reassemble his forward military deployment along the borders with Israel; he did not send the Fedayun against Israel or resume border incidents; and he did not hamper Israeli shipping in the Straits of Tiran. He was prevented from taking any of these actions, not by the formal political pronouncements and convoluted phraseology of the diplomats at the U.N., but by the reality of the Sinai campaign, which had fundamentally changed power relations between Israel and Egypt and clearly returned Israel's deterrent capability. Dulles had foreseen it; he told Eban, "Will Nasser chase the U.N. force out of Gaza? I don't think he's particularly anxious to meet you face to face again."[83]

The UNEF itself played only a secondary role in generating this new situation of "security and tranquility," as Dulles phrased it.[84] From the very outset the U.N. force was not given the authority to use arms except in self-defense; the U.N. Secretariat and the Advisory Council would not even permit Burns to open fire against infiltrators. The main function of the U.N. force's presence was in providing Nasser with a convenient pretext for his own decision to refrain for the time being from *actively* reinstating the status quo ante. The restoration of the Israeli army's deterrent power was ultimately the main achievement of the Sinai campaign.

A·F·T·E·R·W·O·R·D

Toward the end of 1955 the government of Israel formally resolved not to embark on a preventive war against Egypt, despite the serious blow to the balance of weapons created by the Egyptian-Czech arms deal. Instead, Israel's Cabinet decided to meet the challenge by different means, foremost by procuring arms that would rectify the upset balance and reestablish the Israeli army's deterrent power. Indeed, during the spring and summer of 1956 Israel acquired considerable quantities of armaments from France. What then prompted Israel to embark on a war initiative against Egypt just when the problem of deterrence had been resolved? Had the Israeli government reversed its decision against preventive war? And if so, why did it do so when a preventive war was no longer necessary?

In fact, the Israeli government never reversed its decision, because the Sinai campaign did not represent the delayed implementation of the original proposal for preventive war. Israel embarked on the war against the backdrop of severe problems with Egypt that had obtained even before the Czech transaction; the arms deal only exacerbated these problems and gave them a dimension of urgency, which the rectified arms balance had blunted but not fundamentally resolved. Nasser's nationalization of the Suez Canal and the subsequent British and French decision to launch a military offensive against him provided Israel with an opportunity to resolve these underlying problems.

The preventive war proposed in the autumn of 1955 was intended to negate the *consequences* of the Czech deal—that is, the grossly upset weapons balance. The main motivation for preventive war concerned genuine fears that Egypt might in the near future attack Israel and manage to overpower it. Indeed, a preventive war is by definition a war initiative against an enemy, provoked by fears that a given situation might take a turn for the worse.

This was not the case of the Sinai campaign; Israel was in no immediate danger in the autumn of 1956. The war was fought to contend with the *motivations* of the Czech deal—with the tensions and dissensions between Israel and Egypt that had existed since the beginning of the 1950s and that were aggravated in 1954 when Nasser set about putting his pan-Arab policies into action, including signing the agreement with Czechoslovakia.

Israel's most pressing problem vis-à-vis Egypt since the early 1950s had been the nebulous and uncertain situation created by the Egyptian-Israeli Armistice Agreement and the two country's contradictory interpretations of that agreement. Egypt's interpretation was restrictive: The agreement did not annul the state of belligerency between it and Israel and did not abrogate Egypt's belligerent rights. Israel's interpretation was broad: The agreement did nullify the state of belligerency. But so long as actual hostilities did not erupt, Israel seemed willing to accept this provisional situation of uncertainty, although it posed many risks for Israel. But this very same ambiguity was what permitted Egypt to harass Israel through Fedayun raids, border tensions, and the blockade against Israeli navigation in the Suez Canal and the Straits of Tiran, and made the situation intolerable for Israel.

Israel had hoped that the U.N., under whose auspices the Armistice Agreements had been signed, would be more liberal in its interpretation, but that organization tended to follow the restrictive interpretation, much to Israel's dissatisfaction. It was no coincidence that Israel embarked on the Sinai campaign at the very height of a crisis in relations between Ben-Gurion and the U.N. secretary general and when it became apparent that the latter was in fact a loyal custodian of the problematic status juris.

The first announcement issued by the IDF spokesman after the paratroops had landed in the Mitla Pass declared that the main reasons for the military assault were the Fedayun incursions and the closure of Israel's transportation routes. But although there were no Fedayun units at the Mitla Pass, Abu Agheila, or el-Arish, the announcement was not an entire fabrication. The 1956 war was launched mainly to effect a change in the status quo that the restrictive interpretation of the Armistice Agreements had created. Indeed, at the very beginning of hostilities Ben-Gurion had announced the unilateral nullification of the Armistice Agreement with Egypt; more than anything else, his declaration expressed one of the major goals of the campaign: abrogation of the ambiguous intermediate status of neither war nor peace.

The nationalization of the Suez Canal and the subsequent French and British willingness to join Israel in a military strike against Nasser seemed to provide Israel with the opportunity to rectify this situation, either by establishing peace with Egypt—a hope that was soon dashed—or by effecting territorial and legal changes that would create a new status quo.

In the spring of 1956 Ben-Gurion had told Moshe Dayan, "The only thing we can gain from the war . . . is Nasser's overthrow."[1] Ben-Gurion probably hoped that the allies' success and subsequently pro-Western regime that would replace Nasser's might lead to peaceful relations with Egypt. In 1955 the Israeli leadership and public alike viewed Gamal Abdul Nasser as Israel's chief enemy. At the Sèvres conference, too, the underlying assumption seemed to be that the joint allied operation would result in a change in leadership in Egypt. But Ben-Gurion saw this as the allies' task, not Israel's. At any rate, it was a fervent hope indeed, but scarcely an operative plan and certainly not a precondition for Israel's consent to join the alliance with Great Britain and France, especially since Ben-Gurion himself had doubts about the allies' ability to attain this goal.

And the hope evaporated when Operation Musketeer crumbled. From this point on, Israel's battle was geared to effecting a change in the status quo through territorial adjustments or legal and contractual modifications.

Superficially, the Suez War did not seem to achieve even this limited objective: Israel did not manage to change the status quo either territorially or legally. It was forced to retreat from all the areas it had conquered, and the Armistice Agreements remained intact. All the hopes that Israel had pinned on its military alliance with Great Britain and France were dashed— Nasser's regime was not overthrown, and the likelihood that the alliance would reduce international criticism and make it easier for diplomatic bargaining was proven illusory. The failure of Operation Musketeer left Israel alone and exposed to tremendous international censure as well as to an obdurate U.N. and U.S. position. All the fruits of victory were denied Israel: It was forced to withdraw from the entire Sinai peninsula, including Sharm al-Sheikh and the Gaza Strip, in exchange for which it received no formal change in the status quo.

But although the situation may not have undergone any formal changes, practically it had been transformed beyond recognition. Operation Kadesh reasserted Israel's deterrent capability; not only did Nasser not dare provoke war with Israel for the next ten years, but until that hasty attempt in 1967 "to salvage the shame of 1956," the Gulf of Aqaba was open to Israeli navigation and Eilat became a booming port. For those next ten years as well, Nasser refrained from sending in the Fedayun and from massively deploying his army in the Sinai peninsula. During the 1960s, when Egypt refrained meticulously from getting entangled in Syria's dispute with Israel over the attempt to divert the headwaters of the Jordan River, Nasser responded to his critics by declaring that until the Arab world was ready for war with Israel, he was not prepared to squabble over "every Syrian tractor that got damaged." More clearly than anything else, Nasser's statement proved just how profound a change had been effected by the Sinai campaign, not in the *status juris* but in the *status de facto*.

To be sure, Israel's deterrent power was reestablished to a certain degree by the procurement of weapons from France, but it was completely reasserted only in the military campaign. Egyptian actions between 1957 and 1967 clearly indicate that the leaders of Egypt were not oblivious to the IDF's fighting ability as expressed in the Suez War, even though they always justly stressed that this campaign was fought not only against Israel but also against the Anglo-French threat.

It is indeed fair to consider a certain reservation regarding Israel's deterrence capability. The Israeli army captured the Sinai peninsula from a thinned-down Egyptian military deployment, and it was the powerful British and French air forces that struck at Egypt's air fields. Moreover, during the second half of the campaign, Nasser had ordered his army in Sinai to retreat. All in all, Nasser could claim, sincerely enough, that the Israeli army's advantage was an illusory one that had been achieved with the aid of two Great Powers. Furthermore, at the end of the Suez War Nasser succeeded in creating an image of himself as victor in the military campaign as well as the political one, emerging as a figure who had fought bravely and wisely against overwhelming odds. The deterrence effect that the Sinai operation had created was therefore a "limited deterrence," and the Egyptians continued to believe that they would be capable of striking Israel as soon as they were once again strong enough. It would be on the force of this belief that Nasser would, in ten years' time, make his greatest mistake. But in the meantime, Israel had bought itself ten years of relative peace and prosperity.

Neither the U.N. nor the Great Powers accepted Ben-Gurion's contention that the Armistice Agreements were no longer valid. But the substantive relations between Israel and Egypt underwent an overwhelming change. No longer did they constitute the ambiguous situation that had obtained until then: Until 1967 the situation was clearly "not war." The Suez War gave Israel unqualified sovereignty over all its territory up to the Demarcation Lines, which became, for all intents and purposes, increasingly established as effective boundaries. From this point of view the Sinai campaign had achieved its goal—the quarrel with Egypt over the interpretation of the Armistice Agreements was settled in Israel's favor.

Israel had three territorial aims in the Sinai campaign: obtaining control of the Straits of Tiran, the Gaza Strip, and the eastern part of the Sinai peninsula. Control of the Straits of Tiran would ensure Israel's freedom of navigation. The instructions Golda Meir received when she left for the St. Germain conference stated that Israel would be demanding effective control of the shore lines of the Straits of Tiran. Control of the straits indeed became a central point of dissension in Israel's struggle to retain the fruits of its victory after Operation Kadesh.

Control of the Gaza Strip was important for Israel to prevent hostile incursions from inside that territory, but this goal was not unequivocal. The Israeli GHQ did believe that only the physical presence of Israeli forces in the Strip could eliminate the danger posed by the Fedayun and the risk of the Strip turning into a springboard from which enemy forces could easily penetrate into the heart of Israel in wartime, but Ben-Gurion was dubious about the need to cope with hundreds of thousands of hostile Palestinians and to assume responsibility for their welfare. When the time came, he was willing to forgo the "bargain" and trade IDF responsibility for that of the U.N.

Control of the eastern part of the Sinai peninsula was vital to prevent the forward deployment of the Egyptian army along the Israeli border. All three goals found expression in the Sèvres Protocol, in which Ben-Gurion insisted on declaring Israel's intention of permanently holding the entire territory east of the el-Arish-Sharm al-Sheikh line. Soon after the Sinai campaign, however, it became obvious that Israel would not be able to realize even one of these goals and would not be able to effect any territorial change in the region.

The illusion that Israel could still effect territorial changes was part of the legacy of Israel's 1948 War of Independence. That war had been fought in undefined territory, and the results of the battles established territorial facts. During the 1950s occasional voices were heard proposing that the "work begun in 1948 be completed"—specifically by taking the Hebron Hills, the suburbs north of Jerusalem, or the Gaza Strip—on the assumption that these areas could be absorbed into the territory of Israel, as such seizures were effected in 1948. But conditions had changed irreparably in the seven years since the War of Independence. The amorphous situation of 1948 no longer existed, and territorial changes in the wake of wars were no longer acceptable for the international community.

When Israel realized this, it tried to make its withdrawal from areas it had conquered contingent on juridical changes. The withdrawal from the Straits of Tiran was made conditional on formal guarantees ensuring it freedom of navigation; withdrawal from the Gaza Strip was made conditional on exclusive U.N. control there; and withdrawal from the Sinai peninsula was made contingent on demilitarization under international accords. The only problem was that Egyptian sovereignty in the Sinai was undisputed; Israel also failed to obtain anything more than informal assurances for its freedom of navigation in the straits and for U.N. supervision of the Gaza Strip. Superficially, then, Israel seemed to have suffered an unqualified defeat, achieving neither its territorial goals nor any of its juridical conditions. Effectively, however, the Sinai peninsula remained demilitarized for the next ten years, Nasser refrained from renewing tensions along the border, and Israel's freedom of navigation in the Straits of Tiran was secured.

Israel had an additional political goal when it embarked on the Sinai campaign: consolidating and strengthening its ties with France and securing France's obligation to arm the Israeli army. Virtually from the beginning of Israel's existence as a state, Ben-Gurion advocated pursuit of the assistance and support of one of the great powers to underpin Israel's security. In the early 1950s he tried in vain to join the various defense pacts that the West was trying to establish in the Middle East. In the mid-1950s France's North African interests intersected with Israel's security interests on the other side of Egypt. At the time, Ben-Gurion viewed maintaining this pact as a central political goal.

Indeed, Ben-Gurion was willing to compromise and go to war alongside Israel's ally at a time and under conditions not totally to Israel's advantage; Challe's "scenario" was not ideal for Israel, but France's friendship was supremely important for Ben-Gurion. In order not to disappoint the French, the Israeli prime minister was ready to go very far indeed.

That same need to retain the informal military pact with France was at the center of Ben-Gurion's considerations after the Suez War as well, when he finally accepted Christian Pineau's suggested formulation for the withdrawal from Gaza. Nevertheless, it must be stressed that Israel did not place itself at France's disposal as a mercenary; it had very powerful motivations of its own for striking at Egypt and had its own score to settle with Nasser. The opportunity to do so in tandem with France, Ben-Gurion thought, served Israel's vital interests perfectly.

France emerged from the war utterly defeated; its position as a world power had been seriously assailed and its control of North Africa was ultimately lost. But for the next ten years it remained a vital bulwark for Israel; until de Gaulle imposed an embargo on Israeli arms sales in the wake of the Six-Day War, France was Israel's main source of weapons, and relations between the two nations flourished.

The main achievement of the Sinai campaign for Israel was the ten years during which Israel enjoyed relative tranquility and could direct its resources and energies to economic and social goals. In retrospect, however, the Sinai campaign also influenced the outcome of the next war. The consequences of the campaign had far-reaching implications for the Six-Day War, determining the political and military conditions under which that war would be fought. Israel's victory in the Six-Day War cannot be understood, nor can its political situation afterward, if we do not take into account the consequences of the Sinai campaign. Israel's military power was strengthened and its army became a modern one based on air and armor power because of its alliance with France, permitting it to win a lightning victory in 1967. The battle experience and self-assurance the IDF had gained during the Sinai campaign had no small influence on the military consequences of the 1967 war.

Paradoxically enough, moreover, in the Six-Day War Israel benefitted from the restrictions imposed in the Sinai campaign. Because of political considerations, the Sèvres Protocol stipulated that the allies rather than the Israeli air force would undertake the assault on Egyptian air force bases. As a result, the Egyptian air force took no precautions against a possible Israeli air force strike, giving Israel the tremendous advantage of total surprise and permitting it to strike at the Egyptian air fields with its planes spread out and totally exposed. The Israeli victory in 1967 was sealed during those first hours of battle, as its air force's capabilities, which had not been revealed in full in the Sinai campaign, could be effectively employed.

But it was not only the military conditions under which Israel went to war in 1967 that had improved in the wake of the unexpected consequences of the Sinai campaign. No less important, the political conditions had also

improved unexpectedly as a result of Israel's political struggle at the U.N.
and in Washington after Suez. At the time this struggle was perceived as a
defeat. In retrospect, however, it is clear that precisely because of that struggle in 1957, Israel's 1967 war initiative was not censured and was even considered justifiable by the United States.

In the course of this struggle in the winter of 1957, Israel's *casus belli*
were defined and clarified; although it was not anchored in any formal resolutions, blockade of the Straits of Tiran and the entry of the Egyptian army
into the Sinai peninsula were recognized as a "red line," Egypt's encroachment of which would be interpreted by Israel as a declaration of war. Indeed,
when Nasser crossed that line in 1967, sent his army into the Sinai, and
again closed the Straits of Tiran, war became inevitable; Israel responded by
initiating hostilities, and its friends in the West viewed it as a justifiable war
of self-defense.

In addition, the informal undertakings that the United States had provided
Israel in the course of the diplomatic struggle over withdrawal eventually
created a bond between the two nations. Informal though it was, the
American president had undertaken a moral obligation to stand at Israel's
side. This obligation turned into an asset of the first order in Israel's security
policy after the Sinai campaign, especially after Lyndon Johnson's election
as American president. During the Suez crisis Johnson had been leader of
the opposition and had consistently demanded that Israel's security needs be
taken into account. In 1967, when he learned that the United States could not
put its 1957 obligation into effect to keep Nasser from blocking the Straits or
massing his army in the Sinai, he saw no way out but to acquiesce to Israel
and permit it to exercise its right to self-defense, which had been specifically, albeit only informally, ratified by America's president during the 1957
crisis. The fact that this time Israel was expected to withdraw from the Sinai
only in exchange for a full peace should also be viewed as a consequence of
that same development. Abba Eban's energetic diplomatic battle in
Washington and New York during the winter of 1957 bore fruit in the summer of 1967.

The triple alliance did not eliminate Gamal Abdul Nasser; in fact, he managed to emerge from the war as a victor, not only in Arab eyes, but for the
entire Third World. The very fact that he could not be overpowered by two
former imperialist powers elevated his stature in every land where the popu-

lation fought to free itself from the bonds of colonialism, and in the ten years after Suez his international prestige reached its apex.

Bulganin had written Eden that the days of colonial enslavement were over, and that Western control of the peoples of Asia and Africa by force had ended. Bulganin was right. The war fought by Great Britain and France was an anachronistic one, and therefore they lost it. It was doomed to failure from the outset because it ran against the course of international developments that could not be stopped.

Not so Israel's war, which differed in its very essence from the one fought by Great Britain and France because it was fundamentally a war of self-defense. For this reason Israel was not ultimately tarnished by the unholy alliance it had entered into with the "imperialist plotters." The emerging nations of Asia and Africa stood alongside Egypt during the U.N. struggle but did not hesitate to form increasingly closer ties with Israel afterward. The decade after Sinai also saw the high point in Israel's relations with the states that had just gained their independence from colonial rule. Paradoxically, both Egypt and Israel emerged as victors, even though they fought against each other.

Israel and Egypt won the war, but both victories led only to another war. Israel's success in the Sinai campaign did not lead to the hoped-for peace but rather brought it back to square one; the conditions were improved, but Israel was forced to recognize that yet a third round of hostilities was inevitable. Nasser's success nurtured his own hopes of being able to beat Israel the next time around. In the end, Israel attained some of its goals in 1957, but not the most important of all, the ultimate goal that Ben-Gurion spoke of when he briefed Israeli army officers in the winter of 1955: "In both our military preparedness and in the belligerent actions imposed on us," he said, "we must never lose sight of the fact that our ultimate goal in our relations with our neighbors is to attain peace and coexistence." But Ben-Gurion went on to say that "After each war we win, we will again face the same problem. . . . We will be confronted by a third round, and a fourth."[2] This was indeed a tragically clear-sighted prediction: Israel was destined to experience a third round, and even two more rounds. The longed-for peace with Egypt was ultimately achieved not by the sword but by reconciliation and compromise.

List of Abbreviations

BGA	Ben-Gurion Archive
COS Archive	Chief of Staff's Bureau Archive
COS Diary	Chief of Staff's Bureau Diary
COS Diary, Doc. Vols.	Chief of Staff's Bureau Diary, Documents and Appendices Volumes
DDEL	Dwight D. Eisenhower Library
DDQ	Declassified Documents Quarterly
DOS Bulletin	U.S. Department of State, Bulletin
FRUS	Foreign Relations of the United States
GAOR	General Assembly Official Record
JCS	Joint Chiefs of Staff
JFDP	John Foster Dulles Papers
PRO	Public Record Office, London
SCOR	Security Council Official Record
SIA	State of Israel Archives
SWB	Summary of World Broadcasts

N·O·T·E·S

CHAPTER 1
THE EGYPTIAN–CZECH ARMS DEAL:
THE FORMATION OF A NATIONAL EMERGENCY

1. The full Egyptian announcement can be found in *Summary of World Broadcasts,* Part IV, The Arab World, Israel, Greece, Turkey, and Persia, 1955-1957 (hereinafter referred to as *SWB*), No. 608, September 30, 1955, pp. 16-18. On the historiographic considerations for beginning this study with the Egyptian-Czech arms deal rather than with the Gaza raid, see Colonel (Res.) Mordechai Bar-On, "The Egyptian-Czech Arms Deal: A Question of Periodization," in *Ma'arachot,* Israel Defense Forces, 306-307, December 1986-January 1987, pp. 38-42 (Hebrew).

2. Nasser's own version of the chain of events leading up to signature of the agreement can be found in his interview with Kenneth Love in *The New York Times* of October 6, 1955. See also Kenneth Love, *Suez: The Twice-Fought War* (New York: McGraw-Hill, 1969), chap. 8: "Enter the Bear." Uri Ra'anan claims that the deal had already been negotiated at the beginning of 1955—see Uri Ra'anan, *The USSR, Arms and the Third World* (Cambridge, MA: MIT Press, 1969).

3. The announcement rocked the entire Middle East. In his survey of the events of the preceding year, Barraclough speaks of the "electrifying effect" it had on the region—see Geoffrey Barraclough, *Survey of International Affairs 1955-1956* (Oxford: Oxford University Press, 1960), p. 95.

4. *Chief of Staff's Bureau Diary* (hereinafter referred to as *COS Diary*), IDF Archive, Givatayim, September 29, 1955. (All citations from *COS Diary* are in Hebrew unless otherwise stated.)

5. Moshe Sharett, *The Diary of Moshe Sharett* (Tel Aviv: Am Oved, 1982) (hereinafter referred to as *Sharett's Diary*), vol. 4, pp. 1176-1177 and 1180. (All citations from *Sharett's Diary* are in Hebrew unless otherwise stated.)

6. For background on the workings of this apparatus see Paul Jabber, *Not by War Alone: Security and Arms Control in the Middle East* (Los Angeles: University of California Press, 1981), chaps. 4 and 5.

7. *Knesset Records,* Israel Government Printing Office, Jerusalem, vol. 19, p. 119. (All citations from *Knesset Records* are in Hebrew unless otherwise stated.)

8. Cited in *Sharett's Diary,* vol. 4, p. 1182.

9. "An Assessment of the Political and Security Situation in Light of Developments in the Region," memo from Isser Harel dated October 19, 1955, in the *Ben-Gurion Archive,* Sde Boker (hereinafter referred to as *BGA*), Letters and Meetings File: September-October 1955. (All citations from *BGA* are in Hebrew unless otherwise stated.) See also *Sharett's Diary,* vol. 5, p. 1233.

10. Memo signed by Abba Eban in *BGA,* Letters and Meetings File.

11. *Sharett's Diary,* vol. 4, pp. 1207-1208.

12. *The New York Times,* October 5, 1955.

13. *Public Record Office,* London (hereinafter referred to as *PRO*), FO/371, 115469, V1023.

14. *Sharett's Diary,* vol. 4, pp. 1206-1207.

15. *Ma'ariv* daily newspaper, October 2, 1955 (Hebrew). *New York Post* editor Paul Sann interviewed Egypt's prime minister; the interview was widely cited in Israeli newspapers on October 15 and served to confirm this public feeling. Nasser, Sann wrote, believed that he was fighting Judaism and Jewish wealth. His mission was to save the world from control and destruction at the hands of the Zionist conspiracy.

16. *Yediot Aharonot,* October 14 and 25, 1955 (Hebrew).

17. *Herut,* September 29, 1955; October 2 and 5, 1955 (Hebrew).

18. *Haboker,* October 21, 1955 (Hebrew).

19. *Davar,* October 2nd, 1955 (Hebrew).

20. U.S. House of Representatives Committee on Foreign Affairs, *Report of the Special Study Mission,* Report no. 2147, Washington, D.C., May 1, 1956.

21. All the following debate and resolution citations are from *Knesset Records,* vol. 19, pp. 64-120.

22. Personal interview with Avraham Ben-Yosef, former assistant to the director general of the Ministry of Defense, 1958.

23. *State of Israel Archives,* Ministry of Foreign Affairs collection 130.02, file 2350/7. All further references to this source—cited as *SIA*—are from the same collection, and only file numbers will be cited. All citations are in Hebrew unless otherwise indicated.

24. *Ha'aretz,* October 24, 1955 (Hebrew).

25. In December of that year Egypt and Syria also declared "weapons weeks" and organized fund-raising activities for arms purchases. See *SWB,* part IV, no. 614, October 21, 1955; no. 630, December 16, 1955; and no. 631, December 20, 1955.

26. A considerable amount of material on the attempts to achieve such a settlement can be found in "Efforts at Discussions with Egypt," *SIA,* 2454/1. For the U.N.'s point of view see E.L.M. Burns, *Between Arab and Israeli* (London: Harrap & Co., 1962), pp. 86-90.

27. See General Burns's report on the operation in United Nations, *Security Council Official Record* (hereinafter referred to as *SCOR*), New York, 1955, Suppl., Doc. S/3430.

28. *SCOR,* ibid., Doc. S/3435.

29. *Yediot Aharonot,* October 17, 1955 (Hebrew). The Foreign Ministry's Research Department reported on October 4, 1955, that the Egyptian representative to the U.N. had calmed Ahmed Shukeiri, the aggressive Syrian representative, asking him not to react too strongly on the Nitzana attack and proposing "moderation and reason in Arab appearances for the outside world" because of the arms deal. See *SIA* 2450/7.

30. *PRO,* FO/371, 115465, V1013/50.

31. *SWB,* Part IV, no. 609, October 4, 1955, pp. 10-11.

32. News of the arms deal was received ecstatically throughout the Arab world: see *SWB,* Part IV, nos. 609, 610, 611, and 612. Ahmed Shauky, commentator for Cairo Radio's "Sauth al-Arab," spoke of thousands of letters of support sent to Nasser's bureau. In a memo dated October 31, 1955, the British permanent under secretary for foreign affairs wrote that reports from Cairo indicated that Nasser was intoxicated with the popularity he had achieved by provoking the West. See *PRO,* FO/371, 11546, V1023/19.

33. For a history of the blockade of the Straits of Tiran and an analysis of the implications in international law, see L. M. Bloomfield, *Egypt, Israel and the Gulf of Aqaba in International Law* (Toronto: Carswell, 1957). With Saudi Arabian consent, Egypt took over the islands of Tiran and Sanafir in January 1950. But, in a memo to the American ambassador in Cairo, Egypt undertook not to disturb vessels sailing "in good faith"; see Cable Caffery to Sec. of State, U.S. Department of State, *Foreign Relations of the United States* (hereinafter referred to as *FRUS*) (Washington, D.C.: Government Printing Office, 1950), vol. 5, no. 774, p. 711. The problem was first raised in the U.N. Security Council in 1954. See *SCOR,* 1954, Suppl., Doc. S/3168, Add. 1. On September 27, 1955, Abba Eban submitted a formal complaint to the chairman of the Security Council on Egyptian instructions regarding the Straits of Tiran. See *SCOR,* 1955, Suppl., Doc. S/3442.

CHAPTER 2
STATUS ASSESSMENT

1. A detailed analysis of the events as perceived through the prism of the Israeli leadership can be found in Michael Brecher, *Decisions in Israel's Foreign Policy* (New Haven, CT: Yale University Press, 1975), chap. 3.

2. Minutes of GHQ meeting, October 26, 1955, *COS Diary,* Documents and Appendices Volumes (hereinafter referred to as *COS Diary,* Doc. Vols.).

3. As soon as the transaction was announced it was obvious that it was the Soviet Union that was involved, not Czechoslovakia. When Sharett met the Soviet foreign minister at the end of October, Molotov continually referred to the sale in the first person plural. See *Sharett's Diary,* vol. 5, p. 1273.

4. Minutes of meeting, October 26, 1955, *COS Diary,* Doc. Vols.

5. Ibid.

6. U.S. Department of State, *Bulletin* (hereinafter referred to as DOS *Bulletin*), vol. 33 (1955), October 31, 1955, p. 688.

7. *FRUS,* 1952-1954, vol. 9, part 1, doc. 536, 538.

8. *Daily Express,* October 20, 1955.

9. "Special Intelligence Compilation" no. 65, *Chief of Staff's Bureau Archive,* IDF Archive, Givatayim (hereinafter referred to as *COS Archive*), January 13, 1956. (All citations from *COS Archive* are in Hebrew unless otherwise indicated.)

10. Pronouncements by Egypt's leaders at the time indicated that a substantive change had indeed taken place in their perception of the IDF's deterrent power. For example, Nasser told a correspondent from *The New York Times* that "after the Egyptian-Czech arms deal Israel will have to think carefully before undertaking a preventive war against Egypt" (cited in *Ma'ariv,* October 6, 1955). In a talk with a *Newsweek* editor he said, "Look at me, I sleep in my bed at night. Look at Sharett—he never spends two nights in the same bed." See Harry Kern, "The Cold War Moves South," in *Tensions in the Middle East,* Middle East Institute, Washington, D.C., 1955.

11. Weekly meeting held on December 1, 1955, *BGA,* Weekly Meeting Minutes File.

12. Ya'acov Herzog, in charge of the U.S. desk at the Foreign Ministry, recorded the talk; a précis was cabled to Eban in Washington: cable no. 454/1113, *COS Archive,* Outgoing Cables File.

13. Minutes of High Command meeting, January 1, 1956, in *COS Diary,* Doc. Vols.

14. Report by Israeli Foreign Ministry's Research Department, *SIA,* 2356/3.

15. See Ehud Ya'ari's instructive analysis, based on captured documents, *Egypt and the Fedayun 1953-1956* (Givat Haviva: Givat Haviva, 1975) (Hebrew).

16. In Yehoshafat Harkaby, *The Israeli Position in the Arab-Israeli Conflict* (Tel Aviv: Dvir, 1968), p. 466 (Hebrew).

17. Baruch Kimmerling, "Prominence of the Arab-Israeli Conflict as a Social Indicator 1949-1970," *State, Government and International Relations,* no. 6, 1974, p. 100 (Hebrew).

18. *Sharett's Diary,* vol. 1, p. 54. See also Moshe Dayan, "Israel's Border and Security Problems," *Foreign Affairs,* vol. 33, no. 2 (January 1955), pp. 250-267.

19. *Sharett's Diary,* vol. 2, p. 329.

20. Political debate, August 18, 1952, in *Knesset Records,* vol. 12, p. 2985. The same mood pervaded an internal briefing distributed in the Israeli Foreign Ministry less than two months after the Egyptian revolution: "We do not view Naguib's rule as one of enmity. . . . Deposing King Farouk eliminated from the arena one of the major figures advocating vengeance on Israel, for whom personal honor overrode national shame. . . . We cannot presume that the new regime in Egypt today intends to renew belligerence against Israel by the adventurism of a second round." *SIA,* 2409/2. The document is dated September 17, 1952.

21. *Knesset Records,* vol. 18, p. 673.

22. Gamal Abdul Nasser, "The Philosophy of the Revolution," *Ma'arachot,* Israel Defense Forces, November 1954 (Hebrew). The pamphlet was probably written by Mohamed Hassenein Heikal but is attributed to Nasser.

23. *Knesset Records,* vol. 19, p. 674.

24. Nasser, "The Philosophy of the Revolution," pp. 40, 44.

25. *SIA,* 2403/12.

26. Report of the Israeli Foreign Ministry's Research Department on "Glubb's Actions in Preparation for the Second Round," *SIA,* ibid.

27. "More Arab Threats to Renew War with Israel," document prepared by the Foreign Ministry's Research Department, July 4, 1949, *SIA,* 2401/12.

28. Cited in "Collection of Arabic News Clippings," Foreign Ministry's Research Department, *SIA,* ibid.

29. Letter sent by Sasson to Sharett, *SIA,* ibid.

30. David Ben-Gurion, *What Did We Fight For? What Did We Gain?* (Tel Aviv: Central Committee of the Israeli Labor Party/Information Department, 1957?) (Hebrew).

CHAPTER 3
CRISIS DIPLOMACY

1. *Sharett's Diary,* vol. 5, pp. 1231-1232.

2. Sharett described the meetings in great detail in his diary; see ibid., pp. 1243-1276.

3. In his memoirs Abba Eban writes that Sharett did not expect much from his trip but felt he had to go and do his best—see Abba Eban, *An Autobiography* (Jerusalem: Steimatzky, 1977), p. 194. See also the skepticism expressed by Israel's ambassador to France, Ya'acov Tsur, *Paris Diary: The Diplomatic Campaign in France* (Tel Aviv: Am Oved, 1968), p. 185 (Hebrew).

4. *Sharett's Diary,* vol. 5, p. 1252.

5. Evelyn Shuckburgh, *Descent to Suez: Diaries 1951-1956* (London: Weidenfeld & Nicolson, 1986), p. 297.

6. *Sharett's Diary,* vol. 5, pp. 1275-1276.

7. "Record of a Meeting between the Secretary of State and the Israeli Prime Minister," *PRO,* FO/371, 115537, V1076/4.

8. *Sharett's Diary,* vol. 5, p. 1152.

9. Eban, *An Autobiography,* p. 182.

10. *Sharett's Diary,* vol. 5, p. 1253.

11. Abba Eban took notes on the second talk in Geneva and telegraphed the details to Jerusalem in cable no. 749, *SIA* 2449/5.

12. Israeli Foreign Ministry Research Department report quoting the ambassador's discussion with an American journalist, *SIA* 2540/3 (English).

13. *Sharett's Diary,* vol. 5, p. 1259.

14. Eban's report of his meeting with Francis Russell, *SIA* 2540/7. See also *Sharett's Diary,* vol. 5, p. 1259.

15. "U.S. Objectives and Policies with Respect to the Near East" (NSC 5428), *Joint Chiefs of Staff* (hereinafter referred to as *JCS*) 1887/126, October 31, 1955, pp. 946-949, *Declassified Documents Quarterly* (hereinafter referred to as *DDQ*), 1987, 000390. See also "Memorandum of Discussion at the 263rd Meeting of the National Security Council," *FRUS* 1955-1957, vol. 14, *Arab-Israeli Dispute 1955,* pp. 661-668.

16. *Sharett's Diary,* vol. 5, p. 1260.

17. Ibid., vol. 5, pp. 1274-1275. See also Eban's report to Russell in "Memo. of Conversation," *PRO,* FO/371, 115469.

18. Dwight D. Eisenhower, *The White House Years: Waging Peace 1956-1961* (New York: Doubleday & Co., 1965), p. 529.

19. *Sharett's Diary,* vol. 5, p. 1254. For details on Sharett's meeting with Edgar Faure, see Tsur, *Paris Diary,* pp. 187-188.

20. *Sharett's Diary,* vol. 5, p. 1249.

21. *Ma'ariv,* October 27, 1955.

22. *Sharett's Diary,* vol. 5, p. 1268.

23. "Foreign Minister's speech at Lod Airport on his return from Geneva, November 1st, 1955," *SIA* 2449/5.

24. Research Department's weekly review, November 2, 1955, ibid.

25. *The New York Times,* October 28, 1955.

26. "Record of Meeting between Mr. Macmillan and Mr. Dulles at Geneva on November 9, 1955," *PRO,* FO/371, 115469, V1023/25.

27. Report to Jerusalem in telegram no. 749, *SIA* 2449/5.

28. DOS *Bulletin,* vol. 33, November 21, 1955, p. 845. Also cited in Noble Frankland, ed., *Documents on International Affairs 1955,* RIIA (Oxford: Oxford University Press/RIIA, 1957).

29. *Sharett's Diary,* vol. 5, p. 1267.

30. *PRO,* FO/371, 115469, V1023/25.

31. Ibid., V1023/23.

32. Shimon Peres, *David's Sling: The Secrets of Israel's Strength* (Jerusalem: Weidenfeld & Nicolson, 1970), pp. 29, 34-39 (Hebrew).

33. In his May 25 report to his defense minister, Peres wrote that the French "were not unaware of the high cost of their technological revolution and for that reason the [French] military considered themselves full partners in the military-industrial efforts to locate new markets." *Peres Archive*, Overseas Trips File. (All entries in the *Peres Archive* are in Hebrew unless stated otherwise.)

34. Ibid., pp. 36-37.

35. Sylvia Crosbie, *A Tacit Alliance: France and Israel From Suez to the Six Days War* (Princeton, N.J.: Princeton University Press, 1974), pp. 41-46.

36. Report on trip, May 25, 1955, *Peres Archive*, Overseas Trips File.

37. Quoted by Shimon Peres in his lecture to his senior staff at the Ministry of Defense, November 11, 1955. Peres Archive, "Overseas Trips File."

38. Peres's cable to Nachmias, September 28, 1955, *Peres Archive*, Incoming Cables File.

39. Chief of Staff's telegram to Nishry, no. 953-14, September 28, 1955, *COS Archive*, Military Appendix File.

40. Tsur, *Paris Diary*, pp. 188-189.

41. See Tsur's cable to Walter Eytan, director general of the Israel Foreign Ministry, on November 14, *SIA* 2449/2A, in which Tsur reported that the Quai had succumbed to pro-Arab pressures and would be providing arms to Egypt.

42. *France Observateur*, November 6, 1955 (French). For more on arms procurement from France, see Chapter 10.

CHAPTER 4
PREVENTIVE WAR

1. *BGA*, Meetings File, September 30, 1955.

2. Moshe Dayan, *Diary of the Sinai Campaign* (New York: Schocken, 1965), p. 12.

3. *Knesset Records*, vol. 19, p. 233.

4. *COS Diary*, November 13, 1955.

5. *BGA*, Weekly Meeting Minutes File, March 31, 1955.

6. *Knesset Records*, vol. 19, p. 676.

7. Address delivered to senior commanding officers on December 16, 1955, in *BGA*, Lectures File.

8. Reported in cable no. 454/1113, *COS Archive,* Outgoing Cables File.

9. Minutes of meeting between Ben-Gurion and "working intelligentsia" on December 12, 1955, *BGA,* Letters and Meetings File for November-December 1955.

10. See Ezer Weizman, *Yours the Sky, Yours the Earth* (Tel Aviv: Ma'ariv, 1975), pp. 112-114 (Hebrew).

11. Cited by General Dan Tolkowski at an address to senior commanders and General Staff members on November 11, 1976: "The Air Force Between the War of Independence and the Sinai Campaign" (private copy) (Hebrew).

12. Several studies have been written in an attempt to explain the Arab-Israeli conflict in terms of deterrence. See for example Avner Yaniv, *Deterrence Without the Bomb* (Lexington, MA: Lexington Books, 1987); Jonathan Shimshoni, *Israel and Conventional Deterrence* (Ithaca, NY: Cornell University Press, 1988); John J. Mearsheimer, *Conventional Deterrence* (Ithaca, NY: Cornell University Press, 1983).

13. *COS Diary,* October 11, 1955.

14. Ibid., October 13, 1955.

15. Minutes of a conference of senior commanders on November 24, 1955, *BGA,* Letters and Meetings File for November-December 1955.

16. Excerpts from Ben-Gurion's address to senior commanders are in the Hebrew version of Moshe Dayan's autobiography, *Milestones* (Jerusalem: Idanim, 1976), pp. 174-175. The full address is in *BGA,* Letters and Meetings File for August-September-October 1955.

17. No minutes were taken at this meeting and the only record is that preserved in *COS Diary.* The instructions issued by Dayan to the general staff on October 26, three days after the meeting with Ben-Gurion, for which a full record is available, probably conformed with what had been decided at that meeting.

18. International law grants certain rights and obligations to "belligerents." For the Arab view on belligerency, see Henry Cattan, *Palestine and International Law* (London: Longmans, 1976); *Colloque des Juristes Arabes sur la Palestine* (Algiers, 1967) (French); R. R. Baxter, "The Definition of War," *Revue Egyptienne de Droit International,* vol. 16, 1960.

19. Ehud Ya'ari, *Egypt and the Fedayun 1953-1956* (Givat Haviva: Givat Haviva, 1975) (Hebrew).

20. In his final report to the Security Council on July 21st, 1949, Ralph Bunche, mediator of the Armistice discussions in 1949, declared that "The Armistice Agreements provide for a definite end to the fighting in

Palestine. Each Agreement incorporates what amounts to a non-aggression pact between the parties." *SCOR,* 1949, Suppl., Doc S/1357.

21. The noted American jurist Philip Jessup recommends that such a situation be granted legal status; see Philip Jessup, "Should International Law Recognize an Intermediary Status between Peace and War?" *American Journal of International Law,* vol. 48, 1954, pp. 98-103.

22. *COS Diary,* October 23, 1955.

23. *Knesset Records,* vol. 19, pp. 231-233.

24. Moshe Dayan, *Diary of the Sinai Campaign,* p. 12.

25. Minutes of General Staff meeting, *COS Archive,* October 26, 1955.

26. *BGA,* Weekly Meeting Minutes File, March 3, 1955.

27. Ibid., March 10, 1955.

28. Mila Ohel, "The Yarkon Mission," *Ma'arachot,* Israel Defense Forces, no. 197, January 1969 (Hebrew).

29. *COS Diary,* October 28, 1955.

30. E.L.M. Burns, *Between Arab and Israeli* (London: Harrap & Co., 1962), pp. 97-98.

31. *SWB,* Part IV, no. 619, pp. 15-18.

32. *COS Diary,* November 8, 1955.

33. *BGA,* Weekly Meeting Minutes File, November 8, 1955.

34. Moshe Dayan, *Story of My Life* (New York: William Morrow and Co., 1976), p. 181. More details can be found in the Hebrew version, *Milestones* (Jerusalem: Idanim, 1976), p. 165.

35. DOS *Bulletin,* November 21, 1955, p. 845.

36. *BGA,* Weekly Meeting Minutes File.

37. *Sharett's Diary,* vol. 5, p. 1240.

38. A précis of the address can be found in *COS Diary,* December 16, 1955.

39. Ibid., November 10, 1955. See also Moshe Dayan, *Diary of the Sinai Campaign,* pp. 12-15.

40. *BGA,* Weekly Meeting Minutes File.

41. Ibid.

42. Ibid.

43. *COS Diary,* December 5, 1955.

44. *BGA,* Weekly Meeting Minutes File.

45. *COS Diary,* Doc. Vols.: summary of meeting, December 15, 1955.

CHAPTER 5
OPERATION KINNERET

1. For the agreement, see *League of Nations Treaty Series,* vol. 22, 1924. For a succinct description of the quarrel over the Jordan River and the Sea of Galilee, see Nisan Bar Yaacov, *The Israeli-Syrian Armistice: Problems of Implementation 1949-1966* (Jerusalem: Magnes Press, 1968), chap. 7; and Shabetai Rosenne, *Israel's Armistice Agreements with the Arab States* (Tel Aviv: Blumstein Publications, 1951), pp. 52-63.

2. General Burns's memoirs reveal that in 1955, the Israeli representatives submitted 22 complaints to the Armistice Commission for sniper fire directed at Israeli fishermen, but never demanded an urgent session of the commission. Burns suspected that the incident that took place the day before Operation Kinneret, in which an Israeli patrol boat was fired on, was a fabricated provocation. See E.L.M. Burns, *Between Arab and Israeli* (London: Harrap & Co.), p. 148. See also General Burns's report to the Security Council, which describes the entire background to the battle: *SCOR,* 1955, Suppl., Doc. S/351.

3. *BGA,* Weekly Meeting Minutes File, March 10, 1955.

4. Ibid., December 15, 1955.

5. Cable from Sharett no. 754/136, SIA 2446/11.

6. Cable from Abba Eban no. 566/978, December 7, 1955, *BGA,* Letters and Meetings File.

7. *Sharett's Diary,* vol. 5, p. 1307.

8. Cable from Eban no. 589/235, December 13, 1955, *BGA,* Letters and Meetings File. See also *Sharett's Diary,* vol. 5, p. 1309.

9. *Ma'ariv,* December 18, 1955.

10. *BGA,* Weekly Meeting Minutes File, December 15, 1955.

11. Yoram Peri, "The Ideological Character of the Israeli Military Elite," *State, Government and International Relations,* no. 6, Autumn 1974

(Hebrew). The article presents findings of research carried out among IDF reserve officers who held senior positions in the 1950s.

12. S. E. Finer, *The Man on Horseback* (London: Pall Mall Press, 1962), p. 141.

13. Chief of staff's meeting with journalists, December 26, 1955, *COS Diary,* Doc. Vols. Such meetings were held regularly and approved by the defense minister.

14. *Knesset Records,* vol. 19, p. 674. "I know of no army in the world more loyal to the supreme authority of the state and its democratically elected officials than the Israeli Defense Forces."

15. Sharett's cable to Ben-Gurion no. 325/281, December 13, 1955, *BGA.*

16. Dwight D. Eisenhower, *The White House Years: Waging Peace 1956-1961* (New York: Doubleday & Co., 1965), p. 25.

17. Cable from Eban no. 599/134, February 18, 1956, *SIA,* 2455/4.

18. Cable no. 611/312, December 20, 1955, and cable from Minister Ben-Dor in Paris, December 18, 1955, ibid.

19. Address to senior commanding officers, December 16, 1955, *BGA,* Letters and Meetings File for December 1955.

20. *SIA,* 1208/22.

21. Ben-Gurion's letter to Abba Eban, *BGA,* Letter and Meetings File.

22. Minutes no. A/14 of Knesset Foreign Affairs and Security Committee, December 27, 1955, in *BGA,* ibid.

23. *BGA,* Weekly Meeting Minutes File, December 15, 1955.

24. Ibid., December 7, 1955.

25. *SCOR,* 1955, Suppl., Doc. S/3514, p. 23.

26. *SWB,* Part IV, no. 632, December 23, 1955.

27. Ya'acov Tsur, *Paris Diary,* p. 206.

28. Cable from Tsur no. 0/89, *BGA,* Letters and Meetings File for December 1955.

29. Cable from Nishri to the Chief of Staff and Head of Intelligence, no. 499/NP, December 20, 1955, *BGA,* ibid.

30. *BGA,* Weekly Meeting Minutes File, December 15, 1955.

31. *BGA,* Letters and Meetings File for December 1955.

32. The following citations are from *COS Diary,* Doc. Vols.

33. *BGA,* Letters and Meetings File.

CHAPTER 6
DEFENSIVE DEPLOYMENT

1. From the chief of staff's broadcast on Army Radio, April 23, 1956, in *COS Diary,* Doc. Vols.

2. bid., minutes of senior command staff meeting, February 8, 1956.

3. *BGA,* Weekly Meeting Minutes File, February 2, 1956.

4. *Ha'aretz,* May 16, 1956.

5. Ibid., June 11, 1956.

6. In 1960 Israel Baer was convicted of espionage for the Soviet Union and sent to prison, where he died of a heart attack a few years later.

7. Israel Baer, "Real and Imaginary Solutions for our Security," in his compilation of his essays entitled *On Security* (Tel Aviv: Am Oved, 1959), p. 189 (Hebrew).

8. Israel Baer, "What to Prepare For and How," ibid., p. 287.

9. Yosef Tabenkin, "In the Fullness of Our Strength," *Me-Bifnim,* vol. 18, no. 4, April 1956 (Hebrew).

10. Reuven Cohen, "On the Alert," in ibid.

11. Shimon Avidan, "Security Problems in the State of Israel," in Zvi Ra'anan, ed., *Army and War in Israel and Elsewhere* (Merhavia: Hapoalim, 1955), p. 988 (Hebrew).

12. Binyamin Kaplan, "Only One Choice," in ibid., p. 999.

13. Efraim Reiner, "To Stand in Defend and Win in Peace," in ibid., p. 995.

14. *COS Diary,* January 29, 1956.

15. bid., Doc. Vols., chief of staff's address, January 1, 1956.

16. bid., minutes of senior command meeting, February 8, 1956.

17. Ibid., minutes of General Staff discussion, January 23, 1956.

18. *BGA,* Weekly Meeting Minutes File, February 16, 1956.

19. *COS Diary,* Doc. Vols., General Staff discussion, August 2, 1956.

20. *BGA,* Weekly Meeting Minutes File, February 22, 1956. Over half a million work days eventually were mobilized.

21. *COS Diary,* March 8, 1956.

22. *Knesset Records,* vol. 19, p. 676.

23. *COS Diary,* Doc. Vols.

24. *BGA,* Weekly Meeting Minutes File, April 5, 1956. Nitzana was one of the major Israeli assault bases in the Suez war.

25. For a detailed description see Mordechai Bar-On, *Challenge Quarrel* (Sde Boker: Ben-Gurion University, 1991), pp. 78-80 (Hebrew).

26. *BGA,* Weekly Meeting Minutes File, April 27, 1956.

27. By the time the Sinai campaign began, Israel had three times as many vehicles at its disposal than it had a year earlier.

28. Moshe Dayan, "Reprisals as a Means of Ensuring Peace," *Israel Defense Forces Monthly Review,* August 1955 (Hebrew).

29. *Sharett's Diary,* vol. 5, p. 1385.

30. See, for example Geoffrey Blainey, *The Causes of War* (New York: The Free Press, 1973), chap. 3, pp. 35-56.

31. *Sharett's Diary,* vol. 6, p. 1385.

CHAPTER 7
"THE ALPHA PLAN"

1. For a general discussion on the development of American strategy in the Middle East during the 1950s, see John C. Campbell, *Defense of the Middle East: Problems of American Policy* (New York: Praeger, 1960), chaps. 4-7, pp. 39-98. In May 1954 all American ambassadors to the Middle East convened at a meeting where the American policy was crystallized: see *FRUS,* 1952-1954, vol. 9, part 1, doc. 211, pp. 506-510.

2. It should be recalled that England was still considered a first-rate power at the time, capable of raising considerable resources. See George Kennan's 1954 appraisal in his *Realities of American Foreign Policy* (Princeton, NJ: Princeton University Press, 1954), chap. 3.

3. Considerable material on Dulles's trip can be found in *FRUS,* 1952-1954, vol. 9, part 1, doc. 1-53, pp. 1-162. An official summation and detailed report was published by the State Department on June 15, 1953: DOS *Bulletin,* vol. 28, pp. 831-834. See also "Important Points of

Trip" in *John Foster Dulles Papers* (hereinafter referred to as *JFDP*), Subject Series, Box 73, ME File.

4. *FRUS,* 1952-1954, doc. 592, pp. 1164-1170; doc. 725, pp. 1406-1409. The statement was made on April 9, 1954, in a speech in Dayton, Ohio, and again on May 1 in an address in Philadelphia before the American Council for Judaism, a blatantly anti-Zionist organization.

5. U.S. Senate Committee on Foreign Relations, *Study of U.S. Foreign Policy* (Washington, DC: Government Printing Office, 1959).

6. Foreign minister's report on his talk with McGee on October 26, 1950, in *SIA* 2408/9.

7. *FRUS,* 1952-1954, doc. 921, p. 1694. The "Alpha Plan" was shrouded in secrecy and not known in Israel at first. However, since the beginning of 1955, a change could be detected in the American attitude toward Israel and it was increasingly evident that the United States was interested in quickly concluding the Israeli-Arab conflict. See "The U.S. and the Resolution of the Israeli-Arab Conflict," *SIA* 2446/3.

8. "Notes on Arab-Israel Dispute," December 15, 1954, *PRO,* FO/371, 111095, VR1070/10.

9. The British Foreign Ministry's archive contains over 30 files crammed with material on the "Alpha Plan," arranged chronologically from the beginning of January 1955—*PRO,* FO/371, 111095-115887. The last three chapters of Shuckburgh's diaries also contain a great deal of material on the plan. See also Wilbur Crane Eveland, *Ropes of Sand: America's Failure in the Middle East* (New York: Norton, 1980), pp. 125-131 and 155-158.

10. Internal Memo by G. G. Arthur, May 17, 1954, *PRO,* FO/371, 111119.

11. *PRO,* FO/371, 115866, VR1046/34.

12. See Byroade's discussion with Nasser in April of 1955 in *PRO,* FO/371, 115867, VR1076/57.

13. See "Present Trends in Egyptian Foreign Policy," *SIA* 2409/2.

14. *PRO,* FO/371, 115869, VR1076/100.

15. Ibid., FO/371, 115867, VR1046/56.

16. See the report on the meeting between Herzog and Burgos, *SIA* 2455/5.

17. On Nasser against the Baghdad Pact see Mohamad H. Heikal, *The Lion's Tale: Suez Through Egyptian Eyes* (London: Andre Deutsch, 1957), chaps. 5, 6, pp. 52-70.

18. Ben-Gurion's cable to Sharett, December 4, 1955, *SIA* 2455/4.

19. Jean Lacouture, *Nasser and His Heirs* (Tel Aviv: Am Oved, 1972), p. 104 (Hebrew).

20. Evelyn Shuckburgh, *Descent to Suez: Diaries 1951-1956* (London: Weidenfeld & Nicolson, 1986), p. 256. See also memo of conversation between Dulles and Macmillan on May 12th, 1955, in *PRO,* FO/371, 115870.

21. See letter from the ambassador in Israel in *PRO,* FO/371, 115867, VR1046/36G.

22. In *Sharett's Diary,* vol. 4, p. 976.

23. *PRO,* FO/371, 115866, VR1076/102.

24. Shuckburgh, *Descent to Suez,* p. 266. See also *PRO,* FO371, 115869, VR1076/102.

25. Dulles to Macmillan, August 19, 1955, in *FRUS* 1955, doc. 201; and Macmillan to Dulles, undated, ibid., doc. 203, pp. 370-371.

26. The full version of Dulles's address appears in several places, e.g., Noble Frankland, *Documents in International Affairs 1955* (Oxford: Oxford University Press/RIIA, 1957), pp. 362-365. For the official version see DOS *Bulletin,* vol. 33, 1955, pp. 378-380.

27. *SWB,* Part IV, sec. 600, September 2, 1955, pp. 10-11.

28. "Reaction to August Speech," *JFDP,* Subject Series, Box 1, Alpha File.

29. *Sharett's Diary,* vol. 4, p. 1147.

30. "Information Briefing to Overseas Embassies" no. 1071, September 13, 1955, *SIA* 2466/3.

31. *Sharett's Diary,* vol. 4, p. 1159.

32. Abba Eban, *An Autobiography* (Jerusalem: Steinmatzky, 1977), p. 184.

33. Ibid., p. 190.

34. Shuckburgh memo dated October 14, 1955, *PRO,* FO/371, 115480, VR1054/5.

35. The full version of the address can be found in Frankland, *Documents in International Affairs 1955,* pp. 382-385.

36. Nasser's statement to *News Chronicle* correspondent, *SWB,* Part IV, no. 621, p. 11.

37. Report on conversation between British Ambassador Trevelyan and Nasser, November 16, 1955, *SIA* 2446/13.

38. See Nasser's interview on Cairo Radio at the end of November in which he repeated familiar Arab formulas: "The question of the refugees concerns all the Arab states and none of them can consider it separately"—Summary of Arab Broadcasts," daily survey no. 1827, November 29, 1955, *SIA* 2455/7.

39. *SWB*, Part IV, no. 623, p. 9.

40. *The Times,* November 14, 1955.

41. David Ben-Gurion, *The Sinai Campaign* (Tel Aviv: Am Oved, 1958), pp. 33-36 (Hebrew).

42. *Sharett's Diary,* vol. 5, p. 1303. See also Sharett's critique of the Guildhall speech at his meeting with the British ambassador on December 30 in *SIA* 2446/4.

43. Sharett's cable from New York to Jerusalem on November 11, 1955, *SIA,* ibid.

44. Sharett to Washington, January 17, 1956, in *SIA,* ibid. See also Eban's response: "Several blazing bonfires of public criticism have been prepared for Eden and [Selwyn] Lloyd on their arrival"—cable no. 81/78, January 11, 1956, *SIA* 2455/8.

45. Ibid., 2446/4.

46. Ibid., 2449/5.

47. Ibid., 3446/4.

48. Elath's cable to Jerusalem, November 24, 1955, *SIA* 2455/7.

49. Ibid.

50. Draft memo in Eban's cable to Jerusalem no. 1531/841, November 17, 1955, *SIA* 2455/4. Ben-Gurion's alterations appear in his cable to Washington no. 295/280, November 28, 1955, ibid.

51. A report on the conversation is in *SIA,* ibid.

52. Shiloah's letter to the foreign minister and ambassador, December 12, 1955, *SIA,* ibid.

53. Eban's cable to Jerusalem no. 611/312, December 20, 1955, *SIA,* ibid.

54. Cable from Washington to Jerusalem no. 596/424, December 12, 1955, *SIA,* ibid.

55. See Eban's cable to Jerusalem, November 21, 1955, in which he noted that the State Department was critical of Eden's Guildhall address, a speech in which Eden's "appetite for fame and desire to gratify the Arabs" had precluded his position as mediator, passing that role back to Dulles: *SIA* 2455/7. See also Eban's cable to Jerusalem, January 14, 1956: "The Guildhall address has been critically received in America both because of its public nature and because it mentions the 1947 resolution, which raised Israeli fears and Arab hopes to a degree that jeopardizes the chances of any mediation"—*SIA* 2455/8.

CHAPTER 8
THE PEACE BROKERS: ROBERT ANDERSON'S MISSION

1. Voluminous documentation on Anderson's mission was published in *FRUS,* 1955-1957, vol. 15, pp. 1-346. On the launching of the mission, see "Editorial Note" on p. 16 and doc. 14, "Memorandum of Conversation, White House, January 11, 1956," pp. 20-22.

2. The *SIA* contains a detailed review of these contacts: "Discussions and Contacts on the Possibility of a Settlement between Israel and Egypt 1949-1955," *SIA* 2454/2.

3. See, e.g., statements by Egypt's envoy to the Lausanne talks, Abdul Muneim Mustafa. See also Gideon Raphael's evaluation, "Summary and Lessons from the Contacts and Negotiations with Egypt 1949-1955," *SIA,* ibid.

4. Raphael's report to Jerusalem, June 9, 1952, *SIA* 2410/2. The talks with Azmi continued after the revolution as well—see the report on the talks held November 29, 1952, *SIA* 2593/22.

5. See *SIA* 2453/12. See also *FRUS,* 1952-1954, vol. 9.

6. See the meeting between Divon and Saddeq on May 28, 1952, two months before the revolt, in *SIA* 2532/3.

7. See Sasson's cable to Shiloah, February 24, 1953, *SIA* 2532/2.

8. See Israel's proposals to Nasser on January 29, 1953, and his evasive reply on May 13, 1953: "Egypt has no aggressive intentions against Israel but cannot think in terms of peace, considering the internal and regional situation"—*SIA* 2453/12.

9. Sasson in Rome to Eytan in Jerusalem, December 28, 1953, *SIA* 2410/2.

10. On Johnston's mission see Georgiana Stevens, "The Jordan River Valley," *International Conciliation,* no. 506, January 1956; K. B. Doherty, "Jordan Water Conflict," ibid., no. 553; Michael Brecher, *The Foreign Policy System of Israel* (Oxford: Oxford University Press, 1972), chap. 5, pp. 173-224; Don Peretz, "The Jordan River Partition," *Middle East Journal,* vol. 9, no. 4. See also Eric Johnston's report on

his first round of contacts, November 17, 1953, *FRUS,* 1952-1954, vol. 9, part 1, doc. 732, pp. 1418-1423.

11. See Haim Herzog's reports to Jerusalem dated February 4th, March 12, and April 22, 1953, *SIA,* 2477/20. Contacts continued even after Ghaleb was replaced by Colonel Abbas al-Shafi.

12. See Raphael's report, November 29, 1952, *SIA* 2593/22.

13. Staff at the American embassies in Cairo and Tel Aviv served as intermediaries for these contacts. See *FRUS,* 1952-1954, vol. 9, part 1, docs. 809, 810, 812, and 814, pp. 1530-1541.

14. The "Lavon Affair," as the episode was known in later years, has merited a great deal of study in Israel, most of it concerning the domestic political dissension that it elicited during the 1960s. For a description of the affair see Aviezer Golan, *Operation Susanna* (Jerusalem: Idanim, 1976) (Hebrew). See also Isser Harel, *And One Brother Rose Up Against the Other* (Jerusalem: Keter, 1982) (Hebrew), and *The Anatomy of Treason: "The Third Man" and the Disgrace in Egypt* (Jerusalem: Idanim, 1980) (Hebrew). Sharett makes several references to the *Bat Galim* in his diary—see vol. 3, pp. 629, 681-688, 940, 950.

15. Chapters from Auerbach's journal were published in the Hebrew daily *Yediot Aharonot* on September 16 and 25, 1974. See also the special file on Auerbach's mission in *SIA* 2453/21.

16. "Discussions and Contacts," *SIA* 2454/2. See also cable from Jerusalem to Paris, December 21, 1954, *SIA* 2453/20.

17. See Elmore Jackson, *Middle East Mission* (New York: Norton, 1983), chap. 2. See also *Sharett's Diary,* vol. 4, p. 1131.

18. *BGA,* Letters and Meetings File for November-December 1955, Letter to Ben-Gurion, December 12, 1955.

19. In the course of the talks Nasser replaced his demand for reinstatement of the 1947 borders with reinstatement of the "1948 borders," i.e., the proposals made by Count Bernadotte in September 1949.

20. Pearson gave a copy of his report on his meeting with Nasser to the Israeli Foreign Ministry; see *SIA* 2456/3.

21. Cable from ministry official Schneerson to Ambassador Elath, December 12, 1955, and Eytan's letter to Elath, December 4, 1955, *SIA* 2446/4.

22. Teddy Kollek, *For Jerusalem* (Jerusalem: Steimatzky, 1978), pp. 115-116. The main source for the Anderson talks in Jerusalem are the notes kept by Ya'acov Herzog. These notes were later published by Ben-Gurion in his article "The Secret Negotiations between Israel and Nasser," which appeared in a four-part series in the Hebrew daily

Ma'ariv, on July 2, 9, 16, and 23, 1971. A very superficial description of the Egyptian side of things can be found in Mohamed Hassenein Heikal, *Cutting the Lion's Tail,* pp. 91-94. The best summary of the different mediation efforts can be found in Saadia Touval, *The Peace Brokers* (Princeton, NJ: Princeton University Press, 1982), chap. 5.

23. For the American considerations, see Anderson's conversation with Eisenhower and Dulles in *JFDP,* Subject Series, Box 10, File Israel Relations.

24. Abba Eban's cable to Jerusalem, November 16, 1955, *SIA* 2455/4.

25. *BGA,* Letters and Meetings File for December 1955; see also *SIA* 2455/8. Details on the proposal appear in *SWB,* Part IV, no. 633, December 30, 1955. The Knesset debated the initiative—see *Knesset Records,* vol. 19, pp. 633-635.

26. Wilbur Crane Eveland, *Ropes of Sand: America's Failure in the Middle East* (New York: Norton, 1980), pp. 155-156.

27. *DDQ,* 1982, 000316, and *DDQ,* 1985, 000562, January 1, 1956. See also Isser Harel's report to Sharett on November 27, 1955, *Sharett's Diary,* vol. 5, p. 1316.

28. The Israeli part of the contacts are described here in detail; events in Cairo are described only if Anderson reported on them to the Israelis. See David Ben-Gurion, "The Secret Negotiations," *Ma'ariv,* July 2, 1971.

29. See Heikal, *Cutting the Lion's Tail,* p. 93. Heikal also describes this episode in *Nasser: The Cairo Documents* (London: New English Library, 1972), pp. 64-65, where he writes that Nasser referred to that meeting as the "Pee Pee discussion."

30. See Gideon Raphael's "Proposals for Conducting the First Stage," January 19, 1956, *SIA* 2454/2, in which he writes that "the most important thing is to test the opponent's sincerity. There is no better test than his willingness to engage in direct negotiations."

31. Ben-Gurion, "The Secret Negotiations," *Ma'ariv,* July 2, 1972.

32. Ibid.

33. Ibid., July 9, 1972.

34. Ibid.

35. See Dulles's notes on a conversation with the president and his notes on Anderson's report to senior State Department officials, *DDQ,* 1984, 001825.

36. Ben-Gurion, "The Secret Negotiations," *Ma'ariv,* July 2, 1972. See full text in *FRUS,* 1955-1957, vol. 15, Attachment to doc. 103, pp. 185-187. The last quotation is translated from the Hebrew text and does not conform verbatim with the text of the *FRUS* document; the differences, however, are merely semantic.

37. Ibid. Heikal's description of events corroborates Anderson's report: "'If I agreed to it [a face-to-face meeting with Ben-Gurion],' said Nasser, 'my people would prevent me from going. Or, if I did arrange to go, they would kill me when I got back.'" Heikal, *Cutting the Lion's Tail,* p. 94. See also Anderson's reports on his conversations in Jerusalem in *FRUS,* 1955-1957, doc. 181, pp. 333-336.

38. Ben-Gurion, "The Secret Negotiations," *Ma'ariv,* July 23, 1972.

39. Ibid.

40. *Dwight D. Eisenhower Library* (hereinafter referred to as *DDEL*), Eisenhower Personal Diaries, Ann Whitman Files, entry for March 12, 1956, *DDQ,* 1977, 252A. Quoted also in *FRUS,* 1955-1957, doc. 187, p. 342.

41. Dulles to Lodge, March 31, 1956, *JFDP,* Subject Series, Box 10. At the end of March, talk could be heard in the White House on the need to abandon Nasser and concentrate on King Saud of Saudi Arabia—see *DDQ,* 1978, 447A, March 28, 1956.

42. See Eveland, *Ropes of Sand,* pp. 168-171. In mid-March Anthony Eden told Shuckburgh that Nasser had to be got rid of, that it was a case of "him or us"—see Shuckburgh, *Descent to Suez: Diaries 1951-1956* (London: Weidenfeld & Nicolson, 1986), p. 346.

43. *PRO,* FO/371, 121707, VR1071/50.

44. Cable sent by the British Ambassador in Baghdad, *PRO,* FO/371, 121709, VR1071/47.

45. H. Justus's interview with Ya'acov Herzog in the Hebrew daily *Ma'ariv,* August 6, 1971, p. 21.

CHAPTER 9
THE STRUGGLE OVER THE ARMISTICE AGREEMENTS

1. Henry Cabot Lodge's comment regarding Hammarskjöld's mission in April of 1956 hints at the concern that gripped American policy makers: "This resolution [to send the Secretary General to the region] gives us thirty more days of peace." See Henry Cabot Lodge, *As it Was* (New York: Norton & Co., 1976), p. 84.

2. "The Foreign Ministry's line . . . was to keep interested parties in a state of tension, threatening to resume activities [on the project] at any minute"—*Sharett's Diary,* vol. 5, pp. 1355-1360.

3. E.L.M. Burns, *Between Arab and Israeli* (London: Harrap & Co., 1962), p. 105. A concise description of the development of the dispute between Israel and Egypt in 1955 can be found in Yosef Tekoa's cable to the Israeli delegation to the U.N. cable no. 540/555, September 11, 1955, *SIA* 2448/5.

4. Burns, *Between Arab and Israeli,* pp. 103-106. See also David Ben-Gurion, *The Renewed State of Israel* (Tel Aviv: Am Oved, 1969), vol. 1, p. 476 (Hebrew).

5. On the rationale behind the policy of reprisals, see Moshe Dayan, "Reprisals as a Means of Ensuring Peace," and "Military Actions in Peacetime," *Ma'arachot,* Israel Defense Forces, May 1959 (Hebrew). For a scholarly analysis, see Dan Horowitz and Shlomo Aharonson, "The Strategy of Controlled Retaliation," *State and Government,* vol. 1, no. 1, Summer 1971 (Hebrew).

6. See Brian Urquhart, *Hammarskjöld* (New York: Alfred Knopf, 1973), p. 137; Burns, *Between Arab and Israeli,* pp. 134-135; Mohamad Hassenein Heikal, *Nasser: The Cairo Documents* (London: New English Library, 1976), pp. 155-157; David Ben-Gurion, *The Renewed State of Israel* (Tel Aviv: Am Oved, 1969) (Hebrew), vol. 1, p. 496.

7. See Burns, *Between Arab and Israeli,* p. 135, for a description of the proposals made to calm the tensions in Gaza. See also Yosef Tekoa's memo, "U.N. Chief of Staff's Proposal to Alleviate Tensions," April 15, 1956, *SIA* 2448/2. General Burns informed Sharett of Nasser's proposal on June 7, 1955—see *SIA* 2446/11.

8. *Knesset Records,* vol. 20, pp. 1307-1308. The Herut Party's Menachem Begin said, ". . . I say that today—yes even today—we must . . . take a military initiative."

9. Brian Urquhart, *Hammarskjöld* (New York: Alfred A. Knopf, 1973), pp. 138-139.

10. *SCOR,* 1956, Suppl., Doc. S/3559, March 13, 1956.

11. Ibid., 717th Mtg. to 728th Mtg.

12. Ibid., 1956, Suppl., Doc. 2/3575, April 4, 1956.

13. *COS Diary,* Doc. Vols., February 8, 1956.

14. Meeting with senior editors, ibid.

15. Directive issued by the Operations Branch, April 3, 1956—see *COS Diary,* Doc. Vols.

16. *COS Diary,* April 3-4, 1956.

17. See U.N. Observers' Staff report in *SCOR,* 1956, Suppl., Doc. S/3596, Rev. 1, April 9, 1956. Egypt's version of events appears in its complaint of April 6, 1956, in *SCOR,* 1956, Suppl., Docs S/3676 and 3577.

18. See Moshe Dayan, *Milestones* (Jerusalem: Idanim, 1976), pp. 185-186.

19. Ibid., p. 186. Ben-Gurion's April 9 reply to General Burns appears in the communiqués published by the Security Council President in *SCOR,* 1956, Suppl., Doc. S/3584.

20. *COS Diary,* April 6, 1956.

21. "Report on Arab Broadcasts," IDF Intelligence Branch, *Israel Defense Forces' Archive* (hereinafter referred to as *IDF Archive*), April 10, 1956.

22. Ben-Gurion's reply in cable to Washington, no. 877/259, April 10, 1956, *SIA* 2455/5.

23. The stenogram dated April 11, 1956, is in *COS Diary,* Doc. Vols.

24. For the full text of the Egyptian-Israeli Armistice Agreement, see Meron Medzini, ed., *Israel's Foreign Relations: Selected Documents 1947-1974* (Jerusalem: Ministry of Foreign Affairs, 1976), vol. 1, p. 168.

25. *Sharett's Diary,* vol. 5, p. 1392.

26. *SIA* 2448/5.

27. *COS Diary,* April 12, 1956.

28. *Sharett's Diary,* vol. 5, p. 1392.

29. *COS Diary,* April 12, 1956.

30. Ibid.

31. *Sharett's Diary,* vol. 5, pp. 1392-1393. Ben-Gurion told Dayan that "Reprisal today means war and they both must be considered. . . . there's no guarantee that [Nasser] will go to war, but this time it's impossible to be certain, and the opposite should be assumed." Meeting *BGA,* Weekly Meeting Minutes File, April 13, 1956.

32. Dag Hammarskjöld Library, U.N. Press Releases, Note no. 1282, April 19, 1956.

33. Urquhart, *Hammarskjöld,* p. 145.

34. *SCOR,* 1956, Suppl., Doc. S/3594, May 2.

35. See secretary general's communiqué to Ben-Gurion, April 13, 1956, *SIA* 2448/3.

36. *SCOR,* 1949, 433rd Mtg., August 4, 1949, p. 11.

37. The address was published in *Ot,* vol. 1, no. 1, September 1960, under the title "Israel and the Arabs: War and Peace" (Hebrew).

38. The termination of the Israeli War of Independence and of the Korean War changed the concept of "armistice" in international law from that of truce within a state of war to that of a measure by which war could be terminated. See Nathan Feinberg, *The Legality of a "State of War" After the Cessation of Hostilities Under the Charter of the U.N. and the Covenant of the League of Nations* (Jerusalem: Magnes Press, 1961); L. M. Bloomfield, *Egypt, Israel and the Gulf of Aqaba in International Law* (Toronto, Carswell, 1957); Julius Stone, *Legal Controls of International Conflict* (New York: Garland, 1973); and Paul Mohn, "Problems of Close Supervision," *International Conciliation,* no. 478 (February 1952):49-99.

39. In 1907 the Hague Convention on the Law of War ratified the classic interpretation of armistice. Even Lauterpacht, the most prominent authority on international law, defines the concept according to its traditional interpretation: see F. L. Oppenheim, *International Law* (London: Longman, Green & Co., 1952), pp. 546-547. For the Arabs' contentions, see Henry Cattan, *Palestine and International Law* (London: Longmans, 1976).

40. Sasson's letter to Sharett, September 27, 1949, *SIA* 2403/12.

41. See Dayan's address to senior commanders on January 15, 1956, *COS Diary,* Doc. Vols.

42. *Knesset Records,* vol. 20, p. 1686.

43. See the secretary general's interim report in *SCOR,* 1956, Suppl., Doc. S/3594, May 2.

44. *BGA,* Weekly Meeting Minutes File, April 27, 1956.

45. For the full text, see Dayan, *Milestones,* p. 191.

46. "Intelligence Extracts," IDF Intelligence Branch, *IDF Archive,* May 15, 1956.

47. The British and the Americans had planned possible military intervention down to the smallest detail. See *PRO,* FO/371, 121759, VR1076/13, "Record of Tripartite Discussions in Washington"; and 121733, VR1073/45, "Anglo-American Joint Planning." The British plans included aerial bombing of Israeli airfields, marine shelling of the coast, and even the occupation of Eilat. See Foreign Office Brief of January 7, 1956, in *PRO,* FO/371, VR1073/46, and VR1073/63.

48. *Knesset Records,* vol. 20, p. 1686.

49. Urquhart, *Hammarskjöld*, p. 150.

50. Heikal, *Nasser*, p. 153.

51. *BGA*, Sinai Campaign File, Ben-Gurion's letter to Eban, October 9, 1956.

52. *COS Diary*, May 2, 1956.

53. *PRO*, FO/371, 121740, VR1073/160.

54. The memoirs of two senior U.N. observers are strikingly anti-Israeli in tone. See General Carl Von Horn, *Soldiering for Peace* (London: Cassel, 1966); and Commander Elmo H. Hutchison, *Violent Truce: A Military Observer Looks at the Arab-Israeli Conflict 1951-1955* (New York: Devin Ader, 1958). General Burns's book is much more balanced, but he too occasionally lapses into outright anger at the Israelis.

55. Carl Von Horn, *Soldiering for Peace*, p. 283.

56. Heikal, *Nasser*, p. 158.

57. A copy of the letter can be found in *SIA* 2436//5.

58. General van Bennike, "Report to the Secretary General," in *SCOR*, 1953, Suppl., Doc. S/3122, October 27.

59. Commander Hutchison relates that the Israelis refused to permit an Arab peasant from Kalkilya to use the water from his own well, which, after the Armistice Agreement with Jordan, was three meters inside Israeli territory. See Hutchison, *Violent Truce*, p. 121.

60. Nisan Bar-Ya'acov, *The Israeli-Syrian Armistice: Problems of Implementation 1949-1966* (Jerusalem: Magnes Press, 1968), p. 67; Hutchison, *Violent Truce*, p. 107.

61. David Ben-Gurion, *Diary*, MS in Ben-Gurion Research Center, Sde Boker, September 3, 1956 (Hebrew) (hereinafter referred to as *Ben-Gurion's Diary*).

62. Kidron's cable to Eytan and Eban in Jerusalem, no. 361/774, June 20, 1956, *SIA* 2448/5.

63. Von Horn, *Soldiering for Peace*, p. 76. The fact that the U.N. headquarters was located in the residence of the former British high commissioner may have contributed to this feeling.

64. Pablo de Azcarate, *Mission in Palestine 1948-1952* (Washington, DC: The Middle East Institute, 1966), pp. 100-109.

65. The first Soviet veto benefitting the Arabs was cast on January 22, 1954, on a proposal to divert the waters of the Jordan River. See *SCOR*, 1954, Ninth Year, 656th Mtg., January 22.

66. Ibid., 1949, Fourth Year, 16th Session, p. 2.

67. *Sharett's Diary*, vol. 3, p. 815.

68. Ibid., vol. 2, p. 423.

69. Ibid., 1956, Suppl., Doc. S/3596, May 9.

70. See Pierson Dixon's May 25 report to Selwyn Lloyd in *PRO*, FO/371, 121741, VR1074/302; 121739, VR10076/219; 121739 and VR1074/225.

71. *SCOR*, 1956, Suppl., Doc. S/3600.

72. Ibid., Doc. S/3605, June 4.

73. Ibid., Doc. S/3594, May 9.

74. Trevelyan to Foreign Office, July 5, 1956, in *PRO*, FO/371, 121710, VR1071/173.

75. Foreign Office to Washington, July 8, 1956, in ibid., VR1071/75.

76. Washington to Foreign Office, July 10, 1956, in ibid., VR1071/76.

77. By the end of June Hammarskjöld was beginning to feel that he had lost Ben-Gurion's trust. The secretary general emotionally expressed his admiration for Ben-Gurion in a conversation with Kidron and practically pleaded for an invitation to visit the region. Kidron did not recommend it; punning on Hammarskjöld's first name—"dag" means "fish" in Hebrew—Kidron wrote the Foreign Ministry that "The fish is dead so why try to revive it?" But Ben-Gurion sent Hammarskjöld a formal invitation and proposed that the fundamental problems be discussed rather than minor details. Their correspondence makes it clear that the secretary general had planned to consider "peace-brokering" this time, and not just the cease-fire. See *SIA* 2448/5.

78. Before leaving for the Middle East, Hammarskjöld informed the British foreign secretary that the Soviet foreign minister, Dimitri Shepilov, had agreed to support his efforts. See *PRO*, FO/371, 121710, VR1071/93, July 17, 1956.

79. Letter dated July 21, 1956, in *SIA* 2448/5 (English).

80. Cited in Walter Eytan's minutes, *SIA*, ibid. (Hebrew).

81. Hammarskjöld's letter to Lloyd in *PRO*, FO/371, 121710, VR1071/91.

82. Burns, *Between Arab and Israeli,* p. 143.

83. Copy of Hammarskjöld's letter dated July 24, 1956, and Ben-Gurion's reply—see Eytan's cable to the U.N. delegation no. 466/434, July 29, 1956, *SIA* 2448/5.

CHAPTER 10
THE FAILURE OF ARMS PROCUREMENT IN THE UNITED STATES

1. Moshe Dayan, *Milestones* (Jerusalem: Idanim, 1976), p. 165.

2. At a meeting convened on December 1, 1955, to examine arms procurement needs—*BGA,* Weekly Meeting Minutes File.

3. Abel Thomas, *Comment Israel fut sauve* (Paris: Albin Michel, 1978), pp. 26-28 (French).

4. Israel's foreign minister told the Knesset on January 1, 1956, that "Our main demand is addressed to the American Administration." *Knesset Records,* vol. 20, p. 679.

5. The Israelis expended a great deal of energy during the winter of 1956 trying to buy six British Centurion tanks for training; the tanks arrived after the Sinai campaign. See Selwyn Lloyd's October 10, 1955, report to the British Cabinet's Near East Committee in *PRO/Cabinet* (CAB), 130/11, Gen 507.

6. Israel ordered six Meteor aircraft from Britain in 1955 for "training purposes" and another six for night fighting. After repeated delays, these were delivered in the summer of 1956.

7. The figures have been taken from material prepared for the chief of staff's lecture to the Knesset Committee on Foreign Affairs and Security on May 21, 1956: *COS Diary,* Doc. Vols.

8. Eban's cable to Jerusalem no. 749 dated October 31, 1955, in *SIA* 2449/5. (See Chapter 3.)

9. The full text is in DOS *Bulletin,* vol. 33, p. 845.

10. *Knesset Records,* vol. 20, p. 679.

11. Minutes of a discussion on arms procurement held on December 1, 1955, in *BGA,* Weekly Meeting Minutes File.

12. Dwight D. Eisenhower, *The White House Years: Waging Peace, 1956-1961* (New York: Doubleday & Co., 1965), p. 25.

13. "Outstanding Valid Licenses Issued Since August 1955," *JFDP,* Subject Series, Box 10, Israel Relations 1951-1957, File 4.

14. Evelyn Shuckburgh, *Descent to Suez: Diaries 1951-1956* (London: Weidenfeld & Nicolson, 1986), pp. 328-329.

15. A copy of the Israeli Embassy's official note is in *SIA* 2356/3 (English).

16. Colonel Katriel Shalmon's letter to the chief of staff, November 23, 1955, *SIA* 2456/3.

17. Memo dated December 6, 1955, *SIA* 2456/3 (English). Also in *FRUS* 1955-1957, vol. 19, doc. 436, pp. 823-825.

18. Report on "Foreign Minister's Meeting with the Secretary of State on December 8th, 1955," *SIA* 2456/3.

19. Cable no. 589/235, December 13, 1955, *SIA* 2455/8. Abba Eban believed that "there was a great chance, almost a certainty, [to receive arms from the U.S.] which Operation Kinneret had sabotaged." Eban's cable to Jerusalem, December 18, 1955, ibid.

20. See Eban's report on his January 5, 1956, discussion with Allen in his cable from Washington no. 670/80 in *SIA*, ibid., and Ben-Dor's report on his December 17, 1955, conversation with Russell, *SIA* 2455/4.

21. The full text of the letter is in *SIA* 2455/8 (English).

22. See cable from Jerusalem to Washington no. 521/423, January 24, 1956, and further details in cable no. 522/384, January 25, 1956, both in *SIA*, ibid.

23. Eban's cable to Sharett no. 756/407, January 25, 1956, *SIA*, ibid.

24. Sharett's briefing in his cable to Eban no. 542/705 dated January 29, 1956, in *SIA*, ibid. The full text of the memo appears in *SIA* 2455/5 (English).

25. The full text appears in "Information for Overseas Embassies" no. 1108, February 8, 1956, *SIA*, ibid.

26. *DDEL*, Eisenhower Personal Diaries, Ann Whitman files, Box 9, Entry for February 8, 1956, *DDQ*, 1986, 1670.

27. Sir Evelyn Shuckburgh writes in his diary that the president and Sir Anthony Eden gave orders to plan maneuvers of the Royal Air Force and the U.S. fleet in the Mediterranean in order to deter Israel from aggression. See *Descent to Suez*, p. 829.

28. Eban's cable to Sharett no. 855/686, *SIA* 2455/5.

29. Klutznick's letter is dated February 7, 1956—*JFDP*, Sel. Corr., Box 104, Klutznick file.

30. Blaustein's letter is dated February 29, 1956—ibid., Box 100, Blaustein File. Veteran Zionist leader Abba Hillel took advantage of his contacts in the Republican Party and met with President Eisenhower on April 26, 1956—see Memo. of Conversation, *DDEL,* WH Memo. Series, Box 3, File 3 (1956).

31. *Ha'aretz,* January 26, 1956. Similar reports appeared on January 31, 1956.

32. DOS Press Release No. 65, *JFDP,* Sel. Corr., Box 106, ME File.

33. DOS Press Release No. 96, February 24, 1956, *JFDP,* ibid., Box 51, Arab States File.

34. *American Foreign Policy Current Documents,* 1956, Doc. 182, pp. 589-590.

35. Meeting described in Eban's "Most Confidential" cable to Sharett no. 964/394, *SIA* 2455/5.

36. The conversation was reported in the Israeli Foreign Ministry American desk's cable to Washington, January 10, 1956, *SIA* 2455/8.

37. Note to Secretary, January 3, 1956, *DDQ,* 1984, 000380.

38. Letter from Dulles to Byroade, February 28, 1956, ibid., 000379.

39. Memo. for the Secretary, March 1, 1956, ibid., 002553.

40. Memo. from the Secretary of State to the President, March 28, 1956, *FRUS* 1955-1957, vol. 15, doc. 222, pp. 419-421.

41. In a letter to Henry Cabot Lodge Dulles called it "a very comprehensive plan"—*DDQ* 1982, 002505.

42. Letter Dulles to Arthur Dean, March 27, 1956, *JFDP,* Subject Series, Box 10, Israel Relations File. Also in *DDQ,* 1986, 000765.

43. Memo of Conversation, March 30, 1956, *JFDP,* ibid., Israel Relations File 2. Also in *DDQ,* 1982, 002564.

44. Telegram from Washington no. 70/1123, March 29, 1956, *SIA* 2455/5. See also Dulles's Notes from Talk with Eban, *JFDP,* ibid., File 3.

45. Israeli Foreign Ministry's American desk cable to Washington no. 846/1251, April 4, 1956, *SIA* 2455/5.

46. *Sharett's Diary,* vol. 5, p. 1380.

47. Sharett's telegram to Eban no. 833 dated March 30, 1956, *COS Archive,* Foreign Ministry Cable File.

48. *COS Diary,* April 3, 1956. See also *Sharett's Diary,* vol. 5, pp. 1385-1386.

49. Eban's cable to Sharett, March 29, 1956, ibid. See also Dulles's reply to journalists' questions in News Conference of April 17, DOS Press Release no. 198, *JFDP,* Sel. Corr., Box 106, ME File, p. 5.

50. Eisenhower suggested releasing a radar system and even some Nike antiaircraft missiles, but no such action was implemented at the time. See Memo. of Conversation, March 28, 1956, *DDEL,* WH Memo. Series, Box 4, File 4.

51. Memo. of Conversation with the President, April 6, 1956, *FRUS,* doc. 249, pp. 481-482.

52. See Memo. of Conversation with the President, ibid. See also Memo. for MacArthur from Haines, ibid., Box 3, File 3; Memo. for the President, September 28, 1956, ibid., File 3; and Dwight D. Eisenhower, *Waging Peace,* p. 29.

53. Eban's telegram to Jerusalem, May 12, 1956, *SIA* 2455/5.

54. Cable from Washington to Jerusalem no. 624/314 dated August 28, 1956, ibid.

55. See a very detailed and more balanced analysis of the development of Israeli-American relations since the Republicans took office and up to the nationalization of the Suez Canal by Reuven Shiloah, *SIA,* ibid.

CHAPTER 11
SUCCESS IN FRANCE

1. Ya'acov Tsur, *Paris Diary,* p. 195.

2. In his memoirs Christian Pineau writes that, unlike the military, the Quai d'Orsay had no "Israeli lobby" but only an "Arab lobby"—Christian Pineau, *1956: Suez* (Paris: Robert Laffont, 1976), p. 65 (French).

3. Tsur's cable no. 731, November 11, 1955, *SIA* 2455/7.

4. Peres's lecture to chief Defense Ministry staffers on November 11, 1955, in *Peres Archive,* Lectures and Reports File.

5. Ibid.

6. Ibid. See also Shimshon Arad's cable to Washington no. 1507, November 16, 1955, *SIA* 2455/7, indicating that the American military attaché in Rome had been explicitly instructed to inform the Italian Foreign Ministry that negotiations on Israeli arms procurement would take place only in Washington.

7. *Peres Archive,* Agreements File.

8. Tsur, *Paris Diary*, p. 201; see also his cable to Jerusalem no. 680, November 19, 1955, *COS Archive*, Cables File, and cited in cable no. 222/325, November 21, 1955, *SIA* 2455/7.

9. See Tsur's comment: "American pressure and the desire to maintain great-power solidarity seem to be prime factors in the transaction's delay"—*Paris Diary*, p. 202.

10. Ibid., p. 213.

11. *Journal Officiel de la République Française*, Assemblée Nationale, Debats, November 28, 1955 (French).

12. Tsur, *Paris Diary*, pp. 203-204.

13. *BGA*, Weekly Meeting Minutes File, December 1, 1955.

14. Peres's lecture to chief Defense Ministry staffers, December 12, 1955, in *Peres Archive*, Lectures and Reports File.

15. A senior French Foreign Ministry official told Tsur that Pinay made a specific commitment from which he could not deviate—*Paris Diary*, pp. 208-209. See also Shuckburgh's diary entry to the effect that Macmillan and Dulles had forced Pinay into promising not to send the dozen jets to Israel: Evelyn Shuckburgh, *Descent to Suez*, p. 313.

16. Tsur, *Paris Diary*, p. 206.

17. Peres's lecture to senior Defense Ministry staffers, December 28, 1955, in *Peres Archive*, Lectures and Reports File; see also cables from Paris no. 650, December 24, 1955; no. 41, January 3, 1956; and no. 240, January 10, 1956, in *Peres Archive*, Incoming Cables File.

18. Cable from Paris no. P/25, December 13, 1955, ibid.

19. Cable from Paris no. SP/106, December 15, 1955, ibid. (Hebrew).

20. Peres's cable to Defense Minister no. 0/133, December 12, 1955, *SIA* 2455/8.

21. Minutes of General Staff meeting, January 5, 1956, *COS Diary*, Doc. Vols.

22. Peres's lecture to senior Defense Ministry staffers, March 3, 1956, *Peres Archive*, Lectures and Reports File.

23. Tsur, *Paris Diary*, pp. 223-224. And indeed, shortly thereafter the French Foreign Ministry sent Egypt 40 MX-13 tanks that had been contracted for under an "old agreement."

24. *Ha'aretz*, February 10, 1956.

25. Cable from Paris no. SP/448, March 6, 1956, *COS Archive,* Foreign Office Cables File.

26. Tsur, *Paris Diary,* pp. 230-231.

27. Tsur's cable to Jerusalem no. 0/112, January 31, 1956, *SIA* 2455/8.

28. Tsur, *Paris Diary,* p. 226.

29. *Ha'aretz,* March 1, 1956. See also cable from Paris no. SP/420, March 1, 1956, *Peres Archive,* Incoming Cables File.

30. Mordechai Bar-On, *Challenge and Quarrel* (Sde Boker: Ben-Gurion Research Center, 1991), p. 127 (Hebrew). See also Shimon Peres, *David's Sling: The Secrets of Israel's Strength* (Jerusalem: Weidenfeld & Nicolson, 1970), p. 47.

31. *Journal Officiel de la République Française,* March 9, 1956.

32. *Le Monde,* March 25, 1956 (French); Christian Pineau, *1956: Suez* (Paris: Robert Laffont, 1976), p. 38.

33. Peres, *David's Sling,* p. 42.

34. Abel Thomas, *Comment Israel fut sauve* (Paris: Albin Michel, 1978), p. 19.

35. *Peres Archive,* April 1956 Trip File.

36. See Ben-Gurion's April 4 letter to Sharett: "Shimon [Peres] can also meet with Pineau or another Foreign Minister. . . . I find all these departmental considerations very strange." Michael Bar-Zohar, *Ben-Gurion* (Tel Aviv: Am Oved, 1971), vol. 3, p. 1180 (Hebrew).

37. The texts are cited in David Ben-Gurion, *The Renewed State of Israel* (Tel Aviv: Am Oved, 1969), vol. 1, p. 497 (Hebrew).

38. Cable from Paris no. 20, April 1, 1956, *Peres Archive,* Incoming Cables File.

39. *COS Diary,* April 23, 1956.

40. Sylvia Crosbie interviews Paul Grossin, a leading French security figure, who affirms that Israeli intelligence had provided French security services with information on Egyptian involvement as early as the summer of 1955; see Sylvia Crosbie, *A Tacit Alliance: France and Israel from Suez to the Six Days War* (Princeton, NJ: Princeton University Press, 1974), p. 58.

41. *COS Diary,* June 1, 1956.

42. *COS Diary,* June 6, 1956.

43. Ibid.

44. Details of the Vermars conference are taken from the report prepared by Harkaby for the defense minister, *COS Diary,* June 22, 1956. Many details can also be found in Moshe Dayan, *Milestones* (Jerusalem: Idanim, 1976), chap. 14 (Hebrew).

45. A week later the French consented to speed up the rate of delivery, and when fighting broke out in the Sinai, Israel already had 60 Mystère jets on its soil.

46. Dayan, *Milestones,* p. 207.

47. *BGA,* Weekly Meeting Minutes File, June 27, 1956.

48. Tsur, *Paris Diary,* pp. 270-272.

49. *Ha'aretz,* July 1, 1956.

50. Ibid., July 3, 1956.

51. Ibid., July 5, 1956.

52. Bar-On, *Challenge and Quarrel,* p. 160.

53. Cable from Paris no. G/144, July 18, 1956, *Peres Archive,* Incoming Cables File.

54. Synopsis of Tevet's description as adapted by Bar-on in *Challenge and Quarrel,* pp. 161-163.

55. The poem, "A True Dream," became famous when Ben-Gurion unexpectedly read it into the record during a Knesset session on October 15.

56. See William B. Quandt, "Influence Through Arms Supply: The U.S. Experience in the Middle East," in Uri Ra'anan, Robert Pfaltzgraff, and Geoffrey Kemp, eds., *Arms Transfer to the Third World: The Military Building in Less Industrial Countries* (Boulder, CO: Westview Press, 1978).

CHAPTER 12
WAITING IN THE WINGS: AUGUST–SEPTEMBER 1956

1. This chapter treats Israel's reactions to the Suez crisis during its first stages. The crisis itself lies beyond the scope of this study, and thus only the main stages are outlined here. Hundreds of books and articles have been written on Suez; an extensive bibliography can be found in Roger Louis and Roger Owen, eds., *Suez 1956: The Crisis and Its Consequences* (Oxford: Oxford University Press, 1989). Keith Kyle's *Suez* (New York: St Martin's Press, 1991) makes use of the most recently available archival material.

2. English text in *SWB,* part 4, July 28, 1956.

3. "France and the Middle East: Note by the Secretary of State for Foreign Affairs," *PRO,* PREM/11, 1099, Egypt Committee, August 7, 1956.

4. Ben-Gurion told Dayan that Israel's present concern had to be getting the armaments as quickly as possible and training personnel. "When the equipment is here, we'll see what can be done. For now, let's rest easy, so long as there is no serious provocation from Egypt." *BGA,* July 29, 1956.

5. See "Suez Canal: Egyptian Motives," *PRO,* PREM/11, 1100. On the surprise the announcement elicited in Paris, see Christian Pineau, *1956: Suez* (Paris: Robert Laffont, 1976), p. 71 (French). Dulles admitted that he had not expected nationalization when he made his decision to withdraw American support for the "High Dam" plan—see DOS Press Release no. 184 of August 2, 1957, *JFDP,* Sel. Corr., Box 100, Aswan Dam File.

6. The nations of Western Europe imported 2 million barrels of Mideast oil a day, over two-thirds of which passed through the Suez Canal— *Joint Chiefs of Staff,* Note no. 2105/38, *DDQ,* 1978, 370A. Britain's dependence was the highest, with about 80 percent of all its energy resources coming from the Middle East and some 4,500 British ships plying the canal each year.

7. Anthony Eden, *Full Circle: The Memoirs of Anthony Eden* (London: Cassel, 1967), p. 424. See also Dulles's assessment in his address before the National Security Council on August 30, 1956: Memorandum of discussion at the 295th Meeting of the NSC, *FRUS 1955-1957,* vol. 16, doc. 149, pp. 324-332.

8. "Memo. on Relations between the U.K., the U.S. and France in the Month Following the Nationalization of the Suez Canal Company in 1956," *PRO,* FO/800, 728, October 31, 1957.

9. Hugh Thomas, *Suez* (New York: Harper Colophon, 1966), p. 31.

10. An interesting analysis of the "Munich syndrome" can be found in Lord Beloff, "The Crisis and its Consequences for the British Conservative Party," in Louis and Owen, eds., *Suez 1956: The Crisis and its Consequences,* pp. 319-334.

11. Winston S. Churchill, *The Second World War* (London: Cassell & Co., 1948), vol. 1, p. 231.

12. Shortly before nationalization, a senior State Department official told Ya'acov Herzog that the United States was suffering from its identification with the European colonial powers—see minutes of meeting, June 8, 1956, *SIA* 2455/5. Selwyn Lloyd describes the U.S. attitude in his memoirs as well—see *Suez 1956: A Personal Account* (London: Jonathan Cape, 1978), p. 59.

13. Dwight D. Eisenhower, *The White House Years: Mandate for Change 1953-1956* (New York: Doubleday & Co., 1965), p. 250.

14. The most prominent of such scholars is Herman Feiner—see *Dulles Over Suez* (London: Heineman, 1964).

15. Cable Foster to Department of State, July 27, 1956, *FRUS* 1955-1957, vol. 16, doc. 2, pp. 3-5. An amusing description of that evening's meeting, to which the unsuspecting ministers had been hastily summoned, can be found in the Earl of Kilmuir, *Political Adventure* (London: Weidenfeld & Nicolson, 1964), p. 268.

16. Cable Prime Minister to President, No. 3358, *PRO,* FO/800, 726. Also in *FRUS* 1955-1957, vol. 16, doc. 5, pp. 9-11.

17. Robert Murphy, *Diplomat Among Warriors* (New York: Doubleday & Co, 1964), pp. 379-381. The meeting is also noted in Harold Macmillan, *Riding the Storm* (London: Macmillan, 1971), p. 105. For Murphy's report from London, see *FRUS* 1955-1957, vol. 16, docs. 22, 24, 25, 33, pp. 37-62.

18. Note by the Secretary to the Joint Chiefs of Staff, July 31, 1956, *Joint Chiefs of Staff,* 2105/38, *DDQ,* 1978, 379A.

19. Conversation with the President, July 30, 1956, *DDEL,* WH Memos., Box 4, File 6.

20. Letter from President Eisenhower to Prime Minister Eden, July 31, 1956, *JFDP,* Subject Series, Box 11, U.K. File; also in *FRUS* 1955-1957, vol. 16, doc. 35, pp. 69-71. See also Message from President Eisenhower to Prime Minister Mollet, ibid., doc. 39, pp. 77-78. See also the text of the president's letter to Eden dated September 6, 1956, in Eden, *Full Circle,* pp. 466-467. When Dulles returned to Washington from his consultations in London on August 3, he affirmed that the U.S. "did not want to meet violence with violence"—see Press Release no. 425, *JFDP,* Sel. Corr., Box 110, Suez Canal File.

21. Egypt Committee, 15th Mtg., Confidential Annex, *PRO,* CAB/134 (also in *PRO,* PREM/11, 1104). See also General Maurice Challe, *Notre Revolt* (Paris: Presses de la Cite, 1968), p. 25 (French).

22. See the official summaries, published after the campaign, in General Charles Keightley, "Operation in Egypt: November to December 1956," *Supplement to London Gazette,* September 10, 1957. See also the description of the commander of the land forces, in General Hugh Stockwell, "Suez from the Inside," *Sunday Telegraph,* October 30, November 6, and November 13, 1956. For a very detailed treatment of the French preparations, see Paul Gaujac, *Suez 1956* (Paris: Charles-Lavauzelle, 1986) (French).

23. The minutes of the first London conference, as well as the full text of the 18 nations' resolution concluding that conference, can be found in

DOS, *The Suez Canal Problem, July 26-September 22, 1956* (Washington, DC: Government Printing Office, 1957).

24. It was Dulles who first suggested that an international "Suez Canal Board" be set up; after minor changes, this proposal became the resolution adopted at the conclusion of the conference—see *JFDP,* Sel. Corr., Box 110, Suez Canal Conference File.

25. Israel had to settle for observer status at the conference. See Ya'acov Tsur, *Paris Diary,* p. 280, and the report on Eliahu Elath's discussion with Harold Caccia on July 31, 1956 in *PRO,* FO/371, 121706, VR1052/25.

26. Pineau, *1956: Suez,* p. 96.

27. This was also the Americans' hope; in his statement to the first Tripartite meeting convened in London on July 29, Robert Murphy said that the Americans believed that the Arab-Israeli problem had to be kept distinct from the present issue. See Cable Foster to State Department, July 29, 1956, *FRUS* 1955-1957, vol. 16, doc. 21, pp. 35-36. See also Watson Adams's minutes in *PRO,* FO/371, 121696, VR1022/10, and remarks of the British Foreign Office director general to the Israeli ambassador in early October: "We did not wish to see the problem of Israel injected into the Suez Canal problem"—Memo. on Meeting with Elath, October 8, 1956, *PRO,* FO/371, 121706, VR1052/31.

28. *PRO,* FO/371, 121706, VR1052/23.

29. Cabinet Egypt Committee, "France and the Middle East," August 7, 1956, *PRO,* CAB/134, 1216, also in *PRO,* FO/371, PREM/11, 1099, p. 271.

30. Pineau, *1956: Suez,* p. 82.

31. The British-French talks included a statement that "a lift of the blockade on Israeli ships passing through the canal should be shown to proceed from general principles and not appear as a mark of favor to Israel": "The Suez Canal Crisis: Anglo-French Discussion," *PRO,* PREM/11, 1099.

32. *COS Diary,* July 29, 1956.

33. *Ben-Gurion's Diary,* August 3, 1956.

34. *COS Diary,* August 5, 1956.

35. Egypt Committee, 24th Mtg., Confidential Annex, September 9, 1956, *PRO,* CAB/134, 1216.

36. *COS Diary,* August 2, 1956.

37. *Ben-Gurion's Diary,* August 2, 1956. See also Moshe Dayan, *Milestones* (Jerusalem: Idanim, 1976), p. 220 (Hebrew).

38. Dwight D. Eisenhower, *The White House Years: Waging Peace 1956-1961* (New York: Doubleday & Co., 1965), p. 677.

39. See Haim Laskov and Meir Zorea in *Ma'ariv,* October 10, 1956.

40. *Ben-Gurion's Diary,* September 1, 1956.

41. *COS Diary,* September 14, 1956.

42. On the Cairo discussions see Robert Menzies, *Afternoon Light* (London: Cassell, 1967), pp. 162-169. See also a personal report sent to Eden in Eden, *Full Circle,* pp. 470-473.

43. Menzies's memo can be found in Cairo cable to FO no. 2000, September 9, 1956, *PRO,* PREM/11, 1100. Nasser's response is in cable no. 2010, ibid.

44. Cairo cable to FO no. 1936, September 6, 1956, *PRO,* PREM/11, 1100.

45. See précis of Henderson's report in Summary of Development in Suez Situation, September 4, 5, 6, 7, 10, 1956, *DDQ,* 1986, 001477. Some details can be gleaned from Loy Henderson's testimony in *Dulles Oral History Collection.*

46. Cabinet Mtg., September 6, 1956, Confidential Annex, *PRO,* CAB/128.

47. The British debated at length on whether and when to approach the U.N.; see, for example, Lord Salisbury's letter to Eden and Eden's memo of August 26, 1956, *PRO,* PREM/11, 1100.

48. Egypt Committee, 19th Mtg., Confidential Annex, *PRO,* PREM/11, 1216.

49. *Journal Officiel de la République Française,* September 7, 1956.

50. See Egypt Committee, 25th Mtg., *PRO,* CAB/134, 1216.

51. The new plan was presented to the Cabinet by the chiefs of staff on September 12: *COS* 56(350), "Alternative to Musketeer," *PRO,* PREM/11, 1104.

52. Cable from Paris no. G/246, August 31, 1956, in Peres Archive, Cables File.

53. *COS Diary,* September 4, 1956.

54. *COS Archive,* Special "French Connection" File, Report no. 27, September 7, 1956.

55. Moshe Dayan, *Diary of the Sinai Campaign* (Tel Aviv: Am Hasefer, 1965), p. 25 (Hebrew).

56. *COS Diary,* September 17, 1956.

57. On September 4 a daily report was instituted in the State Department— "Summary of Developments in the Suez Situation." Almost all the material is available in *DDQ,* 1987, 000859. On September 4 the daily report referred to "disturbingly grave reports of intransigent British and French attitudes." See also Dulles's detailed assessment in the National Security Council meeting of September 31, 1956 in *DDQ,* 1987, 000859.

58. Memo. of Conference with the President, September 6, 1956, *FRUS* 1955-1957, vol. 16, doc. 303, pp. 650-652.

59. See first draft of Dulles's proposal for an association of users dated November 9, 1956, in *DDQ,* 1986, 001931, and ibid., 1987, 000265.

60. Memo. of Conversation with the President, September 8, 1956, *DDEL,* WH memos, Box 4, File 6. Also in *FRUS* 1955-1957, vol. 16, doc. 191, pp. 434-435.

61. See Makins's cable to FO, no. 1831, September 7, 1956; no. 1804, September 6, 1956,; and no. 1832, September 7, 1956, in *PRO,* PREM/11, 1100. The formal proposal was presented to the British ambassador on September 7: Makins's cable to FO, no. 1838, September 8, 1956, ibid.

62. DOS Press Release no. 486, *JFDP,* Sel. Corr., Box 110, London Conference.

63. FO cable to Washington no. 4067, September 1956, *PRO,* PREM/11, 1100.

64. *Hansard* (Commons), vol. 558, no. 207, cols. 299-309.

65. DOS Press Release no. 508, *JFDP,* Sel. Corr. Box 110, Suez Canal 2nd Conference File. See also internal memo "Points to be Raised with Harold Macmillan, *JFDP,* Alph. Subseries, Box 7, Suez Problem File.

66. Eden, *Full Circle,* p. 483.

67. FO Cable to Makins no. 4102, September 8, 1956, *PRO,* PREM/11, 1100.

68. Gledwyn Jebb's cable to FO no. 295, September 9, 1956, ibid.

69. Pineau, *1956: Suez,* p. 109. See also Ambassador Dillon's report from Peres, September 21, 1956, in which he relates that the French accuse the United States of not supporting the allies: Memo. from Dillon to Secretary of State, *FRUS* 1955-1957, vol. 16, doc. 248, pp. 551-552.

70. Egypt Committee, Memo. by Foreign Secretary, August 18, 1956, *PRO,* PREM/11, 1099.

71. Eden, *Full Circle,* p. 484.

72. *COS Diary,* September 29, 1956. See also Shimon Peres's report labeled "The Sidon Affair" in ibid., Doc. Vols.

73. Cable from Paris, September 20, 1956, in *Peres Archive,* Cables File.

74. *COS Diary,* September 25, 1956.

75. *Ben-Gurion's Diary,* September 25, 1956.

76. Ibid.

77. Ibid., September 27, 1956.

78. The full document from which these extracts have been taken is in *COS Diary,* September 28, 1956.

79. For a full account of the mission, see Mordechai Bar-on, "With Golda Meir and Moshe Dayan in the 'St Germain Mission,'" *Ma'ariv,* June 5-8, 1973. This publication was drawn from *COS Diary,* September 29-October 1, 1956. A short description can also be found in Golda Meir, *My Life* (Tel Aviv: Ma'ariv, 1975), p. 216 (Hebrew). See also Dayan, *Milestones,* pp. 233-240; Shimon Peres, *David's Sling: The Secret's of Israel's Strength* (Jerusalem: Weidenfeld & Nicolson, 1970), pp. 161-164 (Hebrew). A description from the French vantage point can be found in Abel Thomas, *Comment Israel fut sauve* (Paris: Albin Michel, 1978), pp. 146-158.

80. Unless otherwise noted, all the following citations are from *COS Diary,* September 29-October 1, 1956.

81. For the atmosphere at the meetings, see Mordechai Bar-On, *Challenge and Quarrel* (Sde Boker: Ben-Gurion Research Center, 1991), pp. 200, 206 (Hebrew).

82. Peres, *David's Sling,* p. 162.

CHAPTER 13
THE JORDANIAN BORDER FLARES UP

1. Sir John Baggot Glubb, *A Soldier with the Arabs* (London: Hodder & Stoughton, 1957), pp. 323-325.

2. General Ali Abu-Nuwar, who soon afterward became the commander of the Arab Legion, admitted to General Burns that, after Glubb's dismissal, discipline in the Jordanian army deteriorated. See E.L.M. Burns, *Between Arab and Israeli* (London: Harrap & Co., 1962), p. 155.

3. On the Arab Legion's politicization and nationalist pressure among its ranks, see P. J. Vatikiotis, *Politics and the Military in Jordan: A Study of*

the Arab Legion 1921-1957 (London: Frank Cass, 1967), pp. 118-136. The rift between General Abu-Nuwar and the king was exposed only half a year later—see King Hussein of Jordan, Uneasy Lies the Head (London: Heineman, 1962), chap. 10.

4. The royal decree dispersing parliament and the Jordanian prime minister's proclamation are in SWB, Part IV, June 29, 1956, p. 34.

5. Ben-Gurion's diary entry for this incident reads, "Once again nighttime infiltrators have killed a driver, between Yahud and Wilhelmina. This cannot be ignored." BGA, July 15, 1956.

6. General Burns submitted a detailed report on the incident to the Security Council—SCOR, 1956, Suppl., Doc. S/3658, August 3, 1956.

7. The IDF view at the time was that the king and those planning Iraqi intervention were interested in keeping the border "hot" in order to persuade public opinion of the need for the Iraqi intervention. See Mordechai Bar-On, Challenge and Quarrel (Sde Boker: Ben-Gurion Research Center, 1991), p. 225 (Hebrew).

8. In response to a proposal to conquer the West Bank, Ben-Gurion declared that he "prayed that Jordan would not disintegrate, since that would be a very dubious blessing"—Ben-Gurion's Diary, April 24, 1956.

9. On September 28 Ben-Gurion wrote in his diary, "We will not sit by idly if Babylon conquers Amman." See also entries on September 30 and October 1, 1956. On October 2 he wrote that he had learned from the French consul in East Jerusalem that "There is trouble in Jordan, bedlam, the danger of collapse. . . . the French Consul is . . . panic-stricken. Europeans are not safe. . . . He fears entire families will be slaughtered before the IDF manages to enter Jerusalem."

10. Ibid., July 10 and 11, 1956.

11. Ibid., September 10, 1956.

12. On the operation see E.L.M. Burns, Between Arab and Israeli (London: Harrap & Co., 1962), p. 166; Michael Bar-Zohar and Eitan Haber, The Paratroop Book (Tel Aviv: Lewin-Epstein, 1969), p. 125 (Hebrew). Reporters for the IDF weekly Bamahane began to take part in and report on reprisal raids; see Uri Dann and Avraham Vered, "The Attack on the Enemy's Fortress," Bamahane, IDF, September 18, 1956 (Hebrew).

13. For a description of the battle see Uri Millstein, The History of the Paratroops (Tel Aviv: Shalgi, 1985), vol. 1, pp. 383-384 (Hebrew).

14. Ha'aretz, September 16, 1956.

15. COS Diary, September 21, 1956.

16. *Ben-Gurion's Diary,* September 24, 1956.

17. *COS Diary,* September 24, 1956. See also Ya'acov Erez, ed., *Conversations with Moshe Dayan* (Tel Aviv: Massada, 1981), p. 32 (Hebrew).

18. *COS Diary,* September 26, 1956. For a detailed description of the operation, see Uri Dann and Avraham Vered, "The Assault on the Hussan Outposts," *Bamahane,* IDF, October 3, 1956 (Hebrew). See also Mordechai Gur, "Company D: The Story of a Paratroop Company," *Ma'arachot,* IDF, 1987, pp. 244-246 (Hebrew).

19. *Ben-Gurion's Diary,* September 30, 1956.

20. Lloyd to Prime Minister, January 25, 1956, *PRO,* FO/800, 731.

21. *PRO,* FO/371, 121722, VR1073/20.

22. The plan was approved by a Cabinet defense committee on October 2 and reported to the full Cabinet the following day. See *PRO,* CAB/130, 120.

23. Egypt Committee 31st Mtg., Confidential Annex, *PRO,* CAB/134, 1216.

24. *Ben-Gurion's Diary,* October 1, 1956; Memo of Conversation of Dulles with Senators, *JFDP,* Alpha. Subs., Box 7.

25. Lawson's conversation with Ben-Gurion was reported in a cable to Washington, no. 457, October 2, 1956, *SIA* 2453/10.

26. See cable to Washington no. 489/311 and report of another talk between Ben-Gurion and Lawson on October 5, 1956, in the cable sent by the U.S. desk on October 7, 1956, *SIA,* 2453/10.

27. Ben-Gurion noted the following intelligence item in his diary: "Abu-Nuwar may be demanding that the Iraqi army be placed under his command. . . . Iraq believes that Abu-Nuwar is an Egyptian agent"— *Ben-Gurion's Diary,* October 4, 1956. See also Egypt Committee 33rd Mtg., *PRO,* CAB/134, 1216, October 8, 1956.

28. See Ben-Gurion's letter to Hammarskjöld, June 26, 1956, *SIA* 2448/5 (English). For the U.N.'s position see *U.N. Yearbook,* New York, UN Department of Public Information, 1957, p. 33.

29. George Schwarzenberger, *Power Politics: A Study of World Society* (London: Stevens & Co., 1964), p. 191.

30. Hammarskjöld's letter to Ben-Gurion of July 24, 1956, in *SIA* 2448/5 (English).

31. Cited in Foreign Ministry cable to the U.N. delegation no. 466/434, July 29, 1956, ibid.

32. Hammarskjöld's letter to Ben-Gurion, July 31, 1956, *SIA* 2448/5 (English).

33. Hammarskjöld's letter to Ben-Gurion, August 18, 1956, ibid. (English).

34. Ben-Gurion's letter to Hammarskjöld, August 23, 1956, ibid.

35. *Ben-Gurion's Diary,* September 3, 1956.

36. Kidron's cable to Foreign Ministry, September 4, 1956, *SIA* 2448/5.

37. Hammarskjöld's letter to Ben-Gurion, September 12, 1956, ibid. (English).

38. Eban's cable to Golda Meir, no. 3761, September 13, 1956, ibid.

39. Hammarskjöld's letter to Ben-Gurion, September 26, 1956, ibid. (English). The letter also appears in Brian Urquhart's biography *Hammarskjöld* (New York: Alfred A. Knopf, 1973), p. 157.

40. *Ben-Gurion's Diary,* September 26, 1956.

41. Ben-Gurion's letter to Hammarskjöld, September 26, 1956, *SIA* 2448/5 (English).

42. Hammarskjöld's letter to Ben-Gurion, October 3, 1956, ibid. (English).

43. *SCOR,* 1956, Suppl., Doc. S/3659, September 27, 1956.

44. *Knesset Records,* vol. 21, pp. 57-65.

45. *Ben-Gurion's Diary,* July 17, 1956.

46. Ibid., October 8, 1956.

47. *COS Diary,* October 7, 1956.

48. "We wanted to avoid military action and hoped we would be able to . . . at least until the Security Council session had concluded. . . . But three days ago, on October 9th, 1956, things went too far." Moshe Dayan, *Diary of the Sinai Campaign,* pp. 40-41 (Hebrew version).

49. For a description of the battle, see Uri Dann and Avraham Vered, "Six Hours at Kalkilya," *Bamahane,* IDF, October 15, 1956.

50. Anthony Eden, *Full Circle: The Memoirs of Anthony Eden* (London: Cassell, 1967), p. 512. The British consul in Jerusalem informed the Foreign Ministry of Hussein's appeal to the British. See Dayan, *Diary of the Sinai Campaign,* pp. 48-49 (Hebrew version).

51. A précis of Westlake's message can be found in the Israeli Foreign Ministry's bulletin to embassies dated October 13, 1956, *SIA* 2453/10.

52. The announcement appears as an appendix in Dayan, *Diary of the Sinai Campaign,* pp. 181-182 (Hebrew version). Westlake met with Foreign Minister Golda Meir again in order to attempt to resolve the crisis—see British desk cable, October 14, 1956, *SIA* 2453/10.

53. *Knesset Records,* vol. 21, pp. 64-65.

54. See Foreign Ministry bulletin to embassies, October 17, 1956, *SIA* 2453/10. See also *PRO,* FO/371, 121706.

55. Ben-Gurion's diary was replete with comments indicating these suspicions—see, for example, the entry for October 6, 1956.

56. Ibid.

57. FO to Nichols, cable no. 1009, October 19, 1956, *PRO,* FO/371, 121706. See also Nichols's conversation with Golda Meir on October 19 in cable to London, *SIA* 2453/10.

58. Memo. of conversation with the president, October 15, 1956, *DDEL,* WH Memo Series., Box 4, File 4. See also Dulles's October 16 reply to reporters to the effect that the U.S. was committed to assisting any nation attacked and that this commitment included Jordan if it were attacked by Israel—DOS Press Release no. 543, *JFDP,* Sel. Corr. Series, Box 110, Suez Canal—Security Council File.

59. *Ben-Gurion's Diary,* September 28, 1956.

60. *Sharett's Diary,* vol. 3, p. 673.

61. Ibid., p. 840.

62. Moshe Dayan, "Military Actions in Peacetime," *Ma'arachot,* IDF, May 1959 (Hebrew).

63. In *BGA,* Weekly Meeting Minutes File, March 17, 1955.

64. Moshe Dayan, "Reprisals as a Means of Ensuring Peace," *Israel Defense Forces Monthly Review,* August 1955 (Hebrew).

65. Ibid.

66. Moshe Dayan, *Milestones* (Jerusalem: Idanim, 1976), pp. 112-113. He writes, "I had determined to put an end to the shameful results of the battles between our units and the Arabs and the equanimity of the IDF Command, which, throughout the ranks, put up with the base failures and the worthless excuses."

67. Ibid., p. 250.

68. *BGA,* Weekly Meeting Minutes File, October 12, 1956.

CHAPTER 14
GENERAL CHALLE'S SCENARIO

1. Maurice Challe, *Notre Revolt* (Paris: Presses de la Cité, 1968), p. 26 (French).

2. See Moshe Dayan, *Milestones* (Jerusalem: Idanim, 1976), p. 240.

3. The directives document drawn up by Moshe Dayan during the flight from St. Germain to Israel is in *COS Diary,* October 2, 1956.

4. For a full description of the French delegation's visit see Mordechai Bar-On, *Challenge and Quarrel* (Sde Boker: Ben-Gurion Research Center, 1991), pp. 212-220 (Hebrew).

5. *COS Diary,* Doc. Vols., October 3, 1956.

6. Dayan, *Milestones,* pp. 241-243.

7. See Colonel Uzi Narkiss's report of his discussions with Colonel Simon in *COS Diary,* Doc. Vols.

8. *COS Diary,* October 5, 1956.

9. Challe, *Notre Revolt,* p. 26.

10. For the Anglo-French approach see *SCOR,* 1956, Suppl., Doc. S/3654.

11. See, for example, Anthony Nutting, *No End of a Lesson: The Story of Suez* (London: Clarkson N. Potter, 1967), pp. 58-59.

12. See Mahmoud Fawzi, *Suez 1956: An Egyptian Perspective* (London: Shorouk International, 1986), pp. 62-79. The French perspective is presented in Christian Pineau, *1956: Suez* (Paris: Robert Laffont, 1976), part 2, chap. 5 (French). The British viewpoint can be gleaned from Selwyn Lloyd, *Suez 1956: A Personal Account* (London: Jonathan Cape, 1978), chap. 10.

13. Cable Dixon to FO, no. 814, October 9, 1956, *PRO,* PREM/11, 1121.

14. Cable Dixon to FO, no. 830, October 11, 1956, ibid.

15. Hammarskjöld submitted the six points to the Security Council on October 12 (741st Mtg). The wording of the six points is taken from the final resolution: *SCOR,* 1956, Suppl., Doc. S/3675, October 13, 1956.

16. *SCOR,* 743rd Mtg., October 10, 1956.

17. Brian Urquhart, *Hammarskjöld* (New York: Alfred A. Knopf, 1973), p. 168.

18. Lloyd, *Suez 1956*, p. 163. Urquhart also notes that Lloyd "arrived in London in a mood of cautious optimism over the possibility of a negotiated settlement"—*Hammarskjöld*, p. 170.

19. Urquhart, *Hammarskjöld*, p. 168.

20. Harkaby's cable to the Chief of Staff, October 10, 1956, *COS Diary*.

21. See Operations Branch, "Kadesh 1" Campaign Order, *COS Diary*, Doc. Vols.

22. *COS Diary*, October 7, 1956.

23. Dayan, *Milestones*, p. 245.

24. Challe, *Notre Revolt*, p. 27.

25. Hugh Thomas, *Suez* (New York: Harper Colophon, 1966), p. 100.

26. For a description of his resignation, see Nutting, *No End of a Lesson*, pp. 105-106. Nutting resigned only after the Cabinet decided to approve the "collusion."

27. This description is based on a comparison of Nutting's version of the Chequers discussion and the version provided Nahmias and included in his cable no. G/553 dated October 15, 1956, in *Peres Archives*, Incoming Cables File.

28. *COS Diary*, October 13, 1956.

29. See Meir Amit's report of October 18, 1956, in *COS Diary*, Doc. Vols.

30. "Operation Windstorm," p. 3, *Peres Archives* (Hebrew). Peres drew up this document immediately after the Sèvres talks, when the events were still fresh in his mind.

31. Cable to Paris dated October 16, 1956, in *COS Diary*, Doc. Vols.

32. The talks at Hotel Matignon were not recorded. On October 18 Selwyn Lloyd drafted a report describing the discussions; the document, however, is obfuscating and not reliable—see Memo by Lloyd, October 18, 1956, *PRO*, FO/800, 728. Nutting's version of what Selwyn told him the day after the talks seems more credible—see *No End of a Lesson*, pp. 98-99. Eden's memoirs up to this point are very precise; after October 16, however, they become vague and inexact. The same can be said of the archival material: Most files include no documents between October 16 and October 29. The Egypt Committee ceased meeting. The Americans virtually halted contacts with the allies: "From about this time on, we had an uneasy feeling that we were cut off from our allies"—see Dwight D. Eisenhower, *Mandate for Change*, p. 56.

33. A copy of the document was cabled to Ben-Gurion that very evening— see *COS Diary,* October 17, 1956.

34. Incoming cables on October 17, 1956, in *Peres Archives,* Cables File.

35. Cable to Paris, October 16, 1956, ibid.

36. Cable from Paris, October 16, 1956, ibid. At this point neither the Israelis nor the British knew whether they would be meeting. Nutting refers to a brief talk he held with Lloyd immediately after his return from Paris, in which Lloyd indicated that he "hoped that we would not have to be directly associated with these talks with the Israelis . . . but he could not rule this out"—*No End of a Lesson,* p. 98.

37. *COS Diary,* October 17, 1956.

38. "Operation Windstorm," p. 5, *Peres Archives.*

39. Bar-On, *Challenge and Quarrel,* p. 247.

40. Minutes of Dayan's talk with Challe, *COS Diary,* October 21, 1956.

41. *COS Diary,* October 22, 1956.

CHAPTER 15
"COLLUSION": THE SÈVRES CONFERENCE

1. Mordechai Bar-On, *Challenge and Quarrel* (Sde Boker: Ben-Gurion Research Center, 1991), pp. 250-251 (Hebrew).

2. *COS Diary,* October 23, 1956. All following quotations are from this source unless otherwise specified.

3. Bar-On took extensive notes during the conference proceedings. His detailed report as well as his description of the site and of the atmosphere appear in *COS Diary,* October 21-24, 1956. Unless otherwise noted, this report is the source for the quotations from the actual sessions in the rest of this chapter. Moshe Dayan's references to the events in his memoirs, *Milestones,* are drawn from Bar-On's report— see pp. 254-266. Many years after the events, Pineau and Abel Thomas published their own recollections of the conference—see Christian Pineau, *1956: Suez* (Paris: Robert Lafont, 1976), pp. 126-137 (French); and Abel Thomas, *Comment Israel fut Sauve* (Paris: Albin Michel, 1978), pp. 160-195.

4. *COS Diary,* October 23, 1956.

5. It is probably on the basis of this discussion that in his memoirs Pineau said that Ben-Gurion was "too concerned with an *idée fixe,* too convinced of his own judgment and the justice of his cause"—see *1956: Suez,* p. 128.

6. Moshe Dayan, *Milestones* (Jerusalem: Idanim, 1976), p. 257 (Hebrew).

7. Selwyn Lloyd, *Suez 1956: A Personal Account* (London: Jonathan Cape, 1978), p. 183. A more neutral British account can be found in a brief memoir written by Lloyd's private secretary thirty years after the events. See Donald Logan, "Collusion at Suez," *Financial Times,* January 8, 1986.

8. Cabinet Confidential Annex., 72nd Conclusions, *PRO,* CAB/28, 30.

9. *COS Diary,* October 23, 1956.

10. Bar-On, *Challenge and Quarrel,* pp. 271-272.

11. Eden never mentioned the conversation. Lloyd never changed his contention that the discussion concerned only the Anglo-French reaction in the event of an Israeli assault. See Lloyd, *Suez 1956,* p. 186.

12. *COS Diary,* October 24, 1956.

13. Bar-On, *Challenge and Quarrel,* p. 273.

14. "Something on 'the Old Man's' position at Sèvres," *COS Diary,* October 24, 1956.

15. Three copies of the protocol were signed. Eden's copy was burned; the French copy was lost; the Israeli copy is in *BGA* and is not open to the public. Logan relates that it was the French who drew up the document; in fact, however, Patrick Dean was an active partner in its composition and even argued over some of the wording. On the atmosphere during the signing, see Bar-On, *Challenge and Quarrel,* p. 265.

16. *COS Diary,* October 24, 1956; see also Dayan, *Milestones,* pp. 278-279.

17. The caricature is in the author's personal collection.

18. See Eden's official biographer, Robert Rhodes-James, *Anthony Eden* (London: Weidenfeld & Nicolson, 1982), p. 532.

19. For more on this see Mordechai Bar-On, "In the Web of Lies," *Iyunim,* vol. 2 (Sde Boker: David Ben-Gurion Research Center, forthcoming) (Hebrew).

20. David Ben-Gurion, *Uniqueness and Destiny: On Israel's Security* (Jerusalem: Ma'arachot, 1971), pp. 218-225 (Hebrew).

21. "Operation Windstorm," *Peres Archive,* p. 28. A slightly edited version also appears in Shimon Peres, *David's Sling: The Secrets of Israel's Strength* (Jerusalem: Weidenfeld & Nicolson, 1970), p. 170 (Hebrew).

22. The communiqué can be found in Pineau, *1956: Suez,* p. 137.

23. Cabinet Confidential Annex., 74th Mtg., October 24, 1956, *PRO,* CAB/28, 30.

24. Taken from the parliamentary debates cited in Peter Calvocoressi, *Suez: Ten Years After* (New York: Pantheon Books, 1967), pp. 84-85.

25. See also Mordechai Bar-On, "David Ben-Gurion and the Sèvres Collusion," in Roger Louis and Roger Owen, eds., *Suez 1956: The Crisis and Its Consequences* (Oxford: Oxford University Press, 1989), pp. 145-160.

26. *Ben-Gurion's Diary,* October 24, 1956.

CHAPTER 16
OPERATION KADESH: POLITICAL DIMENSIONS

1. Tuvia Ben-Moshe, "Liddell-Hart and the IDF: A Reassessment," *State, Government and International Relations,* no. 15 (Hebrew); Meir Pe'il, "The Indirect Approach Is Best," *Ma'arachot—Armor,* IDF, January 1973 (Hebrew); Avraham Ayalon, "The War of Independence, Operation 'Kadesh,' the Six-Day War: A Comparison," *Ma'arachot,* IDF, Summer 1968 (Hebrew).

2. See Yigal Allon, *Curtain of Sand* (Tel Aviv: Hakibbutz Hame'uhad, 1968), p. 69 (Hebrew); Dan Horowitz, *The Constant and the Variable in the Israeli Concept of Security,* Leonard Davis Institute for International Relations, The Hebrew University of Jerusalem, 1982 (Hebrew).

3. In *COS Diary,* October 25, 1956.

4. For greater detail see Mordechai Bar-On, "The Influence of Political Considerations on Operational Planning in the Sinai Campaign," in S. I. Troen and M. Shemesh, eds., *Suez—Sinai Crisis 1956: Retrospective and Reappraisal* (London: Frank Cass, 1990), pp. 196-217.

5. *COS Diary,* October 25, 1956.

6. Minutes of General Staff meeting held on October 25, 1956, in ibid., Doc. Vols.

7. Cable from Paris dated October 25, 1956, in *Peres Archive,* Incoming Cables File.

8. Cable to Paris on October 26, 1956, in ibid., Cables File.

9. Cited in *COS Diary,* relayed orally to Dayan by Colonel Nehemia Argov, Ben-Gurion's military aide.

10. *Ben-Gurion's Diary,* October 26, 1956.

11. Cable from Nahmias, October 27, 1956, *Peres Archive,* Incoming Cables File.

12. Mordechai Bar-On, *Challenge and Quarrel* (Sde Boker: Ben-Gurion Research Center, 1991), p. 285 (Hebrew). For the reserve call-up, see also Robert Henriques, *One Hundred Hours to Suez* (London: Collins, 1957), pp. 49-54.

13. "Timetable of events leading up to Suez Operation," *PRO,* FO/800, 728, October 27, 1956.

14. Cable from Paris, October 26, 1956, *Peres Archive,* Cables File.

15. The entire cable can be found in Dwight D. Eisenhower, *The White House Years: Waging Peace 1956-1961* (New York: Doubleday & Co., 1965), pp. 68-70. Excerpts are in Abba Eban's exhaustive documentation of Israel's diplomatic efforts at the U.N. and in Washington, *The Political Campaign in the U.N. and the U.S. after the Sinai Campaign, October 56-March 57* (hereinafter referred to as *The Political Campaign*) (Washington, D.C., 1957), pp. 7-8 (Hebrew). Also in *FRUS* 1955-1957, vol. 16, doc. 388, p. 795.

16. *Ben-Gurion's Diary,* October 28, 1956.

17. See Eden's message to Guy Mollet in cable FO to Paris no. 2363, November 1st, 1956, *PRO,* PREM/11, 1132.

18. *COS Diary,* October 29, 1956.

19. Bar-On, *Challenge and Quarrel,* p. 290.

20. *COS Diary,* October 28, 1956.

21. Discussion at the Southern Command, *COS Diary,* ibid.

22. *COS Diary,* October 29, 1956; cited also in Bar-On, *Challenge and Quarrel,* pp. 298-299.

23. For a detailed description of the drop, see Rafael Eitan, *Raful: The Story of a Soldier* (Tel Aviv: Ma'ariv, 1968), pp. 64-65 (Hebrew).

24. Text in *COS Diary,* October 29, 1956.

25. Ezer Weizman, *Yours the Sky, Yours the Earth* (Tel Aviv: Ma'ariv, 1975), p. 155 (Hebrew).

26. Moshe Dayan, *Milestones* (Jerusalem: Idanim, 1976), p. 277 (Hebrew).

27. Ibid. See also Moshe Dayan, *Diary of the Sinai Campaign,* pp. 81-82 (Hebrew version).

28. Cited in Uri Milstein, *The Wars of the Paratroops* (Tel Aviv: Ramador, 1968), p. 81 (Hebrew).

29. *Ma'ariv*, October 8, 1956, p. 5.

30. Moshe Dayan, *Diary of the Sinai Campaign*, p. 85 (Hebrew version).

31. See Nasser's article in *The Egyptian Gazette*, October 6, 1956, and his interview in the *Sunday Times*, June 24, 1962. Nasser apparently forced this decision on his High Command. Heikal describes the dramatic meeting at the Egyptian GHQ in which Nasser personally phoned each of his battalion commanders and instructed them to retreat—see *Cutting the Lion's Tail*, pp. 180-181.

32. Anthony Eden, *Full Circle: The Memoirs of Anthony Eden* (London: Cassell, 1967), pp. 525-528. For the text of the ultimatums see *PRO, PREM/11*, 1105, pp. 501, 503; and Noble Frankland, ed., *Documents of International Affairs 1956*, p. 261.

33. Sir Humphrey Trevelyan, *The Middle East in Revolution* (Boston: Gambit Inc., 1970), pp. 114-115. See also Trevelyan's cable to the British Foreign Office in *PRO*, PREM/11, 1105, p. 495.

34. Cable from Paris in *Peres Archive*, Incoming Cables File. Hugh Thomas quotes British officers at command headquarters as saying that the bombardment was postponed also because American transport planes were parked at Cairo West airfield to evacuate American citizens from Egypt—see *Suez* (New York: Harper Colophon, 1966), p. 142. Cabinet discussions indicate that the bombings had always been intended to begin at nightfall—Cabinet 76th Conclusion, *PRO*, PREM/11, 1105, p. 396.

35. Cited by Mordechai Bar-On in BBC broadcast, November 14, 1986.

36. Cable to Paris, October 31, 1956, in *Peres Archive*, Outgoing Cables File.

37. Memo. of Conversation with the President, October 29, 1956, *FRUS* 1955-1957, vol. 16, doc. 411, pp. 833-839.

38. Eisenhower sent another message to Ben-Gurion on October 28, but by the time Ben-Gurion answered it, the British and French ultimatums to Egypt and Israel had already been issued. This permitted Ben-Gurion to reply that "in all fairness, he had to consult with the British and French Governments." See *SIA*, 2459/1, and *FRUS* 1955-1957, vol. 16, doc. 414, pp. 843-844.

39. Henry Cabot Lodge, *As It Was* (New York: Norton & Co., 1976), pp. 93-94. See also *SCOR*, 1956, Suppl., Doc. S/3706.

40. Dulles to Cabot Lodge, October 29, 1956, 9:30 P.M., *JFDP*, Telephone Conversation Memo. Series, Box 11.

41. *SCOR,* 1956, 748th Mtg.

42. The American proposal was labeled Doc. S/3710—*SCOR,* 1956, Suppl. A detailed description of the events that day at the U.N. can found in the cable sent by the British delegate Pierson Dixon to the Foreign Office: Cable no. 989, October 30, 1956, *PRO,* PREM/11, 1105.

43. Dulles to Knowland, October 30, 1956, *JFDP,* Telephone Conversations Memo. Series, Box 11.

44. Abba Eban, *The Political Campaign,* p. 20.

45. Dulles to Senator George, October 31, 1956, 12:48 A.M., *JFDP,* Telephone Conversation Memo. Series, Box 11.

46. *General Assembly Official Record* (hereinafter cited as *GAOR*), 1956, Annex, Resolution A/3256.

47. Eban, *The Political Campaign,* p. 28. See also Brian Urquhart, *Hammarskjöld,* (New York: Alfred A. Knopf), part 1, chap. 7.

48. On Lester Pearson's role in UNEF's establishment, see John A. Munro and Alex I. Inglis, eds., *Mike: The Memoirs of the Right Honorable Lester B. Pearson* (Toronto: University of Toronto Press, 1973), vol. 2, chap. 11. See also Terence Robertson, *Crisis: The Inside Story of the Suez Conspiracy* (New York: Atheneum, 1965), pp. 186-203, 212-229.

49. *GAOR,* 1956, Annex, Doc. A/3290. The vote was 57 in favor of the resolution, 19 abstentions, and no objections. On the proposals that culminated in the establishment of the U.N. force, see Rosalyn Higgins, *U.N. Peacekeeping 1946-1967* (Oxford: Oxford University Press/RIIA, 1969), part 2, chap. 2.

50. *COS Diary,* November 4, 1956.

51. Eban, *The Political Campaign,* p. 34. Eban's response is included in his memo to the secretary general on November 3 in *GAOR,* 1st Emergency Special Session, Doc. A/3279.

52. Minutes of General Staff meeting, November 11, 1956, *COS Diary,* Doc. Vols.

53. *PRO,* Cab/134, 1216, p. 279; and *PRO,* PREM/11, 1105, pp. 182, 185.

54. *GAOR,* 1st Emergency Special Session, 565th Mtg., p. 79, and Doc. A/3287.

55. *COS Diary,* November 4, 1956.

56. Cable from Paris, November 4, 1956, *Peres Archive,* Incoming Cables File.

57. Eban, *The Political Campaign,* p. 40. The entire text of Israel's reply can be found in Meron Medzini, *Israel's Foreign Relations: Selected Documents 1947-1974* (Jerusalem: Ministry for Foreign Affairs, 1976), vol. 1, pp. 555-556. The document is labeled A/3291 in U.N. documentation.

58. *COS Diary,* November 5, 1956.

59. General Sir Charles Keightley, "Operations in Egypt," *London Gazette,* p. 5334.

60. See *SCOR,* 1956, Suppl., Doc. S/3736.

61. The text of the cables to Eden and Mollet can be found in Noble Frankland, ed., *Documents of International Affairs 1955.*

62. Conclusion of Cabinet Mtg., no. 79, November 6, 1956, *PRO,* CAB/28, 30, PREM/11, 1105. See the Foreign Office cable to the U.N. delegation, no. 1615, dated November 6, 1956, in *PRO,* PREM/11, 1105, p. 102.

63. Bulganin's cable to Ben-Gurion arrived after Israel announced its compliance with the U.N. cease-fire resolution. For the text, see Meron Medzini, *Israel's Foreign Relations,* vol. 1, pp. 557-558.

64. Minutes of meeting with the defense minister, November 6, 1956, in *COS Diary,* Doc. Vols.

65. *Ha'aretz,* November 7, 1956.

66. *Knesset Records,* vol. 21, pp. 197-200.

67. Ibid.

<h1 style="text-align:center">CHAPTER 17
WITHDRAWAL</h1>

1. *GAOR,* 1st Emergency Special Session, Doc 3309.

2. Cited in David Ben-Gurion, *The Renewed State of Israel* (Tel Aviv: Am Oved, 1969), vol. 1, p. 527 (Hebrew).

3. "Correspondence Between the Government of Israel and the United Nations," Foreign Ministry collection, *SIA* 2448/13, December 13, 1956.

4. Cited in Michael Bar-Zohar, *Ben-Gurion* (Tel Aviv: Am Oved, 1971), vol. 3, p. 1921 (Hebrew).

5. Shimon Peres, *David's Sling: The Secrets of Israel's Strength* (Jerusalem: Weidenfeld & Nicolson, 1970), p. 175 (Hebrew).

6. Bulganin's letter to Eisenhower is in DOS, *U.S. Policy in the Middle East, September 1956-June 1957* (Washington, DC: Government Printing Office, 1957), pp. 183-187.

7. Edward Crankshaw, ed., *Khrushchev's Memoirs* (Tel Aviv: Adi, 1971), p. 312 (Hebrew).

8. Memo. of the 302nd Mtg. of the NSC, November 1, 1956, *FRUS* 1955-1957, vol. 16, doc. 455, pp. 902-916.

9. On November 6 the American ambassador in Moscow cabled Washington that continued fighting "makes it increasingly difficult for [the Soviets] to maintain complete inaction." See Bohlen cable to the Department of State, *FRUS,* ibid., doc. 520, pp. 1016-1017. See also Charles Bohlen, *Witness to History 1929-1969* (New York: Norton, 1973), p. 433. On November 7 Henry Cabot Lodge advised Herbert Hoover that he had been reliably informed that the Soviets were urging the Arab delegations at the U.N. to hold tight until the volunteers had arrived—see Cable Lodge to Secretary of State, no. DELGA 22, *DDQ,* 1987, 000270.

10. On November 7 Hammarskjöld told Eban that he concurred with Washington's opinion that Israel's refusal to evacuate the Sinai would result in armed Soviet intervention and a third world war—see Eban's cable to Ben-Gurion no. 857/110, *SIA,* 2459/1.

11. Eban cabled that "publication of the sixth paragraph of the Prime Minister's address today had caused Israel's position to plummet in world and public opinion"—cable dated November 7, 1956, *SIA,* ibid.

12. See the text in Meron Medzini, *Israel's Foreign Relations,* vol. 1, p. 563. Also in *FRUS* 1955-1957, vol. 16, doc. 549, pp. 1062-1063.

13. Cable from Washington to Jerusalem no. 945/380, November 7, 1956, *SIA* 2459/1.

14. *Ben-Gurion's Diary,* November 8, 1956.

15. Cable from New York no. 859/130, November 7, 1956, *SIA* 2459/1.

16. Eban's cables to Ben-Gurion nos. 854/320 and 872/97, ibid.

17. Cited in Abba Eban, *The Political Campaign,* p. 53.

18. Golda Meir's cable to Ben-Gurion no. 870/297 dated November 8, 1956, *SIA* 2459/1.

19. For a description of the atmosphere in the prime minister's bureau see Bar-Zohar, *Ben-Gurion,* vol. 3, pp. 1280-1281.

20. *Ben-Gurion's Diary,* November 8, 1956.

21. Moshe Dayan, *Milestones* (Jerusalem: Idanim, 1976), pp. 317-318 (Hebrew). The text of Ben-Gurion's message to President Eisenhower on withdrawal is in *FRUS* 1955-1957, vol. 16, doc. 560, pp. 1095-1096.

22. *BGA,* Broadcast to the Nation, November 8, 1956.

23. Abba Eban, *The Political Campaign in the U.N. and the U.S. after the Sinai Campaign, October 1956-March 1957* (Washington, DC, 1957), p. 60 (Hebrew).

24. Text in Ben-Gurion, *The Renewed State of Israel,* vol. 1, p. 537.

25. Address to senior commanding officers, November 29, 1956, in David Ben-Gurion, *The Sinai Campaign* (Tel Aviv: Am Oved, 1958), pp. 233-241 (Hebrew).

26. See Brian Urquhart, *Hammarskjöld* (New York: Alfred A. Knopf, 1973), p. 176.

27. E.L.M. Burns, *Between Arab and Israeli* (London: Harrap & Co., 1962), p. 138.

28. John A. Munro and Alex I. Inglis, eds., *Mike: The Memoirs of the Right Honorable Lester B. Pearson* (Toronto: University of Toronto Press, 1973), p. 244. See also Rosalyn Higgins, *U.N. Peacekeeping 1946-1957* (Oxford: Oxford University Press/RIIA, 1969), vol. 1, p. 231.

29. Munro and Inglis, eds., *Mike,* p. 246. See also Eden's letter to Eisenhower on November 5, 1956, in which he writes that the British government would be delighted to transfer responsibility to the international organ as quickly as possible—see Cable FO to Washington no. 5181, *PRO,* PREM/11, 1105, p. 158.

30. Cable Dixon to FO no. 1070, November 5, 1956, *PRO,* PREM/11, 1105, p. 121.

31. *GAOR,* 1st Emergency Session, Res. 98 (ES-1), November 3, 1956.

32. Ibid., Res. 100 (ES-1), November 5, 1956.

33. On November 11 General Keightley, commander in chief of the allied Musketeer forces, that "I assume my aim is to assist . . . to establish or become a U.N. force"—Cable Allied CinC to Ministry of Defense, London, November 8, 1956, *PRO,* AIR/20.

34. Cable Dixon to FO no. 1069, November 5, 1956, *PRO,* PREM/11, p. 125.

35. *Knesset Records,* November 7, 1956, p. 200.

36. In Eban, *The Political Campaign,* p. 78, and also in *Ben-Gurion's Diary,* November 10, 1956.

37. Report on morning discussion of the Israeli U.N. delegation, November 20, 1956, *SIA* 2349/4.

38. Eban's cable to Jerusalem no. 193/302,, November 23, 1956, in *SIA* 2459/1.

39. Analysis of Hammarskjöld's documents in Kidron's cable no. 982/1082, November 21, 1956, *SIA* 2459/1.

40. Eban's cable no. 987/520 dated November 22, 1956, *SIA,* ibid.

41. Contemporary documents abound hinting at Hammarskjöld's animosity toward Israel. See, for example, Pierson Dixon's report on his discussions with the secretary general: "He seemed to be by far more preoccupied and incensed with the Israelis than with us"—Cable Dixon to FO no. 1070, November 5, 1956, *PRO,* PREM/11, 1105, pp. 121-122. Ben-Gurion was very sensitive to Hammarskjöld's feelings. "After Russia, Hammarskjöld is our enemy no. 1"—*Ben-Gurion's Diary,* November 12, 1956.

42. Cable Nichols to FO, December 18, 1956, *PRO,* FO/371, 121706, VR1052/39.

43. Argaman's cable to Jerusalem no. 157/392, January 12, 1957, *SIA,* 2349/14.

44. Ya'acov Tsur, *Paris Diary,* p. 316.

45. See report on a conversation held on December 6, cable to Herzog no. 224/511, December 6, 1956, *SIA* 2459/1.

46. See Eytan's cable to Paris and London dated November 30, 1956, in *SIA* 2459/14.

47. *COS Diary,* December 3, 1956.

48. *COS Diary,* December 6, 1956.

49. Official communiqué to Eban dated December 7, 1956, *SIA* 2448/13. See also Kidron's cable no. 103/414 dated December 8, 1956, *SIA,* 2459/14.

50. *COS Diary,* December 6, 1956. See also Burns, *Between Arab and Israeli,* p. 243.

51. Herzog's cable to Eban no. 104/112, December 10, 1956, *SIA* 2459/1.

52. Kidron's cable to Herzog no. 166/206, December 17, 1956, ibid., 2459/14.

53. Copy of Burns's cable to Dayan, December 20, 1956, in *SIA* 2459/1.

54. Eban's cable to Herzog no. 185/345, December 20, 1956, ibid.

55. Herzog's cable no. 162/101, December 19, 1956, *SIA,* 2456/1.

56. Ben-Gurion's cable to the foreign minister no. 163/95, December 19, 1956, *SIA*, 2456/14.

57. DOS Press Release no. 624, Sec. Dulles's News Conference, December 8, 1956, *JFDP*, Sel. Corr., Box 106, ME File, p. 11.

58. Report of discussion in Eban's cable to Jerusalem no. 174/153, *SIA* 2459/1 and 2459/7.

59. The memo appears in the cable sent by the Israeli Foreign Ministry's American Desk to Washington, cable no. 948/348, *SIA* 2459/1 (English).

60. Eban's cable to Ben-Gurion no. 75/198, ibid.

61. Eban's cable to Ben-Gurion no. 181/1455, December 10 (20?), 1956, ibid.

62. Eban's cable to Ben-Gurion no. 265/386, January 6, 1957, ibid.

63. Herzog's cable to Eban no. 975/208, January 8, 1957, ibid. That day Eban told Ralph Bunche of the decision; see Kidron's cable to Herzog no. 280/383, ibid.

64. *COS Diary,* January 15, 1957.

65. Herzog's cable to Foreign Minister Meir and to Abba Eban, no. 953/256, January 1, 1957, *SIA* 2459/1.

66. Eban's cable to Herzog no. 229/302, December 9, 1956, ibid., 2459/14.

67. Eban's cable to Ben-Gurion no. 181/1455, December 10, 1956, ibid., 2459/1.

CHAPTER 18
DIFFICULT DECISION

1. This section is based largely on an analysis of the minutes of the talks that Abba Eban held with Hammarskjöld on January 5, 8, 14, and 23, 1957. The minutes can be found in *SIA* 2448/7.

2. On January 25 Eban handed the secretary general an official document stipulating Israel's position on the Armistice Agreement—ibid. 2459/10.

3. "The Americans are worried lest the Israeli Government issue formal notice that could be interpreted as defiance of the General Assembly"— Eban's cable to Herzog, January 11, 1957, ibid.

4. Eban's memo to Hammarskjöld, January 2, 1957, in ibid. 2448/7 and 2448/13.

5. Hammarskjöld's memo to Eban, January 5, 1957, ibid.

6. Herzog's cable no. 999/430, January 13, 1957, ibid., 2459/2 and 2459/14.

7. Meeting with the defense minister, January 7, 1957, *BGA,* Weekly Meeting Minutes File.

8. Ben-Gurion's cable to Eban, January 7, 1957, *SIA* 2459/2 and 2459/14.

9. Herzog's cable to Eban no. 37/407, January 22, 1957, *SIA* 2459/2 and 2459/14.

10. The memo was submitted to the General Assembly on January 24, 1957, and labeled *GAOR,* Doc. A/3511.

11. *Knesset Records,* January 23, 1954.

12. Minutes of the discussion are in *SIA* 2448/7.

13. *GAOR,* Doc. A/3512, January 24, 1957—see also *SIA* 2448/7.

14. See Abba Eban, *The Political Campaign in the U.N. and the U.S. after the Sinai Campaign, October 1956-March 1957* (Washington, DC, 1957), pp. 165-166 (Hebrew).

15. *SIA* 2448/6.

16. DOS Press Release no. 53, February 5, 1957, *JFDP,* Sel. Corr., Box 119, ME File.

17. Extract from Memo. brought to the President by King Saud, *DDQ,* 1986, 000772.

18. Shiloah's cable to Herzog no. 191/84 dated February 4, 1957, in *SIA* 2459/2.

19. Moshe Dayan, *Milestones* (Jerusalem: Idanim, 1976), p. 328.

20. Ibid.

21. Ben-Gurion's reply to Eisenhower is in *SIA* 2448/6 (English). See also *FRUS* 1955-1957, vol. 17, Arab-Israeli Dispute 1957, doc. 68, pp. 109-112.

22. Ben-Gurion's cable to Golda Meir no. 410/118, February 8, 1957, *SIA* 2459/11.

23. Cable from Washington no. 203/704 in ibid. 2459/2 and 2448/6.

24. Eban's cable to Ben-Gurion no. 212/31 dated February 12, 1957, *SIA* 2459/2. The following citations from cables exchanged February 11-13 are in *SIA* 2459/15 and 2459/21.

25. The Cabinet decisions taken on February 15 were cabled to the Israeli embassies in Washington, London, Paris, and Rome by Eitan—see *SIA* 2459/3 and 2459/15.

26. Eban cabled Dulles's reactions to Herzog—no. 222/1082, February 15, 1957, in ibid.

27. Eban's cable to Herzog no. 309/250, February 16, 1957, ibid.

28. Ben-Gurion's reaction in his cable to Eban, ibid.

29. Dwight D. Eisenhower, *The White House Years: Waging Peace 1956-1961* (New York: Doubleday & Co., 1965), p. 185.

30. *JFDP,* Alph. Subs., Box 7, Suez Problem File.

31. For a description of the meeting at the White House, see Sherman Adams, *First Hand Report* (New York: Harper & Row, 1961), pp. 280-285.

32. White House Press Release, February 21, 1957, *JFDP,* Alph. Subs., Box 7, Suez Problem File.

33. *Ben-Gurion's Diary,* February 21, 1957. See also Eban, *The Political Campaign,* p. 221.

34. For the development of the Jewish lobby in Washington, see I. L. Kenen, *Israel's Defense Line* (Buffalo, NY: Prometheus Books, 1981); Eduard Tivnan, *The Lobby: Jewish Political Power and American Foreign Policy* (New York: Simon and Schuster, 1987), chap. 2.

35. *The New York Times,* February 8, 1957.

36. Ibid., February 26, 1957.

37. The Cabinet decisions are in Herzog's cable no. 492/89, February 22, 1957, in *SIA* 2459/3 and 2459/15. Abba Eban's address to the government can be found in his *The Political Campaign,* pp. 241-243.

38. *Knesset Records,* February 22, 1956.

39. The exchange of cables on February 17-18 is in *SIA* 2459/3.

40. Conversation with senior commanding officers on March 1, 1957, in Michael Bar-Zohar, *Ben-Gurion* (Tel Aviv: Am Oved, 1971), vol. 3, p. 1293 (Hebrew).

41. A detailed report of the "breakthrough" discussion with Dulles was submitted in Shiloah's cable no. 214/1263 dated February 25, 1957. The English version was sent in Shiloah's cable 251/1481, February 26, 1957. Both are in *SIA* 2459/3 and 2459/15. See *FRUS* 1955-1957, vol. 17, doc. 143, pp. 254-267.

42. See the agreed version of the Israeli announcement regarding the Straits in Eban's cable to Herzog no. 224/117, February 27, 1957, ibid 2459/15.

43. Eban's urgent cable to Ben-Gurion no. 318/401, February 25, 1957, ibid. In a "strictly personal" cable from Eban to Herzog, no. 253/320 dated February 26, Eban expressed his extreme dismay at the "catastrophic error" and offered to tender his resignation.

44. Herzog's cable to Eban no. 149, February 25, 1957, ibid. and 2448/6.

45. Précis of discussion with Hammarskjöld in Kidron's cable to Herzog no. 320/822, February 26, ibid. The full minutes of the conversation are also in ibid.

46. Shiloah's cable to Herzog no. 217/225, February 26, ibid., 2459/3. See the American version in *FRUS* 1955-1957, vol. 17, doc. 159, pp. 291-295.

47. Emil Najar's cable to Eytan no. 423/321, January 30, 1957, ibid., 2459/10.

48. Conversation between Ambassador Tsur and Guy Mollet in Tzur's cable to the Foreign Ministry's director general no. 0/171, February 22, 1957, ibid.

49. Pineau's original draft is in Shiloah's cable 254/405, February 27, *SIA,* 2459/3.

50. Eban's cable to Ben-Gurion no. 221/708, February 27, ibid.

51. The agreement is included in Hammarskjöld's report to the General Assembly—*GAOR,* Doc. A/3563, February 26, 1957. See also Brian Urquhart, *Hammarskjöld* (New York: Alfred A. Knopf, 1973), pp. 208-209.

52. Eban's cable to Herzog no. 223/92 dated February 27, *SIA* 2459/3.

53. Cable from Golda Meir and Abba Eban to Ben-Gurion no. 225/81, February 27, ibid. For Golda Meir's discussion with Dulles, see *FRUS* 1955-1957, vol. 17, doc. 162, pp. 299-303.

54. Herzog's cable no. 158/137, February 28, *SIA,* ibid. The Cabinet's corrections are in Herzog's cable no. 159, February 28, ibid.

55. Report on the last meeting with Dulles in Eban's cable to Ben-Gurion no. 325/636, March 1, 1957, ibid. The American version is in *FRUS* 1955-1957, vol. 17, doc. 175, pp. 325-329.

56. Urquhart, *Hammarskjöld,* p. 210.

57. *Ben-Gurion's Diary,* February 28, 1957.

58. Minutes of meeting with senior army officials, *COS Diary,* Doc. Vols., March 1, 1957.

59. Eban's cable to Herzog no. 326/113 dated March 1. Golda Meir's text went through several stages, detailed in Eban, *The Political Campaign,* pp. 273-276.

60. The text of Golda Meir's address is in "Copy of Cable Received," March 3, 1957, *SIA* 2448/7 (English). See also Meron Medzini, *Israel's Foreign Relations,* vol. 1, pp. 604-607.

61. For Henry Cabot Lodge's text see Medzini, ibid., pp. 608-611.

62. DOS Press Release, no. 103, *JFDP,* Sel. Corr., Box 115, Israel File. Minutes of conversation with Arab diplomats in *FRUS* 1955-1957, vol. 17, doc. 177, pp. 332-336.

63. Golda Meir, *My Life* (Jerusalem: Steimatzky, 1975), p. 255.

65. The president's cable is in *SIA* 2448/6. See also Meron Medzini, *Israel's Foreign Relations,* vol. 1, pp. 611-612, and *FRUS* 1955-1957, vol. 17, doc. 182, pp. 347-348.

66. Eban's cable to Ben-Gurion no. 262, March 2, *SIA* 2459/3 and 2459/15.

67. Ben-Gurion's cable to Golda Meir and Abba Eban no. 175/246, March 3, ibid.

68. Herzog's cable no. 117/25, March 4, 1957, ibid.

69. *COS Diary,* March 3, 1957.

70. Golda Meir's letter to the secretary of state, March 6, 1957, *SIA* 2448/6. See also *FRUS* 1955-1957, vol. 17, doc. 200, pp. 377-378.

71. *COS Diary,* March 6, 1957.

72. E.L.M. Burns, *Between Arab and Israeli* (London: Harrap & Co, 1962), p. 257.

73. For a detailed description of the episode from the U.N. perspective, see ibid., pp. 260-270.

74. Eytan's circular no. 908, March 13, 1957, *SIA* 2459/13.

75. Herter's letter to the Israeli foreign minister, March 14, 1957, ibid. (English).

76. The ministry spokesman's announcement in Cable to Embassies, circular no. 915, March 13.

77. Golda Meir's conversation with Hammarskjöld, cable 925, March 20, 1957, *SIA* 2459/13.

78. Tsur's cable to the director general no. 0/129, March 16, ibid., 2459/15.

79. Report of discussion with Dulles, Shiloah's cable no. 325/184, March 19, ibid.

80. Dayan, *Milestones,* p. 344.

81. Ibid.

82. *COS Diary,* September 17, 1956.

83. Eban's cable to Ben-Gurion no. 325/636, February 1, 1957, *SIA* 2459/3.

84. See Dulles's briefing to American ambassador to Cairo, Raymond Hare, before Hammarskjöld's visit to Cairo, cable dated March 19, 1957, in *JFDP,* Sel. Corr., Box 115, Egypt File. See also Dulles's personal message to Nasser in *FRUS* 1955-1957, vol. 17, doc. 236, pp. 445-447.

AFTERWORD

1. Record of the weekly meeting with the Minister of Defense, April 5, 1956, *BGA,* Sde Boker, Weekly Meetings File 1956.

2. A Lecture to Senior Officers, December 16, 1955, reprinted in Ben-Gurion, *Yichud ve Ye'ud (Identity and Destiny): Talks on Israel's Security* (Tel Aviv: Ma'arachot Publication, 1971), pp. 218-225 (Hebrew).

R·E·F·E·R·E·N·C·E·S

PRIMARY SOURCES

(Document Collections, Archives, Diaries, etc.)

American Foreign Policy Current Documents.

BBC Summary of World Broadcasts, Part IV, The Arab World, Israel, Greece, Turkey and Persia, 1955-1957.

Ben-Gurion Archive, Sde Boker (Hebrew).

Ben-Gurion, David. "Diary." MS in Ben-Gurion Archive (Hebrew).

Chief of Staff's Bureau Archive, IDF Archive, Givatayim (Hebrew).

Dag Hammarskjöld Library.

Dayan, Moshe. *Diary of the Sinai Campaign.* Tel Aviv: Am Hasefer, 1968 (Hebrew).

———. *Diary of the Sinai Campaign.* New York: Schocken, 1965 (English).

John Foster Dulles Oral History Collection, Princeton University, Princeton, NJ.

John Foster Dulles Papers, Princeton University, Princeton, NJ.

Declassified Documents Quarterly

Dwight D. Eisenhower Library, Abilene, KS.

Foreign Relations of the United States (*FRUS*). Washington, DC: Government Printing Office, various years.

Frankland, Noble, ed. *Documents on International Affairs 1955.* Oxford: Oxford University Press/RIIA, 1957.

Hansard, Debates of the British Parliament and House of Lords, London.

IDF Chief of Staff's Bureau Diary.

IDF Chief of Staff's Bureau Archive, IDF Archive, Givatayim.

Journal Officiel de la République Française.

Knesset Records, Jerusalem (Hebrew).

League of Nations Treaty Series.

Medzini, Meron, ed. *Israel's Foreign Relations: Selected Documents 1947-1974.* Jerusalem: Ministry for Foreign Affairs, 1976.

Public Record Office, London.

Peres Archive, IDF Archive, Givatayim.

Sharett, Moshe. *Moshe Sharett's Diary.* Tel Aviv: Am Oved, 1982 (Hebrew).

Tsur, Ya'acov. *Paris Diary: The Diplomatic Campaign in France.* Tel Aviv: Am Oved, 1968.

United Nations General Assembly Official Record.

United Nations Security Council Official Record.

U.S. Department of State. *Bulletin.*

U.S. Department of State. *Unclassified Documents Quarterly,* Washington, DC.

U.S. Department of State. *The Suez Canal Problem July 26-September 22, 1956.* Washington, DC.

U.S. Department of State. *U.S. Policy in the Middle East, September 1957-June 1957.* Washington, DC.

U.S. House of Representatives, Committee for Foreign Affairs. *Report of the Special Study Mission,* no. 2147, Washington, DC, May 1, 1956.

U.S. Senate Committee on Foreign Relations. *Study of U.S. Foreign Policy.* Washington, DC, 1959.

SECONDARY SOURCES

Adams, Sherman. *First Hand Report.* New York: Harper & Row, 1961.

Allon, Yigal. *Curtain of Sand.* Tel Aviv: Hakibbutz Hame'uhad, 1968 (Hebrew).

Avidan, Shimon. "Security Problems in the State of Israel," in Zvi Ra'ana, ed., *Army and War in Israel and Elsewhere.* Merhavia: Sifriat Hapoalim, 1955 (Hebrew).

Ayalon, Avraham. "The War of Independence, Operation 'Kadesh,' the Six-Day War: A Comparison." *Ma'arachot,* IDF, Summer 1968 (Hebrew).

Azcarate, Pablo de. *Mission in Palestine 1948-1952.* Washington, DC: The Middle East Institute, 1966.

Baer, Israel. "Real and Imaginary Solutions for our Security," in Israel Baer, *On Security.* Tel Aviv: Am Oved, 1959 (Hebrew).

———. "What to Prepare for and How," in Israel Baer, *On Security.* Tel Aviv: Am Oved, 1959 (Hebrew).

Bar-On, Mordechai. "In the Web of Lies," *Iyunim,* vol. 2, Sde Boker (Ben-Gurion Research Center, forthcoming) (Hebrew).

———. *Challenge and Quarrel.* Sde Boker: Ben-Gurion Research Center, 1991 (Hebrew).

———. "David Ben Gurion and the Sevres Colllusion," in Roger Louis and Roger Owen, eds., *Suez 1956: The Crisis and Its Consequences.* Oxford: Oxford University Press, 1989, pp. 145-160.

———. "The Influence of Political Considerations on Operational Planning in the Sinai Campaign," in S. I. Toren and M. Shevish, eds., *Suez-Sinai Crisis 1956: Retrospect and Reappraisal.* London: Frank Cass, 1990, pp. 196-217.

——— (Col.-Res.). "The Egyptian-Czech Arms Deal: A Question of Periodization," *Ma'arachot* 306-307, IDF, December 1986-January 1987, pp. 38-42 (Hebrew).

Bar-Ya'acov, Nisan. *The Israeli-Syrian Armistice: Problems of Implementation 1949-1966.* Jerusalem: Magnes Press, 1968.

Barraclough, Geoffrey. *Survey of International Affairs 1955-1956.* Oxford: Oxford University Press, 1960.

Bar-Zohar, Michael. *Ben-Gurion.* Tel Aviv: Am Oved, 1971 (Hebrew).

Bar-Zohar, Michael, and Eitan Haber. *The Paratroop Book.* Tel Aviv: Lewin-Epstein, 1969 (Hebrew).

Baxter, R. R. "The Definition of War," *Revue Egyptienne de Droit International,* vol. 16, 1960.

Ben-Gurion, David. *What Did We Fight For? What Did We Gain?* Central Committee of the Israeli Labor Party—Information Department, n.d. (Hebrew)

———. *Uniqueness and Destiny: On Israel's Security.* Jerusalem: Ma'arachot, 1971 (Hebrew).

———. *The Renewed State of Israel.* Tel Aviv: Am Oved, 1969 (Hebrew).

———. *The Sinai Campaign.* Tel Aviv: Am Oved, 1958 (Hebrew).

Ben-Moshe, Tuvia. "Liddel-Hart and the IDF: A Reassessment," *State, Government and International Relations,* no. 15, 1980 (Hebrew).

Blainey, Geoffrey. *The Causes of War.* New York: The Free Press, 1973.

Bloomfield, L. M. *Egypt, Israel and the Gulf of Aqaba in International Law.* Toronto: Carswell, 1957.

Bohlen, Charles. *Witness to History 1929-1969.* New York: Norton, 1973.

Brecher, Michael. *Decisions in Israel's Foreign Policy.* New Haven, CT: Yale University Press, 1975.

———. *The Foreign Policy System of Israel.* Oxford: Oxford University Press, 1972.

Burns, E.L.M. *Between Arab and Israeli.* London: Harrap & Co., 1962.

Calvocoressi, Peter. *Suez: Ten Years After.* New York: Pantheon Books, 1967.

Campbell, John C. *Defense of the Middle East: Problems of American Policy.* New York: Praeger, 1960.

Cattan, Henry. *Palestine and International Law.* London: Longmans, 1976.

Challe, Maurice. *Notre Revolt.* Paris: Presses de la Cité, 1968 (French).

Churchill, Winston S. *The Second World War.* London: Cassell & Co., 1948.

Cohen, Reuven. "On the Alert," *Me-bifnim,* vol. 18, no. 4, April 1956 (Hebrew).

Colloque des Juristes Arabes sur la Palestine. Algiers, 1967 (French).

Crankshaw, Edward, ed. *Khrushchev's Memoirs.* Tel Aviv: Adi, 1971 (Hebrew).

Crosbie, Sylvia. *A Tacit Alliance: France and Israel from Suez to the Six Days War.* Princeton, NJ: Princeton University Press, 1974.

Dann, Uri, and Avraham Vered. "Six Hours at Kalkiliya," *Bamahane,* IDF, October 15, 1956 (Hebrew).

———. "The Assault on the Hussan Outposts," *Bamahane,* IDF, October 3, 1956 (Hebrew).

———. "The Attack on the Enemy's Fortress," *Bamahane,* IDF, September 18, 1956 (Hebrew).

Dayan, Moshe. *Milestones.* Jerusalem: Idanim, 1976 (Hebrew).

———. "Military Activities in Peacetime," *Ma'arachot,* IDF, May 1959 (Hebrew).

———. *Story of My Life.* New York: William Morrow & Co., 1976.

———. "Israel's Border and Security Problems," *Foreign Affairs,* vol. 33, no. 2 (January 1955), pp. 250-267.

———. "Reprisals as a Means of Ensuring Peace," *Israel Defense Forces Monthly Review,* August 1955 (Hebrew).

Doherty, J. B. "Jordan Water Conflict," *International Conciliation* no. 553.

Eban, Abba. *An Autobiography.* Jerusalem: Steimatzky, 1977.

———. *The Political Campaign in the U.N. and the U.S. after the Sinai Campaign, October 1956-March 1957.* Washington, DC, 1957 (Hebrew).

Eden, Anthony. *Full Circle: The Memoirs of Anthony Eden.* London: Cassell, 1967.

Eisenhower, Dwight D. *The White House Years: Mandate for Change 1953-1956.* New York: Doubleday & Co., 1965.

———. *The White House Years: Waging Peace 1956-1961.* New York: Doubleday & Co., 1965.

Eitan, Rafael. *Raful: The Story of a Soldier.* Tel Aviv: Ma'ariv, 1985 (Hebrew).

Erez, Ya'acov, ed. *Conversations with Moshe Dayan.* Tel Aviv: Massada, 1981 (Hebrew).

Eveland, Wilbur Crane. *Ropes of Sand: America's Failure in the Middle East.* New York: Norton, 1980.

Fawzi, Mahmoud. *Suez 1956: An Egyptian Perspective.* London: Sharouk International, 1986.

Feinberg, Nathan. *The Legality of a "State of War" After the Cessation of Hostilities Under the Charter of the U.N. and the Covenant of the League of Nations.* Jerusalem: Magnes Press, 1961.

Finer, Herbert. *Dulles Over Suez.* London: Heineman, 1964.

Finer, S. E. *The Man on Horseback.* London: Pall Mall Press, 1962.

Gaujac, Paul. *Suez 1956.* Paris: Charles-Lavanzelle, 1986 (French).

Glubb, Sir John Baggot. *A Soldier with the Arabs.* London: Hodder and Stoughton, 1957.

Golan, Aviezer. *Operation Susanna.* Jerusalem: Idanim, 1976 (Hebrew).

Gur, Mordechai. "Company D: The Story of a Paratroop Company," *Ma'arachot,* IDF, 1977 (Hebrew).

Harel, Isser. *And One Brother Rose Up Against the Other.* Jerusalem: Keter, 1982 (Hebrew).

———. *The Anatomy of Treason: "The Third Man" and the Disgrace in Egypt.* Jerusalem: Idanim, 1980 (Hebrew).

Harkaby, Yehoshafat. *Israel's Position in the Arab-Israeli Conflict.* Tel Aviv: Dvir, 1968 (Hebrew).

Heikal, Mohamed Hassenein. *Nasser: The Cairo Documents.* London: New English Library, 1976.

———. *Cutting the Lion's Tail: Suez Through Egyptian Eyes.* London: Andre Deutsch, 1957.

Henriques, Robert. *One Hundred Hours to Suez.* London: Collins, 1957.

Higgins, Rosalyn. *U.N. Peacekeeping 1946-1957.* Oxford: Oxford University Press/RIIA, 1969.

Horowitz, Dan. *The Constant and the Variable in the Israeli Concept of Security.* Leonard Davis Institute for International Relations, the Hebrew University of Jerusalem, 1982 (Hebrew).

Horowitz, Dan, and Shlomo Aharonson. "The Strategy of Controlled Retaliation," *State and Government,* vol. 1, no. 1, Summer 1971 (Hebrew).

Hussein, King of Jordan. *Uneasy Lies the Head.* London: Heineman, 1962.

Hutchinson, Commander Elmo H. *Violent Truce: A Military Observer Looks at the Arab-Israeli Conflict 1951-1955.* New York: Devin Ader, 1958.

Jabber, Paul. *Not by War Alone: Security and Arms Control in the Middle East.* Los Angeles: University of California Press, 1981.

Jackson, Elmore. *Middle East Mission.* New York: Norton, 1983.

Jessup, Philip. "Should International Law Recognize and Intermediary Status Between Peace and War?" *American Journal of International Law,* vol. 48, 1954.

Kaplan, Binyamin. "Only One Choice," in Zvi Ra'anan, ed., *Army and War in Israel and Elsewhere.* Merhavia: Sifriat Hapoalim, 1955 (Hebrew).

Kenen, I. L. *Israel's Defense Line.* Buffalo, NY: Prometheus Books, 1981.

Kennan, George. *Realities of American Foreign Policy.* Princeton, NJ: Princeton University Press, 1954.

Kern, Harry. "The Cold War Moves South," *Tensions in the Middle East,* Middle East Institute, Washington, DC, 1955.

Kilmuir, Earl of. *Political Adventures.* London: Weidenfeld & Nicolson, 1964.

Kimmerling, Baruch. "Prominence of the Arab-Israeli Conflict as a Social Indicator 1949-1970," *State, Government and International Relations,* vol. 6, 1974 (Hebrew).

Kollek, Teddy. *For Jerusalem.* Jerusalem: Steimatzky, 1978.

Kyle, Keith. *Suez 1956.* New York: St. Martin's Press, 1991.

Lacouture, Jean. *Nasser and His Heirs.* Tel Aviv: Am Oved, 1972 (Hebrew).

Lloyd, Selwyn. *Suez 1956: A Personal Account.* London: Jonathan Cape, 1978.

Lodge, Henry Cabot. *As It Was.* New York: Norton & Co., 1976.

Louis, Roger, and Roger Owen, eds. *Suez 1956: The Crisis and Its Consequences.* Oxford: Oxford University Press, 1989.

Love, Kenneth. *Suez: The Twice-Fought War.* New York: McGraw-Hill, 1969.

Macmillan, Harold. *Riding the Storm 1956-1959.* London: Macmillan, 1971.

Meir, Golda. *My Life.* Tel Aviv: Ma'ariv, 1975 (Hebrew).

Menzies, Robert. *Afternoon Light.* London: Cassell, 1967.

Milstein, Uri. *The History of the Paratroops.* Tel Aviv: Shalgi, 1985 (Hebrew).

———. *The Wars of the Paratroops.* Tel Aviv: Ramador, 1968 (Hebrew).

Mohn, P. "Problems of Close Supervision," *International Conciliation,* no. 478 (February 1952):49-99.

Munro, John A., and Alex I. Inglis, eds., *Mike: The Memoirs of the Right Honorable Lester B. Pearson.* Toronto: University of Toronto Press, 1973.

Murphy, Robert. *Diplomat Among Warriors.* New York: Doubleday & Co., 1964.

Nasser, Gamal Abdel. "The Philosophy of the Revolution," *Ma'arachot,* IDF, November 1954 (Hebrew).

Nutting, Anthony. *No End of a Lesson: The Story of Suez.* London: Clarkson N. Potter Inc., 1967.

Ohel, Mila. "The Yarkon Mission," *Ma'arachot,* IDF, no. 197, January 1969 (Hebrew).

Oppenheim, F. L. *International Law.* London: Longman, Green & Co., 1952.

Pe'il, Meir. "The Indirect Approach Is Better," *Ma'arachot—Armor,* IDF, January 1973 (Hebrew).

Peres, Shimon. *David's Sling: The Secrets of Israel's Strength.* Jerusalem: Weidenfeld & Nicolson, 1970 (Hebrew).

Peretz, Don. "The Jordan River Partition," *Middle East Journal,* vol. 9, no. 4.

Peri, Yoram. "The Ideological Character of the Israeli Military Elite," *State, Government and International Relations,* no. 6, Autumn 1974 (Hebrew).

Pineau, Christian. *1956: Suez.* Paris: Robert Laffont, 1976 (French).

Quandt, William B. "Influence Through Arms Supply: The U.S. Experience in the Middle East," in Uri Ra'anan, Robert Pfaltzgraff, and Geoffrey Kemp, eds., *Arms Transfer to the Third World: The Military Building in Less Industrial Countries.* Boulder, CO: Westview Press, 1978.

Ra'anan, Uri. *The USSR, Arms and the Third World.* Cambridge, MA: MIT Press, 1969.

Reiner, Efraim. "To Stand in Defense and Win in Peace," in Zvi Ra'anan, ed., *Army and War in Israel and Elsewhere.* Merhavia: Sifriat Hapoalim, 1955 (Hebrew).

Rhodes-Jones, Robert. *Anthony Eden.* London: Weidenfeld & Nicolson, 1982.

Robertson, Terence. *Crisis: The Inside Story of the Suez Conspiracy.* New York: Atheneum, 1965.

Rosenne, Shabtai. *Israel's Armistice Agreements With the Arab States.* Tel Aviv: Blumstein Publications, 1951 (Hebrew).

Schwarzenberger, George. *Power Politics: A Study of World Society.* London: Stevens & Co., 1964.

Shimshoni, Jonathan. *Israel and Conventional Deterrence.* Ithaca, NY: Cornell University Press, 1988.

Stevens, Georgiana. "The Jordan River Valley," *International Conciliation,* no. 506, January 1956.

Stone, Julius. *Legal Controls of International Conflict.* New York: Garland, 1973.

Tabenkin, Yosef. "In the Fullness of our Strength," *Me-bifnim,* vol. 18, no. 4, April 1956 (Hebrew).

Thomas, Abel. *Comment Israel fut sauve.* Paris: Albin Michel, 1978.

Thomas, Hugh. *Suez.* New York: Harper Colophon, 1966.

Tivnan, Eduard. *The Lobby: Jewish Political Power and American Foreign Policy.* New York: Simon and Schuster, 1987.

Trevelyan, Sir Humphrey. *The Middle East in Revolution.* Boston: Gambit Inc., 1970.

Urquhart, Brian. *Hammarskjöld.* New York: Alfred A. Knopf, 1973.

Van Horn, General Carl. *Soldiering for Peace.* London: Cassell, 1966.

Vatikiotis, N. *Politics and the Military in Jordan: A Study of the Arab Legion 1921-1957.* London: Frank Cass, 1967.

Weizman, Ezer. *Yours the Sky, Yours the Earth.* Tel Aviv: Ma'ariv, 1975 (Hebrew).

Ya'ari, Ehud. *Egypt and the Fedayun 1953-1956.* Givat Haviva: Givat Haviva, 1975 (Hebrew).

Yaniv, Avner. *Deterrence Without the Bomb.* Lexington, MA: Lexington Books, 1987.

NEWSPAPERS

Daily Express (England)

Davar (Israel—Hebrew)

France Observateur (France—French)

Ha'aretz (Israel—Hebrew)

Haboker (Israel—Hebrew)

Herut (Israel—Hebrew)

Le Monde (France—French)

London Gazette Supplement (England)

Ma'ariv (Israel—Hebrew)

The New York Post (U.S.)

The New York Times (U.S.)

The Sunday Telegraph (England)

The Times (England)

I·N·D·E·X